EMPOWERING THE NEW
MOBILITY WORKFORCE

EMPOWERING THE NEW MOBILITY WORKFORCE

Educating, Training, and Inspiring Future Transportation Professionals

Edited by

TYLER REEB

Director of Research, Center for International Trade and Transportation, California State University, Long Beach, USA

Associate Director, Federal Highway Administration's Southwest Transportation Workforce Center, USA

ELSEVIER

Elsevier
Radarweg 29, PO Box 211, 1000 AE Amsterdam, Netherlands
The Boulevard, Langford Lane, Kidlington, Oxford OX5 1GB, United Kingdom
50 Hampshire Street, 5th Floor, Cambridge, MA 02139, United States

Notices
Knowledge and best practice in this field are constantly changing. As new research and
experience broaden our understanding, changes in research methods, professional practices, or
medical treatment may become necessary.

Practitioners and researchers must always rely on their own experience and knowledge in
evaluating and using any information, methods, compounds, or experiments described herein. In
using such information or methods they should be mindful of their own safety and the safety of
others, including parties for whom they have a professional responsibility.

To the fullest extent of the law, neither the Publisher nor the authors, contributors, or editors,
assume any liability for any injury and/or damage to persons or property as a matter of products
liability, negligence or otherwise, or from any use or operation of any methods, products,
instructions, or ideas contained in the material herein.

British Library Cataloguing-in-Publication Data
A catalogue record for this book is available from the British Library

Library of Congress Cataloging-in-Publication Data
A catalog record for this book is available from the Library of Congress

ISBN: 978-0-12-816088-6

For Information on all Elsevier publications
visit our website at https://www.elsevier.com/books-and-journals

Publisher: Joe Hayton
Acquisition Editor: Brian Romer
Editorial Project Manager: Aleksandra Packowska
Production Project Manager: Paul Prasad Chandramohan
Cover Designer: Mark Rogers

Typeset by MPS Limited, Chennai, India

Working together
to grow libraries in
developing countries

www.elsevier.com • www.bookaid.org

Dedication

For Noelle, and all the bright paths we travel together.

Contents

4. Strategies to prepare future port and intermodal workers for transformational technologies — 79

Kristin Decas and Aravind Kailas

5. Anticipating and responding to changes in the mobility sector — 97

Lee D. Lambert and Ian R. Roark

Part III The Changing Role of Transportation Providers in the Future Transportation Ecosystem   245

Author biographies

Steve Albert is the executive director of the Western Transportation Institute, Montana State University. He has directed two national University Transportation Centers, and currently directs both the National Center for Rural Road Safety and the West Region Transportation Workforce Center (WRTWC). Since 2007, Albert has served as the rural representative on the USDOT Intelligent Transportation Systems (ITS) Program Advisory Committee, which makes recommendations on national ITS policy, research, and implementation. He also serves as chair of the ITSA Rural ITS Committee and on the TRB Committee on Transportation on Public Lands.

Dr. Allison Alexander, PhD, is a senior manager, Human Capital at ICF. Her work and research focuses on employees in the workplace, with deep experience in the areas of workforce development, workforce planning and staffing, employee assessment, and organizational health assessments. She has worked with clients across various industries, including multiple modes of transportation, to provide high quality and best practice workforce solutions. Dr. Alexander earned her PhD in Industrial Organizational Psychology from Texas A&M University, where her dissertation focused on telework, flexible work arrangements, and employee effectiveness.

Terry Bills is the Global Transportation Industry Director at Esri, responsible for all transportation infrastructure segments worldwide. He has more than 25 years of experience in transportation, working on planning, policy development, information technology, and GIS. He has been a principal planner for a large regional transportation planning agency, as well as the president of a GIS and transportation consulting firm. He was a doctoral candidate at UCLA, where he also earned two masters' degrees.

Rick D. Blasgen is the president and chief executive officer of the Council of Supply Chain Management Professionals (CSCMP), Lombard, IL, United States.

Blasgen began his career with Nabisco, working in a regional customer service center in Chicago, Illinois. While at Nabisco, he held various logistics positions of increasing responsibility in inventory management, order processing, and transportation and distribution center operations management. Blasgen became vice president, supply chain, at Nabisco in June 1998, then vice president supply chain for Kraft in June 2002. He joined ConAgra Foods in August 2003 as senior vice president integrated logistics.

Blasgen has devoted much of his time to furthering a number of company's supply chain management programs and initiatives. This experience has given him a solid foundation for his role at CSCMP where he has responsibility for the overall business operations and strategic plan of the organization. His efforts support CSCMP's mission of leading the supply chain management profession through the development and dissemination of supply chain education and research.

Blasgen was designated by the US Department of Commerce in 2011 to serve as the chair of the Advisory Committee on Supply Chain Competitiveness (ACSCC) providing the administration advice and counsel on issues and concerns that affect the supply chain sector, and continues to chair the committee till date. He is a member of Northwestern University's Transportation Center Business Advisory Committee and a past chair of the Grocery Manufacturers Association Logistics Committee, and a past president of the Warehousing Education and Research Council (WERC). Blasgen is a graduate of Governors State University, earning his degree in business administration and majoring in finance.

Dr. Marlon Boarnet is a professor of public policy and chair of the Department of Urban Planning and Spatial Analysis in the Sol Price School of Public Policy at the University of Southern California and vice president/president elect of the Association of Collegiate Schools of Planning. His research focuses on land use and transportation, links between land use and travel behavior and associated implications for public health and greenhouse gas emissions, urban growth patterns, and the economic impacts of transportation infrastructure. He is a fellow of the Weimer School of the Homer Hoyt Institute for Real Estate, and he is a fellow of the Regional Science Association International. Boarnet has advised California state agencies on greenhouse gas emission reduction in the transport sector, the World Bank on transportation access as a poverty reduction tool, and numerous public and private entities. He has been the principal investigator on over two million dollars of funded research, supported by agencies that include the United States and California

Departments of Transportation, the US Environmental Protection Agency, the California Policy Research Center, the California Air Resources Board, and the Robert Wood Johnson Foundation.

Dr. Austin Brown is Executive Director of the Policy Institute for Energy, Environment, and the Economy at the University of California, Davis. In this role, he builds strong connections between the research and policy communities at the local, state, and national levels with a focus on clean energy and sustainable transportation. Prior to joining UC Davis in June 2017, he spent 9 years in Washington, DC, working for the Department of Energy, the National Renewable Energy Laboratory, and as Assistant Director for Clean Energy and Transportation at the White House Office of Science and Technology Policy in the Obama Administration.

Flora Castillo served as the Vice President of Transportation for UnitedHealth Group and Vice President of Community and Strategic Engagement at UnitedHealthcare Community & State. She has more than 20 years of health care and managed care experience, specializing in marketing, public relations, communications, advocacy and business development.

Flora also served as the Vice President of Marketing and Business Growth at PerformCare, a member of the AmeriHealth Caritas Family of Companies.

Castillo has been a Director of the New Jersey Transit Corporation since 1999. She is also a past Chairwoman of the American Public Transportation Association (APTA).

Castillo is actively involved in mentorship programs for young adults, women, and minorities. For her commitment to public service she has received numerous awards and recognitions, including a member of the 2018 National Urban League of Fellows, 2013 Latina Trailblazer Award from the Statewide Hispanic Chamber of Commerce of New Jersey, the 2013 Hispanic Business magazine 50 Influentials, the 2013 Minority Business Leader Award from the Philadelphia Business Journal, and the 2013 Transportation Leadership Award from the Newark Regional Business Partnership.

Born and raised in El Salvador, Castillo immigrated to the United States in 1981. She received her bachelor's degree in public administration from Long Island University, and is also a graduate of the Christine Todd

Whitman Excellence in Public Services Series and The Leadership Inc. Program of Philadelphia.

Wyatt Cmar works at the Harvard Kennedy School Ash Center researching and writing about innovations in smart city technology. Previously, he worked at Diller Scofidio + Renfro as a researcher and graduated from New York University, United States.

Dr. Brian Cronin, a senior director of Human Capital with ICF (www. icf.com), has a PhD in industrial/organizational psychology. He has nearly 20 years of professional experience in conducting large-scale transportation workforce development, labor market analysis, and strategic planning projects. Dr. Cronin has conducted a variety of projects related to the following areas of expertise for public sector agencies, including the US DOT, Caltrans, ALDOT, FAA, NCHRP, AASHTO, TCRP, and FHWA. For each of these studies, Dr. Cronin has provided comprehensive organizational improvement solutions. Dr. Cronin also regularly publishes and presents research for national audiences on related topics such as improving staffing procedures, the use of technology in HR initiatives, and industry-level occupation assessment efforts.

Kristin Decas is the Director and CEO Port of Hueneme. Since beginning her tenure in 2012, tonnage totals have grown 23% from 1.3 million tons in FY 2012 to over 1.6 million metric tons in FY 2018, marking the Port's strongest sustained trade years since its inception. Decas championed the first annual Port Banana Festival, drawing over 12,000 visitors to the Port. Port related businesses generate $1.5 billion in annual economic impact and create more than 13,600 direct, indirect, induced and influenced jobs. She is the current President of the California Association of Port Authorities (CAPA) representing California's 11 deep-water ports. CAPA provides educational leadership and advocacy on issues related to transportation, trade, the environment, land use, energy and other subjects effecting port operations. She has also served on the U.S. DOT's National Freight Advisory Committee (NFAC) and the Marine Transportation System National Advisory Council (MTSNAC). In 2015, Decas served as the national Chairperson of the American Association of Port Authorities (AAPA), a trade association representing more than 130 public port authorities in the Western Hemisphere. Decas is the first woman to run both the Port of New Bedford in its 50-year history and the Port of

Hueneme in its 81-year history. She is also only the fourth woman to chair the AAPA in its 103 years.

Susan Gallagher is the Education and Workforce Program Manager at Montana State University's Western Transportation Institute (WTI) where she leads education, outreach, community engagement, and professional development initiatives. She manages the West Region Transportation Workforce Center (WRTWC), a resource center serving a ten-state region with the goal of communicating promising practices and catalyzing new strategic partnerships to enhance transportation workforce development efforts at all levels. Her professional and research interests focus on expanding student research and experiential learning opportunities, international collaborations, informal STEM education, and transportation access and accessibility.

Dr. Genevieve Giuliano is Margaret and John Ferraro Chair in effective local government in the Sol Price School of Public Policy, University of Southern California, and director of the METRANS joint USC and California State University Long Beach Transportation Center. Her research areas include relationships between land use and transportation, transportation policy analysis, travel behavior, and information technology applications in transportation. She has published over 170 papers and received several awards for her research.

Stephen Goldsmith is the Daniel Paul Professor of the Practice of Government and the director of the Innovations in American Government Program at Harvard's Kennedy School of Government. He currently directs Data-Smart City Solutions, a project to highlight local government efforts to use new technologies that connect breakthroughs in the use of big data analytics with community input to reshape the relationship between government and citizen. He previously served as deputy mayor of New York and mayor of Indianapolis, where he earned a reputation as one of the country's leaders in public–private partnerships, competition, and privatization. Stephen was also the chief domestic policy advisor to the George W. Bush campaign in 2000, the chair of the Corporation for National and Community Service, and the district attorney for Marion County, Indiana from 1979 to 1990. He has written *The Power of Social Innovation*; *Governing by Network: the New Shape of the Public Sector*; *Putting Faith in Neighborhoods: Making Cities Work through Grassroots Citizenship*; *The Twenty-First Century City: Resurrecting Urban America*; *The*

Responsive City: Engaging Communities Through Data-Smart Governance; and, most recently, *A New City O/S: The Power of Open, Collaborative, and Distributed Governance*.

Dr. Stephanie Ivey is the associate dean for research with the Herff College of Engineering and a professor with the Department of Civil Engineering, The University of Memphis. She directs the U of M's Intermodal Freight Transportation Institute, the Southeast Transportation Workforce Center and the West TN STEM Hub. Her technical research includes focus on journey to school in urban areas, transportation planning (particularly related to freight impacts), livability assessment in urban communities, and strategies to engage citizens in the transportation planning process. She has a strong record of STEM workforce and education research, with special emphasis on transportation workforce development, partnerships between industry and academia, and increasing representation of women and underrepresented minorities in STEM.

Ivey is a member of the Executive Committee of the Institute of Transportation Engineers Diversity and Inclusion Committee—STEM Sub Committee, the American Society of Civil Engineers National Engineers Week/Discover-E Task Committee and the TRB Standing committee on Maintenance and Operations Personnel. She also serves on the Federal Reserve Bank of St. Louis Transportation Industry Council and the board of directors for the Greater Memphis IT Council.

Scott Jakovich is the SWTWC project coordinator for the National Transportation Career Pathways Initiative, an FHWA-funded research effort targeting postsecondary education. He has coordinated the development of customized, fast-track, credit-bearing/credentialing courses and career pathways in cooperation with multicollege consortiums, State and Federal agencies, and industry associations, including the US DOL, DOT, California Community College Chancellor's Office, California Energy Commission, Southern California Logistics Technology Collaborative, LINCS Logistics Training Consortium, Pacific Maritime Association, and Homeland Security.

Jakovich previously served as Workforce Development Program Manager for Long Beach City College and its Center for Training and Professional Development, and as board member for the Southern California Regional Training Transit Consortium. Jakovich is also a career project engineer for the aerospace industry and an alumnus of the

University of California at Irvine. He has managed various organizations, engineering teams, and development projects in the design and production of leading-edge analog instrumentation and data acquisition equipment used in the structural analysis of airframes and rocket engines.

Aravind Kailas manages innovation and R&D initiatives to create and commercialize sustainable transport solutions for the Volvo Group. By promoting the company's creative assets and key technology positions in various fora, Aravind has been instrumental in establishing the Volvo Group as a trusted thought leader in California. He has led Volvo's engagement with the public sector and other outreach efforts in the connected and autonomous vehicles spaces, and championed truck platooning activities in the United States to prepare for a commercial product launch. Aravind also spearheaded local partner development for the first Volvo electric truck roll-out in the United States and has launched innovative projects with startups and customers to showcase critically needed technologies and new business opportunities for the Volvo Group.

Dr. Sanggyun Kang is a postdoctoral research associate at the Center for Transportation Equity, Decision and Dollars, University of Texas at Arlington. His areas of research interest are in urban logistics, freight transportation activity, and land use–transportation interactions. Dr. Kang has published multiple papers in top peer-reviewed journals in transportation and urban planning research. Dr. Kang received his PhD in urban planning and development from the University of Southern California in 2017 and MS in urban planning from Columbia University in 2010.

Lee Lambert, J.D., has been Chancellor of Pima Community College since July 2013. Under Chancellor Lambert, PCC is focusing on student success, connecting with the community to further economic development, and fostering a multicultural world that honors our differences as well as our unifying values. He recognizes the need for creativity in responding to challenges and opportunities. In 2017, he was named CEO of the Year by the Association of Community College Trustees. Chancellor Lambert is a founding member of the National Coalition of Certification Centers (NC3), and serves on its Board of Directors.

Saumya Lathia is a data and research analyst at Los Angeles Homeless Services Authority (LAHSA). She received her master of planning (MPL) degree from USC Sol Price School for Public Policy in 2018 and her bachelor of planning (B Plan) degree from CEPT University at Ahmedabad, India in 2016. Prior to joining LAHSA, Saumya served as a research assistant at Sol Price Center for Social Innovation (CSI) and CEPT's Center for Urban Equity (CUE). Her work experience involves extensive community outreach, qualitative and quantitative research, spatial analysis, data analysis, and visualizations. Saumya's research interests include urban and regional inequities, informal economy and housing, urban sustainability, and social justice. She believes in using high-quality research to advocate for vulnerable and under-resourced communities. Her undergraduate thesis, "Gender and Public Spaces: A Case Study of Sabarmati Riverfront" received the Best Gender Thesis Award in 2016. Its wide coverage by local media initiated discussions about urban planning and women's safety among city and state officials of Gujarat, India.

Valerie Lefler is an international expert in rural transportation and mobility as a service in low population density communities. Currently, she is leading the nonprofit Feonix—Mobility Rising an emerging nonprofit partner focused on deploying Mobility as a Service with a focus on underserved and vulnerable populations.

Prior to starting her own business, Lefler worked at the University of Nebraska at Omaha (UNO) where Lefler served as a Principal Investigator on a $1 million grant to improve rural public transportation for the Nebraska Department of Transportation.

Before she was engaged in public transportation, Lefler served as Program Coordinator for the University of Nebraska-Lincoln Nebraska Transportation Center and the Mid-America Transportation Center from 2003 to 2013. She has worked extensively with program sponsors at the state and federal levels, including, but not limited to, the National Science Foundation, the U.S. DOT Federal Highway Administration, U.S. DOT Federal Transit Administration, the U.S. DOT Office of the Assistant Secretary for Research and Technology, the National Academy of Sciences Transportation Research Board, the Nebraska Department of Transportation, and the Nebraska Department of Education.

In 2005 Valerie graduated with distinction from the University of Nebraska—Lincoln with a degree in Business Administration after studying International Economics abroad at the University of Oxford. She received her master's degree in Public Administration with an emphasis in Public Management from the University of Nebraska—Omaha in 2012.

Dr. Thomas O'Brien is the executive director of the Center for International Trade and Transportation (CITT) at California State University, Long Beach and the associate director of Long Beach Programs for the METRANS Transportation Center, a partnership between CSULB and the University of Southern California. He also serves as the director of the FHWA Southwest Regional Surface Transportation Workforce Center (SWTWC). His teaching and research focuses on logistics, supply chain management, and goods movement policy. Dr. O'Brien has a master's degree in urban planning and development and a PhD in policy, planning, and development from the University of Southern California. He is both an Eno and Eisenhower Transportation fellow and a member of the Transportation Research Board's Intermodal Freight Transport Committee and Intermodal Freight Terminal Design and Operations Committee. He currently serves as the chair of the Southern California Regional Transit Training Consortium and on the boards of the National Transit Institute, Council of University Transportation Centers, Los Angeles Transportation Club, Southern CA Roundtable of the Council of Supply Chain Management Professionals, Harbor Association of Industry and Commerce, and the Foreign Trade Association.

Dr. Gary Painter is a professor in the Sol Price School of Public Policy at the University of Southern California. He also serves as the director of the Sol Price Center for Social Innovation and the Homelessness Policy Research Institute. His research focuses on how to activate social innovation processes, which he includes his recent coauthored book entitled, *Payment by Results and Social Impact Bonds: Outcome-based Payment Systems in the UK and US.* Professor Painter also has extensive expertise in housing, urban economics, and education policy. His recent work at the intersection of transportation and labor markets involves developing new models that measure accessibility vis-à-vis public transit. He has been the principal investigator on over three million dollars of funded research, supported by agencies and foundations that include the US and California Departments of Transportation, the Conrad N. Hilton Foundation, the Haynes Foundation, the Russell Sage Foundation, and the Ewing Marion Kauffman Foundation.

Joanne Peterson is the Chief Human Capital & Development Officer for LA Metro. She is a seasoned human resource and labor relations professional with more than 19 years of executive-level experience in the industry. She joined LA Metro in May 2015 as the executive officer of Human Resources and has held positions with the County of Marin and the City of Seattle's Public Utilities. She received her master's degree in Public Administration from the University of Washington and Executive Education focused on The Art and Practice of Leadership from Harvard Kennedy School.

Ian Roark, Ed.D., is the Vice President of workforce development for Pima Community College. In his role, Roark serves to increase PCC's responsiveness to the needs of businesses and industry and align the college's programs to the workforce and economic development priorities of the region. Roark also oversees the workforce development and continuing education division, which serves nearly 6000 students on an annual basis in workforce education, training, and continuing education programs. He has served as co-Principal Investigator for the Pacific Southwest Region University Transportation Center.

Ronald (Ron) Hall is the president of Bubar & Hall Consulting, LLC and the former principal investigator and director of the Tribal Technical Assistance Program (TTAP) at Colorado State University. While at the TTAP, Hall coordinated the National Tribal Transportation Conference from 1998 to 2013. He served on the executive board of the National Local Technical Assistance Program Association from 1997 to 2004 and was the executive board's chairman for 2002. Hall works nationally to understand and support the training, technical assistance, and technology transfer needs of tribal transportation programs. He also played a key role in creating the Committee on Native American Transportation Issues in the Transportation Research Board, and served as the chairman of that committee from 2001 to 2007; he began his second term as chair in 2016. Hall also served on the FHWA Tribal Safety Management System Steering Committee from its beginning in 2008 until 2013. He organized the first two National Tribal Transportation Safety Summits in 2009 and 2012. Hall serves as the Native American transportation safety expert for the National Center for Rural Road Safety.

Hannah Safford is a researcher with the UC Davis Policy Institute for Energy, Environment, and the Economy, and a Ph.D. student in the UC Davis Department of Civil and Environmental Engineering. In these roles, she works to integrate the best ideas from engineering and policy into practical, scalable, and inspiring solutions. Hannah served for 2 years as a fellow in the White House Office of Science and Technology Policy under the Obama Administration and has also held positions at the U.S. Forest Service, the San Francisco Department of the Environment, and the San Francisco Airport. She holds a B.S.E., M.Eng, and MPA from Princeton University.

Dr. Daniel Sperling is Blue Planet Prize Distinguished Professor of Civil Engineering and Environmental Science and Policy, and founding Director of the Institute of Transportation Studies at the University of California, Davis (ITS-Davis). He holds the transportation seat on the California Air Resources Board and served as Chair of the Transportation Research Board (TRB) of the National Academies in 2015−16. Among his many prizes are the 2018 Roy W. Crum award from TRB, its highest research award; and the 2013 Blue Planet Prize from the Asahi Glass Foundation Prize. He has authored or co-authored over 250 technical papers and 13 books, including Three Revolutions: Steering Automated, Shared, and Electric Vehicles to a Better Future (Island Press, 2018) and is a regular contributor to Forbes magazine on-line.

Anne Strauss-Wieder is a nationally respected senior executive and expert. She currently serves as the director of freight planning at the North Jersey Transportation Planning Authority (NJTPA) and has over 40 years of private and public sector experience. She is recognized for her understanding of the freight and logistics industry; successful project facilitation and delivery; innovative combination of economic development with transportation investment; workforce development; stakeholder engagement; work in resiliency and business continuity; and widely used economic impact assessments. Strauss-Wieder is in leadership roles in national advisory committees and professional organizations including appointments to the US Department of Commerce's Advisory Committee on Supply Chain Competitiveness (where she chairs the Workforce Subcommittee) and the US Maritime Administration's Marine Transportation System National Advisory Committee (where she cochairs the Port Working Group). She also chairs the Transportation Research Board's Committee on the Logistics of Disaster Response and Business Continuity and is an emeritus member of the Freight Transportation Logistics and Planning Committee. She developed and teaches a graduate course on freight and public policy at the Rutgers University Bloustein

School. She is often found in the field at ports, in industrial space, in innovative developments, and at other facilities. Strauss-Wieder has a BA and MA in regional science from the University of Pennsylvania and was a 2010 Lead New Jersey Fellow.

David M. Stumpo has 44 years of experience in the public transit industry. He is the founder and CEO of the American Public Transit Exams Institute (APTREX), and executive director for the Southern California Regional Transit Training Consortium (SCRTTC).

Stumpo began his transit career in maintenance washing buses. He is a certified diesel/automotive technician and electrical/electronic troubleshooter on Rail Cars. He has worked extensively for public transit agencies throughout the United States and Canada in senior and executive roles, including SEPTA, DART, San Francisco MUNI and CEO of Coast Mountain Bus Company (formally BC Transit in Vancouver). He has lectured on transit and has published numerous papers. He is an associate professor of business studies at the University of Phoenix.

The APTREX Institute is known for pioneering in the field of transit workforce development specifically for Professional Transit Certification of managerial staff from frontline supervisors to senior and executive management.

Stumpo holds a master degree from LaSalle University, bachelor in business administration from the Wharton School of Business, University of Pennsylvania, and is certified as a CTEM—Certified Transit Executive Manager.

Stumpo has been instrumental in developing the SCRTTC since 2004 as well as overseeing the SCRTTC toward the advancement of the "Learning Model" for transit technicians, supervisors, and overall workforce development.

Dr. Benjamin (Ben) Toney is a proud product of the public school system in Oakland, California, and is a current PhD student in the Urban Planning and Development program at the University of Southern California's Sol Price School of Public Policy. Prior to returning to school, he was a member of the organizing team at Strategic Concepts in Organizing and Policy Education (SCOPE) in South Los Angeles. At SCOPE, he worked to recruit and develop community leaders to advance racial and economic justice agendas through grassroots campaign strategies. His interests include community development, workforce development, regional equity, and foundation/nonprofit strategies for social justice.

Xinge Wang is the Deputy Director of the Transportation Learning Center. Wang is one of this country's leading experts on workforce demand, training capacity, and future projections of workforce needs. In 2015, Wang led the joint research effort of U.S. Department of Transportation, Education, and Labor to identify the future workforce needs to strengthen skills training and career pathways of the transportation industry.

Wang conducted primary research for and was the lead author on a series of research reports to develop an in-depth analysis of return on investment in Pennsylvania's statewide Keystone Transit Career Ladder partnership and New York State's Project Empire partnership. Highlights of this research were published by the Center as *Transit Partnership Training: Metrics of Success* (2010).

Wang received her Master of Science degree in Industrial Relations and Human Resources from the Pennsylvania State University. She is a member of the American Public Transportation Association (APTA) Workforce Development Committee, and a frequent speaker at industry conferences on human capital development. In 2017, Mass Transit Magazine recognized her as one of the Top 40 under 40 in public transportation.

Phillip A. Washington was unanimously selected CEO of the Los Angeles County Metropolitan Transportation Authority (LA Metro) by the LA Metro Board of Directors on March 12, 2015. In his position as LA Metro CEO, Washington oversees an agency that transports 1.4 million boarding passengers on an average weekday, riding on a fleet of 2000 clean-air buses and six rail lines.

Washington came to Los Angeles from Denver, where he was an Assistant General Manager for nearly 10 years, prior to being named CEO in 2009. In Denver, Washington implemented the FasTracks program, one of the largest voter-approved transit expansion programs in the country.

Washington has had numerous prestigious assignments and honors. He was appointed by the Mayor of Denver in 2007, to head the Host Transportation Committee for the 2008 Democratic National Convention. In 2009, he was appointed by Governor Bill Ritter to serve on the State of Colorado's Workforce Development Council to help the State create a 21st century workforce. Washington was named 2013–14 Outstanding Public Transportation CEO of the Year in North America by the American Public Transportation Association (APTA).

Originally from the south side of Chicago—the Chicago Housing Projects of Altgeld Gardens—Washington is a 24-year veteran of the United States Army where he held the rank of Command Sergeant Major, the highest noncommissioned officer rank an enlisted person can achieve. He retired from active duty being awarded the prestigious Defense Superior Service Medal (DSSM) for exceptional service to his country. He holds a B.A. in Business Administration from Columbia College and an M.A. in Management from Webster University. He is a past chair of APTA.

Editor biography

Tyler Reeb leads research, media, and workforce development teams that address challenges and opportunities related to the new mobility workforce, transformational technology, institutional change, and organizational management. He draws from industry benchmarking, labor market analysis, future scenario planning, systems thinking, and enterprise resource planning to produce research-driven reports, publications, and workforce development programs that promote innovation and civic partnerships between leaders in business, government, and education. He serves on the METRANS Executive Committee and directs research, education, and community engagement efforts across the consortium's affiliated centers of excellence, including The Center for International Trade and Transportation, National Center for Sustainable Transportation, MetroFreight, Southwest Transportation Workforce Center, and Pacific Southwest University Transportation Center. He was also the lead author of a successful $1.5 million Federal Highway Administration grant application to fund deployment of the National Transportation Career Pathway Initiative. He is a member of two National Academies of Sciences, Engineering, and Medicine standing committees focused on Education and Training, and Native American mobility issues.

Acknowledgments

This book is a product of teamwork. I am grateful to the Center for International Trade and Transportation (CITT) team for supporting me in bringing this book to fruition and Long Beach State University's College of Professional and International Education for its support of CITT. I extend a special thank you to CITT's Stacey Park and Rachel Brownell for their exceptional editorial assistance at each phase in this project—evidence that they will publish books of their own throughout their promising careers. I would also like to thank the external reviewers who provided valuable insights on the concept of this book to ensure that it struck the right balance between industry, government, and education as well as domestic and international topics. Many of the ideas put forth in this text were informed by initiatives advanced by members of the National Network for the Transportation Workforce, who embody the spirit of communities of practice championed in this book. Lastly, I express deep appreciation to the writers who contributed chapters to this collection for their commitment to empowering the new mobility workforce.

Introduction

Fingerprints on future mobility systems

Days before finalizing this book, I heard one of this volume's expert contributors tell a group of technology, energy, and transportation leaders "my phone is more important to me than my car." Consider the implications of this simple statement. Modern users of the mobility systems that move people and goods can use their smartphones and other mobile devices to order a driver to pick them up and drop them off at locations and times of their choosing in a vehicle of their preference—compact, sedan, sport-utility-vehicle, van, or truck—in cities around the world.

All around the world, at every second in the hour, people are buying consumer goods running the gamut from food to medicine to electronics to bed mattresses in a box. A few quick swipes and fingerprints on a mobile-device screen is all it takes for consumers to get goods delivered to their home or other preferred locations including the trunk of their parked car. A whole host of products can arrive within 2 hours. Soon it will be commonplace that drones will make those deliveries.

Perhaps the easiest way to convey the magnitude of change transforming the mobility systems that move people and goods is to take a moment to reflect on the difference between the telephone workforce today and 20 years ago. Two decades ago, a phone was merely a phone; it was tied to a location and transmitted analog audio. Two decades later, phones are supercomputers that facilitate a new paradigm for human mobility and consumer behavior. In the time it took to read this paragraph, countless commercial transactions were made with mobile computing devices that led to the movement of people and goods throughout the world. This world of digital mobility is the only reality that the Millennial and Digital Native generations have ever known, which means that new workforce development strategies must address the emerging transportation ecosystem, not its prior iteration back when personal phones were merely phones (Fig. 1).

The children riding on tricycles today are fast moving into an Internet-of-Things world where new technologies and consumer attitudes are driving change in personal vehicle, mass transit, active transportation, and goods movement domestically and internationally. Entrepreneurs are developing new business models that offer alternatives to traditional owner-operator

Figure 1 The children riding tricycles today are racing into an Internet-of-Things future.

models; this includes mobility memberships that give subscribers access to a multimodal suite of transportation options with manual and electric bicycles and scooters on local streets and a blend of public- and private-sector vehicular and mass-transit options for longer commutes. Successfully addressing these transformational technologies and societal trends will require leaders in industry, government, and education to challenge core assumptions about the role transportation will play in moving people and goods through 21st-century urban, suburban, exurban, and rural communities. Challenging those assumptions also means embracing the information-based economy as well as workforce realities facing families.

Take a moment to consider the future transportation ecosystem that workforce development professionals must understand in order to develop effective curriculum, experiential learning models, and career pathways to prepare emerging professionals for that brave new world of mobility.

In the personal vehicle sector, companies like Qualcomm and Intel—who made semiconductors and processors for the supercomputers that drove the Internet, e-commerce, and smart phone revolutions—are now investing billions of dollars into the development of self-driving vehicles, A.K.A.:

super computers on wheels [1]. Other Silicon Valley giants like Google, Apple, Lyft, and Uber are investing heavily in the vehicle-to-vehicle, vehicle-to-infrastructure, and smart-city technologies that will enable those driverless vehicles [2]. In the freight and logistics sector, a range of information technology, electrification, and automation trends are creating demands for new skills and competencies in occupations beginning at the entry level and continuing all the way to the c-suite.

Only two decades ago, the logistical arrangements for freight shipments were largely coordinated via fax machines, phone calls, clipboards, and handshakes. On the consumer end of things, in-person shopping was still the preferred mode of shopping. Back then, if you said "Amazon" most people thought of a river. Utter "Amazon" two decades later and most people think of an e-commerce multinational corporate monolith that can ship virtually anything you want anywhere in the world. It is widely known that Amazon is testing unmanned drone parcel deliveries and has patents on a range of drone technologies that would have seemed like science fiction only a few years ago. What is most amazing about this notion is that most of the American public has accepted this future reality and is not surprised by the prospect of flying robots one day replacing delivery drivers [3].

In the active transportation sector, bicycles and scooters are driving considerable change in urban centers. Over the last decade, bike-sharing depots have become ubiquitous in most American cities. Also on the technological horizon are a host of new high-speed rail, crowd-sourced busing, zero-emission, and Hyperloop technologies that could create new opportunities for publically and privately funded mass-transit options.

Predicting the future of mobility is impossible. But one thing is certain, the industry, educational, and governmental professionals who will shape emerging mobility systems will need to collaborate and integrate data and infrastructure systems as never before. Only in this richer context is it possible to comprehend and account for the full implications of the abiding question for this text:

What are the most effective ways to prepare the next generation of mobility professionals to design, develop, operate, and maintain the systems that will move people and goods in the future?

Clearly new transportation systems will increasingly transform the way businesses and communities function in the future. In turn, and equally important to consider, are the ways that members of the new mobility

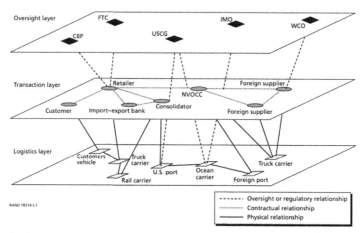

Figure 2 A layered, cross-functional supply-chain model helps identify related regulatory, contractual, and physical challenges facing goods movement stakeholders and related segments of the workforce. Similar models can be applied to human mobility systems.

workforce will have to respond to challenges driven by new consumer preferences, governmental mandates, and the reality that the finite amount of space currently available to move people and goods will become more constrained and congested in the years ahead. All of this means the financial viability and resilience of future mobility systems will be determined by how successful stakeholders across all modes are in synchronizing their efforts across oversight, transaction, and logistics/operational levels as shown in Fig. 2 [4].

Factoring in the jurisdictional layers and cross-functional roles that stakeholders in mobility systems play makes it possible to document and analyze simultaneous interactions occurring at any given step in a human or goods movement mobility system. Such an approach calls for transdisciplinary workforce development research and related strategic initiatives that move beyond traditional business, policy, and educational silos to better address the regulatory, contractual, and physical challenges facing the new mobility workforce.

In 2012, an exemplary group of leaders in industry, government, and education gathered in Washington, DC, to address the most pressing issues facing the new mobility workforce at the National Transportation Workforce Summit. Organized by the Council of University Transportation

Centers with the support of a broad range of key transportation stakeholders, the summit was unique because it convened leadership from the U.S. Departments of Transportation, Labor, and Education to focus on four areas of challenge and opportunity:

- Demographic changes among the user population as well as the future workforce;
- Lack of career awareness and competencies needed in the field;
- Emerging technologies; and
- Increasing and changing demands on transportation agencies.

Those challenges are more relevant today than they were in 2012. Beyond identifying top priorities for the new mobility workforce, the summit embodied the multidisciplinary and nonsiloed approach required to develop that future workforce. A joint report from the summit concluded that transportation employers will need to hire "4.6 million workers—1.2 times the current transportation workforce—in the next decade, due to the industry's employment needs that will result from growth, retirements, and turnover" [5].

In the aftermath of that report, U.S. Department of Transportation officials contended that the nation's transportation systems were fast approaching a "demographic cliff" [6]. Another common reference is the "silver tsunami," a perfect storm of Baby Boomer retirements along with an alarming lack of skilled professionals to assume those critical transportation occupations. In this perfect-storm scenario, transportation jobs remain unfilled, the movement of people and goods grows more inefficient, companies lose revenue, and the national economy suffers. To prevent that scenario, thought leaders in industry, government, and education must develop innovative ways to bridge the gap between the skills job seekers bring and skills that employers need while developing new local, state, and national policy initiatives that support those goals.

Employers across all sectors are increasingly responding to workforce challenges by investing more time and resources into recruiting and developing skilled transportation professionals. Major supply-chain employers are now developing nontraditional apprentice programs to create their own minor leagues of talented professionals after realizing that such efforts are more sustainable than poaching employees from competing firms. Apprenticeships are most commonly associated with training programs for union workers. But there is a growing trend in private-sector firms to develop industry-sponsored apprentice programs to bridge the skills gap between classrooms and workplaces. Investing in apprenticeships can save organizations recruitment and training costs, given that employees can be more accurately placed in positions that match the knowledge and skills gained in the apprenticeship. As a result, these programs help employers to reduce skills gaps. In an Urban Institute study consisting of 900 organizations with apprenticeship programs, approximately 90% of organizations reported they would highly recommend apprenticeship programs to others, because the programs helped meet skill demands and reduce gaps [7].

The emergence of nontraditional apprentice programs is part of a larger trend toward more workplace-learning initiatives formed through employer-educator partnerships. It is commonly observed that K-12 and postsecondary education fails to prepare students for the workplace by emphasizing individualized work and abstract theoretical knowledge over workplace competencies and multidisciplinary understanding. The modern work environment calls for professionals who have in-depth knowledge of their discipline, but a breadth of knowledge in regard to how their field intersects with others.

It seems the days of laissez-faire hiring strategies are long past for employers seeking sustainable workforces. It is no longer sufficient to post a job description on indeed.com or LinkedIn and passively wait for talented applicants. Savvy employers understand that investment in employee talent pipelines, career pathways, and other employer–educator partnerships are keys to long-term viability. Fortunately, longstanding forums exist to bring leaders in industry, education, and government together to address the exponential change and related challenges facing the new mobility workforce.

For decades, the Transportation Research Board (TRB) has engaged thousands of "engineers, scientists, and other transportation researchers and practitioners from the public and private sectors and academia, all of whom contribute their expertise in the public interest by participating on TRB committees, panels, and task forces." Since 1920, TRB's teams of multidisciplinary member specialists, as part of the National Academies of Sciences, Engineering, and Medicine, have given "independent, objective analysis and advice to the nation" that has informed critical public policy decisions and helped document, research, and respond to complex mobility problems [8].

Through its National Cooperative Highway Research Program (NCHRP), TRB has fostered a culture of transportation-focused research and education that has connected leaders in industry, federal agencies, state and municipal transportation departments, and other expert stakeholders to address critical transportation issues facing U.S. communities and businesses. Without the longstanding investments of time and money from public- and private-sector leaders, TRB's nearly 100-year research tradition and rich network of experts working together would not exist. If federal lawmakers had not passed legislation in 1970 to establish the formation of the University Transportation Center (UTC) program funded by the U.S. Department of Transportation, decades of research and valuable professionalizing opportunities for undergraduate and graduate researchers at institutions across the United States would have never materialized.

Said another way, solving the nation's transportation problems is not cheap and longstanding funding for experts to solve those challenges is required to find solutions. Similarly, organizing strategic stakeholders across public- and private-sector spheres to develop communities of practice devoted to recruiting, training, and retaining the new mobility workforce is not cheap or easy. The exponential rates of change driven by ever-changing technologies and new market conditions are upping the stakes and levels of difficulty for the workforce who will design, develop, operate, and maintain the mobility systems that will move people and goods in the future. Fortunately, the answer to this new mobility workforce challenge is simple. All difficult and expensive business and engineering problems require shrewd investment in the most talented and skilled workforces. That means that any thoughtful response to the challenges facing the new mobility workforce should build upon the communities of practice established by the thought leaders who established and contribute to TRB, NCHRP, and transportation centers of excellence located throughout the United States.

This book seeks to build on the work that has preceded it, not repeat or rehash it but rather engage an international roster of subject matter experts to respond to targeted problem statements facing the new mobility workforce. Each chapter provides solutions and analysis to help empower a workforce that has as much to do with semiconductors, microprocessors, and algorithms as it does tires, roads, and rails. This volume will also emphasize, through a series of specific illustrations and case studies some of the most innovative and forward-looking practices that are emerging in transportation organizations that have lasting value as guides to individual and collective action. While this volume emphasizes work largely done in the United States, it also features innovative workforce development efforts being conducted in other countries as well, acknowledging the increasing interconnectedness of mobility systems between countries, economies, and social networks that transcend national boundaries.

Each of the contributing authors recruited for this text embraces the notion that, in the end, mobility problems created by disruptive technologies and societal trends are solved by humans, not machines. These authors understand that students in K-12 and postsecondary schools today need to be inspired before they are trained. Such inspiration is rooted in the idealism that compels every new generation to pursue ethical and new lofty goals. It is imperative that the young girls and boys riding tricycles today grow to understand that their fingerprints may soon cover the mobility systems of the future. Systems that will make their homes, communities and countries safer, healthier, and more prosperous. If today's emerging professionals understand that, then the future of mobility is in good hands.

References

[1] Qualcomm. Develop smart transportation solutions for cities in motion. <https://www.qualcomm.com/solutions/internet-of-things/smart-cities/transportation>, 2018 (accessed 01.11.18).
[2] Forbes. Self-driving cars will keep getting better forever. <https://www.forbes.com/sites/davidsilver/2018/09/04/self-driving-cars-will-keep-getting-better-forever/#4053ee5a217d>, 2018 (accessed 01.11.18).
[3] Amazon Prime Air. <https://www.amazon.com/Amazon-Prime-Air/b?ie = UTF8&node = 8037720011>, 2018 (accessed 01.11.18).
[4] The RAND Corporation. Evaluating the security of the global containerized supply chain. <https://www.rand.org/content/dam/rand/pubs/technical_reports/2004/RAND_TR214.pdf>, 2004 (accessed 01.11.18).
[5] U.S. Departments of Education, Transportation, and Labor. Strengthening skills training and career pathways across the transportation industry. <https://s3.amazonaws.com/PCRN/docs/Strengthening_Skills_Training_and_Career_Pathways_Across_Transportation_Industry_Data_Report_091115.pdf>, 2015 (accessed 01.11.18).
[6] RT&S. FHWA and FTA take on workforce "cliff." <https://www.rtands.com/track-maintenance/off-track-maintenance/fhwa-fta-take-on-workforce-cliff/>, 2016 (accessed 01.11.18).
[7] Southwest Transportation Workforce Center. Jobs Needs and Priorities Report, Phase 2: Southwest Region. (n.d). <https://www.swtwc.org/wp-content/uploads/2016/06/FHWA_Job-Needs-Phase-2-Report-_Southwest.pdf > (accessed 01.11.18).
[8] The Transportation Research Board. About Us. <http://www.trb.org/AboutTRB/AboutTRB.aspx>, 2018 (accessed 01.11.18).

PART I

Keeping Pace with Transformational Technology

Historical perspectives on managing automation and other disruptions in transportation

Austin Brown[1], Hannah Safford[2], and Daniel Sperling[3]
[1]Policy Institute for Energy, Environment, and the Economy, University of California, Davis, CA, United States
[2]Department of Civil & Environmental Engineering, University of California, Davis, CA, United States
[3]Institute of Transportation Studies, University of California, Davis, CA, United States

Contents

Overview

Automation is coming to transportation. Exactly how and when is subject to intense debate, but experts agree that sooner or later, it is

Empowering the New Mobility Workforce.
DOI: https://doi.org/10.1016/B978-0-12-816088-6.00001-8

inevitable. Some believe vehicle automation is a scourge; others believe it is a panacea. Equally uncertain is the impact of this automation on jobs, both for personal mobility and freight.

While automation in transportation is new, automation in other sectors is not. Historical precedents can provide clues about how automation and other technological disruptions in transportation will likely affect the workforce and economy. In this chapter, we explore four instances—in manufacturing, farming, shipping, and food preparation—in which automated labor-saving devices brought deep structural changes to employment and work. These case studies can and should inform preparations and expectations for the automated-vehicle (AV) revolution.

We find many reasons to be optimistic about the net economic and labor effects of vehicle automation. With passenger travel, we know that automation will displace many drivers—for taxis, limousines, Uber, and Lyft—but we also know that AVs will enable workers to more productively use the massive amounts of time currently wasted driving and create jobs at all skill levels. Highly trained professionals such as programmers and data scientists will be needed to develop and optimize AV algorithms. Lower-skilled workers will be needed for customer care, cleaning of cars, and more. New services might be offered in the vehicles, such as personal care, business services, and entertainment. With goods movement, automation of long-haul trucking could increase total freight activity and hence increase demand for workers to load, unload, and stock goods— tasks that are less easily automated.

But the rapid pace at which automation in transportation is occurring warns against complacency. When automation is introduced over generations (as was the case with farming), there was ample time for workers to adjust. Natural attrition of older workers occurs through retirement, and younger workers can be educated and trained to maximize the advantages of automation. If change comes much faster, society as a whole may still benefit but only at the expense of disruptive localized job loss.

Regardless of the exact labor impact, informed public policy is critical for maximizing positive outcomes of AVs, while minimizing costs. Leaders and decision-makers will need to proactively help workers build skills needed in an automated world. Programs should be established soon to support the workers and businesses that automation will inevitably displace in transitioning to new opportunities. And provisions should be put in place to ensure that the benefits of automation in transportation are equitably distributed across geographic regions and socioeconomic classes.

The transportation workforce and economy are changing fast. Society must be prepared to adapt.

History of economic and technological transformation

Through the broad reach of history, technology that helps automate tasks—here broadly defined as reducing the labor input required for a given output—has profoundly transformed our societies and economies. But details matter. Time and scale matter the most. Labor impacts will be most disruptive if change is fast and widespread. But net impacts on jobs are likely to be positive.

Division of labor

For millennia, human beings had only two main jobs—hunting and gathering. They also had only two ways to get around—their left and right legs. It may seem inappropriate to review ancient history, but doing so reminds us of the incredible power we have to change and improve our lives. More or less everything we consider essential today—shelter, clothing, mobility, sanitation, health care, and more—is a product of human ingenuity... and automation.

As societies became more stationary and food supplies more stable, division of labor allowed individuals to develop specialized skills and pass those skills onto future generations. Specialization fostered innovation, allowing people to create and improve technologies, trade knowledge with other parts of the world, and collaborate on projects too advanced for any one person to carry out alone.

Specialization remains important today. Research shows that all else equal, countries with low specialization are able to do less with capital investment than countries with high specialization [1]. This makes intuitive sense, as a low-specialization workforce is less able to take active, value-generating roles in new technology that arrives alongside investment.

Technology substituting for labor

Classic macroeconomic models of the market depend on capital and labor, and allow technology to essentially substitute for labor. When technology substitutes for labor, by definition some jobs in that specific application will be displaced. It might be natural to think that this would have on net reduced labor's share of economic production. Over a century of study, however, this has not been the case [2], as overall growth and new employment in other sectors has more than made up for replaced labor.

Autor and Salomons point out that this has given "grounds for optimism that, despite seemingly limitless possibilities for labor-saving technological progress, automation need not make labor irrelevant as a factor of production" [3]. However, they also find in their recent review that "although automation—whether measured by Total Factor Productivity growth or instrumented by foreign patent flows or robot adoption—has not been employment displacing, it has reduced labor's share in value-added" [3]. So, while technology has only created economic surplus on the net so far, there are some reasons to question whether this trend will continue in perpetuity.

Many areas where technology substitutes for labor also require energy inputs. Smil has extensively reviewed the history of energy technology and shown that energy and technology together effectively have a multiplying effect on labor, allowing much more output per worker [4].

The net effects of technology introduction historically are so strongly and unambiguously positive that it is hard to imagine a counterfactual world. These changes have happened over decades or centuries, and so seem to have a diffuse effect that is hard to measure during the transition. Introductions of technology for labor can also cause local harm such as pollution and job displacement. In short, substituting technology for labor often results in indirect but widespread benefits for the many at the expense of direct adverse effects of the few. These situations in general can make it very challenging for policymakers to maximize public good [5,6].

Impact of automation in other sectors

Understanding how labor-saving technologies affected other sectors in the past provides insight into how automation is likely to affect transportation in the future. The introduction of technology in farming, mechanization in factories, and standardization of freight with containers each had transformative effects on the workforce and the economy.

These industrial examples are well-documented cases of economic substitution of technology for labor. Automation is also increasingly present in our daily lives. Ready availability of labor-saving devices may have contributed to a shift away from in-home services.

Lastly, dining out has changed some of an unpaid service (cooking in the home) to a paid one (eating in a restaurant or ordering take out). While this is not an effect of automation per se, it may be instructive as an example for some aspects of automation in transportation.

Farming

For centuries, farming was a heavily manual occupation: tilling, sowing, irrigation, and harvesting were all done by hand. Most farms were relatively small (since an individual farmer could only manage so much land), and farming employed a high percentage of the workforce (since many workers were needed to produce enough food to support the population). For hundreds of years, well over half of the population was employed in farming and food production [7]. Starting around 1800, with technology developed from the Industrial Revolution, the share of people involved in farming began to fall precipitously. Technological introductions such as the cotton gin (1793), the McCormick Reaper (1834), commercial fertilizer (1843), the gasoline tractor (1892), and hundreds more amplified the person-power of each worker.

This change accelerated dramatically beginning in the early 1900s. The 20th century saw the share of U.S. workers employed as farmers or farm laborers decline steadily from roughly a third in 1910 to less than 1% in 2000 (Fig. 1.1). Farms also consolidated, with the number of farms nationwide dropping as average farm size rose (Fig. 1.2).

Meanwhile, agricultural productivity improved dramatically. Agricultural output in the United States climbed even as inputs remained essentially constant (Fig. 1.3). Agricultural value added per worker in the United States increased to nearly $100,000, a figure that is 10−100 times higher than in less-developed economies [9].

Productivity increases have resulted in food becoming much cheaper and more accessible. The price of wheat, for example, has fallen by more than a factor of 5 (in inflation-adjusted terms) since 1800. Many other commodity food prices have dropped similarly (Fig. 1.4). The share of the average U.S. family's disposable income spent on food decreased from nearly 25% in 1929 to less than 10% in 2014 [10]. Greater agricultural productivity and lower food prices have done much to improve health and quality of life worldwide despite a rapidly growing population.

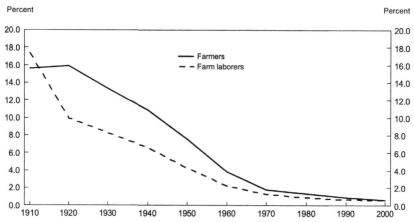

Figure 1.1 Percent of total U.S. employment accounted for by farmers and farm laborers. Combined employment fell from about 30% to about 1% over the course of the 20th century. *From I.D. Wyatt, D.E. Hecker, Occupational changes during the 20th century, Bureau of Labor Statistics, Monthly Labor Review. <https://www.bls.gov/opub/mlr/2006/03/art3full.pdf>, 2006 [8].*

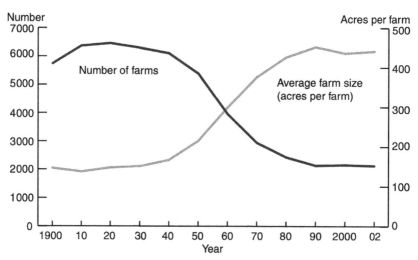

Figure 1.2 Introduction of new farming technology was one reason that farm size grew and farm number dropped beginning in the mid-1900s. *From C. Dimitri, A. Effland and N. Conklin, The 20th century transformation of U.S. Agriculture and Farm Policy, Economic Information Bulletin Number 3, Economic Research Service, U.S. Department of Agriculture. <https://ageconsearch.umn.edu/bitstream/59390/2/eib3.pdf>, 2005.*

Index (1880 = 100)

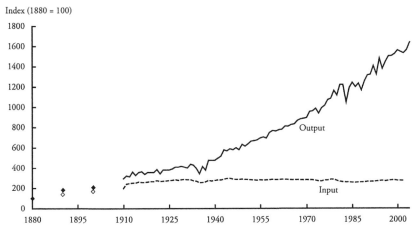

Figure 1.3 Farm productivity has increased dramatically since 1880. *From J.M. Alston, et al., A brief history of U.S. agriculture. In Persistence Pays: U.S. Agricultural Productivity Growth and the Benefits from Public R&D Spending, 2010, Springer Verlag, New York.*

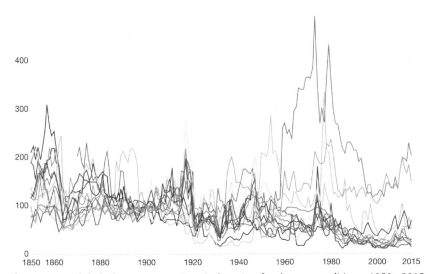

Figure 1.4 Global long-term price index in food commodities, 1850−2015. Commodity price index in food items dating from 1850 to 2015, measured relative to real prices in 1900 (i.e., 1900 = 100). Most food commodities have decreased significantly in real price. *From M. Roser and H. Ritchie, Our world in data, food prices. <https://ourworldindata.org/food-prices>, 2018.*

A major driver of these trends is advancement in farming technology. The adaption of the internal combustion engine to mobile tractors—coupled with the design of tractor attachments for planting, harvesting, threshing, and more—enabled farmers to substantially expand acreage, while new pesticides, herbicides, and fertilizers increased productivity per acre. Improved irrigation systems made it possible to farm well even in water-limited areas. The list goes on.

Not all of the effects of the 20th-century agricultural revolution have been positive. Industrialization of agriculture has increased greenhouse-gas emissions and nutrient runoff while depleting aquifers and soils and limiting the genetic diversity of crops. But the net positive effects for society do not seem to be in doubt. Few would ask to return to an era where most people farmed for a living in tough conditions, food was expensive, harvests were unreliable, and few crops were available. The country accepted and embraced the transition from family farming to large-scale farming because the benefits were large and because the change was gradual. The decline in agricultural employment came mostly through natural attrition rather than large-scale layoffs, and those who remained in the agricultural sector had time to learn new skills and adapt to new practices.

Manufacturing

Factory automation is probably the best-known example of technology replacing labor. The term Luddite, now in general use for someone who fears the advance of technology, has its roots in factory workers who tried to stop the adoption of automated looms in the early 19th century. This is far from the only example of job displacement in manufacturing. Indeed, the labor and economic effects of factory automation remain hot-button political issues today.

In the United States, manufacturing has declined significantly as a share of employment but remained relatively steady as a share of GDP [11] (Fig. 1.5). These trends reflect increasing levels of automation and a shift away from domestic manufacturing of goods that are highly labor-intensive to produce. As with farming, factory automation dramatically lowers end costs of goods. This in turn increases the real purchasing power of consumers. Greater use of technology in manufacturing has also enabled mass production of new types of goods—such as computers and other electronics—that would be impossible using human labor alone.

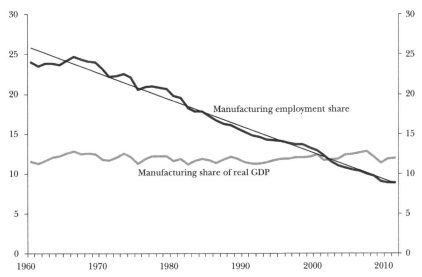

Figure 1.5 Manufacturing value added and employment as a share of the total U.S. economy, 1960−2011. Manufacturing has decreased as a share of employment but remained constant as a share of real GDP since 1960. *From M.N. Baily, B.P. Bosworth, US manufacturing: understanding its past and its potential future, J. Econom. Perspect. 28 (1) (2014) 3−26.*

Also as with farming, the shift from manual labor to automation in manufacturing has taken decades. But in many cases, automating factories is more disruptive than automating farms. Manufacturing jobs tend to be concentrated in "factory towns." Factory automation is therefore more likely than farming automation to cause widespread layoffs in a particular community. This can cause localized economic depression that can persist for generations. Such impacts may not be captured by aggregate metrics but must not be ignored. Possible solutions include offering retraining programs, improved unemployment benefits, and other resources to workers adversely affected by automation.

Shipping

Maritime shipping has been a cornerstone of global trade and economic growth for centuries. Yet as ship technology evolved from sail power to steam power to the power of fossil fuels, shipping technology remained largely the same. Goods were shipped loose, so loading and unloading a ship meant hiring a crew of dockworkers to manually move individual pieces of cargo into and out of the hold. This grueling process could take days. Loose shipping also meant that companies had to be strategic about minimizing cargo exposure to weather, maximizing available storage space, evenly distributing cargo weight, and a host of other factors [12].

Change came with the invention of shipping containers in the 1950s. Little more than a set of standard measurements and connectable corners, this easily overlooked technology revolutionized the shipping industry [13]. Combining lots of individual pieces of cargo in large, standard containers meant that freight could move from ship to train to truck with a tiny fraction of the labor and logistical headaches previously required.

Containerization wrought change more quickly than the introduction of new technology in farming or manufacturing, at both a local and international level. Locally, the dockside workforce experienced large-scale layoffs. Containerization did create some new dockside jobs for laborers such as crane operators, but not nearly enough to absorb the loading/ unloading crews whose services were no longer needed.[1] Dockworkers in some cities were able to fight off containers,[2] but their victory was short-lived. Major ports that eschewed containers are now no longer major ports, having watched their business move to neighboring cities that were more open to change.

Internationally, containerization made long-range shipping across the ocean much more accessible. This opened new avenues for trade and specialization. Easy, low-cost goods movement means that goods will be produced where it is cheapest or where the local economy is otherwise most suitable, rather than where markets are closest. Indeed, Bernhofen et al. found that adoption of containerization was an important determinant of a country's development as a global trade leader [14]. Economic globalization is frequently the subject of political attacks and tariffs seeking to protect domestic industries. Improved access to markets in other countries can undoubtedly undermine some businesses. A business in Iowa producing carpets for $500 each will run into trouble if a new trade route opens U.S. markets to a business in Indonesia producing similar carpets for $50

---

[1] It is difficult to assess the precise magnitude of containerization's effects on the workforce in coastal cities. Gomtsyan [13] finds that even though dockworker employment did decline in some coastal cities following containerization, those declines are correlated with a faster drop in unemployment overall for those cities, implying that it may have created economic growth in other sectors to more than offset job loss by dockworkers.

[2] For a detailed history of the introduction of the shipping container and resulting disputes, see Levinson [12].

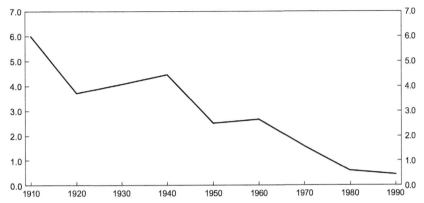

Figure 1.6 Percent of total U.S. employment accounted for by private household ser-vice workers. Employment fell from about 6% to less than 0.5% over the course of the 20th century. *From I.D. Wyatt, D.E. Hecker, Occupational changes during the 20th century, Bureau of Labor Statistics, Monthly Labor Review. <https://www.bls.gov/opub/mlr/2006/03/art3full.pdf>, 2006.*

each. But economists generally argue that, on average, trade improves all participant economies and creates jobs.[3]

Home care

In-home care by private household service workers (such as cleaners, personal attendants, in-home chefs, and other household staff) used to be a major employer in the United States, accounting for 6% of all employment in 1910. By 2000, this figure had fallen to less than 0.5% (Fig. 1.6). The economic research literature in this area is relatively sparse, so we can only observe the correlation and speculate that one contributing factor may be the development of technology for the home that reduces the need for human help. For example, the vacuum cleaner made cleaning easier and modern stoves and ovens, refrigera-tion, and microwaves decreased the time and training needed for food preparation.

Of course, economic and social factors have played a role here too. During some of this period (1910–50 especially), economic inequality decreased in the United States and prevailing wages increased, which may have decreased the number of families that could afford full-time house-hold services [16]. Although economic inequality increased again in the

---

[3] For a review, see Irwin [15].

1980s, employment of household workers continued to decline. Because of these uncertainties, this example should be viewed as tentative at this time.

Food preparation

Each example so far has been in an industry that has seen job losses due to technology substituting for labor. In other cases, technology could create jobs by making it more affordable, and therefore common, to take an unpaid activity and turn it into a paid one. The increase in food-preparation employment is a concrete example of this effect.

Food preparation (i.e., working at restaurants) has grown significantly as a share of employment in the United States (Fig. 1.7). The major factor driving this trend is an increasing share of meals eaten outside the home. The share of meals eaten outside the home was very low before 1910, and grew from less than 20% in 1980 to more than 30% by 2012 (Fig. 1.8). There are many economic and social factors driving this trend, including "a larger share of women employed outside the home, more two-earner households, higher incomes, more affordable and convenient fast food outlets, increased advertising and promotion by large food service chains, and the smaller size of U.S. households." [17].

This is a useful example because it shows that employment in a sector can increase when there is a shift from unpaid labor (here, cooking in the

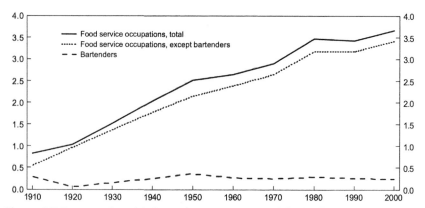

Figure 1.7 Percent of total U.S. employment accounted for by food service occupations. Employment increased from less than 1% to more than 3.5% over the course of the 20th century. *From I.D. Wyatt, D.E. Hecker, Occupational changes during the 20th century, Bureau of Labor Statistics, Monthly Labor Review. https://www.bls.gov/opub/mlr/2006/03/art3full.pdf, 2006.*

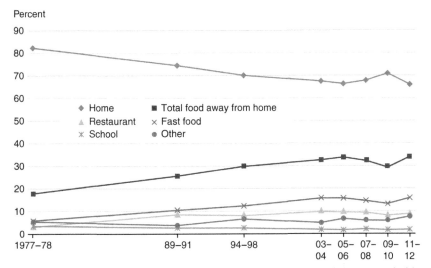

Figure 1.8 Average share of daily calories for U.S. population aged 2 years and older, by source. Since the 1970s, the share of meals eaten outside the home has increased from less than 20% to almost 35%. *From The 30-year upward trend in eating out briefly reversed in 2007—10, Economic Research Service, United States Department of Agriculture. <https://www.ers.usda.gov/data-products/chart-gallery/gallery/chart-detail/? chartId = 79054>, 2016.*

home) to a paid service (eating out) in that sector. Many factors, including increased income and changing social norms, have contributed to the increases in food eaten away from home. This is a useful indicator that if another sector (in the case of this chapter, driving) shifts from an unpaid to paid service, it could increase in-sector employment.

Summary

The introduction of automated and other types of labor-saving technology in farming, manufacturing, and shipping had substantial economic benefits. Cheaper food, goods, and goods movement increased real purchasing power for consumers. Greater productivity freed dollars and people to pursue new opportunities. Factory automation and freight containerization in particular dramatically expanded access to certain goods and markets, benefiting society as a whole.

These benefits were accompanied by some adverse workforce effects. Automation decreased overall employment in U.S. farming and manufacturing, and freight containerization resulted in mass layoffs of dockworkers in coastal cities. In farming, effects were relatively gradual and geographically dispersed. In manufacturing and shipping, however, effects were more concentrated in time and space, making it more difficult for workers to adjust. In the next section, we discuss how lessons from these historical precedents can be applied in the transportation sector to smooth the transition from human-driven cars to AVs.

Impacts of automation in transportation

Automation of the transportation sector is already well underway. Most new cars in Europe, the United States, Korea, and Japan are already partially automated with features such as adaptive cruise control, lane-keep assist, and more. Companies like Google have been testing fully driverless cars for years, and driverless mobility services are being tested at the pilot scale in multiple cities. Some of the effects of vehicle automation on the workforce and the economy are already evident. Others will depend on how automation continues to evolve. In this section, we explore the emerging and likely impacts of vehicle automation on personal mobility and freight. We also consider how these impacts depend on the pace at which automation occurs. Throughout, we assume that vehicle automation occurs alongside two other revolutions in transportation: vehicle electrification and vehicle sharing.[4] We focus on the United States, although we expect many of our conclusions to be applicable to other countries as well.

Effects on personal mobility
Workforce effects

Vehicles account for most passenger-miles traveled in the United States (Table 1.1). The vast majority of vehicle trips are taken in personally owned and driven vehicles. Only a few percent of personal trips use transit, and less than 1% are in a light-duty vehicle with a paid driver (Fig. 1.9). The latter figure is beginning to increase as transportation network companies (TNCs) such as Uber and Lyft continue to gain popularity and market share. But while TNCs have rapidly eclipsed taxis and approached transit in terms of number of trips taken (Fig. 1.9), they are

---

[4] A deeper analysis of the intersections among vehicle automation, sharing, and electrification can be found in Sperling [18].

Table 1.1 U.S. passenger-miles traveled by transportation mode, 2016.

Transportation mode	U.S. passenger-miles (millions)	Percent of total
Air	670,437	12.5
Vehicle	4,580,725	85.7
Transit	56,672	1.1
Rail	39,608	0.7

Source: calculations based on this data: <https://www.bts.gov/content/us–passenger-miles>.

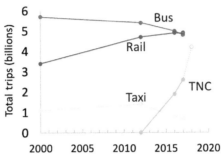

Figure 1.9 TNCs account for a rapidly growing share of travel and may soon pass bus and rail in popularity. The dotted line indicates projections. *From D. Sperling, A. Brown, M. D'Agostino, Could ride-hailing improve public transportation instead of under-cutting it? UC Davis Policy Institute for Energy, Environment, and the Economy. <https://policyinstitute.ucdavis.edu/could-ride-hailing-improve-public-transportation-instead-of-undercutting-it/>, 2018.*

still dwarfed by the personal vehicle. There are also fewer TNC drivers than is commonly perceived. As of 2015, only 0.5% of people in the United States were or had been gig-economy workers, a category that includes many workers besides TNC drivers [18]. This figure may mask the fact that TNCs have pushed to have their drivers classified as independent contractors rather than employees. Nevertheless, the bottom line is unchanged. Drivers-for-hire represent only a very small share of the American workforce.

Far more people are employed to design, manufacture, sell, and service vehicles (approximately 3 million jobs [19]) and related infrastructure [20]. Transportation also directly represents approximately 5% of all GDP [21] (Fig. 1.10).

These jobs will still exist in a world dominated by AVs and may even grow in number, though they may change to be more technical. For instance, TNCs already have many employees developing pricing algorithms and techniques for matching supply and demand. More people will be needed in these roles if, as we expect, TNCs begin to adopt AVs for

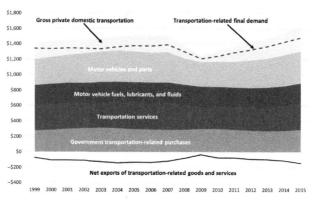

Figure 1.10 Transportation contributions to U.S. GDP. *Figure replicated from Transportation Economic Trends 2017, Bureau of Transportation Statistics, United States Department of Transportation. <https://www.bts.gov/sites/bts.dot.gov/files/docs/ browse-statistical-products-and-data/bts-publications/215901/transportation-economic-trends-2017.pdf>, 2017.*

commercial use. TNCs will also need people to monitor automated fleets and respond to issues in much the same way that employees of bike- and scooter-share companies do now. Vehicle-cleaning and maintenance personnel will become more important as fleet ownership of vehicles displaces personal ownership, since passenger-miles and trips will be more concentrated in a smaller number of shared AVs. It is important to note that worker retraining may be necessary even in jobs that persist. Vehicle and infrastructure maintenance is one good example. Mechanics will need to learn how to inspect and repair advanced sensors and other components absent from conventional vehicles. If AVs are electric as well, mechanics will also need to learn how to install and maintain batteries and charging infrastructure.

Automation may expand and create jobs outside of TNCs. Skilled employees will be in high demand to design hardware and software for AVs. New firms (or new branches of existing firms) may open to provide insurance products appropriate for owners and operators of AVs. A plethora of opportunities may open for service providers. Vehicle passengers no longer occupied with driving will likely look for ways to make the most of their commute time. And as self-driving features make vehicle components like brake pedals, steering wheels, and seatbelts obsolete, it will be possible to redesign vehicle interiors to accommodate in-vehicle services. Some vehicles could double as beauty salons, employing stylists who can give haircuts or manicures while en route. Other vehicles could double as restaurants or bars, employing staff who can provide a mobile happy hour for friends or coworkers. These are just some of the possibilities.

Economic effects

Automation of personal mobility is likely to have substantial net positive economic effects for society as a whole. These positive effects will result from several factors. First, automation frees workers to use time in transit productively instead of wasting it driving. Montgomery [22] estimated that this "unlocked" time could be worth as much as $153 billion (at 100% penetration of AVs).

Second, AVs will drive more efficiently and safely, thereby reducing congestion, oil consumption, and accident rate and severity. Montgomery estimated the total value of these public benefits at up to $633 billion (again, at 100% penetration of AVs). More efficient operation will also enhance productivity in jobs that rely heavily on driving, such as home health care or delivery services. Less time spent driving from stop to stop means more stops completed in any given amount of time.

Third, combining automation with vehicle sharing will enable fuller use of vehicle capacity. The average car is driven only 4% of the time, spending the rest of the time sitting idle as a rapidly depreciating asset. Shared fleets of AVs will have much higher utilization, thereby spreading capital costs over many more users. This in turn increases consumer purchasing power by decreasing travel costs. Travel costs will further decrease if vehicle electrification keeps pace with automation and sharing, since electric vehicles are expected to have much lower operations and maintenance costs than gas-powered vehicles [18].

Shared fleets of AVs will also be able to better respond to real-time changes in demand. Travel demand is highly uneven, spiking both temporally (e.g., during commuting hours) and geographically (e.g., near transit hubs and events). One way for fleet operators to address this problem is by employing enough cars and drivers to meet peak demand without anyone waiting. The downside of this strategy is that it is expensive—and the costs get passed onto customers. Think the lines of taxis that often sit ready at hotels or airports. To have this supply of taxis on hand, fares need to be high enough to compensate drivers not just for active time, but also for time spent waiting.

An alternative that TNCs have adopted is to use "surge pricing" and other cues and incentives to encourage human drivers to work in areas where supply is low and demand is high. These strategies are not always successful. Employing human drivers on a supply-/demand-driven basis may be economically efficient but can make it difficult for TNC drivers to earn a reliable income. What TNCs advertise as flexibility has been deemed exploitation by some drivers and labor groups. Studies so far of driver wages have been mixed, finding incomes of over $19/hour [23] or below $10/hour [24] depending on methodology and specific markets. Human drivers may also avoid certain areas, such as rural communities (where it is more difficult to find customers) or lower-income neighborhoods (where drivers may perceive safety risks). This creates a market failure, may exacerbate socioeconomic stratification, and results in inequitable access to transportation. Shared fleets of AVs have the potential to address all of these issues simultaneously.

Effects on transit

Transit is a significant paid transportation mode, especially in cities, and provides many jobs that may be affected or displaced by automation and new mobility. The interactions of new mobility with transit are already complex and are likely to become more so going forward. Researchers have begun intensive study of key questions such as what modes are disrupted by use of new mobility. The literature so far is mixed [25], but indicates that in urban environments TNCs probably draw from transit ridership on net. In less urban environments, however, TNCs can support transit by serving as an effective feeder system. More affordable new mobility could also potentially compete with personal vehicle ownership, and therefore empower transit for other trips.

The transit industry in the United States is working to figure out how to best accommodate new mobility. Some operators are trying out pilot programs, while others are adopting a "wait-and-see" attitude. Depending on how these new services develop, new mobility could benefit transit (by feeding high-ridership routes from lower density areas), replace transit (by eroding the farebox revenue of transit systems), or become transit (if transit operators start using new-mobility technologies directly or through partnerships). In the most positive futures, transit operators will double down on what transit is good at: providing fixed-route service to move lots of people at once. Transit operators can rely on new mobility to serve the needs of those outside of core lines. This could reinvigorate stagnating transit systems and enrich employment opportunities in the sector at the same time.

Effects on freight
Workforce effects
Unlike personal mobility, where only a small fraction of trips involve a paid driver, all goods movement involves paid employees. In the United States, 1.9 million people work as drivers of heavy and tractor-trailer trucks. Another 1.4 million work as drivers of delivery trucks [26]. The Bureau of Labor Statistics projects [27] that these numbers will increase over the next decade as freight volume continues to grow. Truck driving is only one component of goods movement.[5] Employees are also needed to load and unload goods at origin and end destinations, manage routes and logistics, and monitor performance.

Automation is easiest for the long-haul portion of goods movement, that is, for hundreds of miles along highways. Such automation indisput-ably has the potential to put human long-haul truck drivers out of work. But the physical and psychological demands of extended driving hours and time away from home has made human long-haul truck drivers hard to find anyway [28]. In the short to medium term, at least, automation could help meet commercial needs for long-haul goods movement with-out significant adverse workforce effects. Automation in this model also preserves or grows, at least in the medium term, jobs at both the origin and delivery ends of the supply chain [29].

In the longer term, though, automation of shorter-range delivery could displace human drivers. Minimizing the impacts of this shift will require resources and retraining programs that help drivers transition to other jobs in the freight industry or in other sectors.

Economic effects
Automation is likely to dramatically reduce the cost of goods movement. Driver wages account for 36% of truck operating costs [30], so simply eliminating this expense would be a big financial savings. Automation also enables trucks to safely travel in "platoons," two or more vehicles moving closely together in synchronization. Platooning reduces aerodynamic drag, making all vehicles in the platoon more efficient and cutting down on fuel costs. Moreover, because aerodynamic drag forces are proportional to the second power of speed, these benefits are particularly large for high-way travel, which accounts for the majority of long-haul truck travel [31].

---

[5] Note that in this section, we focus on land-based goods movement. Freight is also transported by rail, air, and sea, but these modes are less relevant to a discussion of vehicle automation.

If automation is accompanied by electrification, fuel and maintenance costs would drop even further. The investment firm Morgan Stanley estimates that automation in freight could yield savings of $168 billion from these and other factors [32]. Cheaper goods movement increases consumer purchasing power, supports specialization, and bolsters economic activity for society overall.

Indeed, automation in freight has the potential to lower the cost of delivery enough to fundamentally transform the way Americans live, shop, and do business. Companies like Amazon have given us a preview of what happens when shipping is free for most transactions: demand for delivery increases and personal travel decreases [33]. Ready availability of cheap or free shipping for a vast online inventory of products makes it difficult for many brick-and-mortar stores to compete. But one study found that on a macroeconomic level, growth in e-commerce from 2007 to 2017 more than compensated for declines in physical retail, while also providing better-paying jobs [34]. Physical stores may also evolve in the future from serving as the point of sale to serving as "showrooms" where customers can test out products in person before ordering online.

Timeframe

One of the most hotly debated questions in transportation research today is "When will AVs be here?" This question is highly relevant to assessments of the likely workforce and economic impacts of automation in transportation since, as historical precedents have shown, slower adoption of automation tends to make it easier to manage adverse impacts but also delays realization of the benefits automation can provide. Predicting the future is always difficult, but particularly so for AVs. One challenge is determining precisely what we mean by "here." Some companies have announced plans to have driverless vehicles available for public use as early as 2020. But it could still take quite some time for AVs to dominate the market. The growth rate of the AV market will depend on factors including how quickly consumers come to accept AVs, how quickly AV technology advances, and the regulatory environment.

A second challenge is that vehicle automation involves the intersection of two industries: one (information technology) that has developed rapidly, and one (transportation) that has been much slower to evolve. Additional research is needed to determine which pace is more likely to dictate the future of AVs. Published estimates of the share of vehicle trips that will be automated by 2030 range from less than 5% [35] all the way to 95% [36]. Given this level of uncertainty, it is important to start establishing retraining programs and resources now for workers likely to be affected by the shift to AVs, in case this shift happens faster than many expect. Decision-makers should also design flexible AV governance policies that can be easily adapted as the AV industry matures.

Summary and net impacts

Automation in transportation is likely to affect both personal mobility and freight, resulting in workforce and economic effects. As was the case for automation in farming, manufacturing, and shipping, we expect automation in transportation to have adverse workforce effects. Automation will inevitably displace some human drivers-for-hire and truck drivers. Yet automation will also expand demand for some existing jobs, as well as create jobs that are entirely new. Moreover, the aggregate economic benefits of automation—including increased productivity from "unlocked" travel time, safer and more efficient travel, and lower goods costs—are likely to far outweigh economic declines associated with job loss in a few sectors. Based on historical precedent and our own analysis, we expect the net impacts of automation in transportation to be positive.

The literature contains additional support for this prediction. Acemoglu and Restrope examined the effect of automation and artificial intelligence on demand for labor, wages, and employment and found that while these technologies do displace labor, displacement is counteracted by increases in productivity and capital accumulation [37]. Hawksworth (2018) argues that artificial intelligence in general could create as many jobs as it displaces [38], though the transportation sector is likely to experience the greatest amount of direct job loss [39]. Almeida examined the job impacts of information technology (IT) adoption in Brazil and found that IT reduced demand for nonskilled labor and shifted the economy towards skilled labor [40]. Montgomery found that automation in transportation is unlikely to cause net job loss, though job loss on a local scale is probable [41]. Montgomery estimated the economic benefits of automation in transportation at up to approximately $800 billion per year [41].

History shows that efforts to hold technological progress back are generally ill-advised, and that technology entering a new sector on net provides massive benefits. While net impacts of automation in transportation are likely to be positive, the magnitude of these benefits—as well as their geographic and socioeconomic distribution—depends on how and at what pace automation develops. Faster adoption of automation may yield benefits sooner but may also make it more difficult for people in certain locations and jobs to adjust. Fortunately, there are steps that policymakers can take to help manage the transition to an automated future, even though the precise nature of this future remains uncertain. These steps are discussed further in the following section.

Managing the transition

Policymakers, including legislators, regulators, city planners, and transit operators, may rightly wonder what position to take when it comes to AVs. Should they welcome this technology and assume only benefits, or should they introduce bans due to the possibility of unintended consequences? Neither extreme is the right course.

Our working hypothesis as a research and policy community should be that this new phase of transportation will yield economic benefits that, on net, outweigh local disruptions. But we should also be vigilant in case they do not. We should set up policy frameworks that allow changes as transportation systems evolve, since it is much more challenging to put such frameworks in place once a new service is widespread.

We are not alone in recommending a managed transition approach. Atkinson found that "[o]f all the concerns being offered for this next uptick in innovation the only real valid one is the need to do more to help workers who lose their job due to technological innovation to transition to new employment" [42]. The Center for Global Policy Solutions found that "certain population groups and areas of the country would be disproportionately affected" by vehicle automation and offered possible policy solutions [43], including automatic unemployment insurance, progressive basic income, education and retraining, automatic Medicaid eligibility, and expanding support for entrepreneurs.

In a recent study of shifting workforce needs from automation [44], the American Center for Mobility recommends these steps:

- Conduct additional research that captures the input of the vehicle operators in different workforce sectors on what training they would be interested in pursuing;

- Identify, in greater detail, the specific skill sets needed by the automotive and technology industries to facilitate the creation and adoption of AVs;
- Establish rapid coursework and training that meets those specific needs;
- Conduct additional research to quantify the overall positive financial impact of AV technology on the economy as a whole, and the potential for job creation.

A managed transition approach

Legislators, regulators, city planners, transit operators, CEOs, and other decision-makers need to strike a balance between embracing the advantages of automation in transportation and treading carefully for fear of unintended consequences. Below, we offer six recommendations to help thread this needle.

Recommendation 1. Work proactively to identify sector-specific impacts and needs associated with transportation in automation

Automation will have differential impacts across the transportation world. Leaders must think critically about how to prepare accordingly. Transit operators may need to shift resources from first-/last-mile bus service (which can be efficiently provided by automated fleets) to longer-distance rail travel. Transportation agencies may need to train workers on how to install "smart" traffic signals that can communicate wirelessly with AVs. Regulators may need to figure out how to set safety standards for design and performance of AV algorithms as well as standard vehicle components. Education professionals may need to expand opportunities for students to learn coding, project management, and other skills that will have increased economic relevance.

Recommendation 2. Provide displaced workers with access to resources and retraining programs

Transportation-sector workers will need resources to adjust to the adoption of automation, particularly if adoption is rapid. Such resources can be funded by the productivity gains associated with automation. This approach has precedent in freight containerization [11]. Some port employers used a portion of the profits associated with adoption of the new, more efficient technology to provide financial benefits and in-kind support to dockworkers. Similarly, policymakers could impose taxes on automated fleet services that are not high enough to kill the industry, but nevertheless yield sufficient revenue to offer displaced workers short-term unemployment benefits and access to retraining programs.

Recommendation 3. Establish protections for gig-economy workers

The emergence of the part-time "gig economy" in the United States has left many people without access to benefits like employer-provided health insurance and retirement savings plans that are often extended only to full-time employees. Gig-economy workers account for only a small fraction of the U.S. workforce today [45], but automation in transportation could expand the number of gig-economy jobs—for instance, for people working as in-vehicle service providers. Policymakers should explore strategies for protecting these workers. One option is to establish mechanisms for employers in the gig economy to offer partial benefits for part-time workers that could be pooled, making it feasible for workers in multiple part-time positions to assemble a compete benefits package.

Recommendation 4. Emphasize equitable distribution of benefits and impacts

Rapid adoption of automation in transportation will affect workers at all levels. The potential for adverse impacts is greatest for lower-income workers, who have the least financial capacity to successfully adjust. We must ensure that automation in transportation does not exacerbate the stark wealth inequality that already exists in the United States. Providing displaced workers with access to resources and retraining programs (Recommendation 2) can help. Establishing fora and processes for policymakers to work with labor representatives and community advocates will enable identification of other strategies for achieving a just transition to an automated future.

Recommendation 5. Ensure that policy frameworks are flexible and adaptable

Automation is indisputably coming to transportation, but it is unclear when and how. Although some policymakers have responded to this uncertainty by taking a "wait and see" approach to AV governance, we recommend against this strategy. It will be much easier to establish effective policy frameworks proactively than to try and impose them once automation is already widespread. However, it should be easy to adjust such frameworks in response to future research insights and developments in AV technology. It is also wise to pilot policy approaches on a limited scale before deploying them broadly.

Recommendation 6. Support further research and data collection

Research insights are key to informed AV governance. The American Center for Mobility notes that further research is particularly needed to:

- Capture the input of the vehicle operators in different workforce sectors on what training they would be interested in pursuing;
- Identify, in greater detail, the specific skillsets needed by the automotive and technology industries to facilitate the creation and adoption of AVs;
- Quantify the overall positive financial impact of AV technology on the economy as a whole, and the potential for job creation.

Another important research need is greater inclusion of economic considerations in modeling studies. Most AV-impact modeling to date focuses on safety, congestion, and environmental outcomes. Models should be expanded to also estimate impacts on factors such as employment and productivity. Pursuing these research objectives will require better data on job numbers and quality in different transportation and service sectors, as well as on other economic metrics. Partnerships among researchers, government agencies, and the private sectors can facilitate collection of such data.

A backup plan if this transition is different

While we argue that past examples demonstrate net benefits of automation under a managed transition, history is not a perfect model. Each example we cite comes from the last two centuries. While that timeframe may seem long, it represents a relatively brief snapshot in the course of human history. It is risky to extrapolate too broadly from these examples.

There has been speculation at least for decades that automation could be the "end of work." Sometimes this is discussed as a benefit, a vision for a short work week and easy labor. Other times it is presented as a future of low employment and nonexistent economic opportunities.

If the replacement jobs we expect do not materialize, policymakers need a course of action. It is never too early to begin developing contingency plans. Policymakers can also pilot approaches to managing the transition in early markets and use the results to inform broader efforts.

One idea to protect workers if automation reduces jobs overall, popularized by Bill Gates, is effectively asking the "robots" to pay—that is, to recapture some of the gained productivity and use it to pay those displaced [46]. This is similar to what port employers did in response to containerization, as discussed in Recommendation 2.

References

[1] A. Rodríguez-Clare, The division of labor and economic development, J. Develop. Econom. 49 (1) (1996) 3–32.

[2] C.I. Jones, P.M. Romer, The New Kaldor facts: ideas, institutions, population, and human capital, Am. Econom. J. Macroeconom. Am. Econom. Assoc. 2 (1) (2010) 224–245.

[3] D. Autor and A. Salomons, Is automation labor-displacing? Productivity growth, employment, and the labor share, BPEA Conference Drafts, March 8–9, 2018, Brookings Paper on Economic Activity, pp. 1–72.

[4] V. Smil, Energy in World History, first ed., Westview Press, Boulder, CO, 1994.

[5] W.C. Mitchell, M.C. Munger, Economic models of interest groups: an introductory survey, Am. J. Polit. Sci. 35 (2) (1991) 512–546.

[6] G. Tullock, Public choice, in: S.N. Durlauf, L.E. Blume (Eds.), The New Palgrave Dictionary of Economics, Palgrave Macmillan, United Kingdom, 2008.

[7] M. Roser, Employment in Agriculture, <https://ourworldindata.org/employment-in-agriculture>, 2019.

[8] I.D. Wyatt and D.E. Hecker, Occupational changes during the 20th century, Bureau of Labor Statistics, Monthly Labor Review. <https://www.bls.gov/opub/mlr/2006/03/art3full.pdf>, 2006.

[9] M. Roser, Our world in data, employment in agriculture. <https://ourworldindata.org/employment-in-agriculture#long-run-perspective-1300-to-today>, 2019.

[10] M. Roser and H. Ritchie, Our world in data, food prices. <https://ourworldindata.org/food-prices>, 2018.

[11] M.N. Baily, B.P. Bosworth, US manufacturing: understanding its past and its potential future, J. Econom. Perspect. 28 (1) (2014) 3–26.

[12] M. Levinson, The Box: How the Shipping Container Made the World Smaller and the World Economy Bigger, second ed., Princeton University Press, Princeton, NJ, 2016.

[13] D. Gomstyan, Rise of the Machines: Evidence from the Container Revolution, University of Turin, Italy, 2016.

[14] D.M. Bernhofen, K. Richard, E. Zouheir, Estimating the effects of the container revolution on world trade, J. Int. Econom. 98 (2016) 36–50.

[15] D. Irwin, Free Trade Under Fire, fourth ed., Princeton University Press, Princeton, NJ, 2015.

[16] T. Piketty, Capital in the Twenty-First Century, Harvard University Press, Cambridge, MA, 2014.

[17] Economic Research Service, Food-away-from-home, U.S. Department of Agriculture. <https://www.ers.usda.gov/topics/food-choices-health/food-consumption-demand/food-away-from-home.aspx>, 2018.

[18] D. Sperling, Three Revolutions, second ed., Island Press, Washington, DC, 2018.

[19] Bureau of Labor Statistics, Automotive Industry: Employment, Earnings, and Hours. <https://www.bls.gov/iag/tgs/iagauto.htm>, 2019.

[20] Bureau of Transportation Statistics, Transportation's contribution to the economy. <https://www.bts.gov/browse-statistical-products-and-data/transportation-economic-trends/tet-2017-chapter-2>, 2017.

[21] Bureau of Transportation Statistics, Gross Domestic Product (GDP) attributed to transportation modes (billions), 2015. <https://www.bts.gov/content/gross-domestic-product-gdp-attributed-transportation-modes-billions-2015>, 2015.

[22] W.D. Montcomery, Public and private benefits of autonomous vehicles. <https://avworkforce.secureenergy.org/wp-content/uploads/2018/06/W.-David-Montgomery-Report-June-2018.pdf>, 2018.

[23] J.V. Hall, J.J. Horton, D.T. Knoepfle, Pricing efficently in designed markets: evidence from ride-sharing. <http://john-joseph-horton.com/papers/uber_price.pdf>, 2018.

[24] S. Zoepf, S. Chen, P. Adu and G. Pozo, The economics of ride hailing: driver revenue, expenses and taxes. <http://ceepr.mit.edu/publications/reprints/681>, 2019.

[25] R.R. Clewlow, G.S. Mishra, Disruptive transportation: the adoption, utilization, and impacts of ride-hailing in the United States, Institute of Transportation Studies, University of California, Davis, Impacts of Ride-Hailing in the United States. Institute of Transportation Studies, University of California, Davis, Research Report UCD-ITS-RR-17-07.

[26] Bureau of Labor Statistics. Occupational outlook handbook: heavy and tractor-trailer truck drivers. <https://www.bls.gov/ooh/transportation-and-material-moving/heavy-and-tractor-trailer-truck-drivers.htm>, 2018.

[27] A. Hogan, B. Roberts, Occupational employment projections to 2024, Bureau of Labor Statistics, Monthly Labor Review. <https://www.bls.gov/opub/mlr/2015/article/pdf/occupational-employment-projections-to-2024.pdf>, 2015.

[28] U. Staats, D. Lohaus, A. Christmann, M. Woitschek, Fighting against a shortage of truck drivers in logistics: measures that employers can take to promote drivers' work ability and health, Work 58 (3) (2017) 387−397.

[29] S. Viscelli, Driverless? Autonomous trucks and the future of the American trucker, Center for Labor Research and Education, University of California, Berkeley, and Working Partnerships USA. <http://driverlessreport.org/files/driverless.pdf>, 2018.

[30] L.R. Grenzeback, A. Brown, M.J Fischer, C.R. Lamm, Y.L. Pei, L. Vimmerstedt, A.D. Vyas and J.J. Winebrake, Freight transportation demand: energy-efficient scenarios for a low-carbon future, U.S. Department of Energy, Transportation Energy Futures Series <https://www.nrel.gov/docs/fy13osti/55641.pdf>, 2013.

[31] M. Taiebat, A.L. Brown, H.R. Safford, S. Qu, M. Xu, A review on energy, environmental, and sustainability implications of connected and automated vehicles, Environ. Sci. Technol. 52 (2018) 11449−11465.

[32] Morgan Stanley. Autonomous cars: self-driving the new auto industry paradigm, Morgan Stanley Blue Paper. <https://orfe.princeton.edu/~alaink/SmartDrivingCars/PDFs/Nov2013MORGAN-STANLEY-BLUE-PAPER-AUTONOMOUS-CARS%EF%BC%9A-SELF-DRIVING-THE-NEW-AUTO-INDUSTRY-PARADIGM.pdf>, 2013.

[33] D. Weideli, Environmental analysis of US online shopping. <https://ctl.mit.edu/sites/ctl.mit.edu/files/library/public/Dimitri-Weideli-Environmental-Analysis-of-US-Online-Shopping_0.pdf>, 2013.

[34] M. Mandel, How ecommerce creates jobs and reduces income inequality, Progressive Policy Institute. <https://www.progressivepolicy.org/wp-content/uploads/2017/09/PPI_ECommerceInequality_2017.pdf>, 2017.

[35] HIS Markit, Autonomous vehicle sales forecast to reach 21 mil. globally in 2035, according to HIS Automotive. <https://ihsmarkit.com/country-industry-forecasting.html?ID = 10659115737>, 2016.

[36] Rethinkx, New Report: due to major transportation disruption, 95% of the U.S. car miles will be traveled in self-driving, electric, shared vehicles by 2030. <https://www.rethinkx.com/press-release/2017/5/3/new-report-due-to-major-transportation-disruption-95-of-us-car-miles-will-be-traveled-in-self-driving-electric-shared-vehicles-by-2030>, 2017.

[37] D. Acemoglu and P. Restrepo, Artificial intelligence, automation and work, NBER Working Paper No. 24196, <https://www.nber.org/papers/w24196>, 2018.

[38] J. Hawksworth, AI and robots could create as many jobs as they displace, World Economic Forum. <https://www.weforum.org/agenda/2018/09/ai-and-robots-could-create-as-many-jobs-as-they-displace/>, 2018.

[39] PWC UK, How will automation impact jobs? <https://www.pwc.co.uk/services/economics-policy/insights/the-impact-of-automation-on-jobs.html>, 2018.

[40] R.K. Almeida, C.H.L. Corseuil and J.P. Poole, The impact of digital technologies on routine tasks: do labor policies matter? World Bank, <https://elibrary.worldbank.org/doi/abs/10.1596/1813-9450-8187>, 2017.

[41] D. Montgomery, R. Mudge, E. Groshen, J.P. Macduffie, S. Helper, C. Carson, America's workforce and the self-driving future, SAFE. <https://avworkforce.secureenergy.org/wp-content/uploads/2018/06/SAFE_AV_Policy_Brief.pdf>, 2018.

[42] R.D. Atkinson, ICT innovation, productivity, and labor market adjustment policy, in: L. Pupillo, E. Noam, L. Waverman (Eds.), Digitized Labor, The Impact of the Internet on Employment, Palgrave Macmillan, Cham, Switzerland, 2018, pp. 179–200.

[43] Center for Global Policy Solutions, Stick shift: autonomous vehicles, driving jobs, and the future of work. <http://globalpolicysolutions.org/report/stick-shift-autonomous-vehicles-driving-jobs-and-the-future-of-work/>, 2017.

[44] Michigan State University, Automated vehicles will create a shift in workforce demands. <https://msutoday.msu.edu/news/2018/automated-vehicles-will-create-a-shift-in-workforce-demands/>, 2018.

[45] S. Kessler, *Gigged: The End of the Job and the Future of Work*, Macmillan, 2018, p. 180.

[46] K.J. Delaney, The robot that takes your job should pay taxes, says Bill Gates, Quartz, <https://qz.com/911968/bill-gates-the-robot-that-takes-your-job-should-pay-taxes/>, 2017.

[47] C. Pasma, Basic income programs and pilots. <http://nke.beta.niagaraconnects.ca/wp-content/uploads/sites/2/2014/05/Basic_Income_Programs_and_Pilots.pdf>, 2014.

CHAPTER TWO

The great transformation: the future of the data-driven transportation workforce

Terry C. Bills
Global Transportation Industry Director, ESRI, CA, United States

Contents

Introduction

The great economic historian Karl Polanyi spent his career describing the emergence of a market society in Europe as the great transformation. This "great transformation" was responsible for changing preexisting economic and social relationships and led to the emergence of the modern state and market-dominated economies.

While the current transformation is nowhere as significant as the era that Polanyi described, the current digital transformation will nevertheless have significant consequences for modern societies, and especially the modern workforce. As we move to an increasingly digital world, one in which business processes will be increasingly supported by intelligent information systems and automated workflows, new career opportunities will open for the workforce of the future. At the same time, it will introduce tremendous challenges for transportation agencies as they transition to this new environment. What follows is meant to describe these

Empowering the New Mobility Workforce.
DOI: https://doi.org/10.1016/B978-0-12-816088-6.00002-X

workforce changes driven by technology, and what transportation agencies can do to help meet these challenges of the future.

There has never been a more challenging time in transportation than today. As the core business of Departments of Transportation (DOTs) shifts from construction to preservation, transportation professionals must increasingly manage complex transportation systems under continually constrained revenues. Limited resources challenge DOTs as they attempt to maintain existing infrastructure while satisfying an ever-increasing set of performance expectations from the public.

These trends are occurring in the context of a dynamic regulatory environment, which requires a greater emphasis on comprehensive information systems to help support better decision making regarding where and how scarce public resources are allocated.

Six significant trends that are changing the way that transportation professionals plan, construct, operate, and maintain key transportation infrastructure:

1. *Requirements for data-driven decisions.* The latest transportation authorization acts mandate that the transportation planning process must be driven by decision-making processes that rely on good information systems and defensible analysis.

2. *Move to performance-based planning (PBP).* Both the Moving Ahead for Progress in the 21st Century Act (MAP-21) and the Fixing America's Surface Transportation (FAST) Act specifically require a performance-based approach to transportation decision making that supports national performance goals related to safety, mobility, goods movement, preservation, and environmental sustainability.

3. *"Digitalization" of the transportation processes.* Transportation agencies, driven by the requirements of doing "more with less" and to better improve their processes, are moving to the latest technologies across their organizations. From the way they collect essential information about their existing assets, to the way transportation projects are constructed and maintained, the digital revolution is transforming transportation agencies across all modes of transportation.

4. *Civil integrated management.* Concurrent with the digitalization of transportation processes, there has been a recognition that transportation agencies need to do a better job with respect to integrating information from the various stages of the infrastructure life cycle. Historically, large transportation agencies have been characterized by relatively "siloed" information within their various departments. Driven by the need to capture greater efficiencies in their processes, transportation

agencies have come to recognize that considerable efficiencies could be gained by greater interoperability between their various software systems and a better integration of the information generated at each stage of the infrastructure life cycle.

5. *Greater emphasis on asset preservation.* As many of our transportation assets age, there is a greater emphasis on being more effective in the way we manage and maintain our existing infrastructure. Current Federal transportation requirements mandate that transportation agencies need to demonstrate that they have implemented a transportation asset management plan (TAMP). These plans must focus on preserving core transportation assets and include a lifecycle cost and risk management analysis of their critical infrastructure assets.

6. *Collaboration and public transparency.* Effective planning to ensure the most strategic use of scarce public resources requires a greater collaboration between agencies. Interagency barriers need to be overcome to maximize the return on taxpayer investments. Transportation planning agencies need to consider requirements across program areas—not just pavements and bridges but also active transportation and transit—that address all critical deficiencies. Our mobility challenges require smarter planning.

At the same time, there are greater expectations from the public for greater transparency with respect to the way public dollars are allocated. Smart DOTs are taking proactive measures to ensure greater transparency and public engagement to help secure greater public consensus and support for continued transportation spending.

All these trends significantly impact the way DOTs conduct their business and meet their mission goals. Collaboration and communication within and among agencies are becoming much more important. This highlights the need for robust and accessible information systems to support increasingly complex management and decision support processes. And more fundamentally, this is creating the requirement for new skills and knowledge sets among the transportation workforce to meet these challenges. As transportation agencies continue to incorporate newer technologies into their business processes, this will require a workforce with greater technical skills. As Erik Brynjolfsson and Andrew McAfee [1] argue in their book, "The Second Machine Age: Work, Progress, and Prosperity in a Time of Brilliant Technologies":

Rapid and accelerating digitization is likely to bring economic rather than environmental disruption, stemming from the fact that as computers get more powerful, companies have less need for some kinds of workers. Technological progress is going to leave behind some people, perhaps even a lot of people, as it races ahead.

However, for those workers with the right education or training, they write, "there's never been a better time." The rest of this chapter is focused on highlighting the changes to the workforce that will be required as we move to a greater emphasis on integrated technologies to plan, construct, operate, and maintain our transportation infrastructure.

Digital transformation

Utah DOT (UDOT) would, on the surface, seem an unlikely candidate to be one of the most technologically progressive among the DOTs. A small state with just over three million people, and without a history of being the center of technological invention, there is little to suggest that Utah and its DOT would subsequently be awarded the highest rating among DOTs from *Governing Magazine* for taking care of its transportation infrastructure. But two factors in their history led them to their status among DOTs.

In the first instance, Dale Peterson, a former Research Director at the DOT, in 1977 originated the concept of "good roads cost less." By that he meant that if the roads were properly maintained over their life cycle, that the full life cycle costs of their infrastructure were reduced by practicing good asset management and preservation practices. As a result, every new engineer at the DOT was initially trained in these concepts, and it became a central "way of doing business" for the way UDOT practiced asset management.

As the DOT [2] states:

Transportation Asset Management is a strategic approach to managing the existing transportation infrastructure. It promotes more effective resource allocation and utilization, based upon quality information, to address facility preservation, operation and improvement. This concept covers a broad array of DOT functions, activities and decisions: transportation investment policies and priorities; relationships and partnerships between Utah DOT and public and private groups; long range multi-modal transportation planning; program development for capital projects and for maintenance and operations...

A central component of UDOT's approach was to understand the location and condition of all their assets. But in 2010 Utah recognized that their traditional (manual) practices of collecting asset condition information were not meeting their requirements. As a former Director of Asset Management at the agency stated [3]: "we knew we had somewhere between 80,000 and 120,000 signs on the State highway system, but that was not very precise..."

As a result, a number of the agency Directors began the process of specifying a data collection initiative for the agency. The Directors of Planning, Engineering, Asset Management, and Safety (among others) all coordinated to identify the critical data requirements for a comprehensive data collection effort. The goal was to deploy state of the art collection methods to improve and develop rigorous safety, maintenance and preservation programs, among others.

Consequently, the agency contracted with a major data collection company (Mandli) to use mobile light detection and ranging (LiDAR), 360-degree digital video, along with laser systems to measure rut and crack measurements on the roadway, along with highly accurate positioning systems. From the resulting LiDAR and digital video data, the contractor was able to extract every agency asset, from "fence post to fence post" with a 2-cm level of accuracy. For the first time the agency now had a complete asset inventory, and knew the condition of every asset (Fig. 2.1).

UPLAN—The second major factor originated in the agency's Planning Department. The former Director of Planning was always frustrated by the

Figure 2.1 Digital video image from Utah DOT's data collection effort. *DOT,* Departments of Transportation.

lack of information and data sources to support good planning decisions. On his own initiative, he began to collect data from a wide number of state agencies and metropolitan planning organizations (MPOs), along with transit agencies and utilities throughout the state. Eventually, the number of data sets numbered over a thousand and introduced significant data management challenges as he attempted to organize all this information in the agency's geographic information system (GIS) database. Standard desktop models of data access were not sufficient to allow multiple planners to work with and analyze the data that he had collected.

It was at this time (2010) that cloud-based GISs were being developed, and UDOT was one of the first to take advantage of the benefits of organizing all of this information in the cloud and making the data available agency-wide. Known as UPLAN, this GIS made all the information he had collected, together with all the asset and LiDAR data available to all UDOT employees, including making a large subset of the data widely available to the public (Figs. 2.2 and 2.3).

Included in the UPLAN data was a comprehensive set of environmental data, which were used to create a GIS-based environmental prescreening tool, with which transportation planners could assess the potential environmental impacts of proposed and planned projects. With the Planning and Environmental Linkages (PEL) tool, transportation planners can view critical environmental attributes such as streams, wetlands, rare plant habitats, historic sites, and other attributes simultaneously with planned transportation projects.

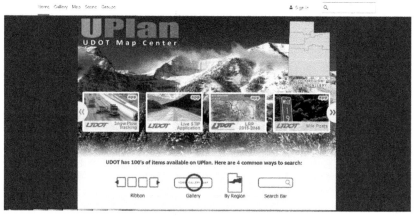

Figure 2.2 Utah DOT's UPlan front-page. *DOT*, Departments of Transportation.

Figure 2.3 UPlan's organized map applications.

For any proposed project, the planner can simply draw (digitize) the location of the project on their computer screen and the tool will automatically generate a PEL report that summarizes all the resources that are intersected by the project's footprint. This report and an accompanying factsheet that provides information related to the project needs, forecasts, conditions, and other current and planned work in the area are shared with stakeholders to facilitate discussion about the potential resource impacts.

The overall impact of UPLAN for UDOT was transformational. In a perpetuating cycle, employees began to want more information. With UPLAN, they could access groups of content related to road planning, asset management, and more critical road and highway information. UDOT also started sharing its visual data with partners, who could use the maps themselves.

The application led to significant productivity improvements in the agency's work. As an example, UDOT used the application to identify potential railway line corridors in a 200–mile-by-200–mile study area in parts of three states. Using UPLAN, the agency developed 26 potential corridors, totaling more than 4000 miles. Screening the 26 alternatives for engineering and environmental feasibility took just 2 months, at a cost of only $400,000. As John Thomas, the former Planning Director indicated [4], "If UDOT had done that before UPLAN, it would have taken at least three years and several million dollars to do the same work."

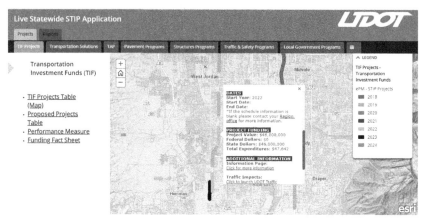

Figure 2.4 Utah DOT's Statewide Transportation Improvement Program (STIP). *DOT, Departments of Transportation.*

The transformation extended all the way to the top of the agency: when the Executive Director briefs the legislature on the proposed transportation projects, he briefs them personally with the UPLAN GIS application (Fig. 2.4).

Data-driven decisions and performance-based planning

Good planning begins, as we have seen, with organizing your information. For UDOT that started with UPLAN which served to create not only a "system of record" for the agency, but which also integrated with many of their authoritative business systems. This allowed them to create a single source of truth that is trusted throughout the organization. While this proved valuable for everyday business activities, it is especially valuable in helping guide the project planning process. Through GIS, information from transportation models, asset management systems, roadway inventories, and transportation monitoring systems can all be brought together to support the entire planning process. Having all relevant data and information sources easily accessible and centrally located removes a large amount of frustration from the equation.

Furthermore, once these information sources are organized through the GIS, information products in the form of targeted and easy-to-use applications can be built to assist functional area planners in performing deficiency and needs analyses. The results of these analyses can be organized to give planners wide and easy access to relevant data, as illustrated in the graphic given in Fig. 2.5 from UDOT.

Current transportation legislation stipulates that states and MPOs must follow a PBP approach to plan development and project selection. Such a management approach is designed to inform investment decisions by focusing on projects that help achieve widely shared goals and priorities, improve the project and program delivery process itself, and provide greater transparency and accountability to the public.

The following elements form the core of a PBP process:

Strategic direction—Where do we want to go? In the transportation planning process, stakeholders articulate a strategic direction that is based on a shared vision of the future. This includes defining the goals, objectives, and performance measures that will help track results.

Planning analysis—How are we going to get there? Driven by data on performance, along with public involvement and policy considerations, agencies conduct analyses that inform investment and policy priorities. This includes analysis of trends and current deficiencies and the

Figure 2.5 Utah DOT's freight planning map applications. *DOT*, Departments of Transportation.

identification of strategies (and alternatives) required to achieve performance goals.

Programming—What will it take? Programming involves selecting specific investments to include in an agency capital plan, a transportation improvement plan (TIP), or a statewide transportation improvement plan (STIP). In a PBP approach, agencies make programming decisions based on whether those decisions support performance targets or contribute to desired trends. This step often includes the development of an investment plan and the prioritization of projects based on their ability to help meet the performance goals outlined.

Implementation and evaluation—How did we do? A PBP approach is based on the premise that following these processes will lead agencies to their desired goals. To help ensure success, the final steps involve a process of monitoring, evaluation, and reporting. These steps provide feedback that is used in the next planning phase.

This entire planning process depends on having a solid information infrastructure that facilitates effective coordination and communication. This infrastructure brings together the disparate data sources required for monitoring, modeling and analysis, and project prioritization. An effective GIS-based project planning framework can help orchestrate the entire workflow by administering, standardizing, and ensuring consistency throughout the entire process.

Figure 2.6 Virginia DOT's open data map portal. *DOT*, Departments of Transportation.

Figure 2.7 Virginia DOT's maintenance map applications. *DOT*, Departments of Transportation.

As the example given in Figs. 2.6 and 2.7 illustrates, various data sources can be organized into a coherent portal with individual applications developed for each of the various functional or modal areas. These applications can be the result of various modeling scenarios or different analyses of network performance, infrastructural deficiencies, or highway safety, among others. The important point is that these apps no longer represent disparate and ad hoc files that are siloed and often inconsistent.

The analytic part of the PBP process begins with a clear understanding of current system performance and deficiencies. Deficiencies are derived from previously defined performance goals, which can be measured and monitored with performance dashboards, network maps, and other data inputs. This helps to understand current system performance and areas where performance is falling short of expectations.

System performance is measured across multiple dimensions and includes asset management, safety, freight, nonmotorized transport, and overall network performance.

Critical inputs, which assist the planner in understanding current network performance, include the following:

- Outputs from travel demand forecasting models
- Results from highway safety analyses

- Forecasts from asset and maintenance management models
- Trends in current performance measures
- A variety of other information inputs (Fig. 2.8)

Each input contributes to an accurate and comprehensive view of current system performance and a thorough analysis of existing deficiencies by functional topic.

After the analysis of the current system performance and identification of deficiencies, agencies need a formalized process for incorporating asset management needs, bundling individual needs, creating new projects, and submitting and evaluating potential projects. Projects can be defined by any number of different agencies, such as local governments, MPOs, or the DOT itself. Each entity needs access to a centralized process, which allows projects to be defined in some detail before being subjected to initial screening and scoring.

As shown in the example (Fig. 2.9), the North Carolina DOT utilizes a GIS-based application that allows the project submitter to define the project location and boundary. After these parameters have been defined, the project submitter then enters the project details.

Next, the project proposer can see an evaluation and preliminary score for the project, including a preliminary environmental analysis.

These can be maintenance, safety, or new capacity projects, and each is scored differently. The scoring is based on previously agreed on criteria and represents the project's ability to help meet performance goals and its

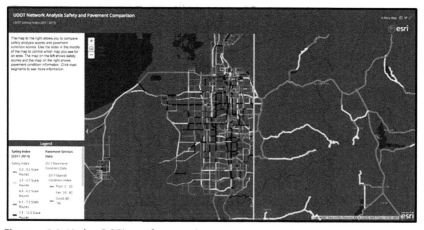

Figure 2.8 Utah DOT's safety and pavement condition comparison. *DOT,* Departments of Transportation.

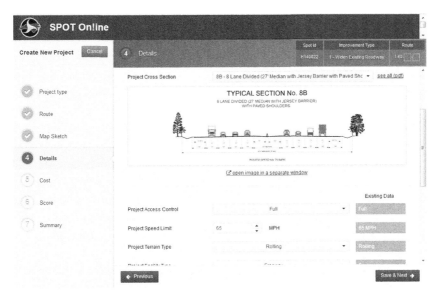

Figure 2.9 North Carolina DOT's project prioritization application. *DOT*, Departments of Transportation.

consistency with overall system requirements. Agencies can develop their own scoring criteria based on their specific goals and objectives. Scoring formulas can be based on an infinite number of variables.

A final step in the process of developing an investment plan and a program of projects involves comparing a set of alternative portfolios to optimize investments across asset classes. For many DOTs, this has been perhaps the most difficult part of the planning process. All too often, the current year's allocation is a factor of the previous year's budget allocation by asset class.

However, that is neither a strategic nor a data-driven approach to resource allocation. Under a PBP process, project selection is driven by its ability to help achieve overall goals. Recently, there has been significant progress in identifying various methodologies to help transportation planners make strategic decisions with respect to project selection and resource allocation. The recent National Cooperative Highway Research Program (NCHRP) Report 806 titled "Guide to Cross-Asset Resource Allocation and the Impact on Transportation System Performance," provides a framework for using an analytic hierarchy process methodology to put an agency's goals at the center of its decision process.

A number of State DOTs have begun to adopt these methodologies to help them make more strategic decisions which optimize their resource commitments across multiple asset classes. With the recognition that State DOTs never have sufficient resources to do all that is needed, these decision methodologies help planners and decision makers determine the most strategic mix of projects to achieve the agency's goals. The results of these analyses are then displayed in the GIS to help facilitate intelligent what-if analyses and help decision makers understand the trade-offs and analyze alternative portfolios of projects, as this example illustrates (Figs. 2.10 and 2.11).

Effective performance-based planning ultimately requires considerable coordination not only within but across agencies (DOTs, MPOs, regional transportation planning organizations [RTPOs], and transit agencies) as well. This ensures that all parties can coordinate and collaborate on the development of shared goals, objectives, performance measures, and targets.

GIS and effective information technology (IT) provides a framework to facilitate data sharing and collaboration within or between agencies. The state DOT, MPO, and local governments can all share the same information and have the same understanding with respect to project definitions. In addition, they can collaborate on analyses, modeling, and other project alternatives and share results, leading to a comprehensive and cohesive planning framework.

The final step in a PBP process is effectively communicating the plan's components to the public. In the past, comprehensive transportation plans were often presented in written documents that received little attention from the public. These documents were limited by technical jargon and presentation formats that the average reader could not understand. But a

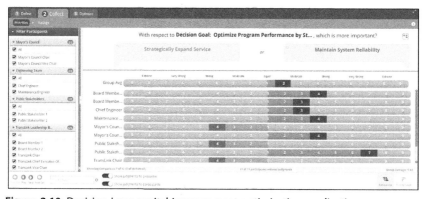

Figure 2.10 Decision Lens capital improvement optimization application.

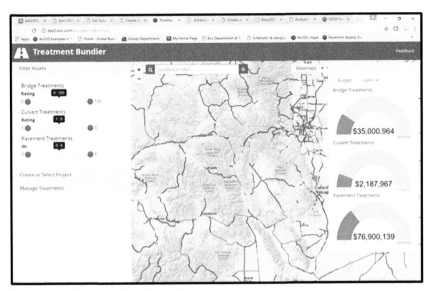

Figure 2.11 Treatment bundler with project costs.

Figure 2.12 Regional Transportation Alliance of Southwestern Pennsylvania's Story Map.

new generation of planners has discovered the benefits of more effective web-based and multimedia presentation formats to convey their plans. These multimedia presentations combine high-quality graphics, maps, text, and videos to present each element of a plan. For example, in the graphic above (Fig. 2.12), the Regional Transportation Alliance of Southeast Pennsylvania recently created and shared a Story Map application called Imagine Transportation 2.0 that explained its vision to the public.

Transformation of the planning process—There are two critical lessons to be gained from this review of current planning processes at DOTs. The first is that the role of information and good information management plays an increasingly central role in the planning process. From the ability to gather data and information from across their organizations, DOTs increasingly must grapple with being able to organize this information and to make it widely available not only to their own planners, but also to other agencies. This collaborative framework is central to the ability to make strategic, data-driven decisions, impacting resource allocations across the State transportation system.

As we have seen, the way that DOTs are now collecting information is changing, the way in which they organize that information is changing, and the tools to analyze and understand that information are changing; and that leads to the second critical lesson, that the skill sets required to support this transformation are also changing. From the greater technical skills increasingly required in the way we collect roadway asset data, to the modeling skills required to understand the transportation networks 20 years in the future, and the changing analytical skills required of planners to make more informed recommendations, these tasks require greater technical training and understanding, and that is the challenge ahead for most State DOTs. We will need a new generation of workers who are trained in these new skill sets, which will require changes in the way we train the coming transportation workforce, from the University level on down. We will return to this theme in a final section.

Civil integrated management

In the previous section, we saw how DOTs are transforming their data and information infrastructures to help them better plan transportation improvements for their transportation systems. But these same trends are occurring across all the business functions of a State DOT. Sometimes referred to as the process of digitization, the vast majority of business tasks and workflows are transitioning to digital processes. Across the board, whether the ways that maintenance and inspections are conducted, management of the right of way, or even the ways that transportation projects are designed and constructed, each of these workflows is moving to significantly greater computerization and in some cases automation.

While these trends have often introduced painful transitions for many agencies, they also hold out significant promise for increases in productivity, and for cost savings. These are especially true in terms of the role of information in the transportation infrastructure life cycle (Fig. 2.13).

Transportation professionals often speak of a project life cycle, from planning through design, construction, operations and maintenance (O&M) (and sometimes decommissioning). But practice in many DOTs over the years is that each of these different stages of the life cycle was represented by a separate Division, each with its own business systems and information systems. In many cases, not only did the different Divisions maintain their own databases of basic information, but often this pattern was replicated even within Divisions.

These "siloed" databases were one of the greatest barriers to better decision-making within DOTs. As a Federal Highway Administration [5] report stated:

The goal of data integration is to consolidate or link the data that exist in separate files or database systems so they can be used to make decisions within and across asset types. States and local agencies know that without an integrated set of data they can never make strategic and comprehensive transportation investment decisions.

It is not just the disparate databases that are the problem within DOTs, but this problem is often compounded by the different software

Figure 2.13 Transportation life cycle.

systems that each Division uses, and the difficulty (or often inability) of integrating information from these various software platforms. Nowhere is this problem more acute than in the planning, design, and construction phases of the project life cycle.

An analysis conducted by the National Institute of Standards and Technology (NIST) in 2004 [6] among US architectural and engineering firms documented the extent of the inefficiencies from this problem. Titled "Cost Analysis of Inadequate Interoperability in the US Capital Facilities Industry," NIST was able to put a range of dollar and time costs associated with the lack of integration between these various software tools and systems within the construction industry. Key findings include:

- Because of the prevalence of paper processes and the lack of good data organization during the typical project, 40%—50% of an engineer's time is spent locating and validating the information they need to perform their job through the life cycle of the project.
- The lack of integration of project information impacts the project delivery cycle. More effective data and information communication could reduce project delivery time by 20%—50%.
- Modern large-scale infrastructure projects require access to large amounts of information during the construction process. Poor communication and the lack of interoperability between different software systems waste up to 30% of project costs.
- More effective data management practices from the early project stages could save up to 14% of the O&M costs.

The goal of civil integrated management is to address these inefficiencies by creating a seamless flow (and management) of information throughout the infrastructure life cycle. Sometimes referred to as BIM (building information modeling), this effort brings together several emerging trends in the infrastructure industry.

The first is the increasing use of 3D technologies to plan, design, and construct major infrastructure. These technologies first emerged in the building construction industry, where they found efficiencies by being able to bring together the various design elements into a "de-conflicted" unified design. The 3D representations of the building design allowed the designers to identify any conflicts prior to construction, with the resulting decline in change orders and other design adjustments during construction.

Advances in the technology and integration with other design components has led to the emergence of 4D (project scheduling) and 5D (project costing), giving the contractor much greater information and control over the project. And while there are often different conceptions of what BIM is (or is not), an essential component is the much greater reliance of 3D technologies in the planning and design phases of the project.

It is often the case that different software systems are used for planning and design, and increasingly there is greater interoperability between these different software systems, so they can not only share data and information, but also often use the information in parallel as seen in Fig. 2.14.

The second major element of CIM is the effort to integrate and manage the data and information from each stage of the life cycle, creating what has been labeled, *whole life cycle information management.* This component is designed to address the inefficiencies identified in the NIST Study. As the Federal Highway Administration defines it [7], "Civil Integrated Management (CIM) is the technology-enabled collection, organization, managed accessibility, and the use of accurate data and information throughout the life cycle of a transportation asset" [7]. As represented by the drawing given in Fig. 2.15, the goal of whole life cycle information management is to capture the inefficiencies common in the transition from one phase to the next in the life cycle.

If data could be collected and managed systematically in the early phases of a project lifecycle, it could deliver significant value in the later phases (O&M) of the project life cycle. This approach has found strong support in the European Case, with the Governments of Germany, the

Figure 2.14 3D GIS side by side with project 3D design.

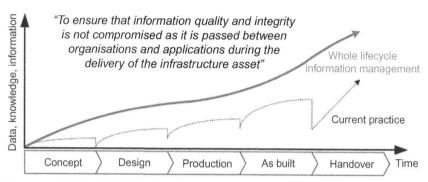

Figure 2.15 Whole life cycle information management phases. *Crossrail.*

United Kingdom, and the Scandinavian countries having adopted formal requirements for the use of CIM in nationally funded projects.

In the case of Germany, all government funded transportation projects will be required to follow BIM standards by 2020. In announcing the initiative, Alexander Dobrindt, the German Minister of Transport and Digital Infrastructure said [8]:

> *"We are launching an initiative for the digitalization of the construction industry... By applying the most sophisticated digital methods, construction projects are to be realized more efficiently and slippages in terms of timeframe and budget are to be prevented." The Minister highlighted the gains from collaborative workflows and greater transparency and said "The aim of this action plan is to usher in a culture change in the field of major projects.... More collaborative partnerships are to produce more cost transparency and a better ability to meet deadlines."*

Crossrail—A perfect example of these concepts put into action is the Crossrail project in the United Kingdom. It represents the largest infrastructure project in Britain, funded at over \$20 billion and initiated in 2008. Crossrail is made up of over 150 km of new track, starting on the far west side of London, with 42 km of tunnels under London, and terminating on the far East side of London. It connects with the existing London Underground, and contains over 40 new or upgraded stations along its path. In operation, Crossrail will carry over 200 million passengers per year; a 10% increase in current capacity.

From the start, the Crossrail Team understood that they were actually constructing two railways: the physical railway (the tracks, stations and tunnels, signaling and communication equipment) and the "virtual" railway. As a result, from the early design stages, every effort was made to manage the information generated by the project, with the understanding that at completion, the Crossrail Team would be handing over not only the physical railway, but also its digital twin for use in O&M.

The project generated over two million computer-aided design (CAD) drawings, eight million supporting documents, one million different assets, and the GIS that helped to manage much of this data has over 50 million features, totaling over 12 terabytes of data. At the heart of the information system, the Crossrail Team created a Common Data Environment (a federated data architecture) that integrated all their major business systems, including the eventual asset management system.

Much of this information is accessed through *Crossrail Maps*, which is their GIS portal for organizing these vast stores of data and making it easily accessible. They widely view the map or location as the way into the other information systems.

And the result? The main benefit Crossrail identifies is simplicity. By giving the user a simple-to-use map interface which is easy to understand and navigate, Crossrail Maps opens up all of the relevant information in an easily discoverable fashion. That includes maps and data in 2D and 3D, which allows the user to isolate any feature (utilities, for example) from the completed railway, and to easily locate the needed information. While Crossrail has not established a specific dollar value for this data availability, all agree that the project was greatly aided by taking such an approach.

More specific benefits that Crossrail identified include saving 5000 person-manhours per year associated with their tunnel boring operations, and a 75% time savings on property acquisition, and saving their asset protection engineers 80% of their time per year. Perhaps just as important was the interoperability achieved by following the PAS 1192-2 and PAS 1192-3 processes and procedures, required under British regulation. Crossrail standardized on two key technology platforms, and ensured interoperability between the two systems. While Crossrail is an exemplar of the benefits of applying CIM concepts to transportation, these practices are receiving widespread adoption throughout the transportation industry.

Whole life cycle information management

Data collection—We have already highlighted how the digital revolution is transforming transportation agencies across all modes of transportation. In this section, we highlight how these new technologies are changing the required skills needed to succeed in the transportation field. Much like the infrastructure life cycle, a great deal of transportation starts with data collection.

It was not so long ago that most of the data collection in the field was done on paper, often with the standard yellow pad, or with a Xeroxed form. This information was collected in the field and brought back to the office to be entered into a mainframe computer for storage and analysis. While that manual process still takes place, it is increasingly being replaced by much more integrated and computerized systems.

There has been a proliferation of mobile field data collection technologies introduced in the last 10 years. As asset management and maintenance management systems become more widely adopted in transportation agencies, there has been a corresponding adoption of computerized inspection and work order management systems to integrate field workers directly back into corporate databases (Fig. 2.16).

From a standard iPad or tablet, the field worker can collect a wide range of information, and have that data automatically update the database back in the office, ensuring greater data accuracy and timeliness. The efficiency gains from mobile workforce management have spread across most transportation sectors, and similarly allow supervisors to track progress through dashboards, as shown in the example from Vermont DOT and their rail crossing inspection system (Figs. 2.17 and 2.18).

At the same time, LiDAR and other laser-based technologies are being widely used for data collection among transportation agencies. We have already highlighted UDOT's LiDAR data collection efforts, which allowed the agency to collect all their surface assets, and assess their current condition through this automated data collection methodology. But the skill sets required for these newer data collection technologies are

Figure 2.16 Mobile workforce management.

Figure 2.17 Taking information and map products to the field.

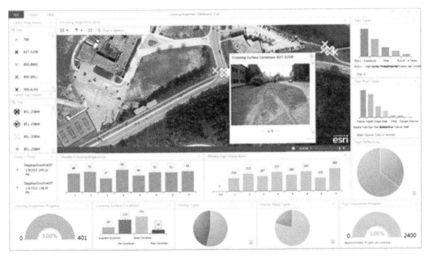

Figure 2.18 Vermont DOT's rail crossing inspection dashboard. *DOT*, Departments of Transportation.

also changing. As the President of Mandli Communications (who performed the data collection for UDOT) stated [9]:

It is our belief that one of our roles in the industry is to help develop the next generation of Geospecialists. It has been our practice to hire individuals into the entry level roles of the organization who have degrees or are in the process of earning a degree in the geospatial sciences or engineering fields. Those that show strength in the areas we are looking for will find opportunities and advancement to higher level roles both inside and outside the company.

LiDAR and photogrammetry technologies have significantly changed the way that data are collected, whether ground based, aerial, or drone collected, and are rapidly becoming standard technologies across the transportation market. These technologies generally require higher levels of training, and knowledge of geomatics, geography, and surveying together with GIS skills. The Bureau of Labor Statistics (BLS) currently estimates [10] that jobs in the field of photogrammetry are expected to grow by approximately 19% between 2016 and 2026 and will be one of the fastest growing occupations in the United States during the same period. The opportunities for these career paths are quite strong across transportation, but do require higher levels of technical training than traditional data collection techniques (Fig. 2.19).

Data management and data analysis—We have already highlighted the importance of good information, and effective information management for transportation decision making. As a result, transportation agencies will increasingly need to rely on professionals who have good IT skills and who also possess good communication skills. Whether managing databases on pavement and bridge condition, to constructing crash databases which bring together information from across the agency, database management and data integration skills will be a critical requirement for

Figure 2.19 Mandli's LiDAR and pavement condition collection vehicle.

the transportation agencies of the future. These skills will be especially important in the era of connected vehicles, where information from connected cars will be used for real-time traffic management and safety alerting.

There is a wide range of IT skill sets that will be required in the future DOT. From those database-trained workers who will be required to manage and maintain existing data sets, to workers who will have more advanced data integration skills, to programmers able to develop transportation-related applications, to the data scientists and business intelligence analysts who will derive the insights which will guide future transportation decision making. In each case, these are largely new or changing employment classifications for transportation agencies and they have often struggled to compete with private sector salaries.

Cloud engineer, security analyst, machine learning engineer, business intelligence analyst, data scientist, and computer vision engineer are all new job classifications that will be required in the modern DOT, and for which there are few existing classifications. As a recent McKinsey Report [11] stated:

> DOTs will have to evolve from a predominantly engineering-focused culture to one that integrates classical engineering, new engineering skills, technology capabilities, general problem solving, and financial acumen. To succeed, they'll need a talent acquisition and development plan that speaks to a generation of innovators interested in making a positive impact on their communities.

Similarly, there will be a significantly increased demand for GIS analysts, GIS programmers, and GIS trained business intelligence analysts in DOTs. As we have seen, GIS and good data management are critical to supporting almost all the workflows within a DOT. As DOTs move to performance-based planning, the role of performance monitoring will increase, and the ability to integrate information from multiple sources and present complex information will be highly valuable to DOT Executives (Fig. 2.20).

Like the demand for those trained in geomatics, the US Department of Labor Employment and Training Administration [12] estimates that demand for geospatial technology is growing at almost 35% per year, with positions at many different levels of skill and training.

Construction and construction management—just as most workflows within a DOT are being fundamentally transformed, so is the case for the construction of major transportation projects, and how construction projects are managed. We have already mentioned the move to CIM and

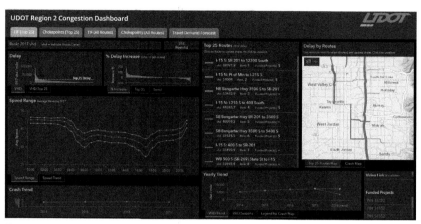

Figure 2.20 Utah DOT congestion monitoring dasboard. *DOT,* Departments of Transportation.

3D design technologies, and most DOTs now have active programs to encourage the growth of 3D design for their major transportation projects. To support this trend, they will require a new generation of design engineers who are conversant in the latest 3D design software programs, such Bentley's Open Roads and Autodesk's Autocad Civil 3D and Infraworks.

Even highway construction is becoming more automated, with the introduction of automated machine guidance (AMG) and machine control technologies, as applied to road grading and paving. AMG uses data from sources such as 3D engineered models to guide construction equipment during earth work and paving operations. Machine control, on the other hand, directly controls the hydraulics on the grader through a motorized total station, in which the operator is simply driving the equipment. By some estimates [13], AMG can increase productivity by up to 50% on some operations and cut survey costs by as much as 75%.

Because of these technologies and their reliance on greater ground precision, the technical requirements of transportation construction workers have increased significantly, as knowledge of survey and geomatics now become required skills in road building. The role of surveyors within the construction process is enlarged, as they become responsible for establishing the vertical and horizontal control for the project, and they acquire and validate the digital terrain models used in the project. The BLS forecasts [14] growth of 11% between 2016 and 2026 for both surveyors and survey technicians, with a college degree required for a surveyor, and a high school diploma required at the technician level.

Operations and maintenance—The technical data and information requirements for many of the domain areas within DOTs are similarly being transformed by technology. We have already mentioned the requirement that the DOT must demonstrate they have implemented a TAMP, which includes a life cycle cost and risk management analysis of their critical infrastructure assets. As a result, most DOTs have now established a Director of Asset Management and are implementing computerized asset and maintenance management systems (CMMS). These systems depend on having a complete inventory of existing assets, their current condition, as well as a host of other characteristics which impact their life cycle (such a weather conditions, traffic volumes, and materials used in construction).

From this information, degradation curves are calculated, which helps forecast the timing and the prescribed treatment to most strategically prolong the life of the asset. Whether bridge or pavement management, these are becoming more exacting sciences, and require access to good information and sophisticated modeling techniques. Best practice maintenance regimes have jettisoned the traditional "worst first" maintenance philosophy, and used complex decision support models to prioritize the most critical and strategic maintenance activities, since funds are never sufficient to keep all assets in good condition in the current environment. Instead, asset engineers forecast the levels of degradation (measured by indices like the international roughness index—IRI) likely to occur given fixed maintenance budgets and develop longer range maintenance and capital improvement plans like the one shown in Figs. 2.21 and 2.22.

Similarly, under the guidance and encouragement of the US DOT, most states have invested heavily in intelligent transportation systems (ITS), with the hope of gaining greater operational efficiencies from existing infrastructure. Yet ITS systems have evolved significantly to now include vehicle-to-vehicle communication and vehicle-to-infrastructure communication, often under the heading of connected vehicles. Relying on dedicated short-range communications (DSRC), each vehicle will be continuously communicating a wide range of information (braking, collision warning, weather, speed, among others), which will be used for a wide array of applications within DOTs.

The challenge for many DOTs will be the sheer volume of data, as vehicles will transit 10 information packets per second; surely defining what is often called "big data." To leverage the information generated from this vast amount of DSRC data will require the latest in big data

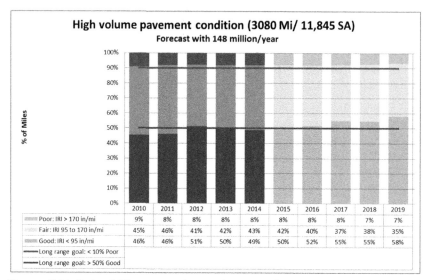

Figure 2.21 Utah DOT pavement condition analysis. *DOT,* Departments of Transportation.

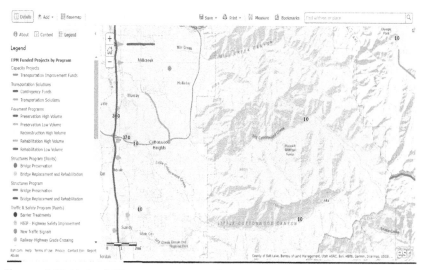

Figure 2.22 Utah DOT pavement resurfacing projects. *DOT,* Departments of Transportation.

capabilities, and require skill sets that many DOTs do not currently possess. Data scientists, together with analysts trained in artificial intelligence and machine learning technologies, will all become part of the necessary staffing for DOTs.

Figure 2.23 Citylabs' Streetlytics data product.

Additionally, there is a virtual explosion of new data sources to help transportation professionals better understand currently changing mobility patterns. Leveraging anonymized cell phone data, a number of companies are able to provide detailed mobility data for almost any geographic region. One such data provider—Citilabs—can provide detailed demographic information and trip purpose for drivers on every street segment for all major cities within the United States (Fig. 2.23).

The ability to effectively utilize these new data sources will similarly depend on having data scientists and business analysts trained in big data techniques to manage and interrogate such large data sources. Current estimates [15] are that demand for data scientists will increase by 28% by 2020 with the strongest demand in the private sector.

Digital transformation and the new workforce

While full digital transformation is not yet a reality for many DOTs, many are moving aggressively in this direction. Reflecting this trend, several DOTs have created a new position of Chief Data Officer, to help organize and manage the rapidly growing stores of data and information that are required to manage complex transportation networks.

Colorado DOT is one such example, where senior staff brought in the Chief Data Officer from New York State to help lead their digital transformation. As Barbara Cohn, the new Chief Data Officer, states [16]:

> the real-time information is ever flowing... because it is coming at us so quickly, that is causing the digital transformation.... How do we analyze all that information? You cannot consume all that information without a digital transformation.

Colorado DOT recognizes that information will be their greatest asset going forward and have embarked on an aggressive effort to effectively organize their corporate data and information sources, aiming to make that information available through a "system of engagement." Designed to support each of the agency's workflows with the right information and with targeted GIS maps and visualization, the effort is a central part of the agency's transformation to a data-driven organization. As Barbara Cohn explains [16]:

> In our architecture vision and in our road map, we are starting with the geospatial area... (because) everything about transportation is about where, about location.

Because DOTs and other transportation agencies are coming to recognize the importance of data and information in their organizations, this is leading to a sea change in the skill sets that will be required for the future transportation workforce. The future transportation knowledge workers will need to be much more versed in emerging technologies, in informational technology and good data management practice, and in data analysis and structured decision-making methodologies. Attracting, training, and developing those workforce skills will remain a central challenge for most DOTs.

The opportunities that these technological changes open for the future workforce are significant. The required technical skills will move many transportation-related jobs into more advanced skill categories and will create enviable career paths for many transportation workers. At the same time, transportation agencies will have difficulty identifying, hiring, and retaining qualified candidates. Since these digital skills will be rewarded throughout all sectors of the economy, public sector transportation agencies may have difficulty competing for the best workers.

As a result, the transportation agencies which will be the most successful in the future will have to be much more creative in their workforce development efforts, working more collaboratively with various educational institutions in the community. Starting with high schools and community colleges, transportation agencies need to develop stronger relationships with these local educational centers, to communicate their labor force requirements, and to work with these organizations to help train these future workers.

Over the years, many US schools have abandoned their technical training programs in favor of college preparatory courses. Yet the experience from Germany and other countries, which follow an integrated course of study together with an apprentice program, has delivered not only strong results, but also higher wages for their workers. Transportation agencies could develop summer internships and other programs in conjunction with local high schools and community colleges to help interest students in transportation careers and to help build the needed skills in these students. At the same time, many of these more technical skills—survey technician, model network coders, data entry technicians—can lead to opportunities for further training and advancement throughout the career pathway.

Secondly, transportation agencies and State DOTs in particular need to develop much stronger relationships with their local universities. The opportunity for students to participate directly in transportation-related research through courses in planning, IT, and civil engineering can provide a strong pathway for jobs upon graduation. Internships and course related research can help interest students in these transportation positions; and similarly, transportation agencies can assess and help train their future workers.

Finally, for some of the more skilled technical positions, transportation agencies will need to develop their own training and technological advancement programs. Hiring bright and energetic young workers and then training them in the required skills constitutes a winning combination for both the worker and the agency. It is unlikely that many transportation agencies would be able to afford a highly trained and experienced database administrator or data scientist, yet they still need these skills in their organizations.

This fact will necessarily force them to take advantage of effective training programs to develop these skill sets among their own workforce. Having a close relationship with the local university would help facilitate these workforce development programs and help the university design courses meeting the transportation community's needs.

Meeting the challenges of the great digital transformation will require new and more creative thinking on the part of transportation agencies.

Going forward, the greatest challenge is not only understanding the importance of effective information management and new analytical technologies for improved decision-making, but also how to attract, train, and retain the workforce of the future.

References

[1] E. Brynjolfsson, A. McAfee, *The Second Machine Age: Work, Progress, and Prosperity in a Time of Brilliant Technologies*, W. W. Norton and Company, New York, 2014.

[2] State of Utah Department of Transportation, Asset management. <https://www.udot.utah.gov/main/f?p = 100:pg:0::::V,T:,982>, 2018.

[3] Private correspondence with Stan Burns, former Director of Asset Management at Utah DOT.

[4] Esri. Esri News for State and Local Government. <https://www.esri.com/library/newsletters/state-local/winter-2015-2016.pdf#page = 14>, 2015/2016.

[5] A. Vandervalk-Ostrander, J. Guerre, F. Harrison, *Review of Data Integration Practices and their Applications to Transportation Asset Management*, Federal Highway Administration, 2003.

[6] M.P. Gallaher, A.C. O'Connor, J.L. Dettbarn Jr., L.T. Gilday, *Cost Analysis of Inadequate Interoperability in the U.S. Capital Facilities Industry*, National Institute of Standards and Technology, Gaithersburg, MD, 2004.

[7] Scan management. Scan 13-02 advances in Civil Integrated Management. <http://onlinepubs.trb.org/onlinepubs/nchrp/docs/NCHRP20-68A_13-02.pdf>, 2015.

[8] Federal Ministry of Transport and Digital Infrastructure. *Phased introduction of Building Information Modelling* (BIM) until 2020. <https://www.bmvi.de/SharedDocs/EN/PressRelease/2015/152-dobrindt-bim.html>, 2015.

[9] Private correspondence with Ray Mandli, President of Mandli Communications.

[10] Geospatial at UCLA. What are the prospects for employment in GIS and related industries? <https://gis.ucla.edu/blog/gis-employment-outlook>, 2016.

[11] S. Fuchs, R. Shehadeh, *The Department of Transportation of the Future*, McKinsey & Company, 2017.

[12] United State Department of Labor. *High Growth Industry Profile—Geospatial Technology*. <https://www.doleta.gov/brg/indprof/geospatial_profile.cfm>, 2004.

[13] D. Townes, *Automated Machine Guidance with Use of 3D Models*, Federal Highway Administration, 2013, p. 1.

[14] Bureau of Labor Statistics, U.S. Department of Labor. *Occupational Outlook Handbook, Surveying and Mapping Technicians*. <https://www.bls.gov/ooh/architecture-and-engineering/surveying-and-mapping-technicians.htm> (accessed 23.09.18).

[15] L. Columbus, "IBM predicts demand for data scientists will soar 28% by 2020," *Forbes*. <https://www.forbes.com/sites/louiscolumbus/2017/05/13/ibm-predicts-demand-for-data-scientists-will-soar-28-by-2020/#558420b37e3b>, 2017.

[16] Esri Video. Barbara Cohn, Colorado Department of Transportation. <https://www.esri.com/videos/watch?videoid = 8CHwkwo6A6w>, 2018.

CHAPTER THREE

Mobility management for smart cities professionals

Stephen Goldsmith[1] and Wyatt Cmar[2]

[1]Daniel Paul Professor of the Practice of Government and Director of the Innovations in American Government Program, Harvard Kennedy School, MA, United States
[2]Program Coordinator for the Innovations in Government Program, Harvard Kennedy School, MA, United States

Contents

Introduction

Imagine a single mother working as a hostess in a snowy city. She begins her day hours before her shift because she has to prepare her child for daycare. Her usual bus stop, which is a 10-minute walk, drops her off a few blocks away from her workplace. But she needs to drop off her child before she goes to work and needs to account for the weather

Empowering the New Mobility Workforce.
DOI: https://doi.org/10.1016/B978-0-12-816088-6.00003-1
63

conditions. At the time of this writing, this single mother and her child would face a lengthy and cold commute without access to the convenience of a personal vehicle. But in the not too distant future, employers and municipal leaders will work together to provide mobility alternatives for citizens at every socioeconomic level. In this positive future scenario, she uses her smartphone to consider the best route and mode options. Her employer and the city have provided a limited number of transportation credits, so she decides to leave after rush hour when transit costs are reduced and to take an Uber Pool to daycare, before taking a bus from the daycare center to work.

This hypothetical scenario illustrates a rare moment in the history of transportation when two forces are converging to spur transformative change. First, unprecedented leaps in the progress of networked technology allow for the sharing, tracking, and automation of multimodal mobility networks. Second, and as a result of this expanded capability, citizens are rightly demanding more responsive transportation options. However, to fully realize the opportunity at hand requires a third critical element: engaged governmental leaders who develop and implement new mobility solutions in order to meet their constituencies' demands. By prioritizing user experience rather than the operation of disparate transportation agencies, policymakers can empower a new mobility workforce to usher in an era of efficient, sustainable, and equitable transportation.

This new era will be founded on the idea of mobility management, a new approach to facilitating the deployment of transportation options across a region. Unlike the old system of transportation governance in which a city possessed a series of agencies tasked with discrete purviews and goals, mobility management instead prioritizes optimization at the system level. Like the users they cater to, mobility managers will be multimodal in their thinking and agnostic in their considerations of different transportation modes.

The Old Operating System

Before considering the way that cities should manage service delivery in the modern era, one must first understand the ways that city governments used to operate and the socioeconomic- and policy-driven reasons that shaped those modes of governance.

In the past, transportation policymakers have not regulated broad, networked mobility but have instead managed individual modes: cars, taxis, transportation network companies (TNCs), bikes, scooters, buses, and subways. This antiquated form of management is the "Old Operating System" wherein local governments structure themselves to meet the organizational demands of specific agencies and private providers as opposed to the transportation needs of end-users. The rationale behind the Old Operating System is simple: budgeting, management, and goal setting for monolithic providers was, in the era before massive amounts of consumer data and feedback, much easier than it would have been to cater to atomized users' needs (Fig. 3.1).

In addition to neglecting the transportation requirements and aspirations of users and restricting creative problem solving, the Old Operating System also myopically focused on single modes of transportation. These modes—regulated taxis, heavy rail and fixed bus routes, among others—are still elements of a robust, efficient transportation network, but narrowing focus on each one encumbers the implementation of new technologies or planning solutions integrated across various modes that better reflect currently desirable transportation patterns. A number of experts in the field of transportation still push a "cars versus transit" narrative that, while enticing as a newspaper headline, detracts from the larger question of trying to optimize transportation networks for users at a system-wide scale.

The formation of the Old Operating System was based on rule compliance aggravated by a lack of data available to both government and the private sector. Even 10 years ago, the idea that a passenger at a bus stop would know when the next bus would arrive seemed farfetched. Acquiring high-quality useable information was far more encumbered than it is now. There were no outcries on Twitter when the train stopped mid-track during Monday morning rush hour. Neither was there any Uber-like application where citizens could evaluate their transportation experience in real time.

On Creating a Competitive Environment
As Deputy Mayor of New York City, I was responsible for the Taxi and Limousine Commission. At the very moment when taxi fleet owners should have been rapidly innovating, regulators were instead enforcing uniformity on the types of vehicles and the number of inspections that had to occur each year. Policymakers should instead champion the creation of a competitive environment that promotes service enhancements rather than allowing for old business models to insulate themselves with barriers to entry into their market. –*Stephen Goldsmith*

Figure 3.1 Cities should foster innovation as opposed to insulating competitors from competition.

The Old Operating System was not only inadequate for the development of a holistic transportation management system, but expressly prevented any such transformation from happening because of narrow organization. The hardening of the vertical silos and culture of unresponsiveness was further aggravated by federal and state regulators whose funding and rules inhibited flexibility and change. Federal funding flowed to streets or buses not to transportation and brought with it a mass of limiting rules that controlled both capital and labor expenditures.

But there is hope. Unlike traditional transportation providers, users care little about the organizational distinctions between individual modes and wish primarily to optimize their overall transportation experience. A more flexible transportation system managed holistically might be able to grow with an ever-evolving city, but such a system would require a completely new form of organization, including new payment and tracking systems, more dynamic routing services, a better user interface, and a completely new operating system.

What is the New Operating System?

The New Operating System involves more interconnected planning and management tools to improve mobility while reducing unnecessary expense and environmental impact. The technological foundation of the Old Operating System—one we consider today as distinctly analog—has been replaced in large part by digital systems. We still operate the public sector in its hierarchical, agency-designed fashion, but today's citizens live in socially networked systems: systems that government needs to consider, not as a compliance oriented regulator and information monopolist, but as a platform provider that furthers the efficient operation of a distributed system.

Digital, networked technology enables a mobility management platform that would have been unthinkable until recently. Unlike the heyday of the Old Operating System in which government accumulated very little third-party data and shared even less, both cities and companies now have troves of real-time maps capturing volumes of information concerning streets, sidewalks and vehicles. They have the capacity to know precisely how many passengers are in circulation at any given moment, and even have a ballpark idea of the general level of demand for their services (Fig. 3.2).

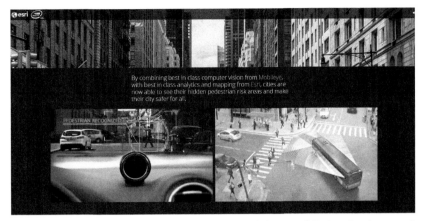

By combining best in class computer vision from Mobileye, with best in class analytics and mapping from Esri, cities are now able to see their hidden pedestrian risk areas and make their city safer for all.

Figure 3.2 The City of New York worked with Mobileye and Esri to implement the Vision Zero program to reduce passenger fatality to the lowest rate in more than 100 years. Smart cities around the country are implementing similar programs.

Most residents and city employees possess smartphones equipped with easy-to-use apps. The low cost of mobile computing power allows cities to manage vast amounts of information on the fly. Open data portals and common transit feeds allow seamless connectivity. Data feeds from private, public, and nonprofit providers, and Internet of Things (IoT) devices combined with predictive analytic tools enable instantaneous planning, dynamic pricing, and operations changes. Citizens are experiencing a tremendous growth in their power to be multimodal and to make choices concerning the duration, cost, and comfort of their trips. They are quickly incorporating new modes of transportation—most recently microtransit modes such as dockless bikes and electric scooters—and expect to switch seamlessly between public and private mobility options.

One of the chief concerns driving the Old Operating System was that, without a tight regimen that controlled both the public employee and the regulated provider, corruption could flourish as unscrupulous fleet owners put unsafe vehicles on the street. Corruption, while still existent, has been severely reduced by the proliferation of electronic records keeping and oversight from outside agencies and third-party watchdogs armed with open data. Public workers in many situations now focus more on solutions and less on process.

In addition to the adoption of leading technologies, the New Operating System requires complex procurement decisions, data- and cost-sharing agreements, new technology development, as well as public—private partnerships. The future of mobility demands a new culture and skillset from government transportation leaders, as well as restructuring for a new office, its powers, and sources of data. All of these forces inevitably lead city agencies to the reality that they must make profound changes in order to thrive and continue to meet the demands of their constituencies—and these changes start with a new kind of workforce.

Hiring the right people for the New Operating System

Hiring the right individuals and providing them with the appropriate leadership, vision, training, and work culture is foundational to enabling the New Operating System. Without onboarding the appropriate workers, cities will struggle to create the tools and agreements that will enable them to keep pace with recent leaps in mobility. In many of today's agencies, public employees establish themselves through the careful management of prescheduled rules, but the New Operating System instead rewards innovative thinking, tough negotiation, thoughtful data analytics, and constructive partnership building. The very best employees will often plan on spending only some time, not a lifetime, in government jobs. Hiring takes time and bringing the best tech talent into a government agency is an especially difficult challenge as private-sector demand for those same skills has skyrocketed.

In the short run, enlisting the help of universities can assist in filling some of the employment gaps. In Los Angeles, for example, the Information Technology Agency created the Data Science Federation, a coalition of leading academics working with data from a number of local universities. The Data Science Federation acts as a conduit for the city to deliver problem statements and project proposals to local university talent. Professors and graduate students may respond to these prompts and begin work within city government, receiving compensation, or academic credit for their contributions.

As an example of their work, LA DOT sponsored the Data Science Federation and a group of researchers from UCLA to produce a unified record of active transportation projects. Over the course of a 6-week sprint in 2016, students helped create a platform that integrated a number of different data feeds into a comprehensive map that may be used to monitor the status of the city's transportation projects [1] (Fig. 3.3).

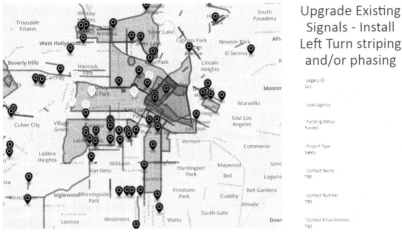

Figure 3.3 Protectionism is a fundamental flaw in the Old Operating System.

Cities also have the option of developing their own tech talent in-house. San Francisco is one of the city's leading the charge: in 2014, it started its own Data Academy, which provides tool- and skill-focused workshops for city employees. The Data Academy hosts 2- to 3-hour workshops for city employees, during which they can learn a range of topics including data analysis and visualization. City officials found a collateral benefit: the training on common tools and open data has helped foster collaboration across city government. Staff members have begun informal working groups outside of the Data Academy, further engendering cross-departmental sharing.

Finally, some cities will find that in lieu of full-time hires they instead need to bring in short-term contractors to help with the most pressing projects. Some of the major challenges that cities face on this front are determining which outside vendors to hire, how to appropriately structure agreements, and how to leverage the relationships to build internal capacity within government.

Encouraging collaboration

Elected officials must address the place for all types of vehicles on the road, whether public, private, high-, or low-occupancy. A data sharing platform is a fundamental component of this structure. Government officials need to carefully consider information sharing arrangements as a condition of licensing. Indeed, private companies have proprietary intellectual property (IP) that needs protection, like their algorithms that speed the matching of a request and driver or the analysis of demand, but they should also be required to share certain information as a condition of operating on the city's streets. Vendors who license curb space for parking or advertising need to protect the public's privacy and security while also negotiating with government about what anonymized information will be shared and under what circumstances. Furthermore, diverse cities coexisting within a region must consider establishing common platforms and shared planning initiatives.

Undoubtedly, these negotiations require leadership: a mobility manager, for instance. Thus, government officials need to establish a leadership structure for integrated mobility, asking questions like: who does the mobility manager work for and what data do they receive? How should a region balance the subsidizing of public and private rides with the need to regulate the marketplace and to improve equitable access?

As the array of private mobility providers—and the IoT infrastructure on which they rely—expands, so too do the opportunities for public-private collaboration. Rideshare companies, delivery services, carshares, bikeshares, insurance companies, cell phone service providers, and car rental services all collect data that is invaluable to the real-time management of transportation as well as the long-term planning of cities.

The new mobility manager will be able to sit down at the table with the applicable agencies and companies and be able to mediate between public needs and concerns regarding IP, the privacy of their customers' data and the protection of the provider's data-centric business models. The new mobility manager will also understand the power that the city wields in terms of having the right to regulate the streets. A new generation of public officials will be able to structure agreements with mobility-sector companies that are mindful of business needs while protecting citizens' safety and convenience.

The National Association of City Transportation Officials outlined a menu of items that the new mobility leadership should maintain in order to succeed, noting that they should understand, at least in aggregate, the trends in the origins and destinations of different trips and be able to glean from that information the speed of those trips [2]. This will help not only from the standpoint of improving traffic management and removing impediments to faster mobility, but will also improve cities' understanding of how their citizens would prefer to get around. The use of this data may lead, in the long term, to new planning initiatives that reduce the need for private automotive transportation. Furthermore, cities should have a sense of where transportation providers are delivering their services and if requests for transportation from particular areas are consistently being canceled by drivers. This kind of information will help cities understand how equitably services are being provided, and where they may need to enforce the better provision of services.

With some baseline data, city officials can begin to advocate for a mobility system that is efficient, cost-effective, and mode-agnostic. They can begin to implement the New Operating System.

Cities testing and implementing New Operating Systems

Some cities have already begun to adopt the New Operating System for mobility, appointing a mobility manager, focusing new regulations on the benefits of users, and, in general, fostering better mobility outcomes for all. These cities are establishing new and innovative collaborations, working toward meaningful outcomes as opposed to process benchmarks, and empowering their workers to be innovative and interdisciplinary in their work.

Using Waze data in Louisville, Kentucky

In the Louisville Metro Government, Michael Schnuerle, the city's Chief Data Officer, is developing open source tools to analyze data from Waze and other sources. The city's goals are to reduce collisions, improve pedestrian and bicycle safety, and optimize transportation efficiency. Over the last year, Schnuerle has partnered with Ed Blayney, the City Technology Manager, to create a Mobility Innovation Team that works with traffic, advanced planning, and other departments and external agencies.

Louisville uses Waze data as a far cheaper alternative to traditional traffic studies in which information is manually captured over the course of a few months at a cost of tens of thousands of dollars in order to analyze traffic flow [3]. The data that Louisville receives from Waze helps the city understand the current state of its roads and where improved signal timing might reduce congestion and improve safety. In an internal study comparing a paid traffic study with Waze data, officials found that the results of the Waze analysis and traditional analysis were 90% comparable. With these new data feeds, the city may produce far more traffic studies than before at a fraction of the cost [4].

Louisville also wants to ensure that its efforts are shareable and collaboratively built. The Waze WARP open source cloud platform is a partnership among multiple cities to assist in building a free data analytics platform, instead of cities paying individually to develop similar solutions. It was funded by Amazon, build by developer Slingshot, supported by Waze, and project managed by city governments. Now that WARP exists, other organizations like the University of Pennsylvania and Data for Democracy are beginning to use it for the own applications. The WARP project is an Open Government Coalition project, and part of the city's larger efforts to build a reproducible mobility-focused data warehouse and analytics platform.

As exemplified by the formation of the Mobility Innovation Team, Louisville is using momentum around the Waze data project to build new data partnerships and a culture centered on data-driven performance improvements. By successfully completing a number of small projects and making incremental improvements, city officials are setting the stage for easier buy-in for future projects. This personnel-level work promises to not only save time and money but also open roads up for faster, safer mobility.

Collaborating with Uber in South Bend, Indiana

Carless individuals are often dependent on family and friends to get to places inaccessible by public transit, which in turn limits their choices in terms of employment, healthcare, housing, and education. Even families that own one car are in a similarly vulnerable position due to the risk of being stranded if their vehicle were to break down, or if another family member has a more pressing appointment on a particular day.

South Bend has been working to quantify the costs of unreliable transportation for part-time and shift workers and for their employers. The city found that the employment turnover rate for those facing an onerous commute to work is extremely high. By demonstrating the associated financial and operational costs, South Bend has been able to convince employers to invest in reliable transportation for their employees [5].

Led by Santiago Garces, South Bend's Chief Innovation Officer, the city mapped high concentrations of household origins and employment destinations so they could build a program that would provide shared rides for multiple employees heading in the same direction. Like many cities, South Bend simply is not dense enough to mandate the development of new fixed rail and bus systems to help those who are otherwise rendered immobile. Instead, they began exploring on-demand transportation as a means of getting low-income residents to work.

The city is also intent on fairly distributing the costs of trips to work among the three parties involved: government, business, and employee. To speed along South Bend in their development, Bloomberg Philanthropies awarded the city $1 million as one of the nine winners of their Mayor's Challenge.

South Bend conducted randomized control trials with over 100 employees (wherein 50 receive the new transit benefits and 50 do not) to prove that the on-demand services will reduce turnover and help job-seekers connect with gainful employment opportunities. Already the city discovered significant differences between the group receiving the new transit benefits and those who did not. Transit-rich workers were able to access additional shifts and work longer hours, and their employers experienced significantly less absences and late arrivals. As a result, more local businesses have expressed an interest in sharing the cost to ensure less turnover and more stability within their workforce.

Beyond the significant impact of the program itself, South Bend's initiative reveals strategies that other cities should replicate. South Bend's human-centered design approach—paying close attention to the tradeoffs that employees are willing to make with regard to paying for transportation and getting to proper employment—is indicative of the new way that government should function under the New Operating System.

Coding the curb in Los Angeles

In Los Angeles, Seleta Reynolds and her team at the Los Angeles Department of Transportation (LA DOT) have been hard at work focusing on the city's ample curb space. Their unique approach touches every mode of transportation and centers on user experience.

To address the question of how to make curbside usage more efficient, equitable, and safe, the city first had to gather an understanding of how the space was used. For that reason, Mayor Garcetti announced the Code the Curb initiative in 2016 [6]. The project had a low-tech start with an initial plan to have workers manually record information about curbside signage. Later, they installed curbside sensors and created open source data feeds the public could access. These datasets will allow private companies to quickly build applications to solve problems that might otherwise take the city years to achieve.

To quickly progress to applied research, Reynolds and her team authorized ninety-five product and software companies to create systems that will help the city envision future curbside use [7]. They are acknowledging procurement as a considerable hurdle and have created a new model that allows them to accomplish tasks on a week-by-week, task-order basis rather than a year-by-year RFP basis (Fig. 3.4).

With all of this information coming in from different public- and private-sector transportation providers, the next step for the city is to build out the capacity to direct traffic away from areas of high congestion to less-disruptive, drop-off spaces. By doing so, city officials will likely reduce congestion and the resultant pollution, as well as improve traffic safety conditions, particularly for those getting in and out of vehicles.

Figure 3.4 Map of Los Angeles' streets and curbside space. Scale 1:275,000. *From Maps throughout this chapter were created using ArcGIS® software by Esri. ArcGIS® and ArcMap™ are the intellectual property of Esri and are used herein under license. Copyright © Esri. All rights reserved. For more information about Esri® software, please visit www. esri.com; LA Street & Address File. GIS Data for LA County. <https://egis3.lacounty.gov/ dataportal/2014/06/16/2011-la-county-street-centerline-street-address-file/>* (accessed *30.10.18), [8,9].*

The project is indicative of the New Mobility Operating System because it is holistic in approach and user-centric in design. These case studies from Los Angeles, Louisville, and South Bend all demonstrate how to start implementing New Mobility. Whether the work begins with curbside studies, traffic management, or workforce outcomes, the question is not so much about where to start—it is about when to start, and the time is now.

A long-term view of the New Operating System

In addition to making changes within the structure of individual city governments, the New Operating System for mobility needs to be scalable to a national level, in which cities and regional governments may collaborate and build on one another's work.

One of the central issues preventing cities from better collaborating with one another is a set of divergent data and programming standards that are preventing the good work of one city—even when it is uploaded to an online sharing platform such as GitHub—from effectively being utilized by another. Also, cities often use different programming languages to create their data analysis tools, as well as different information sharing, security, and interoperability protocols for their platforms. There is little incentive to make the code easily legible or available to other cities, and as a result, code developed by cities is often poorly documented or written in a way that is not easily generalizable.

Part of the solution to this problem will be to create common data standards and more cloud-based tools that may be adopted by other cities quickly and with minimal work. Open source, cloud-based tools—whether developed by government or mandated to be developed by the private sector in data sharing agreements—will allow cities to integrate mobility solutions at a much faster rate.

In the long run, the result of an empowered mobility workforce will be a truly integrated system designed not for the ease of governance, but for the utility of the commuters. That is the promise of the New Operating System for mobility—a transportation system that is responsive to the needs of each individual.

Creating the New Mobility Operating System

For the New Mobility Operating System to take hold, cities must take a number of important steps. Following are five of the most important ones.

Empower a mobility manager

Cities need to empower a mobility manager to integrate the datasets and transportation solutions currently demanded by citizens. This individual or team will oversee coordination and regional planning. They will work across agencies and geographies. They will be located wherever it makes the most sense: in the municipal or state DOT, in the City Manager's Office, in a Department of Innovation, a metropolitan planning organization or inside of a regional transit authority. They will need to be master compromisers but also able to structure public—private partnerships that benefit cities. They will need to be able to attract and retain a data workforce that is capable of working with big data and creating new tools, and they need to be able to lead this workforce effectively.

Define data sharing standards

Cities should have a shared, baseline understanding of the data that private mobility providers must give them in order to operate on their roads. Currently, much of the data that is shared from the private sector to cities exists in formats that are challenging for government employees to interpret and make use of. Better data standards allow information to be shared more easily between the public and private sectors as well as with different public sector agencies.

Guarantee privacy

Companies need to have the capacity to share data with the cities in a secure manner. Sharing information with enough detail to be helpful while protecting privacy and security presents a particularly difficult challenge but one that is necessary to address as a baseline issue facing many data-swap deals.

One approach involves ensuring that the data provides sufficient detail for planning purposes but not so much geographic detail that the city or a third party accessing its data could re-identify individual riders. A different approach would be to identify a problem and seek private commercial anonymized data that assists in answering a specific question.

Create the appropriate tools

Cities need to stop working in parallel on the development of digital analysis tools and instead work on a common mobility-planning platform and toward shared goals. The future of mobility management involves creating online cloud-based tools that cities can share with one another to analyze similar datasets they are receiving from their private-sector partners, regulated parties, and IoT sensors.

Cities need to support open systems that facilitate better mobility regardless whether the traveler secures his information from an app built into the car, or a mobile parking app, or some other device. This support would come from maintaining a central, up to date source of information including dynamic pricing, parking availability, and traffic conditions and a payment platform supported by an application programming interface (API) that allows interaction with licensed providers of transit services. An integrated payment app would give cities much more data and allow consumers to better plan out their trips and save money on transfers.

Reframe the problem

To integrate mobility, one need not look further than the all-encompassing needs of transit users. All the solutions lie in creating a user experience focused on them. This would be a change of focus for cities. They would go from focusing on how best to run and manage their organizations to instead considering how to best serve individuals. User-centric design, such as this, is a unifying, organizing principal. It is one that will take us from the Older Operating System to the new.

References

[1] Data Science Federation. DOT active transportation planner. <http://www.datasciencefederation.lacity.org/dot-active-transportation-planner>, 2017 (accessed 23.10.18).

[2] NACTO. City data sharing principles: integrating new technologies into city streets. <https://nacto.org/wp-content/uploads/2017/01/NACTO-Policy-Data-Sharing-Principles.pdf>, 2017 (accessed 28.09.18).

[3] Ed Blayney. How we do free traffic studies with Waze data (and how you can too). <https://medium.com/louisville-metro-opi2/how-we-do-free-traffic-studies-with-waze-data-and-how-you-can-too-a550b0728f65>, 2018 (accessed 25.10.18).

[4] Louisville Office of Performance Improvement and Innovation. Traffic engineering project evaluation metrics, 2018.

[5] Caleb Bauer. South Bend wins $1 million form Bloomberg Philanthropies. South Bend Tribune. <https://www.southbendtribune.com/news/local/south-bend-win-million-from-bloomberg-philanthropies/article_e55f9998-92cc-5c1a-adde-41d15d5a09e9.html>, 2018 (accessed 29.10.18).

[6] Julia Wick. Confused by L.A.'s parking signs? There might soon be an app for that. <http://www.laist.com/2016/03/24/parking_apps.php>, 2016 (accessed 29.10.18).

[7] The Planning Report. A symphony of transportation choices: LADOT GM Seleta Reynolds' composition. <https://www.planningreport.com/2018/05/14/symphony-transportation-choices-ladot-gm-seleta-reynolds-composition> (accessed 29.10.18).

[8] Maps throughout this chapter were created using ArcGIS® software by Esri. ArcGIS® and ArcMap™ are the intellectual property of Esri and are used herein under license. Copyright © Esri. All rights reserved. For more information about Esri® software, please visit <www.esri.com>.

[9] LA Street & Address File. GIS Data for LA County. <https://egis3.lacounty.gov/dataportal/2014/06/16/2011-la-county-street-centerline-street-address-file/> (accessed 30.10.18).

CHAPTER FOUR

Strategies to prepare future port and intermodal workers for transformational technologies

Kristin Decas[1] and Aravind Kailas[2]

[1]CEO/Port Director, Port of Hueneme, CA, United States
[2]Research and Innovation Manager, Volvo Group North America

Contents

Introduction

Connectivity is ubiquitous resulting in a tremendous amount of data generation globally. This has accelerated the mass adoption of smart, information, and communication technologies (aka "Digitization") in enterprise processes. This phenomenon is the catalyst for the evolution of traditional supply chains toward a smart, connected, and highly efficient supply chain ecosystem [1]. These transformational technological shifts will require leaders across the global supply chain to adopt new strategies to prepare port and intermodal workforces of the future for these many changes.

Today, the supply chain is a concatenation of many siloed processes and systems with minimal transparency and agility to maximize customer productivity. Thoughtful application of digital technologies and applications have the potential to breakdown these silos, and bring transparency to all members of the supply chain—from the suppliers of raw materials, components, and parts, to the transporters of those supplies and finished goods, and finally to the customers demanding fulfillment [2]. The

Empowering the New Mobility Workforce.
DOI: https://doi.org/10.1016/B978-0-12-816088-6.00004-3

"digital" supply chain will apply a combination of digital technologies and applications at each part of the supply chain—supplier, warehouse, production, distribution, and customer [2].

Port operations are a complex and a critical part of the supply chain today. Increasingly, the port authorities are taking measures to introduce different digital technologies, electrification, automation, and connectivity applications into their operations to create business value for their customers and increase their competitiveness. Middle Harbor Long Beach (Fig. 4.1) and Trapac Terminal in the San Pedro Complex are highly sophisticated terminals constructed—at hefty price tags of $1.49 billion [3] and $630 million [4,5], respectively—that today make terminal automation a reality. Ship-to-shore cranes robotically move containers to the shore, drop them on zero-emission ground vehicles that respond to sensors in the pavement, and ultimately move them to the staging area where they are mechanically stacked.

The Port of Los Angeles and the Port of Hueneme partnered in a grant application for Zero- and Near-Zero-Emission Freight Facilities (ZANZEFF) funds offered by the California Air Resources Board. They successfully received $50 million to install zero-emission technologies at their ports and pilot hydrogen fuel cell truck technologies. The ports of

Figure 4.1 Equipped with nearly all electric- and zero-emissions technologies, the Port of Long Beach's Middle Harbor Terminal is one of the most environmentally sustainable container terminals in the world.

Long Beach, Oakland, and Stockton also garnered $50 million in ZANZEFF funds, for a similar project that deploys zero-emission technologies, including a zero-emission tugboat and zero-emission truck and cargo equipment. These pilot programs steer the ports to the forefront of technological development that promise to drive a new economy and undoubtedly change the face of the workforce.

"Digitization" is transforming freight movement by integrating trucks into the "digital" logistics chain, with the transport of shipments to factories, warehouses, and end customers being fully transparent and tracked in real time [6]. The Port of Los Angeles is rolling out an all-new digital portal in partnership with GE Transportation to enable total transparency for tracking cargo flow at the port and enabling better planning of supply chain logistics [7]. In March 2018 the Port of Long Beach partnered with GE Transportation to also test a digital solution to enable real-time information sharing among terminal operators, logistics companies, and customers to expedite the cargo movement through the port and onto distribution centers [8].

Applying digital technologies to physical transportation infrastructure systems will generate a wealth of information for the road users that will enhance safety, mobility, and environmental efficiency. That vision includes trucks that will be able to communicate their contents and destinations with other trucks and with technology platforms that will automatically match shipments to trucks with available space, rerouting them as necessary and making the supply chain truly agile for maximum customer productivity. Additionally, there are technologies implemented in the truck itself, such as levels of automation, to make operations safer and more efficient. Complete digitization of the freight sector is a long way away, but, at the time of this writing, foundational parts of that bold digital transition are being implemented or in the works.

Innovation will happen. However, how it is applied and how it affects our society is up to us. Digital technologies and applications have the potential to bring economic prosperity, but not without shaking up the current socioeconomic strata. In the end, technology should be viewed as a range of tools and integrated technological platforms that ultimately benefit humanity. Those technologies must not be implemented "at the cost" of humanity. With this in mind, this chapter presents a ringside view of the workforce preparation at the ports, and suggests a pathway for achieving the right balance between humans and technology without compromising social responsibility and integrity.

Supply chain jobs and their economic significance

At the very foundation of the supply chain lies the human worker and this holds true for commercial seaports. Ports fuel the US economy creating more than 23 million direct, induced, and indirect jobs, generating $4.6 trillion in national economic output, and spawning $1.5 billion in total personal income and local consumption. In 2014, the average salary for direct employees in the port sector was $53,723 [9] or $55,469.01 when adjusted for inflation for 2017 [10], slightly above the US average salary of $50,620 reported by the Bureau of Labor Statistics in 2017 [11]. Conventional port jobs at the entry level include advanced vocational trades, maintenance crews, and wharfingers. Warehouse managers, freight forwarders, expediters, and stevedores constitute some of the more mid-level management jobs. Port directors, logistics analysts, engineers, transportation planners, policy analysts, finance experts, and public relations and marketing professionals sit at the top of the workforce pyramid [12,13].

Unique to the maritime industry, there is another layer to the matrix of the labor force. Union labor, pilots, and tug operators also perch at the apex of the supply chain with extremely high incomes based on practical training and experience, not typically college and graduate degrees. Unionized labor, the workers who offload and load ships, operate cranes and equipment, and stage cargo on-dock reap excellent benefits and high wages compared to other trades. In the United States, the unions with this jurisdiction include the International Longshore and Warehouse Union (ILWU) on the West Coast and the International Longshoremen's Association (ILA) on the East Coast, Gulf, and Great Lakes. Registered Longshoremen and women working at least 2000 hours earn $163,481 per year, clerks make $186,461, and foremen take home $264,509 [14]. Pilots—professionals who safely navigate vessels into port—lead the industry in annual income. On average, they earn $400,000 in annual income, making $192.31 per hour [15].

Technology, however, is taking over and infiltrating the waterfront and a paradigm shift in the workforce has become inevitable. Ports need to modernize and capitalize on emerging technologies or they face competitive disadvantages, higher costs, and inefficiencies that will drive goods movement to more optimal supply chains. At the forefront of this evolution is automation, intelligent transportation systems, Internet and the virtual world, and the development of green and zero-emission technologies. Social justice and environmental groups aggressively advocate for these shifts, but does the workforce? What does labor think about technology? How is industry responding? These are the questions permeating the dialogue among port and transportation professionals while educators and trainers at colleges and trade schools grapple with how to prepare the next generation of workers. As the debate persists, industry leaders are increasingly facing the reality that significant workforce innovations are required to address the skills gaps created by the many transformational changes occurring across the supply chain.

Leaders in industry, education, and government agree that there is no slowing of, nor changing the tide of technology. The port logistics sector is no different and technology transfer into the supply chain continues at a rapid pace. The Internet of Things (IoT), big data analytics, blockchain, and automation and robotics represent the building blocks to this new and dynamic industry and associated workforce.

IoT technologies hold great potential in enhancing many elements of a port enterprise. Web pages, social media, and apps are increasingly becoming the channels of communication. A webinar serves as the office for a business deal. The supply chain becomes optimized and pushed to its competitive limits through the publication of data, including truck-turn times, gate congestion, and dwell times. Port terminal managers track cargo via barcodes and data transfer. Systems can be maintained with high-tech automated, wireless meter-sensing systems, and information trackers. Geographic information systems publish the whereabouts of the physical thing and the human one. But IoT does not come without a cost. It poses risk due the increased exposure of sharing incredible volumes of information among so many different stakeholders across numerous networks. Strict data management, accessibility, business rules, encryption, passwords and other protocols must be properly set up to achieve the safest operations and avoid leaking of data. The demand for these new competencies has opened up an entire new field of work in IoT and cyber security for port and intermodal professionals [16,17].

Big data analytics churn a sea of data into something practical that a business, like a port, can utilize to be more efficient and productive. Operational, administrative, financial, marketing, and commercial tasks can be performed across secure networks. The collected data gets redistributed by the power of technology into usable deliverables. The data and its outputs travel along high fiber-optic systems and wireless networks to be shared in an array of virtual forums. Big data analytics allow ports to take an unlimited stream of available data, organize it, and build platforms to manage and display results. Emails flood the inboxes of port professionals from consultants seeking work to organize real time and historical data into meaningful and transferable products. Many of the ports hire these types of workers internally; others will outsource [16].

Blockchain shares the ledger of an entire supply chain transaction, origin to destination. Stakeholders see information through every system, making the delivery of goods movement completely open and transparent. Blockchain, big data analytics, and IoT can communicate freight location to a shipper, a broker, an agent, and other parties through a portal by using sensors in containers. Additionally, jobs are emerging specific to blockchain, creating similar opportunities for insourcing and/or outsourcing such professionals [16].

Automation is one of the most prevalent emerging technologies affecting the maritime and intermodal sector. Automation builds in significant efficiencies at port terminals where real estate is at a very high premium. It allows for advances in stacking and storing systems that optimize port operations [16]. Environmental regulations also drive innovation toward clean,

TECHNOLOGY = CLEAN AIR
Fun facts:
To date, clean technology driven clean air projects at the California ports have yielded significant air quality improvements. The San Pedro Ports since 2005 realized an 80% reduction in particulate matter, 90% SO_x, and 50% in NO_x. Trapac and Long Beach Middle Harbor run ship-to-shore operations through automation with zero-emission technology. The San Pedro Ports collectively rolled out a $14 billion Clean Air Action Update for deployment of zero-emission truck and handling equipment technologies in November 2017. The Port of Oakland cut CO_2 emissions by 98% for trucks and 75% for ships between 2005 and 2015. As part of its clean air plan, and with the help of its grant funds, the Port of Hueneme is constructing the electrical infrastructure requisite to supporting future electric zero-emission cargo handling equipment. Its shore-side electrification project will deplete particulate matter by 92%, NO_x by 98%, and green house gasses (GHG) by 55% over the 30-year life of the project. San Diego decreased GHG emissions by 3000 metric tons in 2015 alone and rolled out a climate action plan to bring GHG emissions to 10% below 2006 by 2020. Cruise terminal, pier upgrades, and shipyard improvements at the Port of San Francisco collectively reduced particulate matter by 61% and reduce GHG by 6000 tons a year. The efforts of the California ports outpace those of the rest of the world [19].

zero-emission technologies, such as automation. In California, regulation pushed ports to develop shore-side systems so that vessels can plug in at berth and not run their diesel auxiliary engines. Continued pressures from regulators drive the port industry to transition to zero-emission facilities as early as 2030. Automated facilities, which run green, seem to be the answer to appeal to the regulatory vigor. Many ports also turn to solar-panel technologies to meet zero-emission goals and achieve more sustainable operations. The State of California Employment Development Department (CAEDD) forecasts an increase of 130.6% in solar installer jobs between 2016 and 2026 [18].

The universe of jobs affiliated with these technological advances certainly changes the look of the workforce inside the port ecosystem. New jobs include [12,16]:

- Project managers for supply chain automation,
- Automation engineers,
- Mechanical application engineers,
- Solutions architects,
- Blockchain managers,
- Blockchain technologists,
- Blockchain developers,
- Web designers and web developers,
- Social media analysts and specialists, and
- Cyber security managers and specialists.

One of the unique positions evolving out of the virtual world is that of the Scrum Master. Software designs seek to make product delivery faster and more agile. The Scrum Master oversees the process for managing this software and is responsible for the team that has the agility to make fast, organized decisions regarding how information is processed and shared. At the executive level, positions are opening throughout the port industry in supply chain optimization [20]. During the same period of 2016−26 the CAEDD predicts growth of 40% in software developer jobs, 29.7% in operations research analysts, and 20% in trade/labor positions [18].

An emerging workforce is evolving out of the intensifying wave of technology and automation that is creating demands for new skills and professional competencies. Positions in automation, green technology and sustainability, real-time applications, improved transportation networks, efficient freight corridors, and intermodal freight transport are becoming common at the ports (Figs. 4.2 and 4.3).

Figure 4.2 A cargo ship at the Port of Hueneme in the 1960s.

Figure 4.3 A cargo ship and on-dock rail at the Port of Hueneme in the 1960s (note, it's Port of Hueneme not Port Hueneme).

While the opportunities seem endless, the transformations have given rise to a significant debate around technology, automation, and unionized labor. The invention and adoption of the standardized container in 1955 arguably represents the largest technological leap born to the maritime industry prior to today's surge in technology and highly automated systems. Wooden flats, referred to as dunnage, served as the technology of the day to offload and load ships. Such equipment became obsolete with rise of the container. In 1955, Malcom P. McLean, a trucking entrepreneur acquired a steamship company with the idea of moving entire truck trailers full of cargo by way of ship. The goal to increase efficiency and the speed of goods to market drove this innovation. In McLean's mind, truck trailers could be loaded from a truck to a ship, then from a ship to another truck seamlessly and driven straight to the marketplace. Containerization became the new norm and blossomed into what industry primarily relies on today, intermodal transportation [21]. Advanced tech systems emerged to track freight and ensure the appropriate container landed at its port of call and was correctly received, regardless of content or volume. As Tinekye Egyedi, a standardization study expert, noted, the container created the perfect technology gateway. It created "a gateway between different subsystems of transportation that enhances the efficiency of the system (supply chain) as a whole" [22].

The container and the use of new machinery single-handedly disrupted conventional labor jobs, such as stevedore lashing and stevedore knotting. In the 1960s, labor and industry reached a compromise with mutual guarantees that the existing workforce would be protected from job loss. Labor would gain increased wages and benefits, and industry earned the right to introduce new and efficient machinery [23]. Jobs morphed into something new and, perhaps, better. The workforce gained higher-skilled, higher-earning jobs, including crane operators, mechanics, X-ray and laboratory technicians, and new labor-intensive posts emerged, such as lashers, swingmen, and utility tractor rig (UTR) drivers.

Will history repeat itself in the 21st century—the age of data-driven technology and automation—with a comprehensive redefining of critical occupations and competencies required to operate the logistics systems of the future? At the turn of the century, technological advancements fueled an important conversation between labor and management: discussions about what do with the free flow of information as tech processes increasingly displaced traditional manual tasks performed by clerks. In 2002 the ILWU and the Pacific Maritime Association (PMA), representing the employer, sought to balance the advancements in technology with that of labor. The clerical unions in fact became one of the early adopters of a new technology framework in the labor-management contract. Labor accepted the introduction of new technology, allowing for the free flow of information into, out of, and around the Ports, in return for more pay guarantees and increased benefits. This negotiation represents the introduction of technology and information flow into a labor agreement and allowed for the use of technology without human intervention [24].

Seemingly right after the technology discussion around free-flowing information came the introduction of the robot and automated terminal infrastructure and equipment, which became a core element of the ensuing labor-management agreement. To compete in a dynamic global supply chain, ports embraced the rise in automation, such as that seen at Long Beach Middle Harbor and Los Angeles Trapac. Automated and mechanically advanced systems became essential to improve the flow of gate and yard operations to build in significant physical efficiencies to space-constrained terminals [25]. The goal of efficiency complemented pressures in the regulatory arena to go to zero-emission technologies. The 2008-14 Pacific Coast Longshore Contract between the ILWU and the PMA recognized that new technologies and robotics displace traditional longshore jobs and established that a job equivalent involving the installation, upkeep, and cleaning of new technologies fall under ILWU jurisdiction. The parties agreed to discuss the operations of automation and established grievance and arbitration clauses to resolve any disputes. The discussions could not impede the introduction of automation, but rather address who would be doing the work, how jobs change, and the training and education for any new required skills. These provisions established the opportunity to align the kind of work affiliated with automated operations. Important to labor, it also created the flexibility to determine the level of labor and training required to perform that job change [26].

The existing PMA-ILWU Pacific Coast contract preserves the right of industry to introduce automated infrastructure and maintains the recognition that jobs could be lost to the use of new machinery. It leaves open the opportunity to change union jobs so that they support automated and robotic operations. The contract continues to lay out the procedures to determine how many workers are needed and who does that particular work [27]. This contractual chapter between ILWU and PMA does not sunset until 2022 [28].

The evolution of labor and automation continues to unfold in the face of innovation. In 1960, more than 28,000 longshore workers dominated the docks offloading cargo along the West Coast waterfront. Today 14,000 longshoremen and women do the same [29]. Automation cleans the air, creates higher-skilled, better paying jobs, but as the Pacific Coast contract clearly recognizes, jobs can be lost to machinery. There are exceptions, however, that could become the trend. The Marline Steel factory tells a story of automation saving its workforce. Chinese price gouging tactics compromised the company's ability to hold on to market share of its top wire basket commodity. Automation became their front to compete in a world of lower prices and opened new doors for growth. They began manufacturing a new line of products for leading companies, such as Boeing and General Motors [30]. This led to the need for increased workers and higher-skilled positions at better pay grades. It seems inevitable that the jobs will modernize, but the possibility seems real that there may be fewer jobs, or maybe not. The jury is out.

The obvious: bridging workforce with academia strategy

Unless they want their bottom lines to suffer, it is incumbent upon employers help build the bridge between academia and the modern workforce. Most successful professionals get excited about the prospect of telling their story about that game-changing chapter in their professional development. The mentor, the experience, and the life-changing moment are never forgotten. That same spirit of professional inspiration must be given to the next generation of supply chain professionals. Global trade logistic classes, internship programs, and curriculums connecting the college and/or vocational student to a real-world experience are musts in the evolution of the supply chain and port logistics workforce. This is not a new concept and many of the ports are extremely active on this front, but it is an imperative that such initiatives continue.

Leaders in academia must also embrace new levels of proactivity to keep pace with the transformational trends and technologies that are reshaping the supply chain landscape. Despite rapid changes in almost every technology and science field, traditional university curricula are seldom revised to keep up. It is imperative that leaders in academia develop new standards for updating curricula to address ever-changing industry trends. Educators can revisit existing classroom methodologies and tools and explore modifying them to cater to the tech trends and the current generations. Traditional classroom techniques are theory intense and limited in their ability to connect to real-world problems, primarily owing to the time constraints of the academic schedule. One easy option could be to invite practitioners and professionals from the industry to not only infuse an element of practical applicability, but also to enable student interactions that will help them better fit into the workforce.

Furthermore, there are a number of affordable, industry relevant online courses available, which can be merged with the traditional curricula to prepare the students in the classroom for the industry.

In addition to technology training, educational institutions and trade schools are a great venue for potential employers to offer industry-specific training, topical workshops, and meet prospects at career fairs and job expos. Internships, co-ops, and part-time projects provide students the much-needed exposure to how the industry operates and the current realities of a workplace. Such experiences will not only equip the students to adjust to the needs of the workforce, but also be a confidence booster.

Finally, it is also imperative to provide the right exposure and training to the faculty. One approach is to encourage the faculty member to take on small collaborative projects with an industry affiliate or spend the summer semester at a company. This will help ensure that the faculty is in line with the current industrial trends. However, this also means that the industry professionals step up and actively engage academic professionals in R&D projects and guide their work. For example, the Volvo Group has the Academic Preferred Partners Program in the United States and Europe. Another model could be the one adopted by the Volvo Research and Educational Foundations (VREF). VREF invests in programs and projects that contribute to the dissemination and implementation of research findings among both university researchers, practitioners, decision makers and other relevant stakeholders among other goals [31]. Such interactions are a few example initiatives undertaken by the industry and academia for bridging the gap in the workforce.

Communication and messaging strategies to target the workforce

Engaging the workforce is critical for the business sustainability of advanced technologies. In addition to timely engagement with public agencies and lawmakers, actively involving end users and the broader community is very important to gain acceptance for new technology trends. Ensuring dialogues about technology and use-case scenarios are essential to establish a clear understanding of the potential and limitations of the technology. Furthermore, proper communication will also pave the way for the necessary training to ensure that the workforce will be rightly equipped to fully tap into the advanced technology product. The technology provider must thus also consider these issues to effectively introduce the product in the market. Some solutions are pilots and beta products for evaluation by the general public, using traditional and digital media to clearly communicate about the technology usage, offer hands-on-training for the first adopters and provide excellent aftermarket support and incentives such as training and tech support for the early adopters.

Another approach commonly used by transportation solutions providers such as automotive original equipment manufacturer (OEM) and technology developers are tech demonstrations, workshops, and seminars to bring different stakeholders together to discuss the technology concept and its applicability to them (or the society). As an example, in March 2017, the Volvo Group in collaboration with UC Berkeley/PATH, FHWA, Caltrans, LA Metro, and a few other partners successfully demonstrated truck platooning on Interstate 110 South in Southern California. The demonstration of the advanced technology prototype brought together law enforcement officials and a number of end users to talk about the benefits of the technology, the required training, use cases, and other topics such as deployment considerations and timeline [32].

Outside the realm of academia lie alternative and useful forums and mediums to host the discussion of how to develop a workforce to support the emergence of technology in the port sector and supply chain. Traditional tools still hold a valuable platform to entertain this discussion. Port Directors and CEOs continue to read newsletters and trade journals to stay informed about current events and trends in industry. These publications can target the dilemma at hand and serve as part of the solution. Typically, they run quarterly, monthly, weekly or even daily issues. They accommodate the preference of the full spectrum of information consumers using print, social media, email, and online communication channels. Engaging in an open dialogue in publications heavily relied on by decision makers for trusted information can drive the conversation into actionable results. It offers the opportunity to put this most relevant topic under a microscope to such a level that more and more port executives understand how they can get involved and affect positive change in developing their industry's workforce.

Another conventional but still highly utilized networking forum is that of the tradeshow or conference. If the value proposition presents itself to those in high positions, they will travel and attend such events. These arenas offer a primetime opportunity to bring together the educator and the employer. In person, real-time discussions with industry experts and the developers of education and training curriculum and programming can be very powerful. Said another way, it takes two to tango. Industry and academia need to dance and step out of their comfort zone of the typical business trip and cross-pollinate. Managers should seek out the high-profile events of academia as should those in academia attend the leading events of employers. This can be difficult to motivate as results will not be immediate and budgets are tight, but it is necessary. Technology itself can support the convening of the different actors. The meetings can take place in person, during conference calls, or through the Internet via Web conferences and social media posts. It is incumbent on industry and academia to meet in both the real world and the virtual one to strategize about how to develop the most prepared and viable workforce. It will ultimately create a win-win situation. The educator will draw a larger student body and the employer will acquire the "right talent" to advance their business.

Technology and automation present the next generation with an opportunistic future and an affluence of potential career tracks. Academia recognizes its outright obligation to work with industry and government partners to build career pathways to these jobs through every level of education. This workforce challenge drives home one final quintessential point around what constitutes the "right talent." Today a 3-year-old controls the iPhone with more competence than a Baby Boomer. With access to classes in technology and automation from kindergarten up through a graduate degree, is that 3-year-old destined for a bright and successful future, and have the promise to attain a high-tech job at a port or any industry for that matter?

There is another skill set to consider—one that no employer or educator can afford to forget: that of human social skills and proficiencies. Technology serves as a catalyst to improving the goals of society, but without vision and leadership, the technology can be misused, unsuccessful and even cause social ills. A survey of port directors from all regions of the United States performed to support this chapter brought this notion to light. Several responses expressed the need for a workforce adept with high-tech skills and training and experience with virtual mediums. However, every single response called for workers with strong human skill sets. The responses resoundingly identified leadership, interpersonal, communication, and integrity as the drivers to a successful employee, team, and organization [12].

Several experts in psychology find that the individual with a higher emotional quotient outperforms the one with the higher intelligence quotient. Social competence and the ability to influence endure as important characteristics to success. People need to exhibit self-awareness and self-regulation in a work setting. Behavioral control and the ability to manage emotions are paramount to a successful professional. The computer will not lend an individual that ability. Fight or flight, panic, freezing, and irrational behavior can doom a business deal or cause an employee to interrupt a technological function in an operational supply chain application [33,34].

People need the ability to connect with one another to create results, and not just through networks, but also through strong oral and writing skills. Ideas bud from real life interactions and conversations. The art of negotiation stems from a person who exhibits the ability to communicate, listen, and make compromise. The IoT alone cannot negotiate a business deal or a labor-management contract—that requires human not technological capital. However, technology serves a very good purpose in informing the negotiating or any other process by providing critical data and useful and meaningful information. It is up to the individual to capitalize on the power of information and use their interpersonal strengths to get the deal done.

The strategic balance: human and technology

On a concluding note, it is important to remember that technology is intended to make the lives of humans better, implying that the quality of life will not be comprised nor will be the human be replaced and made obsolete by the technology. Humans and technology will coexist though there may be changes to the exact role or job description of the human. When one considers advanced technology systems at the ports that will necessitate additional technical skill sets, this may bring about a certain repurposing of the human-driven task, but will also make the whole process better in some way (e.g., safer, more efficient), and will definitely raise the pay, thereby raising the standard of living and prosperity. In the end, all of these efforts will be facilitated and sustained through positive collaborations between leaders in industry, education, and government who are committed to empowering the next generation of mobility professionals.

Back to the 3-year old, the answer is yes. A strong bridge between the student and academia in the technology sector sets the stage for that 3-year old to land a high-tech, good paying job in the port environment or supply chain. The education must, however, encompass developing the person and providing social skills training. Students must learn to gauge their behavior and enhance relationships. They need to learn that the workplace is an environment where they need to respect others and listen to new ideas. Leaders in academia need to teach the basics in communication, conflict management, negotiation, teamwork, professionalism and ethics, and of the utmost importance, leadership. To succeed, future supply-chain leaders must be able to build a vision informed by actionable goals and related road maps to reach those deliverables. Those future professionals will need educational experiences that teach them necessary skills and competencies but also imbue within them the passion for innovation and creative problem solving to respond to the transformational changes increasingly occurring within the global supply chain. Empowered with those skills and professional attitudes, that 3-year old will be poised to lead supply chain innovations that will spur economic opportunity while promoting more efficient and clean goods movement systems around the world.

References

[1] Pricewaterhouse Cooper Limited, Maximizing the impact of digitization. <https://www.strategyand.pwc.com/media/file/Strategyand_Maximizing-the-Impact-of-Digitization.pdf>, 2012 (accessed 25.10.18).

[2] Pricewaterhouse Cooper Limited, Industry 4.0: How digitization makes the supply chain more efficient, agile, and customer-focused. <https://www.strategyand.pwc.com/reports/digitization-more-efficient>, 2016 (accessed 26.10.18).

[3] Pier E-Middle Harbor, Port of long beach. <http://www.polb.com/about/projects/middleharbor.asp>, n.d. (accessed 29.10.18).

[4] Los Angeles Times, Cost of terminal upgrade at port of Los Angeles doubled over 4 years. <http://articles.latimes.com/2013/nov/18/local/la-me-port-terminal-over-runs-20131119> 2013 (accessed 29.10.18).

[5] Christina. S, PE. Cost of port of Los Angeles TraPac redevelopment program, 2018. Email exchange.

[6] Pricewaterhouse Cooper Limited, The era of digitized trucking: transforming the logistics value chain. <https://www.strategyand.pwc.com/reports/era-of-digitized-trucking>, 2016 (accessed 29.10.18).

[7] Icons of Infrastructure. Los Angeles port joins hands with GE for a digital makeover. <https://iconsofinfrastructure.com/port-of-la-joins-ge-transportation-digital-make-over/> (accessed 20.10.18).

[8] Icons of Infrastructure. Port of long beach follows Los Angeles for digital transformation. <https://iconsofinfrastructure.com/port-long-beach-follows-los-angeles-digital-transformation/>, n.d. (accessed 20.10.18).

[9] Martin Associates, 2014 National economic impact on the U.S. coastal port system: executive summary. <http://aapa.files.cms-plus.com/PDFs/Martin%20study%20executive%20summary%20final.pdf>, 2015 (accessed 29.10.18).

[10] Martin, J. Email exchange.

[11] U.S. Bureau of Labor Statistics. <https://www.bls.gov/home.htm>, n.d. (accessed 20.10.18).

[12] Association of Port Authorities. Port Workforce Needs and Assessment Evaluation Survey, 2018.

[13] Burning Glass. Data on job classifications provided by research assistant.

[14] Pacific Maritime Association, Pacific Maritime Association 2017 annual report. <http://apps.pmanet.org/pubs/AnnualReports/2017/PMA_Annual_Report_2017. pdf>, 2017 (accessed 29.10.18).

[15] Chron, Salaries for harbor pilots. <https://work.chron.com/salaries-harbor-pilots-5915.html>, 2012 (accessed 29.10.18).

[16] Blockgram, The different types of blockchain jobs. <http://blockgram.com/the-different-types-of-blockchain-jobs/>, 2018 (accessed 29.10.18).

[17] Singapore Institute of Purchasing and Materials Management, New and emerging technology in the port-logistics sector. <https://sipmm.edu.sg/new-emerging-technology-port-logistics-sector/>, 2018 (accessed 29.10.18).

[18] State of California Employment Development Department, Top 100 fastest growing occupations in California, 2016–2026. <https://labormarketinfo.edd.ca.gov/occguides/fastgrowingocc.aspx>, 2018 (accessed 29.10.18).

[19] The California Association of Port Authorities, Environmental stewardship at California ports. Flyer, 2018.

[20] Whatis.com, Definition of scrum master. <https://whatis.techtarget.com/definition/scrum-master> (accessed 29.10.18).

[21] World Shipping Council, History of containerization. <http://www.worldshipping.org/about-the-industry/history-of-containerization>, 2018 (accessed 29.10.18).

[22] F.J. Lechner, J. In Boli, The Globalization Reader, John Wiley & Sons Ltd, United Kingdom, 2015.

[23] International Longshore and Warehouse Union, The ILWU story. <https://www.ilwu.org/history/the-ilwu-story/>, 2018 (accessed 29.10.28).

[24] International Longshore and Warehouse Union (ILWU), Pacific Maritime Association (PMA). Pacific Coast Longshore and Clerks' Agreement Contract Document for Clerks and Related Classifications Between Locals 14, 23, 29, 34, 40, 46, 52, and 63 and PMA Members in California, Oregon and Washington for 2002–2008. <https://www.ilwu.org/wp-content/uploads/2010/12/PCCCD_2002-2008.pdf> (accessed 29.10.18).

[25] Journal of Commerce.com, US Ports in no rush to follow shanghai on automation path. <https://www.joc.com/port-news/terminal-operators/shanghai-international-port-group/us-ports-no-rush-follow-shanghai-automation-path_20171211.html>, 2017 (accessed 29.10.18).

[26] International Longshore and Warehouse Union (ILWU), Pacific Maritime Association (PMA). Pacific Coast Longshore Contract Document For International Longshore and Warehouse Union and Pacific Maritime Association for 2008-2014, section 1.72 and section 15. <http://apmanet.org/pubs/laborAgreements/2008-2014%20PCLCD.pdfps>, 2009 (accessed 29.10.18).

[27] International Longshore and Warehouse Union (ILWU), Pacific Maritime Association (PMA). Pacific Coast Longshore Contract Document for 2014-2019. Section 1.72 and section 15. <http://apps.pmanet.org/pubs/LaborAgreements/2014-2019_PCLCD_web.pdf>, 2014 (accessed 29.10.18).

[28] International Longshore and Warehouse Union, West Coast longshore workers ratify contract extension; New agreement will continue until July, 2022. <https://www.ilwu.org/west-coast-longshore-workers-ratify-contract-extensionnew-agreement-will-continue-until-july-2022/>, 2017 (accessed 29.10.18).

[29] Press Telegram. P. Port of L.A.'s automated terminal: future of commerce or blue-collar job-killer? <https://www.presstelegram.com/2017/03/18/port-of-las-automated-terminal-future-of-commerce-or-blue-collar-job-killer/>, 2017 (accessed 29.10.18).

[30] Venturebeat, Automation replaced 800,000 workers... then created 3.5 million new jobs. <https://venturebeat.com/2017/09/07/automation-replaced-800000-workers-then-created-3-5-million-new-jobs/>, 2017 (accessed 29.10.18).

[31] Volvo Research and Educational Foundation, About the Volvo Research and Educational Foundations. <http://www.vref.se/futprogramme/aboutthevref.4.7cd0 18df146d4c36803302ee.html>, 2018 (accessed 20.10.18).

[32] Volvo Trucks, Volvo trucks successfully demonstrates on-highway truck platooning in California. <https://www.volvotrucks.us/news-and-stories/press-releases/2017/march/volvo-trucks-successfully-demonstrates-on-highway-truck-platooning-in-california/>, 2017 (accessed 20.10.18).

[33] Butterworth, G. Surveying the Top 12 Signs of Emotional Intelligence. Camarillo Health Care District Community Advisory Council, 2018.

[34] A. Stein, Supply chain talent: a practical approach to hardening soft skills,, Supply ChainManage. Rev. 19 (4) (2015) 20−26.

CHAPTER FIVE

Anticipating and responding to changes in the mobility sector

Lee D. Lambert and Ian R. Roark

Workforce Development, Pima Community College, Tucson, AZ, United States

> I skate to where the puck is going to be, not where it has been.
> *Wayne Gretzky*

Contents

Introduction

To get a sense of the profound change coming imminently to the mobility workforce, consider a typical workday for commercial truck

Empowering the New Mobility Workforce.
DOI: https://doi.org/10.1016/B978-0-12-816088-6.00005-5

drivers of the future. Their time on the road will require constant vigilance, situational awareness, and calculation, as it does today. However, it will not require them to sit in the driver's seat, hands on the wheel day and night, actually steering the truck down the road. The truck drivers of the future will not drive trucks, because the truck, more precisely an autonomous vehicle, will do the driving.

But the truckers of the future will be busy, interacting with the truck's computer systems, tracking cargo as it progresses through the supply chain, occasionally taking the wheel, and repairing the truck when it breaks down. In short, to retain employment they will need to call upon old skills (turning a wrench) along with new knowledge (information technology, logistics) in a job that will bear little resemblance to commercial trucking of today.

It will not only be the nation's 3.5 million truck drivers who will need to learn new skills to thrive. The US mobility workforce also comprises 750,000 auto mechanics, and 1.03 million employed in the nation's warehouses and fulfillment centers. Also consider the nearly 150,000 employed as aviation mechanics and technicians. For millions whose livelihood depends on transporting people and goods safely and efficiently, it will be a new world.

The future of truck driver training, automotive technology, logistics and supply chain management, and Aviation Technology is of special interest to Pima Community College. Pima offers programs in these areas of study, as well as others that constitute Career and Technical Education (CTE). Pima is located in the fast-growing aviation, logistics, and transportation hub of Tucson, Arizona, 60 miles from the Mexico border. Arizona exports more to Mexico than to its next nine international trade partners. Each day, approximately $1.6 billion in trade is processed at Arizona ports of entry [1]. We are well aware of the opportunity Pima has to be a key player in the economic development of our transnational region, especially in the transportation sector. Hence, we are acutely interested in understanding the future of air and ground transportation, and how the College can become part of a community of practice devoted to leveraging its knowledge for the benefit of our students and region. Given the technological changes accelerating through society, our interest could not have come at a more appropriate time.

The future is now: the four superpowers, industry 4.0, artificial intelligence, Internet of Things . . .

A broad cross-section of thought leaders argue we live in a new era. On January 15, 2018, as part of the World Economic Forum Annual

Meeting, VMware CEO Pat Gelsinger published an article under the headline, "Four New 'Superpowers' Changing the World." The article reads, in part: "The term 'superpowers' conjures an image of major nations shaping the course of global history. But in the digital era ... it's time we expanded that definition to include ... mobile technology, the cloud, artificial intelligence (AI) and the Internet of Things (IoT)" [2]. Klaus Schwab, Founder and Executive Chairman of the World Economic Forum, writes in his 2016 book *The Fourth Industrial Revolution*, "We are witnessing profound shifts across all industries ... Equally, governments and institutions are being reshaped, as are systems of healthcare, education and transportation" [3].

Digital technologies are reshaping every aspect of the economy and our lives, especially employment. Approximately 50% of current work activities can be automated by adapting currently demonstrated technologies, according to a November 2017 McKinsey Global Institute report. By 2020, the research firm Gartner Inc. estimates that AI will create 2.3 million jobs worldwide, while eliminating 1.8 million. *New York Times* columnist Thomas Friedman concludes that for anyone seeking to remain employed in this new era, "self-motivation to learn and keep learning becomes the most important life skill." Training will be especially important in transportation. "Strengthening Skills Training and Career Pathways across the Transportation Industry," a 2015 report issued jointly by the US Transportation, Labor, and Education departments, emphasized the need to hire and train 4.6 million new workers in the transportation sector [4].

Demographic challenges

As discussed by Carleton College economist Nathan Grawe in "Demographics and the Demand for Higher Education," the number of births in the United States has declined nearly 13% since the recession of 2008 [5]. This "birth dearth" will cause stark challenges for workforce development and college enrollment due to population stagnation, especially in Pima County and southern Arizona.

The number of emerging workers' ages 18-24 in Pima County is projected to stagnate or decrease until 2030, as shown in Fig. 5.1.

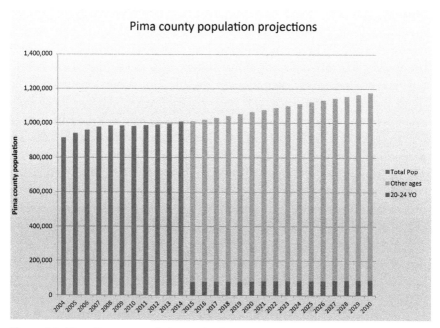

Figure 5.1 Pima County population projections.

The population pyramid shown in Fig. 5.2 also demonstrates stagnation among emerging workers. Even more troubling is the pattern of rapid population increase and decrease around ages 19-24, due to an influx of students who move to Tucson to attend the University of Arizona, only to move away upon graduation.

Particularly alarming is the decrease in the available workforce aged mid-20s to the early 40s, likely due to a Tucson median income of $46,764 that lags the national median of $57,617 and the Arizona median of $51,340, pushing mid-level employees to seek better wages elsewhere. Only at typical retirement ages and above do we see an increase in the available workforce in Pima County, as shown in Fig. 5.2. Pima County's education and workforce development pipeline cannot fill jobs that will open up due to the Baby Boomer generation's departure from the workforce, combined with projected job growth in transportation, manufacturing, and other technical fields.

Interestingly, Pima Community College outperforms other Arizona community colleges in enrolling high school graduates immediately upon their graduation. Of all public high school graduates in Pima County, 43% enroll at Pima within 1 year of graduation—10% points higher than

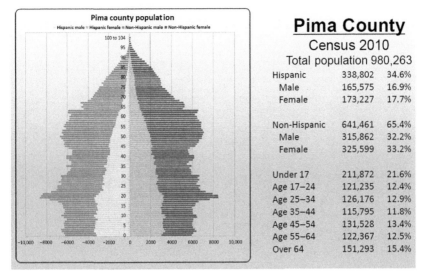

Figure 5.2 Pima County population age distribution.

the average percentage of the state's 10 community colleges. While we are proud of this data point, it is also troubling that 57% of recent high school graduates do not matriculate to Pima. What is that 57% doing after graduating from high school?

Enrollment data provide an answer. When we examine the median age of enrollees in our Applied Technology programs (as shown in Fig. 5.3, which includes transportation technology, as compared to traditionally university transfer-oriented programs of study) we see a noticeable gap in the median age of enrollees. Specifically, the median age of enrollees in programs such as mathematics, communications, sciences, and developmental education hovers around 19-20 years, while the median age of those enrolled in CTE areas such as applied technology, allied health, and nursing programs is 28-30 years.

It is reasonable to conclude many Pima County students, upon high school graduation, enter lower-skilled jobs and meander through the labor market for about a decade—Pima has labeled it "the lost decade"—before enrolling in Pima's Applied Technology programs with the intention of pursuing programs of study that lead to higher wages and gainful employment.

The next-oldest slice of the demographic pie, 35-44-year olds, is also cause for concern. Arizona ranks 49th in labor market participation for

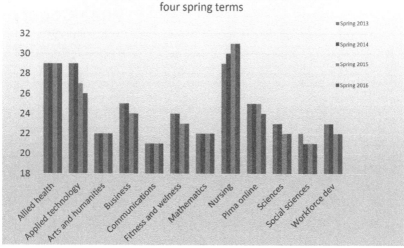

Figure 5.3 Median age of Pima Community College students by division.

workers aged 35-44 years [6]. In Pima County, 25% of the eligible work-forces are nonparticipants in the labor market [7]; out of an estimated 490,000 eligible workers in Pima County, 122,000 are workforce nonpar-ticipants. The low labor market participation skews the real unemploy-ment rate in the region (and for that matter, the nation), acting as a drag on developing the mobility workforce and intensifying the skills gap.

The lost decade: Pima's responses

Pima is employing two strategies to close the labor gap caused by the lost decade:

1. CTE Dual-Credit Academies, and
2. Prior learning assessment (PLA).

CTE Dual-Credit Academies aim to increase the number of graduat-ing high school seniors that matriculate to CTE/workforce programs at the college. We are seeking to align dual credit offering with our guided pathways—roadmaps that lead students to a credential quickly and effi-ciently—and maximize the number of college credits in CTE that stu-dents may earn while in high school. PLA incentivizes the incumbent workers aged 25-64 years to enter CTE programs at Pima.

CTE Dual-Credit Academies

Dual credit enables students to earn college credit while still in high school. Dual credit is high school coursework that is aligned with college coursework and is taught by a high school instructor certified as a college adjunct instructor. CTE Dual-Credit Academies are wholly aligned programs of study. Students can earn an entire certificate from Pima at or before they graduate from high school.

We have designed CTE Dual-Credit Academies in partnership with the Center for the Future of Arizona and have followed the center's Pathways to Prosperity career pathways design, as shown in Fig. 5.4. Our CTE Dual-Credit Academies must include:

- Aligned curricula;
- Engagement with industry for support and work-based learning experiences;
- Alignment with industry-recognized standards;
- Peer-to-peer collaboration among the high school and college faculty;
- Integration of high school guidance and enrollment processes with college student services;
- Seamless enrollment processes for high school parents and students;
- Integration of support services, such as those available through the public workforce system; and
- A welcoming environment for high school students, parents, and staff.

Engagement with external constituents is a key element of the CTE Dual-Credit Academy paradigm. By partnering with the Pima County Joint Technical Education District (a secondary education public school district focusing on CTE) and area high schools, we can align our CTE

Figure 5.4 More than 140, local high school and Pima students who participated in NC3's Career and Technical Education Letter of Intent Signing Day in February 2018.

curricula to maximize college course participation among Pima County youth. Dual enrollment students connect with college faculty and staff to build relationships and familiarity with Pima, while parents, students, and counselors build relationships with college faculty and staff in developing seamless programs and support services. This ecosystem of relationships and college-aligned curricula allows for more students to directly matriculate to Pima upon high school graduation and close the gap posed by the lost decade.

There is no greater testament to the power of the CTE Dual-Credit Academy approach than our participation in the National Coalition of Certification Centers (NC3) National CTE Letter of Intent Signing Day. This annual event, started by Washburn Tech in Topeka, Kansas, is the Career, Technical, and Workforce Education analog to the events that celebrate high school students signing letters of intent to play for college and university athletics teams. We joined National CTE Signing Day 3 years ago. Participation by local high school students has more than quadrupled since then. Local and regional employers in CTE fields also attend the event to support the students as well as inform them about careers with their companies. Some employers give out scholarships to students who commit to working for them while enrolled in our programs.

Last year we began inviting the students' parents to the event, and it is heartwarming to see the smiles on parents' and students' faces as the students sign their letter of acceptance to a CTE program. Pima's Aviation Technology and Automotive Technology programs have the highest attendance at the event. Representatives of our most prominent local auto dealerships stand behind the students when they sign their letters. The high school students proudly wear their NC3 MOPAR CAP LOCAL jerseys and were jubilant when a local dealer announced a scholarship program that will help each student continue to train at Pima.

As a result of the CTE Dual-Credit Academies and such outreach as the CTE National Signing Day, we have already seen a decrease in the median age in our Applied Technology programs as shown in Fig. 5.3. This is possible only through curriculum alignment and student-centered relationships. The students already have college credit for their transportation program of study and a relationship with a local employer. Thus they are incentivized to finish their educational journey with us as they progress toward gainful employment, and we are glad to make inroads in resolving the lost decade issue.

Prior learning assessment

PLA broadly refers to the awarding of college credit to students for learning that occurred outside the scope of formal higher education coursework and prior to students' enrollment at the institution. PLA is often used to certify and award college credit to students for formal military training, demonstrated mastery of college course outcomes without having to take the classes, industry-recognized credentials, and career experiences. PLA takes many forms across the United States and includes such practices as allowing challenge examinations to count for coursework, articulating industry-recognized credentials toward coursework, recognizing formal military training, and utilizing portfolio assessment tools to evaluate work and life experience.

At a minimum, colleges view PLA as a common-sense means to help students attain degrees and certificates by closing the gap between what they know and can demonstrate versus the time and cost involved in taking classes that would be redundant. However, PLA is increasingly viewed as a means to address larger issues of student access and student success, and is a critical means to addressing the skills gap in technical education. Sherman and Klein Collins state:

> [T]he U.S. economy will need 106 million Americans to hold postsecondary credentials in 2025. Based on current attainment rates, the country is projected to fall 19.8 million credentials short of that goal. Increased enrollment in—and successful completion of—postsecondary learning programs is critical to achieving it. Prior learning assessment, or PLA, can help more workers complete training and degree programs sooner by giving them college credit for knowledge and competencies they have gained outside of the classroom. PLA can save students time and money, and the boost in credit earning might also have a motivating effect for some students [8].

In addition, students with PLA credits were 2.5 times more likely to persist to graduation than students without PLA credits [9].

The need for a robust PLA regimen at Pima is evident in the context of economic development, the labor market, and accompanying skills gap in technical fields in Southern Arizona. According to Pima County, Southern Arizona high-tech employers see promising opportunities for expansion in current and emerging markets, but additional skilled workers are needed in order to take advantage of those opportunities [10].

The Pima County Workforce Investment Board (WIB) states:

Greater focus must go toward developing highly skilled, homegrown talent . . . . [The] current workforce, including dislocated workers and Veterans with technical backgrounds, represents an untapped potential talent pool. Career-ladder development and non-traditional delivery of education [are] needed to allow current workers to move up into high-technology occupations, diminishing the need to import outside talent to address unmet demand [11].

In response to these needs, we launched a task force to address the PLA policy and practice gaps at Pima. In order to delve into the issues and ensure a thorough and sustainable PLA regimen launch, the task force included members from key areas of the college and also included an official from our regional public workforce system, Arizona@Work, Pima County. Since the launch of the task force in October 2015, we have developed and implemented a comprehensive PLA system that addresses student services, curriculum alignment, policy and compliance, and outreach to the targeted populations. We are launching PLA in two areas. Our Building Construction Technology Program will issue college credit to students who have earned NCCER credentials outside of the college in building and construction trades, and our Public Safety and Emergency Services Institute will issue college credit to professional firefighters who have demonstrated knowledge and skills through their experience and professional training with fire service agencies via an electronic portfolio assessment.

The implications for transportation technology training are great; 30% of Pima's coursework has been identified by faculty and deans as eligible for PLA, including coursework in Aviation Technology (career field experience and FAA industry-recognized credentials), automotive technology (industry-recognized credentials in Automotive Service Excellence), and logistics (career field experience and portfolio assessment). The full launch for PLA in these program areas is slated for Spring 2019.

Centers of Excellence

Dual-Credit Academies and PLA are two of an array of means Pima is employing to meet its overarching strategic end: providing the talent—the human capital—that will allow existing employers to expand their operations and draw new employers to our region. Another way we will achieve our goal is by establishing Centers of Excellence (CoE). As stated in in our *Educational Master Plan*, "a Center of Excellence (CoE) can be defined as a team, a shared facility, or an entity that provides leadership, best practices, support and/or training for a focus area. In higher education and at 2-year colleges, the term refers to a collection of academic or technical programs that are strategically aligned to pursue excellence in a particular discipline or field of study" [12].

A CoE's relevancy depends on its link to a leading-edge sector of the economy such as the mobility sector. The first of six CoEs to be brought online by Pima will be one focused on applied technology. (The other five are in health professions, information technology, public safety and security, the arts and humanities, and hospitality.) We are investing more than $45 million, with additional funding to come from a capital campaign, to expand existing programs and start new ones across three verticals:

1. Transportation technology (e.g., automotive technology, diesel technology, autonomous and connected vehicles),
2. Manufacturing/advanced manufacturing (machine technology, welding/fabrication, mechatronics, automation, process control optics, quality, design), and
3. Infrastructure (construction, utility technology, mining, and HVAC).
   The characteristics of successful CoEs include:

- Offering formal degree and certificate programs in CTE, yet providing flexibility through short-term training opportunities via stackable credentials and multiple on-ramps of emerging and incumbent workers;
- Solidifying and deepening partnerships with business and industry, community partners, and high schools;
- Providing thought leadership in workforce development at the highest level;
- Concentrating resources and expertise through shared faculty and industry partners using best practices;
- Integrating credit, noncredit, and industry-recognized credentials throughout CTE/workforce programs;
- Providing faculty and staff with state-of-the-art professional development opportunities with industry; and
- Using real-time regional economic development and local labor data to better understand and respond to community, business, and industry needs [12].

When fully realized, CoEs will be best-in-class: programs and facilities recognized regionally, nationally and internationally as preeminent in their sector. That is the plan. What follows is the hard part: execution.

Speed, adaptability, and convergence

October 6, 2017, was an important day for Pima's Centers of Excellence initiative. More than 130 business, industry, and community partners gathered at a summit to provide insights on our plan to create a CoE for Applied Technology at our Downtown Campus. As external participation is critical, the summit featured a panel comprising regional and national leaders from the business and economic development sectors. The panel was asked, "From the perspective of industry, what do you consider the most important considerations for Pima as we move forward with establishing the Center of Excellence?" The response from panelist Joe Snell, President and CEO of Sun Corridor, Inc., our regional economic development organization, resonated with all in attendance. "Pima Community College will need to be able to deliver education and training with speed, adaptability, and in recognition of the convergence of technological and economic trends that is upon us" (Fig. 5.5).

Education and training organizations such as Pima must adopt leadership and action platforms that recognize the need for speed, adaptability,

Figure 5.5 More than 150 leaders from the business, economic development, government, and education sectors met at PCC in Fall 2017 to discuss the needs and expectations of a Center of Technology in Applied Technology.

and convergence. Our relevance and capabilities in meeting the workforce needs of the not-so-distant future will depend on our ability not to keep pace with the needs of today, but in our ability to forecast and respond to changes beyond the horizon. Thus, it is worthwhile to dive deeper into each concept as it relates to CoE:

- Speed (responsiveness): CoEs will utilize real-time regional economic development and local labor data so they can move quickly to supply high quality, in-demand programs and employees.
- Adaptability (flexibility, exploration, and investigation): CoEs will nurture collaboration, professional development, and critical thinking—skills required in the next generation of productivity—and will facilitate career guidance and action research by practitioners with real-world experience.
- Convergence (exposure and expertise): CoEs will deepen partnerships with external constituencies and will be a community hub for open resources that facilitate the exchange of knowledge, work-based learning and apprenticeships, and seminars and forums on thought leadership.

To make CoEs a reality, Pima will have to overcome institutional challenges. Our curriculum adoption and planning processes have long lagged in the timeliness required to respond to ever-advancing technology and keep up with the pace of business in transportation, manufacturing, health sciences, and other fields. We have, for far too long, expected industry and our students to adjust their business cycles and work—life schedules to meet our antiquated paradigms of seat time, semester scheduling, and static certificates and degrees. Our legacy systems are built on linear models of default high-school-to-college matriculation and educational models predicated on occupational specificity and longevity within one specific career field.

On each of these counts, we must retool. We must be able to respond at or before the point of need of business. We need to be flexible in programming and modalities to meet the needs of businesses and workers in a complex society, and move past paradigms of occupational and job specificity that are rapidly disappearing in the workplace.

Applied transportation technology at Pima

Speed. Adaptability. Convergence. These three considerations constitute the rallying call for transformational change for Pima's CTE/workforce development programs. Through redesign, investment, and

Checking under the hood

By Lee D. Lambert, J.D., Chancellor, Pima Community College

I became Chancellor of Pima Community College in July 2013. But even before taking over as CEO, I knew the College had to overcome internal challenges if it was to become a leader in the transportation sector. That's because during the interview process in Spring 2013 I had requested and received a tour of the College's Automotive Technology Center.

You can tell a lot about a community college by touring its ATC. My walk-through revealed the need to improve Pima's commitment to industry partnerships, support for professional development of its faculty, curriculum currency, preparation of students for career success, and other indices of excellence in Automotive Tech.

After taking over as CEO, it became apparent that Automotive Tech was symptomatic of a larger problem. Pima's Workforce approaches were not connecting with the community in a holistic and comprehensive manner. I spent my first year engaging the community as much as I could, and external constituents told me repeatedly it was not clear whom one should speak to at Pima about meeting employer needs. Ostensibly a multi-campus community college district, Pima actually comprised six siloed campuses that worked separately and were responsible for their own initiatives. This led to fragmentation, miscommunication, inconsistencies and a lack of follow-through.

In response, I established a Vice President for Workforce Development, a position that would become the business community's single point of contact for all things Workforce related. Additionally, being mindful of growing external concerns related to the relevancy of higher education, the skills gap, demographic shifts and the impact of the digital age, I directed the Provost to assess Pima's capacity to adapt. The assessment resulted in an Education and Facilities Master Plan that encapsulates our comprehensive, long-range planning approach and ambitiously articulates our vision through 2025.

The bottom line for leaders: Kick the tires. You never know what it may reveal, and how those revelations can drive transformation at your institution.

Figure 5.6 "Checking Under the Hood" Word doc.

innovation, we are keeping pace with transformational technology in the context of education and training in applied transportation technology: automotive technology, Aviation Technology, logistics and supply chain management, and truck driver training.

Automotive technology, partnerships, and industry-recognized standards

Each day, the automotive industry impacts nearly every facet of our lives. Automobiles meet our personal transportation needs, form a large part of the US manufacturing sector, and are the backbone of the networks that supply most good and services. At our NC3 CTE Signing Day event at our West Campus, one of our key partners in the automotive industry reminded us, "We are here to celebrate all of these CTE programs, but remember how you got here today. Whether it was by car, truck, or bus, you were brought here by the automotive industry." It follows that a college that recognizes these impacts and connections is one that ensures its Automotive Technology program is of high quality and is connected to local industry.

Pima's Automotive Technology Program offers certificates and degrees in maintenance and light repair, serving about 250 students annually. The program is currently accredited as a National Automotive Technicians Education Foundation (NATEF) Master Level Program and is moving toward the ASE Education Foundation accreditation for the next accreditation period. Previously, Pima had under-invested in the program's facilities, faculty training and equipment, and had allowed connections with the local industry to fragment. In response, our approach to program improvement was threefold: (1) reengage the local industry, (2) leverage the training network of NC3, and (3) prepare for the program's inclusion and expansion in the CoE in applied technology.

Our reengagement with the local automotive industry was part of a college-wide industry engagement regimen. We networked and researched what our partners wanted and needed from our automotive program and focused on small wins that would demonstrate our commitment to change. We did not defend or justify our current practices; we listened and implemented what we learned. We have shifted to more hands-on learning, as requested by industry, firmed up our National Automotive Technicians Educational Foundation/Automotive Service Excellence alignment in preparation for our next visit, and are bringing industry to the table for every major program decision.

It soon became evident that the changes we were making locally were not going to help the program meet the challenges presented by the Fourth Industrial Revolution. The rapid advent of smart vehicle and IoT technology advancing into the auto shop, and adoption of autonomous vehicles was outpacing our ability to update our curriculum and lab. We needed to leverage the power of a network to learn quickly from other education and industry partners nationally, and to implement training solutions to keep pace with or get ahead of the industry. It was at this juncture that we turned to NC3.

"The National Coalition of Certification Centers (NC3) was established to address the need for strong industry partnerships with educational institutions in order to develop, implement, and sustain industry-driven and industry-recognized portable certifications that have strong validation and assessment standards in the transportation, energy, and aviation sectors" [13]. These certifications are developed by industry partners such as Snap-on, Fiat Chrysler Automobiles, and Starrett, who work with educational providers to develop, test, and deploy the certifications in programs of study.

NATEF serves as the foundation of an automotive technology program on which other quality measures are built. These include original equipment manufacturer (OEM) training programs such as the Fiat Chrysler Automobiles (FCA) MOPAR Career Automotive Program (MOPAR for short) and NC3 certification programs. We then leveraged our NATEF accreditation and relationship with NC3 to take our automotive program to the next level of industry standards alignment.

Upon joining the NC3 network, Pima took advantage of the training offered by NC3 and integrated those certifications into our Automotive Technology Program, including automotive scanner diagnostics, multimeter, electronic and mechanical torque, and precision measurement instruments. We sent our faculty to NC3 certification training and purchased the necessary equipment to deliver the training in our lab, including the most up-to-date training equipment produced by Snap-on. These certifications and trainings enhanced our program and gave our students up-to-date knowledge of industry trends and skills. Since 2015, Pima students have earned over 430 NC3 certifications across our Automotive Technology, Aviation Technology, and Manufacturing Programs.

On this foundation, we were approached by NC3 to participate in MOPAR. In partnership with the Jim Click Holmes Tuttle dealerships, we were vetted by FCA and NC3 and implemented MOPAR in 2016. At the time, we were one of 35 schools asked to be a part of the program. We implemented the training both at Pima and through our CTE Dual-Credit Academy partners. So far, we have opened the door for 49 high school students in MOPAR to continue their training at Pima. We were the first college in the United States to offer the Level 0 course, an online introduction to the maintenance of FCA vehicles, to high school students. In addition, we laid the groundwork for a full-fledged OEM program in our Center of Excellence for Applied Technology.

We will continue our investment in automotive technology by expanding the program space and capacity to double or triple the number of students served, including continuing education in the field. Also, we will add a Diesel Technology Program to address long-haul trucking and mining industry needs. Diesel tech also will fill in labor needs in Tucson's blossoming autonomous and connected vehicle technology sector.

 ## Aviation technology, national labor market pressure, and alternative modalities

Pima's Aviation Technology Program is working to better align with industry needs in order to meet the growing demand for qualified aviation technicians in Southern Arizona and elsewhere. As cited by the Pima Association of Governments (PAG):

> *Careers in aviation maintenance have continued to increase as global economies expand and airlines fly thousands of jetliners to meet air transportation demand. According to Boeing, by 2035, 118,000 maintenance technicians will be needed in North America alone (Boeing, 2016) ... Over the next seven years, local [i.e., Pima County] job growth for aircraft mechanics and service technicians, and avionics technicians is expected to grow by 8 percent and 13 percent, respectively [14].*

Many regional employers are having trouble hiring enough workers to sustain this growth. For example, the region's largest aviation employer, Bombardier Aerospace, with employees about 1,000 workers, reported in April 2016 a nearly 14% increase in its jet-maintenance workforce at Tucson International Airport [14]. Other major employers such as Ascent Aviation Technologies reported similar patterns and needs.

In response, our program is increasing the number of trainees, expanding facilities, and staffing. We have a new Part 65 training and testing program, in which experienced technicians and military veterans are given a fast-track opportunity to prepare for their Federal Aviation Administration (FAA) licensure exams; we assess their current skills and content mastery and then customize instruction through a battery of training modules, closing the skills gap for each enrollee. Since 2016, we have served 83

Part 65 trainees and are currently piloting a new online-classroom hybrid version of the program with 30 additional people. These efforts have led to 113 people (and counting) outside of our regular certificate and degree program to enter the new mobility workforce.

In addition, in 2009 the program launched a high school early-college enrollment program with the Pima County Joint Technical Education District (JTED) that enrolls high school juniors and seniors. High school student enrollment numbers for the early college program were robust even considering the evening schedule and the distance of the ATC from surrounding high schools. We are exploring more online-classroom hybrid options for this training given the initial success of our hybrid Part 65 program.

Finally, as in the automotive technology section, our partnership with NC3 has helped us keep pace with the technological change in industry and enhanced partnerships with other colleges in the NC3 network to share best practices and innovations. We offer these NC3 certifications in our program: precision electrical termination, structural sheet metal and assembly, multimeter, and electronic and mechanical torque. In fact, our Aviation Technology faculty was instrumental in the development of the Precision Electrical Termination and Structural Sheet Metal and Assembly certifications, which were developed in partnership with NC3, Daniels Manufacturing Corporation, and Snap-on. These innovations allow us to close the skills gap, meet the demands of the skilled-labor shortage, and integrate new technologies and certifications into our training. Our employer—partners see an increase in the quality and quantity of our aviation technicians, and our students benefit from increased labor-market value and currency in the new mobility workforce.

Advances in logistics and supply chain management and truck driver training

Pima's participation in the Pacific Southwest Region (PSR) University Transportation Center (UTC) partnership is helping drive advances in our Logistics and Supply Chain Management and Truck Driver Training programs. Pima is one of the first community colleges to become part of a UTC. The collaboration is central to our empowerment of the new mobility workforce. It helps us keep up with technological change and reach disadvantaged populations. At its core, the PSR UTC project epitomizes adaptability and convergence.

The Pacific Southwest Region UTC is funded under the US Department of Transportation's University Transportation Centers program. Established in 2016, Pacific Southwest Region UTC is led by the University of Southern California and includes seven partners: (1) California State University, Long Beach; (2) University of California, Davis; (3) University of California, Irvine; (4) University of California, Los Angeles; (5) University of Hawaii, (6) Northern Arizona University, Arizona; and (7) Pima Community College, Tucson. The Pacific Southwest Region UTC conducts an integrated, multidisciplinary program of research, education, and technology transfer aimed at improving the mobility of people and goods throughout the region. UTC programming is organized around four themes: (1) developing technology to address transportation problems and improve mobility, (2) improving mobility for vulnerable populations, (3) improving resilience and protecting the environment, and (4) managing mobility in high-growth areas. Pima serves as the workforce development arm of the partnership in concert with METRANS.

METRANS is a partnership between the University of Southern California (USC) and California State University Long Beach (CSULB), two of the UTC partners. As part of the partnership, Pima has started and will complete the following activities:

- Implement a wholly online version of the Logistics and Supply Chain Management program with a work-based learning component;
- Implement a hybrid (i.e., partially online) variant of truck driver training;
- Integrate geospatial information system (GIS) technology into Logistics and Truck Driver Training;
- Integrate employability or "soft skills" into these new models; and
- Deliver all of the above to underserved and rural populations, with an emphasis on tribal populations in the PSR region and the American Southwest.

This last point is crucial given Pima's mission to serve the Pascua Yaqui Tribe and Tohono O'odham Nation. The Yaqui have communities in the American Southwest and in Mexican states of Sonora, Chihuahua, Durango, and Sinaloa. Pima has had an extensive and fruitful relationship with the Pascua Yaqui Nation since 2000. The College has an extensive inter-governmental agreement with the tribe that addresses collaboration in several workforce development programs and grants. Pima leadership is now actively working with the PSR UTC consortium to develop and implement workforce development initiatives to empower its local tribal communities.

The Tohono O'odham are the descendants of the ancient Hohokam of the Sonoran desert and American Southwest. The Tohono O'odham Nation is a federally recognized tribe and is the second-largest reservation in Arizona in both population and geographical size, and the third largest in the United States. Tohono O'odham Community College began offering classes in 2000 with Pima's assistance.

Geospatial information system tribal training initiative

Public- and private-sector employers increasingly request that employees demonstrate not just the requisite technical and interdisciplinary skill sets, but also soft skills such as leadership, interpersonal development, project management, and more. Native American populations have historically had barriers to access programming where these skills can be taught and mastered. Those realities drive METRANS and Pima's partnership under the auspices of the PSR UTC with the Tohono O'odham and Pascua Yaqui to provide GIS workforce training that includes soft skills development. The intended benefit of the program is primarily to generate relevant technical career interest by engaging youth, but also to empower tribes by augmenting their own ability to document and quantify road and other infrastructure data through GIS systems. Lastly, the program enables the Tohono O'odham and Pascua Yaqui to identify and record spatially explicit cultural history.

The proposed GIS workforce training program builds on the GIS Tribal Training Initiative launched by the Southwest Transportation Workforce Center (SWTWC) in 2015. That effort serves rural and urban communities in Oklahoma, Los Angeles County, and San Diego County. METRANS and Pima partnered with the Tohono O'odham and Pascua Yaqui tribes to engage rural and urban populations in Arizona. That engagement will include partnerships with the newly founded Tohono O'odham Community College, which Pima Community College helped establish.

The METRANS-Pima Community College GIS Tribal Training program will be integrated with our Logistics and Supply Chain

Management program, with the aim to expand to other colleges and universities throughout the UTC's region. We are leveraging our logistics education expertise in concert with consortium partners to develop and implement a GIS modular pilot curriculum designed to reach tribal youth and other underserved populations. The specific GIS learning models are designed to be completed in order, with the goal of introducing students with no previous GIS knowledge to the ways GIS software is used and how GIS could lead to a career in transportation, logistics, or elsewhere. Modules will stack, with the potential to count toward the Pima Associate of Applied Science in Logistics and Supply Chain Management via PLA. All of the modules use and build on ArcGIS Online tutorials, while integrating specific content customized to the local geography.

The need for introductory employability skills

The 21st-century workforce needs technical and specialized training. However, there exists an alarming gap of general employability skills, or soft skills, within the millennial generation, as evidenced by labor market research conducted at the Southwest Transportation Workforce Center (SWTWC). Individuals with a balanced combination of both soft and technical skills will be more ideal candidates than those lacking foundational workplace skills.

Pima is attempting to close this gap through its partnership with METRANS. We are developing soft skills modules focusing on basic language and communication skills, digital literacy, professional etiquette, interpersonal skills, time management best practices, teamwork and leadership, conflict management and resolution, and systematic thinking. These modules will be incorporated into Pima's Commercial Driver's License (CDL) training and Logistics and Supply Chain Management Programs to produce critically thinking and organizationally savvy candidates capable of problem solving within technology-driven logistics environments.

Logistics and supply chain management

Providing education to the area's indigenous peoples is a challenge, given they often live far from our campuses. In partnership with the PSR

UTC, we are closing that gap by moving all classes in our Logistics program online (with the work-based learning aspects still managed by the system at Pima). This will enable the targeted tribal populations, rural communities, and, eventually, students in major markets to complete the Logistics and Supply Chain Management degree through Pima. As mentioned, the program is developing stackable modules and stackable courses in GIS, supply chain management principles, warehousing operations, transportation operations, customer service operations, demand planning, inventory management, manufacturing and service operations, and supply management and procurement. Eight to ten of the aforementioned courses, with an additional capstone, will be articulated into a 4-year program with Northern Arizona University and others.

Truck driver training

Like our Logistics and Supply Chain Management program, our Center for Transportation Training (CTT) is built on a platform of outreach and collaboration to meet the specific needs of our community as well as the principles animating the PSR UTC.

Through the PSR UTC project, we are redesigning classroom-based CTT courses to be wholly online so that we may further engage underserved populations through the program: women (a generally underrepresented population in the trucking industry), veterans seeking to break into the workforce, nonnative English speakers, and tribal populations (i.e., the Pascua Yaqui and Tohono O'odham) who face challenges commuting from reservations to the workplace.

In response to the international issue of human trafficking, CTT collaborated with Southern Arizona Anti-Trafficking Unified Response Network (SAATURN) to combat human trafficking by offering education and awareness. Pima hosted a seminar January 2017, and SAATURN presented at the regional meeting for National Association of Publicly Funded Truck Driving Schools hosted at Pima November 2017. SAATURN members from the Tucson Police Department and CODAC Health, Recovery, and Wellness are also members of our industry advisory committee. We have added a human trafficking component to our curriculum. Students receive training in human trafficking identification and prevention and are given contact information cards to carry with them in case they suspect human trafficking.

The driver health and wellness curriculum is being updated in collaboration with Pima's employee wellness department and based on recommendations from industry partners. Drivers are given information on exercises they can do in their truck, as well as suggestions for healthy eating habits while on the road.

TuSimple and Pima

Our strategies aim to meet the needs of today's truck driver. But what about the truck driver of the future—the operator of that autonomous vehicle, essentially an 18-wheeled computer? These women and men, who will be among the first to face the aforementioned consequences identified in Schwab's *The Fourth Industrial Revolution* and in Gelsinger's "Four New 'Superpowers' Changing the World," are top-of-mind at Pima, and it is through our deepening relationship with TuSimple that Pima is helping pave a road to their future success.

TuSimple is a San Diego-based autonomous vehicle technology company that aims to advance a Level 4 truck driving solution in Tucson, which is a car that can operate autonomously but only under specified conditions or restrictions, such as road type or speed limit. TuSimple epitomizes the convergence of the four superpowers: (1) mobile technology, (2) the cloud, (3) AI, and (4) the Internet of Things (IoT). In working with TuSimple to embrace the challenges and opportunities brought by these technologies to education and training, Pima has embraced the convergence of training modalities and program areas in order to educate the workforce of the future and mitigate displacements brought about 4IR.

According to the company's website, TuSimple was founded in 2015 "with the goal of bringing the top minds in the world together to achieve the dream of a level 4 autonomous truck driving solution. With a foundation in computer vision, algorithms, mapping, and AI, TuSimple's solution will be safer, more cost-efficient, and reduce carbon emissions" [15]. TuSimple was founded by Mo Chen and Dr. Xiaodi Hou from the California Institute of Technology and has facilities in Beijing, its Chinese headquarters; San Diego, its US headquarters; and Tucson, its production engineering and testing center. TuSimple began testing its autonomous trucks in Arizona in 2016 and then opened its Tucson testing facility in August 2017. Pima was honored to be represented at that opening.

Soon after the opening of the Tucson site, Robert Brown, Director of Public Affairs with TuSimple, reached out to Pima with one aim in mind: "We want to work with you to develop the truck driver training program of the future and prepare the workforce for what our technology will bring about." The conversation followed the main points of the now-famed McKinsey report, which garnered major headlines when it predicted that one-third of the American workforce would be displaced by automation and AI [16]. Would not TuSimple's technology eliminate the need for truck drivers? No, Brown said. "Our technology is meant to empower people. The drivers will still be there; they will just have to be able to do different things than they do now."

Brown explained how the driver of the future will need a CDL license to occasionally drive the truck, such as when it is disconnected from the grid, but will also need diesel technology mechanical training and skills, to maintain the vehicle and perform repairs; basic coding and computer programming skills, to maintain and address issues with on-board IT systems; and an understanding of logistics. TuSimple wanted to meet with the individuals who could lead program development across these disciplines: automotive technology, logistics and supply chain management, IT, and truck driver training.

Brown's request proved to be enlightening yet problematic. It would require that Pima coordinate across three academic divisions (each with its own dean) and four program areas. His request brought to light the fact that Pima is organized for the past and not for the future, and this project will help us "skate where the puck is going to be." The very structure of our divisions and programs will have to change. Pima will have to organize and design programs of study outside of the rapidly faltering, occupationally specific program of study paradigm and its lagging CIP and SOC codes. We will have to embrace the wholesale convergence of educational disciplines and training modalities rather than keep tinkering on the edges of change with a smattering of interdisciplinary projects across job-specific silos. *This* is what empowering the new mobility workforce is all about.

Since that initial conversation, Pima has embraced the TuSimple project as emblematic of the change at hand. Our faculty, staff, and deans are researching and learning more in order to meet TuSimple's needs. While we are helping the company with their current need for CDL-licensed drivers and mechanical technicians, we are also working with them to design the truck driver training program of the future. In our research, we discovered additional areas of convergence and need. For example, TuSimple's autonomous driving platform uses an array of cameras, rather than LiDAR, to scan the surroundings. This is very similar to the optics technology used by the aerospace and defense manufacturing base in Pima County, and thus our Mechatronics/Manufacturing program faculty have been brought into the effort.

Using the TuSimple experience as the model, we are moving forward to deliver training with speed and adaptability in recognition of the convergence required to meet the needs of the new mobility workforce. On the road, in the sky, and in factories and warehouses, Pima Community College is ready to accelerate toward a new era of prosperity.

Acknowledgment

Paul Schwalbach contributed to this chapter.

References

[1] Mexican Visitor to Arizona: Visitor Characteristics and Economic Impacts, 2007–2008, Economic and Business Research Center, University of Arizona.

[2] P. Gelsinger, Four new 'superpowers' you should know about (article written for the World Economic Forum Annual Meeting), 2018. Retrieved from: https://www.weforum.org/agenda/2018/01/the-four-superpowers-shaping-our-world/.

[3] K. Schwab, The Fourth Industrial Revolution, Crown Business, New York, NY, 2016.

[4] U.S. Department of Education, Office of Career, Technical, and Adult Education, Strengthening Skills Training and Career Pathways Across the Transportation Industry, Author, Washington, DC, 2015, August.

[5] N.D. Grawe, Demographics and the Demand for Higher Education, Johns Hopkins University Press, Baltimore, MD, 2017.

[6] Arizona Commerce Authority Office of Economic Opportunity, Arizonans 35-44 Not in the Labor Force. Geographic Profile Survey from the Bureau of Labor Statistics, Washington, DC, 2015.

[7] Arizona Commerce Authority Office of Economic Opportunity, Arizona's Labor Force Participation and Unemployment by County. US Census American Community Survey 2010-2014, Washington, DC, 2015.

[8] A. Sherman, R. Klein-Collins (Eds.), State Policy Approaches to Support Prior Learning Assessment (Research Report Prepared for the Lumina Foundation for Education), Council for Adult and Experiential Learning, Chicago, IL, 2015.

[9] Council for Adult and Experiential Learning, Fueling the Race to Postsecondary Success: A 48-Institution Study of Prior Learning Assessment and Adult Student Outcomes (Research Report Prepared for the Lumina Foundation for Education), Author, Chicago, IL, 2010.

[10] Pima County, Pima County Economic Development Plan, 2015 Through 2017, Author, Tucson, AZ, 2015.

[11] Pima County Workforce Investment Board Pima County One-Stop System Plan: July 1, 2014—June 30, 2017, Pima County Community Services Employment and Training, Tucson, AZ, 2014.

[12] Education Master Plan draft, 2016, p. 116.

[13] National Coalition of Certification Centers, NC3 website, 2018. Retrieved from: http://www.nc3.net.

[14] Pima Association of Governments, Building a skilled workforce: The Tucson Region's Aerospace and Defense Cluster—Workforce Needs and Opportunities in Aviation Technology—Issue White Paper (White paper prepared for Pima Association of Governments Economic Vitality Advisory Committee), Author, Tucson, AZ, 2017. December, p. 6.

[15] TuSimple, TuSimple website, 2018. Retrieved from: http://www.tusimple.com/index-en.html.

[16] J. Manyika, M. Chui, M. Miremadi, J. Bughin, K. George, P. Willmott, et al., A Future that Works: Automation, Employment, and Productivity, McKinsey Global Institute, San Francisco, CA, 2017. January.

PART II

Responding to Socioeconomic Shifts in the Transportation Workforce

CHAPTER SIX

Responding to the demographic and skill shifts in the mobility workforce

Brian Cronin and Allison Alexander
Center for Workforce Strategies, ICF, Austin, TX, United States

Contents

Introduction

Allison and I met about 10 years ago. We both work at a company called ICF as management consultants. Over our careers, we have been heavily involved in conducting transportation workforce development

Empowering the New Mobility Workforce.
DOI: https://doi.org/10.1016/B978-0-12-816088-6.00006-7

projects for state DOTs, transit agencies, and the US DOT. We are industrial-organizational (I/O) psychologists by trade and, over time, we both realized that we had similar reasons for entering the field. We wanted to help people, as anyone interested in psychology might, but we also had an interest in working with businesses to improve the experience of staff and the way organizations function. The I/O field brings these opportunities together.

When you think about it, most people spend a significant portion of their lives at work and even more time commuting to or from their place of employment. Yet many people are not fully satisfied with their jobs, the way their organization is operated, the benefits, or the interactions with their coworkers. Some people are not even sure if they are in the "right" occupation or career. When thinking about the field of I/O psychology, we realized that if we could make a positive impact in one or more of these areas, we could have a big impact on the daily lives of everyday people. This is a big part of why we each entered our field and focused on workforce research.

As I/O psychologists, we are able to use psychological principles paired with strong research methods and available data sources to solve problems in the workplace. Not only can this type of information help organizations improve and gain success, but it can also help to create a better work experience and quality of life for employees. For example, consider an organization that has been accused of discrimination in their hiring practices. We can support the organization by making sure that they have effective selection instruments that do not show bias against any groups; thereby allowing those who are qualified to gain employment, regardless of their sex, race, religion, or other personal characteristics. This helps to create more diverse working groups. As another example, consider an organization where employees are burnt out and overworked. We can apply psychological principles related to job design, satisfaction, and employee recognition to help create a workplace where employees are satisfied and engaged in their work—this not only makes the lives of these employees better, but the organization will also see gains. Likewise, in our roles, we can help build skill pipelines for entire industries such as transportation to attract people from different cultural backgrounds, neighborhoods, and schools to a career where there may be lifelong opportunities they never knew were possible.

In this chapter, we bring our I/O background, our personal experiences, and workforce research expertise together to provide insights and best practices to harnessing the mobility workforce and improving transportation organizations.

The mobility workforce: workforce challenges and trends

In interviews with transportation leaders, frontline workers, and industry stakeholders across the United States, we have seen time and again that tackling the challenges facing the mobility workforce takes dual focus. On the one hand, transportation organizations must have skilled employees ready and available to meet the demands of providing mobility to the American public as well as the US business community. From the leader perspective, this means having the right applicants to hire for specific jobs with unique skills sets while also building training systems to ensure proper career growth. This way, workers always have the right skills at the right time. In many ways, individual employees like this approach because they are rewarded for their individual strengths and get professional development that is tailored for them at the right time of their careers. On the other hand, when we think about developing the workforce for the entire industry, we have come to realize that leaders must look at challenges with a different lens.

At the industry level, it is critical to look for common job and skill needs across mobility jobs and employers. This allows for the identification of skill needs and crosscutting workforce challenges. Focusing at this macro level also allows for the identification of more wide-ranging solutions where resources can be shared, duplication of effort is reduced, and opens opportunities for outside stakeholders to establish valuable professional connections. For example, in the development of FHWA's National Workforce Strategy, our industry level analysis allowed for strategies where the K-12, community college, and higher education communities could support the growth of the mobility workforce pipeline.

As part of our work, we have also partnered with the Council of University Transportation Centers (CUTC), the National Network for the Transportation Workforce (NNTW.org), and researchers across the United States to analyze and propose solutions focused on enhancing the mobility workforce. These research efforts have spent considerable time analyzing the specific challenges facing the industry, which include [1,2]:

- Demographic changes,
- Career awareness and recruitment,
- New technologies and the need for operators and managers who can use them, and
- Rising demand on transportation organizations, requiring a workforce with a wider range of experience.

Each of these challenges is having major impacts on transportation organizations across the nation. Additional consideration around each key challenge is provided below.

Demographic changes

Our research and interviews with transportation executive leaders revealed that many agencies went through a hiring boom in the 1970s and 1980s as the United States began to expand and invest in infrastructure. As a result, the transportation workforce today is older than the national average found in other industries, with more than half its workers over 45 years old and predominately white males in the leadership ranks. There is also a correspondingly high projected loss of these staff to retirement over the next 5–10 years. Baby Boomers (born between 1946 and 1964) will be retiring and leaving vacancies, particularly those at senior and management levels, which will need to be filled. This will, as participants from the Federal Highway Administration to metropolitan transit agencies have indicated, leave significant knowledge gaps in the workforce as more senior leaders depart and new workers are ushered into take their place without the same level of on-the-job experience in many cases.

With evolving age demographics and new skill needs, multigenerational and diverse workforce compositions within transportation organizations are becoming more common. We have seen employees ranging in age from their 20s to their 70s working in the same space and on the same projects. Likewise, there are more women entering the workforce and more staff from different cultural backgrounds. These advancements are good for the industry and will continue; but there are challenges, as we have heard from large DOTs and private sector transportation employers alike from coast to coast. The age differences can create challenges, because, while younger employees likely bring greater comfort with technology, more seasoned employees have experience working in the DOT transit office or the transportation field more generally. They have "been there, done that" so they can often handle crisis a with more ease. Thus, our research has indicated that it is critical for these different age groups to work together to share and exchange knowledge before crises hit or more senior leaders retire. But, at the same time, the organizations must still focus on innovative ways to provide training, experiences, and career opportunities that fit individualized needs of younger staff.

The impending influx of younger workers, the balancing of men and women, along with the increasing diversity in cultures present another set of challenge as well. The new generation expects more support from their employers in terms of work-life balance and flexible work arrangements. Likewise, the diversity in staff presents new needs for HR programs, multilingual communications, and reliance on social media, different holiday considerations, and flexible work environments to attract and retain the best staff.

Career awareness and training

As we have traveled and met with students, educators, and transportation leaders, it has become clear that many students learn about transportation careers while enrolled in school. This might happen in the K-12 school system or in community colleges and universities. The field is different from public safety, medical, or military careers where people might grow up wanting to be a firefighter, doctor, nurse, or helicopter pilot. People typically do not realize how many careers transportation has to offer until they are at a job fair or see a job posting. Thus, people who are not familiar with the industry often make decisions about the jobs they will pursue before they ever learn about opportunities in transportation.

For this reason, we have found that it is paramount for the industry to build career awareness earlier and earlier in the education cycle by working with teachers, students, and guidance counselors. This is an area where the industry has begun to focus over the last 5–10 years and will need to continue to invest in the years to come. It is critical because the industry must reach students—particularly those who want to go into transportation engineering, environmental planning, information technology, and advanced technical careers—early enough to ensure they can take the specialized classes needed in college, and sometimes even high school, in order to gain the necessary qualifications to be hired. This involves strengthening relationships with education providers to influence curriculum, training courses, field trips, career fairs, and preparing materials for guidance counselors to offer to students.

New technologies

Technology is another force that we have seen rapidly changing the dynamics of the mobility workforce. The traditional mandate of transportation agencies designing and building roads has evolved to a focus on extending the capacity and efficiency of existing infrastructure, primarily through technological means. Our clients and other researchers have noted these changes require new ways of doing business and different skill sets for transportation organizations and staff. These technological advancements combined with safety requirements and changing legislation have not only changed how work is performed but, in fact, changed the way transportation services are envisioned and delivered to the public. For example, intelligent transportation systems (ITS), which involve the convergence of communication, computing, sensing, positioning and control technologies, influence not only what transportation agencies do, but also how they plan and conduct projects—in turn influencing the way in which people drive on the roads and the skills necessary to fill transportation positions.

Demand on transportation agencies

Our work with the American Association of State Highway and Transportation Officials (AASHTO) and research for several projects with the Transportation Research Board had also revealed that the demand on transportation agencies has been dramatically increasing over the past few decades. There is a focus on new construction to expand existing systems and repair aging infrastructure but also added emphasis on maintaining and operating existing systems more efficiently through improved data analysis and real-time information systems. This combination of factors is requiring vast increases in the demand for certain occupations and a new set of skills for mobility jobs than in the past.

Quantifying changes in mobility jobs and the mobility workforce

Transportation systems across the nation are multimodal, with wide-ranging career options from archeologist to IT expert to pilot. In our research, we assessed these occupations within the major modes of transportation, including jobs within ports of entry, highways, air travel, transit and rail organizations, motor carriers, marine work, nonmotorized vehicles, and pipeline work. The extensiveness of these modes varies across states and regions of the United States and all are important to consider when assessing the industry's workforce pipeline and estimating projected supply and demand. To assist in this analysis, we use a number of tools to evaluate and project labor market information, which are described further.

Understanding tools available to analyze labor market information

There are numerous tools available to analyze labor market information related to the workforce pipeline. The California Community Colleges Chancellor's Office Vocational Education Research and Technical Advisory Committee (VERATAC) produced an excellent description of these tools recently. The pertinent tools are summarized here to provide guidance on how mobility workforce leaders can gain a better understanding of current and future supply and demand of employees.

Economic Modeling Specialists International (EMSI): EMSI combines multiple sources of publicly available data and allows users to produce industry and occupational employment reports that include college program completion information, basic demographic indicators, GIS mapping, business listings, and economic indicators such as unemployment. These reports can be run at the national, state, and local levels for EMSI subscribers.

Burning Glass/Labor Insight: The Labor Insight Tool developed by Burning Glass allows users to search publicly available job postings found on job boards across the Internet by criteria, such as required education, job titles, certifications, and geographic location. The tool provides trend data on the number of postings for specific occupations within geographic regions so subscribers (i.e., employers) can better understand the skill needs for jobs, how intense the competition for individuals with specified skill sets will be, and the typical salaries for similar positions. This information can help companies to better calibrate recruitment efforts.

Census Bureau: The Census Bureau collects data related to employment and unemployment rates, including details related to occupation type, industry, and class of worker. These statistics are available by age, race, gender, household composition, and a variety of other demographic factors, including geographic location. This information is available for public use through the Census Bureau website.

*Occupation Information Network (O*NET):* The Department of Labor's O*NET system provides detailed information on hundreds of occupations, including: common job tasks and work activities; required knowledge, skills, and abilities (KSAs); tools and technology used on the job; and expected education levels, experience, and job training. This information is available for free through the Department of Labor's website.

Bureau of Labor Statistics (BLS): BLS collects data from a sample of business around the United States related to employment and earnings of workers. This data is used to analyze labor market numbers and trends at the national, state, and local levels, which is publicly available on the BLS website.

We have found these labor market analysis tools to be effective resources that have helped us to better understand the national and local workforce pipeline. As an illustration, Table 6.1 provides results from BLS showing the current age trends across key modes within the entire US transportation industry. As can be seen in this table, the average age for many types of transportation jobs is quite high. For example, the average age of employees is 51.3 years old in bus service and urban transit jobs and 47.1 years old in air transportation jobs. This table also shows that there are many transportation workers who are 65 years and over—individuals who will likely be retiring soon.

In Table 6.2 employment trends over the next 10 years are provided for key occupations across modes. The results are interesting as they show anticipated growth in almost every career field over the next 10 years.

The emerging skill needs of the transportation workforce

In working with the National Network for the Transportation Workforce (NNTW.org), Allison and I have conducted considerable research in the crosscutting, emerging skill needs of the mobility workforce. Our research indicates that across organizations and occupations new skills will be required in four in-demand areas: STEM occupations, CTE/vocational or technical occupations, skilled laborer occupations, and supply chain and logistics occupations. Additional information about each area is provided below.

STEM occupations typically require an advanced degree that comes with technical expertise. As the transportation industry shifts toward a greater reliance and focus on complex technology, there will be increasing demand for individuals in STEM occupations. Our meetings with industry stakeholders and assessment of labor market datasets have shown that STEM professionals are already in high demand with a significant shortage nationally. This presents a challenge for public sector transportation employers, as many STEM professionals chose work in private sector organizations due to higher pay.

Civil engineers are routinely identified as particularly critical to the transportation industry in our research, given that they can fulfill many different roles with their skillset. Civil engineers supervise and perform

Table 6.1 Transportation and warehousing employees, by age category (2017).

	16–19 years	20–24 years	25–34 years	35–44 years	45–54 years	55–64 years	65 years and above	Median age of employees
Transportation and warehousing	1%	7%	20%	21%	25%	20%	6%	45.1
Air transportation	1%	5%	21%	19%	28%	23%	4%	47.1
Rail transportation	0%	5%	19%	30%	25%	19%	2%	44.1
Water transportation	1%	11%	29%	23%	19%	14%	5%	40.1
Truck transportation	1%	5%	17%	22%	28%	20%	6%	46.7
Bus service and urban transit	0%	4%	13%	16%	26%	26%	14%	51.3
Taxi and limousine service	1%	5%	22%	22%	24%	19%	8%	44.7
Pipeline transportation	2%	6%	19%	25%	21%	25%	2%	44.4
Scenic and sightseeing transportation	0%	6%	23%	11%	23%	23%	14%	—
Services incidental to transportation	1%	8%	22%	23%	22%	19%	6%	43.7
Postal Service	0%	5%	19%	17%	28%	28%	4%	49.0
Couriers and messengers	3%	14%	25%	18%	23%	15%	3%	39.1
Warehousing and storage	2%	14%	28%	22%	20%	11%	4%	38.2

Source: Bureau of Labor Statistics (BLS, 2017). Household data Annual Averages. Table 18b. Employed persons by detailed industry and age. Retrieved from: https://www.bls.gov/cps/cpsaat18b.htm.

Table 6.2 Occupational data and projections for transportation jobs.

SOC code	Occupational title	Employment (2016)	Projected employment (2026)	Change in employment, 2016–26	Percent change	Occupational openings, 2016–26 annual average
53–1000	Supervisors of transportation and material-moving workers	396,200	425,800	29,700	7.5%	44,400
53–1011	Aircraft cargo handling supervisors	7600	8100	500	5.9%	800
53–1021	First-line supervisors of helpers, laborers, and material movers, hand	184,400	200,100	15,700	8.5%	21,000
53–1031	First-line supervisors of transportation and material-moving machine and vehicle operators	204,200	217,700	13,500	6.6%	22,600
53–2000	Air transportation workers	275,300	293,200	18,000	6.5%	29,600
53–2010	Aircraft pilots and flight engineers	124,800	129,200	4400	3.5%	12,100
53–2011	Airline pilots, copilots, and flight engineers	84,000	86,900	2900	3.4%	8100
53–2012	Commercial pilots	40,800	42,300	1600	3.8%	4000
53–2020	Air traffic controllers and airfield operations specialists	33,800	35,500	1600	4.9%	3300
53–2021	Air traffic controllers	24,900	25,800	900	3.5%	2400
53–2022	Airfield operations specialists	8900	9700	800	8.8%	900
53–2031	Flight attendants	116,600	128,500	11,900	10.2%	14,200
53–3000	Motor vehicle operators	4,358,900	4,590,600	231,700	5.3%	506,900
53–3011	Ambulance drivers and attendants, except emergency medical technicians	17,300	21,100	3800	21.9%	3100
53–3020	Bus drivers	687,200	730,600	43,400	6.3%	88,900
53–3021	Bus drivers, transit and intercity	179,300	195,400	16,100	9.0%	24,000
53–3022	Bus drivers, school or special client	507,900	535,200	27,300	5.4%	64,900
53–3030	Driver/sales workers and truck drivers	3,293,100	3,456,600	163,600	5.0%	371,500
53–3031	Driver/sales workers	467,900	461,000	−6900	−1.5%	48,200
53–3032	Heavy and tractor-trailer truck drivers	1,871,700	1,980,100	108,400	5.8%	213,500
53–3033	Light truck or delivery services drivers	953,500	1,015,600	62,100	6.5%	109,800
53–3041	Taxi drivers and chauffeurs	305,100	320,300	15,100	5.0%	32,700
53–3099	Motor vehicle operators, all other	56,200	62,000	5800	10.3%	10,700

Code	Occupation					
53–4000	Rail transportation workers	122,900	120,600	−2,300	−1.9%	10,400
53–4010	Locomotive engineers and operators	44,400	42,500	−1,800	−4.1%	3300
53–4011	Locomotive engineers	38,800	37,700	−1100	−2.8%	3000
53–4012	Locomotive firers	1200	300	−900	−78.6%	0
53–4013	Rail yard engineers, dinkey operators, and hostlers	4400	4600	200	3.7%	400
53–4021	Railroad brake, signal, and switch operators	19,300	19,000	−300	−1.6%	1700
53–4031	Railroad conductors and yardmasters	41,800	41,000	−900	−2.1%	3700
53–4041	Subway and streetcar operators	12,800	13,400	500	4.1%	1300
53–4099	Rail transportation workers, all other	4600	4800	100	3.1%	400
53–5000	Water transportation workers	86,300	93,200	6900	8.0%	10,500
53–5011	Sailors and marine oilers	33,800	36,400	2,600	7.6%	4,400
53–5020	Ship and boat captains and operators	42,400	46,100	3700	8.7%	4800
53–5021	Captains, mates, and pilots of water vessels	38,800	42,200	3400	8.8%	4400
53–5022	Motorboat operators	3,600	3,900	300	7.6%	400
53–5031	Ship engineers	10,100	10,800	700	6.5%	1300
53–6000	Other transportation workers	356,500	384,800	28,200	7.9%	55,500
53–6011	Bridge and lock tenders	3700	3800	200	4.9%	400
53–6021	Parking lot attendants	151,600	161,000	9400	6.2%	23,900
53–6031	Automotive and watercraft service attendants	110,000	121,700	11,700	10.6%	20,000
53–6041	Traffic technicians	6600	7200	600	9.1%	800
53–6051	Transportation inspectors	28,200	29,800	1,700	5.9%	2,900
53–6061	Transportation attendants, except flight attendants	18,500	20,000	1,600	8.4%	2,700
53–6099	Transportation workers, all other	38,000	41,200	3100	8.3%	4800
53–7000	Material moving workers	4,678,000	5,000,200	322,100	6.9%	676,000
53–7011	Conveyor operators and tenders	28,100	27,700	−300	−1.2%	3700
53–7021	Crane and tower operators	46,000	49,900	3900	8.6%	5300
53–7030	Dredge, excavating, and loading machine operators	55,100	59,100	4100	7.4%	6600
53–7031	Dredge operators	1800	1900	100	5.0%	200

(Continued)

Table 6.2 (Continued)

SOC code	Occupational title	Employment (2016)	Projected employment (2026)	Change in employment, 2016–26	Percent change	Occupational openings, 2016–26 annual average
53–7032	Excavating and loading machine and dragline operators	50,600	54,700	4100	8.1%	6100
53–7033	Loading machine operators, underground mining	2600	2500	−100	−3.5%	300
53–7041	Hoist and winch operators	2900	2900	0	−0.7%	400
53–7051	Industrial truck and tractor operators	549,900	585,900	36,100	6.6%	65,900
53–7060	Laborers and material movers, hand	3,796,000	4,049,700	253,700	6.7%	566,600
53–7061	Cleaners of vehicles and equipment	369,200	408,700	39,500	10.7%	57,800
53–7062	Laborers and freight, stock, and material movers, hand	2,628,400	2,828,100	199,700	7.6%	388,400
53–7063	Machine feeders and off bearers	87,700	89,200	1600	1.8%	12,000
53–7064	Packers and packagers, hand	710,800	723,800	13,000	1.8%	108,400
53–7070	Pumping station operators	27,300	31,600	4300	15.6%	3900
53–7071	Gas compressor and gas pumping station operators	3900	4000	100	3.4%	500
53–7072	Pump operators, except wellhead pumpers	11,900	13,500	1600	13.8%	1700
53–7073	Wellhead pumpers	11,500	14,000	2500	21.7%	1800
53–7081	Refuse and recyclable material collectors	136,000	153,900	17,900	13.2%	18,900
53–7111	Mine shuttle car operators	1500	1,200	−300	−21.9%	100
53–7121	Tank car, truck, and ship loaders	10,800	11,400	600	5.2%	1400
53–7199	Material moving workers, all other	24,400	26,700	2300	9.3%	3200

Source: Bureau of Labor Statistics (BLS, 2012). 2012 Annual averages—Household data. Table 18b. Employed persons by detailed industry and age. Retrieved from: https://www.bls.gov/cps/cps_aa2012.htm.

the design, construction, and operation of transportation systems (e.g., roads, tunnels, bridges). According to our analysis BLS data, the demand for this occupation is expected to grow by 16.8% nationwide by 2022. In terms of background, the skills needed for civil engineers include complex problem solving, critical thinking, mathematics, and systems analysis. Though employers vary by state and region, they include organizations such as Boeing, HNTB, and Lockheed Martin.

CTE/vocational and other technical occupations are also in-demand. The jobs typically require additional education, training, or certification beyond high school for their employees and are critical to the day-to-day functioning of transportation organizations. For example, bus and truck mechanics and diesel engine specialists have been identified as particularly important across the United States. They work to maintain and repair any types of diesel engines. They also are responsible for the diagnostics and report of buses and trucks, such as those used for public transportation or hauling goods. According to BLS data we reviewed, this occupation is expected to grow 7.3% by 2022 and required skills include repairing; operation, monitoring, and control; equipment maintenance; and quality control analysis. Though employers vary by state and region, they include organizations such as Walmart, UPS, and Penske.

Skilled laborer occupations do not usually require education beyond high school to enter the field but again, we heard in many different organizations, that these jobs are crucial to transportation operations. These occupations are critical for building and repairing transportation infrastructure and often have apprenticeships and on-the-job training as transitional steps in entering full employment. This means employers must invest in employees to get them to right skill levels. The most popular industry for skilled laborer occupations varies according to the specific occupation, but examples include construction, finance and insurance, and manufacturing. Skills needed for these occupations typically include machinery, repairs, coordination, and critical thinking.

Supply chain and logistics occupations have varying requirements in terms of skills and education. The common thread is that these employees contribute to the effective functioning of warehouses and other operations that focus on the movement of goods. We have seen instances of work in these occupations across a variety of industries, including retail trade, manufacturing, and professional, scientific, and technical services with job titles such as logistician, supply chain coordinator, planning analyst, or distribution manager. Skills needed for supply chain and logistics occupations typically include scheduling, logistics, distribution, transportation management, warehousing, critical thinking, and complex problem solving.

How does the industry reach the next generation of workers?

Allison and I have spent the last several years working with industry associations and transportation leaders to identify best practices for reaching the next generation of mobility workers. We have found that to expand the diversity of the applicant pool and ultimately find the best workers, it will be necessary to focus recruiting efforts in ways that will tap populations that are currently underrepresented within the industry. Key strategies from our research are briefly described in this section.

Key strategies to recruit new mobility workers

Meet them where they are. One way to identify new applicants from underrepresented populations is to expand recruitment efforts into organizations where diverse individuals are represented. For example, transportation organizations can present job opportunities at local minority business groups, professional organizations, or alumni associations that already serve as a meeting place for diverse populations. This type of outreach includes expanding recruitment efforts beyond the physical location of the organization and recruiting in new areas, such as nearby cities or local colleges and universities that have not traditionally been used as a source of job candidates. Meeting applicants where they are should also include a focus on economic development in the local community—when there are partnerships in place to help community members prepare for employment opportunities, businesses will be more likely to find needed employees locally and grow their workforce talent.

Identify desired benefits and workplace factors. We have found that many transportation organizations cannot offer the benefits that attracted employees decades ago such as pensions, job security, or generous health care plans because they are cost prohibitive. Likewise, the new generation often prefers benefits that did not exist when Baby Boomers were entering the workforce. Thus, we have seen many organizations moving to more innovative offerings to attract new employees such as flexible work schedules (e.g., in terms of hours worked or work location), customizable benefits packages, and more comprehensive wellness plans that expand beyond a traditional health care plan to include things like stress management, mental health support, and weight management programs.

Promote on-the-job opportunities that will be seen as desirable. We have also noticed that the on-the-job experiences that attract people to the field are rapidly changing. For example, younger workers are looking for work that is meaningful and can make a difference in the world, as well as ample training and career advancement opportunities [3]. For organizations, this means they need to develop career ladders that allow for quicker advancement and movement into different areas of the organization as a means to further promote opportunities for growth and development. Similarly, opportunities such as mentoring and coaching are necessary to provide new employees an opportunity to not only learn about the organization and develop career-related knowledge, but also connect them with another employee who has a similar background, knowledge, or experiences. These types of programs are being highlighted by cutting edge organizations during recruitment to show potential employees valuable elements of the job that will be of interest to them.

Create a workplace culture that values diversity. Research has shown that applicants from underrepresented populations view organizations that value diversity as more attractive than other organizations [4]. As such, we have heard from transportation executives that it is important to create a culture in which people understand the benefits diversity can bring and through which the organization can show their commitment to inclusion and supporting diverse employees. This can be accomplished, for example, by incorporating elements of diversity and inclusion into workplace initiatives or employee development plans, as well as providing opportunities for employees no matter their background, personal characteristics, or beliefs.

Show diversity in leadership positions. Recent studies have also indicated that organizations with diverse leadership teams perform better financially and are likely to have more constructive dialogue than organizations with less diverse leadership boards [8]. Not only can benefits be seen in an organization's performance when leadership is diverse, but when potential employees can see diversity in leadership as well as diversity in employees of the organization, they are more likely to be attracted to the organization and want to work there [5,6]. We have also heard this directly from industry stakeholders. These leaders indicate that connecting employees with diverse mentors can help grow talent within agencies and assist in recruiting underrepresented populations into transportation jobs.

Preparing the future workforce for success: best practices in workforce development

Our work with transportation organizations across the country has shown that is not enough to simply attract the best talent. Once new employees are hired, it is essential to make sure that they receive the proper training and are prepared for success, so they remain with the organization. This section highlights four focus areas that should be considered for improving workforce development and provides examples of the types of strategies that could be effective for transportation organizations. The topics discussed in this section include:

- Early recruiting of the next generation of transportation professionals,
- Passing the torch from Baby Boomers to millennials and future generations,
- Identifying innovative recruitment practices to build the transportation workforce, and
- Continuously planning for the future of the transportation workforce.

Early recruitment of the next generation of transportation professionals

We have found that it is critical to start the recruitment of future employees early, by building knowledge and awareness of available transportation careers and developing interest in students before they have entered post-secondary education and already planned their career path. The strategies described in this section include this idea of focusing on kindergarten through high school students, as well as community college students and programs.

Focus knowledge building efforts on students in grades K-12. Most career paths require planning and preparation, especially when students select courses and curriculum in high school that impacts their available college major options upon graduation. Students need to be reached before this time if they are to be knowledgeable about transportation careers and potentially choose a transportation career path for their future jobs, which means investment on the part of industry. A key to preparing a strong future transportation workforce is to build awareness early in students' academic lives.

The focus on transportation career opportunities and building awareness will look different at varying stages of a student's schooling. For example, in elementary school, DOTs and transit agencies often work to build awareness by focusing on showing students the equipment used for various careers, allowing them to touch things like buses or trains, and providing opportunities for them to ask questions during career days or similar activities. As students get older, focus can move more toward sharing information about the different careers available, and the paths one would need to take to end up in those careers. Once students are in high school, opportunities become more career focused and begin to show actual career requirements and what a day in the life of a transportation employee would look like. We have found that one effective strategy is to bring in higher education partners such as technical schools, community colleges, or universities. These institutions can help to increase awareness and interest by providing hands-on opportunities for students to see transportation career opportunities and the educational paths to get there [7].

Transportation leaders have also shared with us that parents need to be part of the equation. When parents are informed of and involved in these types of opportunities, additional benefits are gained as the parents are able to see the potential careers available and discuss those careers with their children or support them in pursing jobs in the industry. The earlier parents and students are involved in transportation career-related opportunities in schools, the better. Earlier exposure means there is more time to develop interests and for parents to encourage their children to pursue transportation-related opportunities. This strategy also helps to address demographic challenges and a lack of diversity in the workforce—if students and parents from different demographic backgrounds and with diverse characteristics are invited to events that expose them to transportation careers, the number of racial minorities, women, or other groups currently underrepresented in the industry is increased.

Partner with community and technical colleges to develop future employees. Allison and I have found the community and technical colleges are a valuable source of employees for the industry because they help prepare students for a variety of careers in transportation and work directly with employers. Creating partnerships between transportation organizations and community and technical colleges can provide benefits for both sides. For example, transportation organizations benefit because they have input on what is covered in the classroom, ensuring that future employees are learning relevant information and developing knowledge in a way that will benefit the transportation organization. Students and the colleges, likewise, benefit because they are given access to hands-on experiences related to transportation jobs that can develop knowledge beyond what can be found in a book.

Many community colleges and technical schools have programs and courses that directly align with transportation jobs. However, many of these schools do not have transportation-specific equipment (e.g., training ships, rail cars) that can be used for instruction and transportation-related courses [8]. As such, investment in technology, tools, and equipment related to transportation careers is a valuable aspect of forming these partnerships. For example, a transit agency could coordinate with a technical college program to bring buses to a bus maintenance class for observation, or bring students to the transit agency to observe mechanics working on the buses. Developing these relationships helps establish a steady stream of talent to fill future transportation job openings.

Passing the torch from Baby Boomers to millennials and future generations

As the Baby Boomers begin to retire and new employees step into these roles, it will be imperative to share institutional knowledge held by the exiting employees so that it can be kept within the organizations. We have found that transportation organizations are accomplishing this in various ways, as described in this section.

Utilize knowledge management strategies to ensure knowledge is kept. There are many different strategies that transportation organizations can use to build institutional knowledge and sustain the knowledge of employees. Knowledge management (KM), as a discipline, is the process organizations use to collect and maintain organizational knowledge—it involves capturing, retaining, and transferring the knowledge of employees so that important information is not lost as employees retire or otherwise leave their organizations [9]. We have from transportation leaders and employees alike that significant benefits are realized when KM strategies are leveraged. Organizations report more efficient processes, employee development, innovation, and new knowledge creation [10].

The key is to focus on making sure that knowledge is shared *and* stored effectively. For example, if a transportation organization need to capture knowledge from senior leaders, it is beneficial to conduct knowledge interviews with employees before they retire. This strategy involves gathering key insights from employees regarding their day-to-day work on the job, skills required to accomplish job tasks, decision-making processes that must be followed, and other information that may not be captured in procedural manuals. The goal is to gather the tacit or "know-how" type knowledge and the interviews allow employees to talk through their various job requirements and lessons learned. However, this information will be of little value to the agency if it is not stored properly. Thus, we have found that organizations must also focus on retaining the knowledge and developing repositories that store information. Similarly, transportation organizations need to make sure that their new employees can gain this important institutional knowledge going forward, meaning strategies related to "information sharing" must be also incorporated into workforce development efforts. This allows the information to be shared through activities such as mentoring programs, holding brown bags and town hall discussion forums, or developing cross-functional team building activities to share knowledge across the organization [11].

Institute mentoring programs to share knowledge and develop relationships. In our discussions with transportation leaders, they report that retirement-eligible employees are far more likely to share knowledge with younger employees if they have developed personal relationships with those individuals. Research supports their reports. Many studies show that mentoring programs that pair experienced employees (mentors) with newer employees (mentees) are a way to teach new staff about the job or the organization, and share knowledge that will help to prepare the newer employees for future success. Further, not only do mentoring programs serve as a way to develop knowledge in new employees, but they also increase employee commitment to the organization and reduce employee turnover [12], meaning that new transportation organization employees will be more likely to stay with the organizations if they participate in mentoring programs.

A few key elements to consider when implementing a mentoring program are as follows:

- *Program planning:* It is important to set the goals, rules, and structure of the program. The program will be more successful when participants understand this information and what will be expected of them before beginning it.

- *Carefully match mentors and mentees:* Relationships are the key element of mentoring programs, so it is necessary that care is given to making matches that will be successful. The way matches are made can serve different purposes. For example, matching employees on demographic factors can increase minority employee retention because employees form connections with similar individuals. Alternatively, matching based on technical skills can be an effective way to share knowledge that could otherwise be lost.

- *Facilitate interactions between pairs:* Especially at the beginning of the mentoring program, it is important to give support and guidance to pairs that will help them learn from one another and develop relationships that will benefit both the individuals and the organization.

Developing a formal mentoring program that is designed to develop relationships and share information among employees is one strong way that organizations can focus on facilitating the transfer of knowledge and responsibilities from retiring Baby Boomers to the new generation of transportation employees.

Develop succession plans to prepare for departing talent. Succession planning involves a concentrated effort to prepare for the departure of leaders by developing up-and-coming staff to be ready to fill open positions. Succession planning is more than making sure that institutional knowledge stays within an organization; it focuses on preparing individuals to successfully take on leadership positions. Leaders we have spoken with indicate this is an especially important strategy given the current state of transportation organizations—with the large gap in experience between tenured, retiring employees and a young frontline staff with much less experience. Succession planning is beneficial for developing talent from within as it provides newer employees with the ability to improve their skills, have professional development opportunities, and better understand the culture and inner workings of the organization [13]. In general, the transportation industry has been slow to adopt and embrace formal succession planning efforts, even given impending retirements and the technical complexity of many positions, which can require significant time to adequately prepare [14].

To successfully implement succession planning efforts, it is necessary to identify the expected departure rates and determine how many employees will be needed to fill positions that are predicted to become open. It is also important to prepare employees for positions that could become available unexpectedly, and not just those that are known. Once these positions are identified, the organizations will need to identify high potential employees who will likely be successful in the leadership positions. Once identified, these individuals can be invited to participate in leadership development programs, mentoring relationships with the leaders, or other developmental activities to prepare them for taking on leadership responsibilities in the future.

Identifying innovative recruitment practices to build the transportation workforce

Beyond sharing knowledge internally and preparing the current workforce for future success, our work with the industry has highlighted bringing new talent to continue filling open positions in transportation organizations is equally important.

Identify Other Industries with Qualified Employees. If there is a lack of employees trained specifically for transportation jobs in a community, transportation organizations can recruit individuals from other industries to fill open positions. There are many industries that have jobs with skill requirements similar to those in transportation, which could be leveraged to find new employees [15]. Identifying industries that are shrinking or expected to have fewer jobs available in upcoming years is a particularly successful strategy to use in recruiting employees from other industries. When this shrinkage occurs, employees from those industries are often searching for new jobs and willing to move into an organization in a different industry. Data regarding shrinking industries are available from the US Department of Labor, and can be reviewed to identify opportunities to locate and recruit new types of employees.

In our work with the industry, we recommend a simple method to identifying talent pools outside of the industry. The first step is to determine the KSAs needed for transportation jobs that will require a larger or more qualified workforce in the future. This is important so that the transportation organization can identify the target industries or jobs and find qualified employees. To be able to attract individuals from other industries, recruitment methods may need to evolve. For example, partners in other industries could be located who can help introduce potential employees to transportation organizations. When recruiting these individuals, transportation organizations should share how the skills that are required in the other industry are related to transportation skill needs, showing that working for the transportation organization would be a logical career move for the individual. Additionally, it can be valuable to point out the benefits of working in the transportation, whether it be innovation in the way that transportation moves people and helps the local community, a good health plan and benefits, or the types of work arrangements available to support work-family balance.

Continuously planning for the future of the transportation workforce

The final category of workforce development strategies to be considered to help prepare the future transportation workforce for success is to focus on workforce planning. Workforce planning involves a systematic focus on the current workforce as well as the organization's future talent needs. Workforce planning helps organizations gain a clear view of their talent supply and demand and gain a competitive advantage through planned rather than reactive talent management efforts [16]. Two strategies that can be used to focus on workforce planning are described next.

Review new workforce and labor market data that become available. As discussed, there is a large amount of data available to assist transportation organizations in their workforce planning efforts (see Section: Quantifying changes in mobility jobs and the mobility workforce). Resources such as BLS data, Burning Glass analytics software, and data from local workforce offices (e.g., Workforce Investment Boards) can provide data to transportation organizations that can be used to identify workforce-related trends or needs. Utilizing up-to-date data can ensure that transportation organizations fully understand the workforce that will be available and how the labor market of the future may change.

Invest in economic development with the local community. As transportation employees retire or leave the industry, there will be increasing needs to fill their positions. However, if there are not qualified individuals in the local area, it can be difficult to find people to fill these vacancies. The benefits of utilizing this strategy include being able to locate needed talent in the local community, develop partnerships to support development of future employees, and bringing improvements to the local economy because community members are being prepared for success in local jobs.

This strategy involves collaboration with local agencies or educational providers to create skill development opportunities for unemployed or underemployed individuals in the local community. The key element is to first identify what will be needed by the organization (e.g., specific skill profiles) and determine if necessary training is available in the local area. If training is available, the transportation organization can work with the training or education providers to tailor existing courses to meet the organization's workforce needs. If relevant training is not available, the organization may need to work with education providers to create new courses or training programs. Overall, using a strategy that focuses on investment in local community members and preparing them for transportation careers will create a workforce that is more sustainable and available to fill future needs.

Conclusion and recommendations

The current economic climate and workforce makeup of the transportation industry indicates that there will be changes to both the types of work to perform and the types of employees who will be needed. To prepare for and successfully maximize benefits from changes to the demographic makeup and skill requirements for the future mobility workforce, we recommend transportation organizations need to:

- Become aware of the current and impending changes,
- Use available data to analyze needs and opportunities,
- Make plans for action based on identified needs and data trends, and
- Implement workforce development strategies and programs to support their planning, recruitment, and retention of knowledge.

Taking the initiative to address challenge areas and prepare both organizations and employees for future success is one way we can help to improve the work lives of many individuals—by creating varied job opportunities and putting the jobs within more positive, rewarding workplaces.

References

[1] Council of University Transportation Centers, 2012, National Transportation Workforce Summit, Summary of Results, Washington, DC.
[2] National Network for the Transportation Workforce, 2016. Executive Summary & National Overview: US Transportation Job Needs and Priorities, Washington, DC. Retrieved from: www.NNTW.org.
[3] E. Ng, L. Schweitzer, S. Lyons, New generation, great expectations: a field study of the millennial generation, J. Busi. Psychol. 25 (2) (2010) 281−292.
[4] Goldberg, C. (n.d.) Recruiting and maintaining a more diverse workforce. SHRM Enterprise Solutions White Paper Series. Retrieved from: https://www.shrm.org/external/SHRMenterprise/SHRMEnterprise_WhitePaper.pdf.

[5] C. Stewart, How diverse is your pipeline? Developing the talent pipeline for women and black and ethnic minority employees, Indust. Commer. Train. 48 (2) (2016) 61−66.

[6] D.R. Avery, P.F. McKay, Target practice: an organizational impression management approach to attracting minority and female job applicants, Person. Psychol. 59 (1) (2006) 157−187. Available from: https://doi.org/10.1111/j.1744-6570.2006.00807.x.

[7] P.C. Kyllonen, Soft skills for the workplace, Change 45 (6) (2013) 16−23. Available from: https://doi.org/10.1080/00091383.2013.841516.

[8] Z. Simkins, R. Mahjabeen, Measuring the transportation workforce skills gap using new indices and survey of employers and workers, J. Transport. Res. Forum 56 (2017) 19−34.

[9] Southeast Transportation Workforce Center (SETWC, 2015). Choosing transportation: attracting women to the profession. Conference Summary. Retrieved from: http://www.memphis.edu/setwc/docs/ctsummary_final.pdf.

[10] Glitman, K. (2010). Transportation Workforce Development at Community Colleges. University of Vermont Transportation Research Center: Burlington, VT. Retrieved from: https://www.uvm.edu/∼transctr/trc_reports/UVM-TRC-10-002.pdf.

[11] I.R. Edvardsson, S. Durst, The benefits of knowledge management in small and medium-sized enterprises, Proced. Social Behavior. Sci. 81 (1) (2013) 351−354.

[12] S.C. Payne, A.H. Huffman, A longitudinal examination of the influence of mentoring on organizational commitment and turnover, Acad. Manage. J. 48 (2005) 158−168.

[13] J.C. Cavanaugh, Who will lead? The success of succession planning, J. Manage. Policy Pract. 18 (2017) 22−27.

[14] B. Cronin, L. Anderson, D. Fien-Helfman, C. Blair Cronin, A. Cook, M. Lodato, et al., NCHRP Report 693: Attracting, Recruiting, and Retaining Skilled Staff for Transportation System Operations and Management, Transportation Research Board of the National Academies,, Washington, DC, 2012.

[15] Herzog, C., Cleary, J. and Shen, Q. (2012). Public Transportation Occupational Guidebook. Prepared for the John H. Heldrich Center for Workforce Development, Edward J. Bloustein School of Planning and Public Policy, Rutgers, the State University of New Jersey.

[16] Louch, P. (2014). Workforce planning is essential to high-performing organizations. Society for Human Resource Management. Retrieved from: https://www.shrm.org/resourcesandtools/hr-topics/technology/pages/louch-workforce-planning.aspx.

Further reading

Cronin, C.B., Alexander, A., Majumdar, E., Thompson, C., Wolf, B., Lazaro, R., et al. (2018). TCRP Research Report 194: Knowledge Management Resource to Support Strategic Workforce Development for Transit Agencies. Transportation Research Board of the National Academies, Washington, DC. Retrieved from: http://www.trb.org/TCRP/Blurbs/176944.aspx.

CHAPTER SEVEN

Strategies for empowered mobility in Indian country

Ronald C. Hall

President, Bubar & Hall Consulting, LLC, Chair, Transportation Research Board Committee on Native American Transportation Issues, Member Three Affiliated Tribes, Fort Collins, Colorado, United States

Contents

The source of an Indian tribe's power is its people. Indian tribes and their members have the inherent right to govern themselves, a right they have possessed from "time immemorial." As a federal appellate court stated in 2002: Indian tribes are neither states, nor part of the federal government, nor subdivisions of either. Rather, they are sovereign political entities possessed of sovereign authority not derived from the United States, which they predate. [Indian tribes are] qualified to exercise powers of self-government … by reason of their original tribal sovereignty.

Stephen L. Pevar, The Rights of Indians and Tribes *(Pevar, 2012).*

See Fig. 7.1

Empowering the New Mobility Workforce.
DOI: https://doi.org/10.1016/B978-0-12-816088-6.00007-9

Figure 7.1 Winners in the 2001 National Tribal Transportation Conference Equipment Rodeo Competition. Each year equipment operators representing tribes from across the country gather at this annual event to sharpen and compare their skills and advance their knowledge.

Introduction

This chapter seeks to discuss the future transportation workforce for federally recognized tribal governments. The 573 federally recognized tribes each exist as sovereign nations and have significant roles in the mobility operations of their local, state, federal, and in some cases international neighbors. Tribes exist in a complex blend of culture, legal status, economic conditions, demographics, and resource bases. Many tribes are geographically isolated. Though it may seem like tribes have the same workforce issues as any other nation, county or local government and this chapter will make clear that tribes are not on a level playing field with their peers when it comes to managing transportation infrastructure. The opening quote helps illustrate a key element of any sovereign; they are nothing more and nothing less than an assembly of people working hard to ensure a bright future for the next generation. Without trained and motivated people new gadgets and advanced technology has little impact and, in some situations, can be dangerous. Transportation in the 21st century is a defining element for quality of life and thus an important and worthy field of engagement for tribal leaders.

Tribal leadership is a key element to the success of transportation infrastructure organization and must be included in the workforce discussion. The future tribal transportation workforce does not just reside within the transportation program. Extensive coordination is required between tribal programs like transportation and law enforcement, two groups with vastly different priorities and missions. Collection of accurate and consistent crash data is dependent on the field officer responding to the scene of the crash. Field police officers do not take orders from the Transportation Director, and it is necessary for someone in a leadership position to support law enforcement implementation of transportation program related crash data collection. I have worked in the tribal transportation field for most of my professional career. From that vantage point, I have witnessed individuals and entire tribal programs make huge strides. Tribes struggling to understand the multijurisdictional web of roads, laws, regulations, and processes made immediate impact by hiring a few key trained and dedicated individuals to guide their processes. Conversely, I have seen talented and motivated individuals become frustrated, isolated and leave because they were not adequately supported or were perceived as a threat to the leadership structure. Preparing the next generation tribal transportation workforce is as much a leadership issue as it is a technical issue. Understanding and embracing organizational change dynamics is a central tenet in workforce development. This chapter focuses on the dynamics of the future tribal transportation workforce and includes the development of leaders that understand the transportation sector and their role in supporting the transportation mission across tribal programs and with federal, state, and local government stakeholders.

Transportation context for tribal nations

Based on the unique and enduring constitutional relationship between tribes and the federal government, a complex and incomplete set of laws, policies, and regulations have both facilitated and burdened the ability of tribes to self-determine the mobility resources within their lands and communities. Throughout the 242-year history of the United States, and the US policies including genocide, assimilation, reorganization, termination, and now self-determination, one truth is undeniable: Success, and even survival, comes down to people. The tribal transportation workforce of the 21st century is quite different in its composition (women, men, LGBTQ + people, tribal members, nonmember Indians, and non-Indians) compared to the pre-Self-Determination era.

The ability to create and sustain dynamic government agencies assumes the ability to control one's own destiny, and the means to pursue and implement those changes. As sovereign nations, tribes have been fighting an ongoing battle to control their destiny and have explored creative approaches to finding the financial and administrative means to maintain culture, learn from history and establish strategic goals for the future. The transportation sector is a perfect illustration and workforce demands are a critical part of the means tribes must have in place to succeed. At stake is the ability to support economic development to combat some of the highest unemployment and poverty rates in the country, access healthcare, and address rampant highway safety issues that include fatality rates twice that of non-Hispanic whites [1]. At the same time, changes in technology seem to be moving the goal posts to succeed in the transportation world.

Despite the many obstacles that have challenged the evolution of tribal transportation programs, there exists a dedicated core of planners, engineers, equipment operators, transit managers, and other professionals who consistently exceed expectations and outperform the limitations of their allotted assets. In those cases, where tribal leadership has recognized and supported those committed individuals, great strides have been accomplished. Tribes as nations have several tools at their disposal that can and must be exercised to continue progress in the mobility field. By taking a proactive approach from an organic tribal vision of land use, environmental protection, economic development, roadway safety, and sustainability, tribes can successfully recognize, anticipate, and navigate the challenges ahead.

As tribal governments take proactive approaches to land use, mobility management, and information technology a transition in their overall perspectives of the role of government and private industry is taking place. Tribal leaders and staff are finding ways to indigenize the planning process and engage strategic planning as an opportunity for self-determination rather than as a federal requirement to be performed at a minimal level. In the early years of tribal transportation program administration, many tribes structured their operations to perform at the level of the program they inherited from the Bureau of Indian Affairs. Like any federal funds, transportation funds come with several strings attached. Certain funds can only be used for construction and others only for maintenance. Further, to pass an audit you must know the difference between the two or risk having large sums of money owed back to the federal government based on an ineligible expenditure.

For some tribes, the requirement to have a Long-Range Transportation Plan (LRTP) was viewed as a federal requirement to be eligible to expend transportation funds, which it is. Each project must be in the LRTP before any federal funds can be expended. As a result, transportation planning was perceived as the production of a document that met the federal checklist for a planning document. Once the plan was accepted, it was maintained at a minimal level to add new projects. Increasingly, tribal leaders and their planning staff have realized that the LRTP is a process through which important tribal cultural, land use, economic development and environmental protection goals can be advanced. For example, dual language interpretive signs along the road can advance the use and survival of a tribal language. Access roads to a new industrial park or pedestrian/bike trails connecting communities and recreation opportunities can enhance private-sector business development and tourism traffic.

Emergence of tribal transportation as a core function and promising career

Tribes, as the original inhabitants of what is now called the United States of America, have an extensive history of transportation infrastructure development on the continent. It is well documented that the first European visitors commented on the extensive network of roads, trails, and river crossings they encountered. David Wade Chambers wrote:

The first thing to note about early Native American trails and roads is that they were not just paths in the woods following along animal tracks used mainly for hunting. Neither can they be characterized simply as the routes that nomadic peoples followed during seasonal migrations. Rather they constituted an extensive system of roadways that spanned the Americas, making possible short, medium, and long distance travel. That is to say, the Pre-Columbian Americas were laced together with a complex system of roads and paths which became the roadways adopted by the early settlers and indeed were ultimately transformed into major highways [2].

These roads served a vast intertribal trade-based economy. With military dominance by the United States came the transition of land through numerous treaties and the reservation of land by tribes for their homelands. Initially tribal lands were used for imprisonment and the indigenous trade network was rendered inaccessible. It was chaos. Tribes were placed in a state of forced dependency on the federal government for basic necessities because otherwise available food sources were eradicated and the traditional means to self-sustain were rendered illegal. When roads and bridges were needed and developed it was initially the responsibility of the War Department, and later the Department of the Interior's Bureau of Indian Affairs. In 1928, the Indian Reservation Road Program was formalized through legislation as a funded program in the Bureau of Indian Affairs.

The original US Native American workforce development initiatives were entangled with the practice of slavery and dispossession of Native people from their land. Indian Preference in labor has existed in federal law since 1834 [3]. Congress passed the Buy Indian Act in 1910 that authorized a preference for hiring and contracting with Native Americans on Bureau of Indian Affairs construction projects. These early laws had little to do with the tribe as a sovereign entity and were generally oriented toward individuals.

Tribal governments did not have authority to manage federal transportation programs until 1991 with the passage of the Intermodal Surface Transportation Assistance Act (ISTEA). Prior to ISTEA, the administration of the Indian Reservation Roads Program was a federal responsibility performed by the Bureau of Indian Affairs. Only then were tribes able to assume the BIA IRR program functions, but the process took years to implement and, in the end, tribes were handed dilapidated facilities, old equipment, and limited data regarding right-of-way, as-built, and other essential resources. Full integration of Tribal Self-Determination policies within the Bureau of Indian Affairs Indian Reservation Road Program became law with the passage of the Transportation Equity Act of the 21st Century (TEA-21) in 1998 and implementing regulations were promulgated through negotiated rulemaking in 2004. Even further delayed was authority of the US Department of Transportation to implement Tribal Self-Determination Laws, which occurred with passage of the Fixing America's Surface Transportation (FAST) Act in 2015. Implementing regulation for the FAST Act's Tribal Self-Determination provisions have yet to be developed. Tribes have had to create the administrative and technical capacity to operate a program that generally mirrors the functions of state departments of transportation, but with several limiting factors including inadequate funding and perhaps even more important, limited access to incomplete inventory and historical financial records (Fig. 7.2).

The initial transition from a Bureau of Indian Affairs delivered program to a tribally administered activity was gradual and limited. In fact, it is still incomplete and ongoing. Part of the struggle may lie in the fact there was a mashup of two separate worlds of legislative policy and language. Congress passed the first Federal Aid Road Act in 1916 that established a policy of federally assisted state highway program, meaning the federal government provides funds to states to administer on state owned highways [4]. To be eligible for the federal funds states had to create departments of transportation with certain technical capabilities. Thus began the evolution of the state DOT staffed by engineers with specialties like construction, safety, design, environmental and safety. Federal transportation funds passed to the states for planning, design, and construction subject to federal oversight.

This also marks the beginning of the American Association of State Highway Officials (AASHO) in 1914. This organization is what we know today as the American Association of State Highway and Transportation

Figure 7.2 Seated from left to right Neil McCaleb, Assistant Secretary Indian Affairs and Rob Baracker, Designated Federal Official and BIA Albuquerque Area Director prepare to consult with tribal representatives at the National Tribal Transportation Conference in Albuquerque, New Mexico, in 2001. Standing is Ronald Hall, Director of the Tribal Technical Assistance Program at Colorado State University.

Officials (AASHTO), a nonprofit association representing highway and transportation departments in the 50 states, the District of Columbia and Puerto Rico. AASHTO provides education to the public and key decision makers and serves as a liaison between state transportation offices and the Federal government. It develops technical standards for all phases of highway system development and provides an active technical committee structure supporting expertise in virtually every element of planning, designing, constructing, and maintaining transportation services. AASHTO is a vital element of state transportation workforce development especially on a leadership level. It is truly the envy of the world in terms of their focus on transportation expertise, their ability to coordinate and communicate on complex issues of national concern and the unquestioned integrity and weight their findings and recommendations have before Congress and the US Department of Transportation.

It is important to note that tribes are not included in any AASHTO initiatives. Despite the unprecedented investment of resources in AASHTO from a federal and state level for the betterment of the nation's transportation infrastructure, there is no place for tribes and there is no AASHTO equivalent for tribes. This is probably the best representation of the uneven playing field that places tribal transportation officials and their workforce at a tremendous disadvantage compared to their state peers. On one hand, you have a world-class transportation monolith for states and on the other, you have absolutely nothing for tribes. You do the math—it is not equal.

In fairness, I must acknowledge that Congress provided for and the Federal Highway Administration administers a program called the Tribal Technical Assistance Program (TTAP). Initiated in 1991 the TTAP grew to include seven centers with designated geographic service areas that effectively covered the lower 48 states and Alaska. In 2017 the seven centers were closed in favor of a single service provider located in Virginia. Funding for the program to serve 573 tribal governments never exceeded $6 million a year. Though vastly underfunded, this is a direct tribal transportation workforce development program that has provided training and technical assistance to tribes on a wide range of issues. While TTAP is a tribal transportation support program it is certainly no AASHTO.

A changing and challenging industry

The challenge to quickly adapt in our current and quickly evolving technology environment weighs heavily on traditionally slow and methodical departments of transportation. The impact of transportation on economic growth is evident through empirical research and lived experience. An inadequate transportation system can and will discourage investment and economic opportunity since we know business will not move in, and some may move out costing important local jobs. Transportation is the lifeblood of a tourism economy and when an area gets a reputation for being unsafe to drive, tourists will stop coming. Transportation impacts access to essential services like education and healthcare. It has been said if you want to know what someone values, watch how they spend their money. In the United States, efficient transportation is so important that national spending on transportation infrastructure in 2017 reached $300 billion according to the Congressional Budget Office [5]. Tribal governments are part of this equation, but they do not participate in the process as equal partners.

How we operate and maintain our public transportation system is entirely a responsibility of some government entity, except for some private–public partnerships. In the administration of transportation programs (road construction and maintenance, transit, and aviation) the state of practice for all governments is being pushed by technological advances that, properly implemented, will save lives, money, and time. The vehicles on our roads today are changing and the future is autonomous and connected vehicles powered by alternative energy. This will change how we understand and engage transportation. Drone ports are multimodal hubs that will facilitate linkage between air and land or water-based vehicles. Even the highways, signs, guardrails, bridges, and other features are getting smart technology to communicate with the vehicles and merge into the Internet of Things. Much like the first days of the Internet or cell phones, this technology is starting out as a novelty. But if the promise of convenience, safety, economy, and other factors prove true, the technology will become pervasive and quickly evolve into what is needed versus a luxury. Federal, state, and tribal governments are all facing real challenges as they strive to keep pace with private-sector advancements.

Along with the changes in the vehicles and infrastructure are the administrative requirements for a national and statewide system to allocate that $300 billion annual spending in a way that rewards efficiency, addresses priorities, and minimizes fraud, waste and abuse. At least for now, the days of pork barrel infrastructure spending where elected officials negotiate for their favorite projects without verifiable justification are gone. The competition for federal and state funding has produced a national consensus that asset management strategies based on long-range strategic plans drive project development and resource allocation. For example, highway safety is a national priority in the push to reduce fatal crashes. Projects must address safety as a primary justification for award of funding. And you cannot just show a picture of a hazardous intersection or dangerous curve. Crash data including frequency, injuries/fatalities, traffic volume, vehicle type (car, pickup, class of truck), time of day, weather, and causation all tell the story and more importantly, score points in a project proposal. Each crash incident is now a feature in the performance of the road and will factor into future management decisions.

Asset management applies to the whole life cycle of the transportation system including project funding, procurement, construction, mainte-nance, and performance monitoring. This means generation, collection and management of massive amounts of data, which in turn becomes its own form of currency. Without the data your projects/programs are not eligible to compete, or they simply will not score enough points in the right categories. Even if an agency is successful in securing the funding up front, failure to provide detailed reports on the expenditure of the funds including procurement method, materials used, jobs created can result in loss of funding already awarded. There is even a requirement on state pro-grams to report post construction data to show that the funded project addressed issues used to justify the project at the outset, and if not, the threat of loss of future funding.

Since the merger of the Indian Reservation Road Program into the Highway Trust Fund in the Surface Transportation Assistance Act of 1981 there has been a gradual replication of the rules applied to state depart-ments of transportation, even though the resources to meet those stan-dards are not nearly equivalent. Tribal governments face the same technological and administrative changes as states and local governments, but with a different foundation of institutional knowledge and signifi-cantly different financial resources.

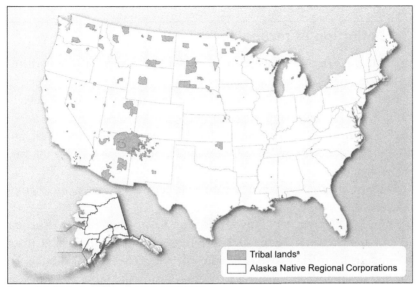

Tribal lands[a]
Alaska Native Regional Corporations

Sources: United States Census Bureau and GAO. | GAO-16-222

New tribal mobility workforce

One could argue that the story of Native America tends to rise and fall based on the technology gap between each tribe and those governments and societies that they encounter. Think about the use of horses as a method of transportation and the advantages European invaders and eventual colonists possessed on first contact. In battle, having a horse versus being on foot was a major advantage. Communication regarding the position or size of an enemy was vastly quicker with messengers on horseback versus on foot. Movement of heavy loads across land, efficiency in trade, and obtaining food all were made more efficient using horses. When tribes acquired and adapted the use of horses, the playing field somewhat leveled. With the emergence of a new wave of technology in the means of transportation and in the administration of transportation programs tribes stand the risk of falling behind once again. The call for proactive use of technology by tribal governments and support for a dynamic workforce could not be louder than today.

I start with a broad definition of "technology" and move to the more specific application of technology in the transportation field. The dictionary definition is as follows: [6]

Definition of *technology*

1a: the practical application of knowledge especially in a particular area, for example, medical *technology*

b: a capability given by the practical application of knowledge, for example, a car's fuel-saving *technology*

2: a manner of accomplishing a task especially using technical processes, methods, or knowledge, for example, new *technologies* for information storage

3: the specialized aspects of a particular field of endeavor, for example educational *technology*.

From this perspective, Native Americans have a long history of acquiring and applying knowledge and therefore technology. It is hard to say the modern use of knowledge is primarily for acquisition of money, but in terms of supporting sustainable tribal programs and services, if they are not properly funded they will not last. So, for some, there is conflict of values when the question of priorities arise. Should the tribe's first priority be the continuation of culture and tradition or the provision of essential services?

Data do not care

Like the viral video and Internet meme of the hapless honey badger, data do not care. Whether the motivation of the tribe is for the provision of high-quality services and transparent expenditure of funds or in the competition for and acquisition of funding, data helps you accomplish both. Ultimately tribal members and the public are entitled to government systems that are efficient, transparent and free from unethical or illegal influences. It would be nice to just take somebody's word that needs for road maintenance or construction funds are in the hundreds of millions of dollars, but a graphic story complete with full color pictures will not get you one dollar any more. The competitive world of transportation funding has shifted to a data driven system. The future tribal workforce must have the skills and tools to support an organization that effectively manages data. This includes the methods for data acquisition, integration, analysis, and security.

There is a logical progression that may be easy to articulate but difficult to put into practice. The success of a tribe in today's federal funding dependent world is increasingly dependent on the tribe's ability to properly manage data. (Not all tribes are dependent on federal funds, but it is safe to say that a clear majority are.) Since passage of the Indian Self-Determination and Education Assistance Act of 1975 (ISDEA) (also called Public Law 93-638) the United States' official Indian Policy is to recognize the right of each federally recognized tribe exist and be the primary source of local program policy and direction. While it seems self-apparent that tribes as independent nation states have a right to exist, that has not always been the case.

In discussing the administrative capacity of tribal governments in the transportation sector, one has to discuss finances. Any agency, and the people working within it, can only perform to the extent of its financial resources. While several variables must be considered, and cost factors can vary widely, it is fair to say that transportation-related construction, maintenance, and operations costs are extremely high. Tribes do not have the equivalent capacity as federal and state governments to generate tax revenue based on a series of US Supreme Court decisions and failure of federal tax policy. As a result, tribes are in a forced dependency on federal funding sources to operate transportation programs, and as a result must structure their programs to meet the funding eligibility and reporting requirements associated with the funds.

The profile of that tribal transportation workforce will be driven by the federal and state transportation programs that are largely being homogenized into asset management frameworks with standardized attributes. This national standardization of data collection and reporting elements are the keys to accessing transportation funds related to infrastructure, transit, and safety. Future program sustainability will largely depend on data that clearly justifies funding needs, expenditure, and asset performance. Organizations that have the capacity to perform all aspects of the data collection, management, security and reporting, in addition to the transportation-related functions, will be more successful than those that struggle in any aspect of this paradigm.

The future tribal workforce must include a team that fulfills the requirements of an asset management life cycle. Programmers/developers for the data collection apps, databases for storage and organization of the data, dashboards for visualization of the data at the front line, management, and leadership level. The system should fully support the ever-changing reporting requirements and automate that process to the extent possible. This level of data integration for reporting purposes requires blending asset management data with financial and project management (schedules, milestones, performance measures).

Addressing the critical mass question

Given the complex range of services and responsibilities tribal governments perform, the diversity of skill sets and capabilities of the workforce is considerable. Tribes are to some degree responsible for basic government services like law and order, education (pre-K−12 and higher ed), healthcare, transportation, housing, household water, waste management, natural resource management, environmental protection, land management, facilities, and motor pool to name a few. In doing so, they must have an organizational capacity to perform contract and grant management, human resources, finance and accounting, legal services, communications, information technology, property management, facilities management, and construction. No matter how you look at a basic government structure, there is a wide range of skills and expertise required to maintain just a baseline level of service.

So where does the workforce come from? Unemployment in tribal communities tends to run substantially higher than national averages. For example, the Economic Policy Institute found that between 2007 and 2013 American Indian unemployment rates for American Indians consistently ran nearly twice that of the White Americans (Fig. 7.3).

Several tribal communities are experiencing a workforce shortage for government and reservation based businesses, and many tribes have have too few qualified tribal members to meet their requirements. As of 2012 the US Department of Health and Human Services found there are 5.2 million people who identify as American Indian/Alaska Native (including single race and multirace), but only 22% live on reservations or other trust lands [7]. The reasons for Native American/Alaska Native movement away from tribal land are complex, including long-term impacts from Federal Indian Relocation Policies from the 1950s, a lack of meaningful on-reservation employment opportunities and a shortage of affordable housing. Consider that in Indian Country 56% of Native Americans own their homes while the national homeownership rate is 65% and 71% in rural areas [8].

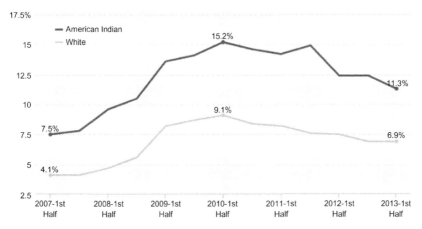

Figure 7.3 "American Indian" refers to individuals identifying as American Indian or Alaska Native alone or in combination with some other racial category. Both American Indian and white data include Hispanics. *Source: EPI analysis of basic monthly Current Population Survey microdata. A. Austin, High unemployment means Native Americans are still waiting for an economic recovery, EPI Issue Brief #372, Economic Policy Institute, 2013 [9].*

Tribal Preference Employment Laws

Since the US Supreme Court decided Morton v. Mancari [10] the preferential hiring of Native Americans by federal agencies and tribes themselves is an exception to the nondiscrimination provisions of the Equal Employment Opportunity Law. This exception is based on the distinct political status tribes and their members have that is cemented in the Indian Commerce Clause of the US Constitution that authorizes Congress "to regulate Commerce with foreign Nations, and among the several States, and with Indian Tribes" [11]. Even with the option of Indian preference in hiring as a legal option, tribes will most likely have to reach outside of the local tribal member labor pool to find employees with the professional skill sets required to address the challenges facing the future mobility workforce. As a result, the preferential treatment in employment or contracting by a tribal government to a Native American individual or business is based on the individual's political status as a member of a federally recognized tribe rather than that person's race. Most tribes having a tribal preference in hiring law to maximize employment opportunities for tribal members do not have enough tribal members to fill the requirements.[1]

This gap in tribal members available for employment in the new mobility workforce is further exacerbated by the education pipeline for tribal youth. The current high school graduation rate for Native American students is 69% compared to the national average of 80% and 28% of Americans complete college, while only 13% of Native Americans hold a college degree [12]. The qualifications of the new mobility workforce largely require some level of academic training. On a tribal level, there is a shortage of educated and technically trained tribal members to fill the needs of the new mobility workforce.

Another challenging element for tribes in the new mobility workforce is worker recruitment and retention. Native American students who attend a college or university are exposed to a wide range of influences and opportunities in federal and state agencies and in the private sector. There is a high level of competition for high achieving Native American graduates particularly in the hard sciences like engineering, information technology, and construction management. Even when a college graduate does take a position with their tribe, the wages are typically much lower than their peers in other agencies. This disparity in compensation leads a significant number of people to leave tribal employment for greener pastures at another agency or company. To make matters even more dire, tribes are exempt from paying Davis Bacon Act wages when they use federal funds in a force account approach rather than competitive contracts. This means a person operating a motor grader for a tribal road maintenance program can receive one-half or less the wage of a person performing the same function for a contractor or a local county road agency. Tribes remain at a distinct economic disadvantage in the competition for and retention of qualified workers in the current environment and are even further disadvantaged in the new mobility era.

The tribal transportation workforce issues largely mirror the challenges facing their national counterparts. The tribal workforce is aging and there is a serious need for new people to bring new skills. The outstanding legal

---

[1] The Council for Tribal Employment Rights (CTER) under the leadership of Conrad Edwards, John Navarro, and legal counsel Daniel Press deserve recognition for their contribution in the development of Tribal Employment Rights Ordinances (TERO) across the country. Established in 1977 CTER has promoted the use of tribal sovereignty to develop and support the Native American workforce by requiring all employers who are engaged in business on reservations give preference to qualified Indians in all aspects of employment, contracting and other business activities.

scholar Charles Wilkinson reminds us that, "Properly understood, modern American Indian history has been made by Indian leaders who seized the initiative, brought forth their grievances and proposed solutions, and more often than not, accomplished the kind of progress they dared to seek" [13]. The challenge stands before the tribal leaders of today and those that will soon follow to sustain and enhance the expertise required to implement transportation programs and negotiate for improved access to resources, both financial and technical. A career in transportation is rewarding in many regards. The ability to support the economy, improve the quality of life, and even save lives through crash reduction are just a few accomplishments that will accompany a nice big pay check. That is the kind of opportunity and future that is possible in the tribal transportation world and there are those who dare to seek.

References

[1] Center for Disease Control and Prevention. Tribal Road Safety: Get the Facts, 2017. Available from: https://www.cdc.gov/motorvehiclesafety/native/factsheet.html (accessed 01.11.18).

[2] R. Dunbar-Ortiz, An Indigenous Peoples' History of the United States, Beacon Press, 2014.

[3] 25 USC §§44, 45, and 46.

[4] 23 USC §145.

[5] Office, 2018. Available from: https://www.cbo.gov/publication/54539.

[6] Merriam-Webster. Application, 2018. Available from: https://www.merriam-webster.com/dictionary/application (accessed 01.11.18).

[7] Department of Health & Human Services (2018). https://minorityhealth.hhs.gov/omh/browse.aspx?lvl = 3&lvlid = 62.

[8] Kunesh, P.H. (2017, Fall). Creating Sustainable Homelands through Homeownership on Trust Lands. *Rural Voices*. Retrieved May 9, 2019, from http://www.ruralhome.org/sct-information/rural-voices.

[9] A. Austin, High unemployment means Native Americans are still waiting for an economic recovery, EPI Issue Brief #372, Economic Policy Institute, 2013.

[10] Morton v Mancari, 1974. 417 U.S. 535.

[11] US Constitution, Article I, Section 8.

[12] L. Camera, Native American Students Left Behind, U.S. News, 2015. Available from: https://www.usnews.com/news/articles/2015/11/06/native-american-students-left-behind (accessed 01.11.18).

[13] C.F. Wilkinson, Blood struggle: The rise of modern Indian nations, Norton, New York, 2006.

CHAPTER EIGHT

Ensuring a competitive and adaptive supply chain workforce

Anne Strauss-Wieder[1] and Rick Blasgen[2]

[1]Director of Freight Planning, North Jersey Transportation Planning Authority, Newark, New Jersey, United States
[2]President and CEO, Council of Supply Chain Management Professionals, Lombard, Illinois, United States

Contents

Introduction

The availability of labor has reached crisis levels in many segments of the supply chain and logistics industry. As the situation exists now, "the unmet and growing demand for workers to operate and support our Nation's supply chains and expanding trade continues to impact the competitiveness of US businesses" [1]. *The New York Times* noted, "The lack of available drivers is rippling through the supply chain, causing a bottleneck of goods that is delaying deliveries and prompting some companies to increase prices" [2]. The *2018 State of Logistics Report*, produced by the Council of Supply Chain Management Professionals noted, "Delivery labor, the primary driver of last-mile cost, increased 9% last year amid low unemployment, higher minimum wages, and intense competition for

Empowering the New Mobility Workforce.
DOI: https://doi.org/10.1016/B978-0-12-816088-6.00008-0
167

drivers among traditional carriers, last-mile specialists, crowdsourcing platforms, and shippers building their own delivery capabilities" [3].

Workforce shortages have been reported in many transportation, logistics, and distribution industry sectors. For example:

- According to an analysis by the US Departments of Education, Transportation, and Labor, "Combining growth and separations, transportation industry employers will need to hire approximately 4.6 million workers, an equivalent of 1.2 times the current transportation employment between 2012 and 2022" [4].
- The American Trucking Associations (ATA) reported that "the driver shortfall is expected to rise by the end of 2017 to the highest level on record" [5]. ATA estimates that "over the next decade, the trucking industry will need to hire roughly 898,000 new drivers, or an average of 90,000 per year" [5].
- Freight railroads, such as the BNSF Railway and the Union Pacific are offering signing bonuses of between $10,000 and $25,000 to attract workers [6].
- The US Maritime Administration reported that the United States was short by 1800 mariners in 2018 [7]. Worldwide, a current shortfall of 16,500 seafarers is anticipated to rise to a shortfall of 147,500 skilled workers by 2025 [8].

Labor availability is one of the highest ranking site selection criteria and has been known to be a deciding factor in industrial real estate locale decisions. *Area Development*'s 32nd annual survey of corporate executives noted that "labor is paramount, and a community that does not have the adequate labor profile is devastating to a project's success in that location, and also limits the economic developer's ability to successfully compete for a project" [9].

The causes of and potential solutions to the workforce shortages are multifaceted. While overarching, various segments of the transportation, distribution, and logistics industry require different types of skills and expertise. Working conditions, locations, and career paths vary. Jobs range from unskilled hourly labor to highly skilled technical positions.

However, one commonality exists—collaborative processes involving multiple organizations are necessary to address the shortfalls. The organizations that are involved or could be involved in addressing workforce challenges consist of the employers, including private sector businesses; federal, state, and local governmental agencies; academic and educational institutions; unions; and associations.

This chapter provides a framework and a series of best practices for advancing solutions. Much of the material presented here is based on work undertaken by and presentations made to the US Department of Commerce's Advisory Committee on Supply Chain Competitiveness and the Advisory Committee's Workforce Subcommittee. That material has been augmented by additional research of best practices and approaches used by organizations and regional level programs.

Framework

An overarching framework has emerged to address workforce challenges:

- *Understand the causes*—Identify the factors that have contributed and/or are contributing to workforce shortages.
- *Market the opportunities*—Build knowledge, awareness of, and interest in transportation, logistics, and distribution careers and jobs.
- *Develop training, skills and expertise*—Develop educational tracks and programs that address the skills and expertise needed by transportation, logistics, and distribution businesses and organizations.
- *Collaborate with employers*—Work early and collaboratively with employers on training, placement, and career paths.
- *Encourage pilot programs and sharing of best practices*—Share the success stories and lessons learned.
- *Enhance accessibility*—Ensure that workers have transportation options for traveling from where they live to where they will work.

Understand the causes of workforce shortages

It is important to understand the underlying causes in order to formulate potential approaches, actions, and partnerships needed to address workforce shortages. Multiple causes have been identified by multiple organizations. Not all of the causes can be addressed through educational initiatives. Some involve outreach, while others involve reviews of regulations. Still other factors are specific to the job and cannot be fully altered.

Some of the factors are contextual, meaning that a factor affects workforce supply and/or the demand across the entire transportation, logistics and distribution industry. Some of the factors relate to specific job requirements or conditions that affect a particular industry segment.

The causes that have been identified related to workforce shortages in the transportation, logistics, and distribution industries include:

- Demographics,
- Work lifestyle,
- Regulations and requirements,
- Compensation, and
- Perception and awareness.

Demographics

Several key workforce shortages and opportunities relate to demographics—specifically, the age, gender and involvement of minorities in the existing workforce. The ATA 2017 *Truck Driver Shortage Analysis* identified the following demographics related to the current driver workforce [5]:

- The average age of drivers in the over-the-road truckload industry is 49 years old, and 52 years old for private fleet truck drivers (compared to an average of 42 years old for the US workforce).
- Female drivers constitute 6% of the overall truck driver population (compared with nearly 47% of the US workforce).
- Nearly 39% of the truck drivers are minorities.

Similar demographic factors can be seen in other sectors of the industry. For example, the International Transport Workers' Federation estimates that women constitute just 2% of the world's maritime workforce [10].

While many workers are choosing to continue remain in the labor force, as older workers do retire, the demand for replacement workers increases. Retirements among truck drivers have accelerated, though the reported rates vary. One benchmark survey reported in an industry publication found that truck driver retirement rates grew from 22% in 2014 to 33% in 2016, sparking concerns that "a wave of retirements is building that will speed up the depletion of the industry's professional driver corps" [11]. Land O'Lakes Chief Supply Chain Officer, Yone Dewberry, noted at an industry conference that "in the past, 10% of drivers were near retirement at any point in time; today it is 25%" [12].

The lower representation of women and minorities in the workforce in certain industry segments presents an opportunity to improve the image of the occupation, as well as market to and recruit from underrepresented groups.

Work lifestyle

The work hours and conditions can be strenuous in the transportation, logistics, and distribution industry, particularly when compared to alternative career opportunities. For example, railroad jobs have been described as "demanding, with irregular work schedules, long hours, and frequent nights away from home" [6].

In trucking, "many drivers are assigned routes that put them on the road for extended periods of time before they can return home, typically a week or two" [5].

Distribution and production facilities often work in shifts, with some facilities operating two or three shifts over a 24-hour period. Accordingly, start and end times can differ substantially from typical business hours and incur additional complications, such as childcare and transit options.

Regulations and requirements

Some current rules, regulations, and practices have also contributed to shortages. For example, the federal age requirement for an interstate commercial driver's license is 21 [13]. According to the ATA [5]:

> This means that interstate motor carriers miss out on the population between 18 and 21. Often, these individuals, at least those that don't go to higher education or the military, obtain employment in construction, retail, or fast food industries, as they can start their careers at a younger age.

Similarly, the trucking industry notes that for certain business segments, such as long-haul trucking and the transportation of hazardous materials, the insurance industry requires drivers to be a minimum of 25 years old [14].

Compensation

Compensation has been an issue in some segments of the transportation, logistics, and distribution industry, reducing interest in entering the occupation or staying with a company. For example, truck driver compensation declined since the 1980s and only recently has increased: "In 1980, the average trucker in America was making an annual salary, adjusted for inflation, equal to more than $110,000 today. Twenty-five years later, truckers make on average about $40,000 a year, working harder, longer hours, and with less job security" [14]. One industry website reported that Swift Transportation pays first-year "rookie" drivers for $41,110, and J.B. Hunt pays rookies $40,000, with additional perks" [15]. Recent trends in driver pay are shown in Fig. 8.1. In distribution, some warehouse jobs may be slightly above minimum wage, although, similar to truck driving, the hourly rates are increasing. According to Salary.com, "The median hourly wage for a Warehouse Worker is $14, as of June 29, 2018, with a range usually between $12 and $16" [16]. Various warehouse job search and working sites report similar ranges, as also shown in Fig. 8.2.

Signing bonuses and increases in pay—even minimal increases in pay—can also lead to increased turnover rates as workers shift among employers. With the significant growth in industrial and distribution operations, wages have increased, as has "poaching" of employees from other businesses. *The Wall Street Journal* noted that "it doesn't take much to lure workers away. 'A guy who makes $10 an hour, you offer $10.25, he's going to leave,' said Tom Landry, president of Allegiance Staffing, which supplies logistics and manufacturing workers. 'That's another tank of gas" [17]. The article further notes that "as poaching becomes a bigger threat, employers are trying to make picker [order selector] jobs more attractive, with perks like employee barbecues and holiday breakfasts, as

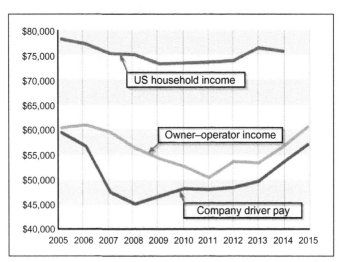

Figure 8.1 Truck driver annual compensation trends. *Source: Overdrive Online (https://www.overdriveonline.com/trucker-pay-has-plummeted-in-the-last-30-years-ana-lyst-stays/).*

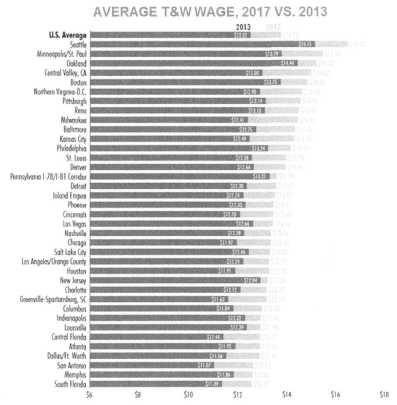

Figure 8.2 Trends in warehouse workers annual compensation. *Source: https://www. cbre.us/research-and-reports/U-S–Industrial–Logistics-Labor-Report-2018.*

well as more-flexible shifts" [12]. Such nonmonetary work benefits and events are being used as one means to attract and retain staff.

Perception and awareness

Perception and awareness of an industry and the related set of occupations can directly affect consideration of working in that field. In some sectors of the transportation, logistics, and distribution industry, poor perceptions exist, which discourage consideration of career opportunities. For example, a 2017 *New York Times* article on truck driving was entitled, "Alone on the Open Road: Truckers Feel like the Throwaway People" [18]. Similarly, exposes of working conditions in some warehouses have appeared in the press.

Sometimes, an industry is not perceived as viable for women or minorities because of the legacy of employment conditions in particular occupations. This perception can impact attracting a diverse workforce. As noted by one woman working in the logistics field, "As a woman working in the sector, a few of my experiences have highlighted this: health and safety gear being produced in large sizes; I've felt that having shorter hair would make for easier compliance; and I've had to manage plenty of quick changes out of tights and into socks and steel-toed boots" [19].

Awareness is another form of perception—potential employees may not know about the industry or the career opportunities within it. The next element of the framework focuses on marketing the opportunities and building awareness of current conditions and career paths.

Market the opportunities

Marketing the opportunities focuses on building awareness of the industry, the value of pursuing careers within it, and addressing negative perceptions. Awareness of the transportation, logistics, and distribution industry can be enhanced. In particular, awareness of career opportunities at the youth level and beyond could stand to improve. Several examples of image-building campaigns and programs are described below.

Overall marketing campaigns, done at a national or regional level can be deployed both to attract potential workers, as well as enhance general public understanding of the industry. As noted by ATA:

> *Unfortunately, the public perception of a truck driver has a tendency to be negative.* Trucking Moves America Forward *is an example of a positive image initiative and will hopefully highlight a demanding but rewarding career for potential drivers [5].*

The mission of the *Trucking Moves America Forward* program is to "establish a long-term industry-wide movement to create a positive image for the industry, to ensure that policymakers and the public understand the importance of the trucking industry to the nation's economy, and to build the political and grassroots support necessary to strengthen and grow the industry in the future" [20]. The campaign is multifaceted and includes videos, posters, a mascot, trailer wraps (shown in Fig. 8.5) and other material. The campaign also highlights career opportunities, as shown in Fig. 8.3.

The Association of American Railroads offers another example of an industry marketing campaign—their Railroad 101 website [21]. In

Figure 8.3 Image campaign trailer wrap focused on the workforce. *Source: Trucking Moves America (http://truckingmovesamerica.com/wp-content/uploads/2018TMAF_2017AR_ FINAL_SINGLES_OPT-2.pdf).*

addition to providing background information on the industry, the site includes a tab for workforce and suppliers. It notes the high level of compensation, long careers, and involvement of military veterans:

The jobs that support railroads are wide-ranging: from engineering and dispatching to law enforcement and information technology to industrial development and more. These highly skilled professionals average $120,900 per year in compensation, including benefits. They tend to spend their entire careers in the industry, and many have family railroad legacies stretching back generations. Railroads are also military-friendly employers, with nearly 25% of current employees veterans [21].

University Supply Chain Management programs have also developed programs that introduce the career opportunities to students. For example, the Rutgers Business School Supply Chain Education Partnership Program "aims to give local high school students a sense of supply chain management as a career. Just as the school year gives way to summer, the Center for Supply Chain Management finds a way to entice teenagers towards a rewarding future. The goal is to show relevance, bringing real-world reference to our students from everyday activities. Students are given hands on experience through visits to industry facilities to explore how SCM management is imperative to every business, large and small" [22].

Enhancing demographic awareness of career opportunities

As noted previously, some demographic segments are underrepresented in the transportation, distribution and logistics industries. Businesses, industry

associations, organizations, educational institutions, and communities recognize the opportunities and challenges of encouraging individuals to
consider less familiar careers.

The Women in Trucking Association (WIT) is an example of a nonprofit focused on the transportation and logistics industry. The organization's mission is "to encourage the employment of women in the
trucking industry, promote their accomplishments, and minimize obstacles
faced by women working in the trucking industry." The Association,
founded in 2007, works to [23]:

- Educate and raise awareness for women's issues,
- Promote career opportunities for women in the industry,
- Improve conditions for women already working in the industry,
- Increase the number of women in leadership positions in the industry,
- Increase the number of women drivers, and
- Serve as a resource about women working in the industry.

As part of the organization's efforts to introduce the industry and
career opportunities at an early age, WIT worked with the Girl Scouts to
create a transportation badge and program (see Fig. 8.4). As noted on their
website, "The purpose of the Transportation Patch is to expose young
girls to careers in the supply chain. From trucks, to boats and airplanes

Figure 8.4 Girl scout transportation badge. *Source: Women In Trucking.*

and pipelines, nearly 800 young girls have now earned the Women In Trucking Transportation Patch" [23]. WIT developed the curriculum and is developing an accompanying activity guide that depicts "the supply chain path of the cookies from the field to the final mile, which is the Girl Scout" [23].

In 2018 WIT introduced Claire, a plush female truck driver doll. The Chief Executive Officer of WIT, Ellen Voie, described the doll's career mission: "The world is wide open for girls today and I'm thrilled to be providing a toy that tells them that whatever they want to be is just great—whether that's a teacher or an ad exec or a professional driver" [23].

The posters produced by Trucking Moves America Forward also represent the diversity of the potential workforce (see Fig. 8.5)" [22].

The marketing- and awareness-building efforts are the introductions. Building skills and expertise is still necessary, as is connecting workers

Figure 8.5 Examples of career posters in trucking. *Source: Trucking Moves America (http://truckingmovesamerica.com/posters/).*

with potential employers. As noted on the Rutgers' program website, the "Rutgers SCM program is the first step in preparing our students to reach higher heights in this field" [22]. Increasing awareness encourages students early on, as well as workers considering alternatives, to consider supply chain professions as a destination career.

Develop training, skills, and expertise

With the building of awareness comes the opportunity to introduce students at a young age educationally to the transportation, logistics, and distribution field and develop programs throughout the educational systems to provide the training classes and opportunities needed.

Federal agencies have recognized the importance of creating these educational programs. Examples include [1]:

- The US Departments of Education, Health and Human Services, and Labor jointly issued a letter in April 2012 indicating their commitment to defining career pathways. Such pathways were defined as: "series of connected education and training strategies and support services that enable individuals to secure industry relevant certification and obtain employment within an occupational area and to advance to higher levels of future education and employment in that area" [24]. The components highlighted in this letter included:
  - Alignment of secondary and postsecondary education with workforce development systems.
  - Services that have, among their goals, a focus on secondary and postsecondary industry recognized credentials, sector specific employment, and advancement over time in education and employment within a sector.
- The US Departments of Education, Transportation, and Labor jointly issued a report in August 2015 entitled, *Strengthening Skills Training and Career Pathways Across the Transportation Industry*. Identified as a data report, the document articulated future transportation Workforce Needs.
- The US Departments of Education, Transportation, and Labor also jointly issued a fact sheet in September 2015 that identified four career path models [4]:
  - Career and Technical Education programs of study, beginning in high school and continuing into postsecondary education or apprenticeship, can provide the foundational and early occupational skills training needed in skilled occupations.

- Preapprenticeship programs for disadvantaged youth and adults can prepare low-skilled and underrepresented populations for entry into these skilled positions.
- Career Pathways systems that are aligned with Registered Apprenticeship programs can expand the number of people who can access these high-demand jobs.
- Significant training at the workplace helps people move from novice to skilled practitioner in their craft.
- The US Department of Labor (US DOL) has provided more than $300 million in grants through the Trade Adjustment Assistance Community College and Career Training Grant Program (TAACCCT) [25].

The US Department of Commerce recognized the criticality of supply chains in creating the Advisory Committee on Supply Chain Competitiveness in 2011 and then establishing workforce development subcommittee within it.

Numerous examples of educational programs, initiatives and curriculum exist. Examples include:

- The North American Marine Environmental Protection Association (NAMEPA) developed the *Marine Industry Learning Guide* [26]. The guide provides lesson plans, resource material, and activities beginning in kindergarten through the 12th grade that introduce students to the maritime industry.
- The Port of Houston Partners in Maritime Education Program was initiated in 2009 among stakeholders that included "industry professionals, academia, chambers of commerce, and economic alliances that could assist in solving the problem of our aging maritime workforce" [27]. The program, which received the 2015 Harvard Ash Center Bright Idea in Government, has organized maritime academies at four area high schools to introduce youth to maritime transportation systems and career pathways in mariner positions, shipbuilding and repair, and port operations. It also helped create 2- and 4-year maritime degree programs and training at higher education institutions so that graduates from the high school programs can continue their maritime studies [27].
- A collaboration that included the New Jersey Department of Education, the North Jersey Transportation Planning Authority (a metropolitan planning organization), the New York Shipping Association, NAIOP New Jersey (a Commercial and Industrial Real

Estate professional organization), several New Jersey universities and community colleges, the Southern Regional Education Board, and multiple private sector freight companies led to the development of the *Global Logistics and Supply Chain Management Curriculum* [28]. Released in 2014, the program provides course work for students, training for teachers, access to tools and technologies, end-of-course assessments, and an opportunity for industry certification and/or dual credit [28].

- The Council of Supply Chain Management Professionals (CSCMP) offers the SCPro Certification program. The certification "is a three-tiered program that assesses progressive knowledge and skills across integrated supply chain activities. This process validates an individual's ability to strategically assess business challenges and effectively implement supply chain improvements through the analysis of real-world case studies and the development of a comprehensive project plan to achieve results such as a positive ROI" [29].

Collaborate with employers

As noted to the Port of Houston and New Jersey examples, collaborations among organizations, and particularly with employers, are crucial. The US Department of Commerce's Advisory Committee on Supply Chain Competitiveness' 2016 Workforce Recommendation letter noted that the transportation, logistics, and distribution industry continued to voice workforce concerns, including [1]:

- Potential mismatches in the skills taught in academic institutions with the skills needed for companies to utilize workers on their first day of employment.
- The need to connect with, leverage, and expand private training programs, including apprenticeship programs within companies.

Further, the July 19, 2018, Executive Order establishing the President's National Council for the American Worker noted the need for collaboration. The Council was tasked with "increasing the number of partnerships around the country between companies, local educational institutions, and other entities, including local governments, labor unions, workforce development boards, and other nonprofit organizations, in an effort to understand the types of skills that are required by employers so that educational institutions can recalibrate their efforts toward the development and delivery of more effective training programs" [30].

Collaborations can take many forms and perform many functions. In addition to the collaborative development of educational programs, collaborations can include apprenticeship programs and career and job fairs.

Apprenticeship programs

Apprenticeships have existed as a proven mechanism for gathering on-the-job experience and credentials in a specific field for centuries. As noted by the US Department of Labor:

> From truck, train, and bus drivers and mechanics, to electrical technicians and vehicle inspectors, apprenticeship programs are training thousands of workers in America's transportation, logistics and distribution industry. Apprenticeship training helps companies innovate and stay competitive in the global economy, and ensures transportation workers have the knowledge and skills needed for today and tomorrow [31].

TransPORTS is one example of a contemporary, organized, nationally-registered apprenticeship program. The organization is one of eight US Department of Labor-contracted industry partners tasked with helping ports, marine manufacturers, supply chain and transportation, distribution and logistics (TDL) employers, and other sponsors develop apprenticeship programs [32]. The five components that distinguish a registered apprenticeship program from company-specific programs and internships include: employer ownership, structured on-the-job training, related technical instruction, rewards for skill gains, and national occupational credential [32]. UPS' Registered Apprenticeship program for US military veterans is another example of the U.S. Department of Labor's program and offers "full-time positions that combine job-related technical instruction with on-the-job experience" [33].

Career days and job fairs

Career days and job fairs are another way in which communities, the private sector, governmental organizations, and educational institutions can introduce students and job seekers to career opportunities. If held at a transportation and logistics operation, the event can also promote awareness of the industry.

Many such events are held throughout the United States by regions, businesses, and other organizations. For example, on April 18, 2018, the Council on Port Performance (CPP) Workforce Development Implementation Team—a collaboration of public, private, nonprofit, and educational organizations in the New York—New Jersey area—held the

Figure 8.6 Council on Port Performance's 2018 Career Awareness and Job Expo. *Source: Port Breaking Waves (https://www.portbreakingwaves.com/tldjobexpo/).*

first Career Awareness and Job Expo at Port Newark/Elizabeth, the largest container Port on the East Coast (Fig. 8.6). The inaugural event attracted approximately 550 high school juniors and seniors and 200 job seekers who visited tables and booths staffed by representatives of 50 organizations and maritime college-level institutions [34].

Encourage pilot programs and sharing of best practices

Pilot programs and the sharing of best practices is another crucial element of the framework. Pilot programs provide test beds to explore new approaches. The sharing of best practices helps all organizations move up the learning curve further to meet workforce challenges.

Example of a pilot program

On July 5, 2018, the US Department of Transportation launched a pilot program that could help address the truck driver shortage. The pilot program will "permit 18 to 20-year olds who possess the US Military equivalent of a commercial driver's license (CDL) to operate large trucks in interstate commerce" [35]. Sponsorship by a participating trucking company is required. The pilot program will operate for three years, after which the safety records of the truck drivers in the program will be compared to the records of a control group of truck drivers.

Best practice examples

One of the ways that trucking companies have addressed the lifestyle challenges of long-distance drivers is to increase the amount of time at home for such drivers. Another is to address driver pay. As one example, US Xpress, one of the nation's largest truckload carriers, announced a new incentive program for current and future team drivers. "The TeamMAX Bonus program allows team drivers to earn total bonuses of $50,000 with up to 4 weeks of paid vacation in a single year" [36]. Several trucking companies are now offering signing bonuses and evaluating hub and spoke distribution patterns that could reduce the time that drivers spend on the road.

Enhance accessibility

The transportation, logistics, and distribution industry has been rapidly evolving as the demands for its services have changed. For example, ecommerce has altered retail distribution channels. Ecommerce fulfillment centers (such as the Amazon fulfillment center, shown in Fig. 8.7), typically have three times the number of workers as a typical distribution center and up to nine times the employment during peak seasons [37].

The resulting higher levels of employment in new locations translate into the need to address the transportation options available to workers. Such buildings may not be located near existing transit options and/or the work shifts may not match with existing transit schedules. As a result,

Figure 8.7 Parking lots for associates at a New Jersey Amazon distribution center. *Source: Google Maps and the North Jersey Transportation Planning Authority.*

workers often have to drive to work or rely on carpooling. The ability to easily move from a place of residence to a place of employment is an increasingly critical consideration both for workers and employers. Worker interest and retention can be affected.

One practice to address the situation is through the use of nonprofit public–private partnerships that can help with last-mile connections to places of employment. The Greater Mercer Transportation Management Association (TMA) in New Jersey is one example. As described on the organization's website:

> The Greater Mercer TMA is a nonprofit public–private partnership dedicated to promoting and providing transportation choices that are designed to reduce congestion, improve mobility, increase safety, and further sustainability in Mercer and Ocean County. Established in 1984, our association consists of large and small employers, local governments, authorities, and state agencies who share a commitment to providing transportation choices that are good for commuters, good for business, and good for the environment [38].

Amazon is one of the partners of this TMA, which provides last-mile connectivity between the fulfillment center and a local transit hub coordinated with the facility's shifts. The Z line bus service, as it is called, also serves other companies in the Business Park [39].

Funding can be an issue for such organizations. TMAs typically rely on both public and private sector funding sources. So far, funding from the Congestion Mitigation and Air Quality (CMAQ) in the Federal Surface Transportation Program, through the US Department of Transportation Federal Highway Administration, has been used to partially finance local TMAs [1].

Moving forward

Transportation, logistics, and distribution drive the United States forward. The industry is crucial to the economic health of the nation, regions, and the global economy. Yet the 2018 CSCMP *State of Logistics Report* was entitled "Steep Grade Ahead" because of the challenges that are affecting the industry.

Workforce issues are among the most pressing. All sectors of the industry have crucial shortages, from unskilled hourly workers to highly skilled logistics professionals. These shortages have been growing.

Still, the path forward does appear bright and optimistic. As discussed in this chapter, multiple efforts are underway to build awareness of the career opportunities beginning at an early age and whenever potential workers consider their employment options. Numerous best practice examples that can be used by businesses, educational systems, and the governmental sector have been identified. All of these programs have been successful because of the collaboration among entities oriented toward a common objective—providing rewarding careers in an exciting and important industry.

References

[1] R.D. Balsgen, A. Strauss-Wieder, Workforce recommendation made by the US Department of Commerce Advisory Committee on Supply Chain Competitiveness, 2016. Retrieved from: https://www.trade.gov/td/services/oscpb/supplychain/acscc/Recommendations/16-04_Workforce%20Development/Workforce%20Recommendation%20-%20Approved.pdf.

[2] The New York Times. "What Does a Trucker Look Like?" It's Changing, Amid a Big Shortage, 2018. Retrieved from: https://www.nytimes.com/2018/07/28/us/politics/trump-truck-driver-shortage.html (accessed 28.07.18).

[3] Council of Supply Chain Management Professionals. The Annual State of Logistics Report, 2018. Retrieved from: https://cscmp.org/CSCMP/Footer/Press_Release/CSCMP_Unveils_the_29th_Annual_State_of_Logistics_Report.aspx (accessed 22.06.18).

[4] US Departments of Education, Transportation and Labor. Strengthening Skills Training and Career Pathways Across the Transportation Industry Fact Sheet, 2015. Retrieved from: https://s3.amazonaws.com/PCRN/docs/Strengthening_Skills_Training_and_Career_Pathways_Across_Transportation_Industry_Fact_Sheet_091115.pdf.

[5] B. Costello, Truck Driver Shortage Analysis, 2017. Retrieved from: http://progressive1.acs.playstream.com/truckline/progressive/ATAs%20Driver%20Shortage%20Report%202017.pdf.

[6] The Wall Street Journal. Why Working on the Railroad Comes With a $25,000 Signing Bonus, 2018. Retrieved from: https://www.wsj.com/articles/why-working-on-the-railroad-comes-with-a-25-000-signing-bonus-1524481201 (accessed 23.04.18).

[7] USNI News. MARAD: U.S. Short Almost 2, 000 Mariners to Supply American Forces in War, 2018. Retrieved from: https://news.usni.org/2018/03/08/marad-u-s-short-almost-2000-mariners-supply-american-forces-war (accessed 22.06.18).

[8] Maritime Training Academy. A Shortage of Seafarers, 2016.

[9] Area Development. 32nd Annual Survey of Corporate Executives Commentary: Labor Is Paramount, 2018. Retrieved from: http://www.areadevelopment.com/Corporate-Consultants-Survey-Results/Q1-2018/labor-is-paramount-Doug-Rasmussen-Duff-Phelps-LLC.shtml (accessed 06.07.18).

[10] ITF Seafarers. Women Seafarers, 2018. Retrieved from: https://www.itfseafarers.org/ITI-women-seafarers.cfm (accessed 06.07.18).

[11] Fleet Owner. "Is a Truck Driver Retirement Wave Beginning to Rise?," 2017. Retrieved from: https://www.fleetowner.com/blog/truck-driver-retirement-wave-beginning-rise (accessed 14.06.18).

[12] Forbes. Shippers Caused The Truck Driver Shortage, 2018. Retrieved from: https://www.forbes.com/sites/stevebanker/2018/07/19/shippers-caused-the-truck-driver-shortage/#282c98d564ff (accessed 19.07.18).

[13] Federal Motor Carrier Safety Administration. What Is the Age Requirement for Operating a CMV in Interstate Commerce?, 2014. Retrieved from: https://www.fmcsa.dot.gov/faq/what-age-requirement-operating-cmv-interstate-commerce.

[14] Forbes. How Trucking Went From One of the Best Jobs in America to One of the Worst, 2016. Retrieved from: http://time.com/money/4325164/trucking-worst-job/ (accessed 19.07.18).

[15] http://www.alltrucking.com/faq/first-year-truck-driver-salary/.

[16] https://www1.salary.com/Warehouse-Worker-hourly-wages.html (accessed 19.07.18).

[17] The Wall Street Journal. Online Retailers' New Warehouses Heat Up Local Job Markets, 2017. Retrieved from: https://www.wsj.com/articles/online-retailers-new-warehouses-heat-up-local-job-markets-1491739203 (accessed 14.06.18).

[18] The New York Times. Alone on the Open Road: Truckers Feel Like "Throwaway People," 2017. Retrieved from: https://www.nytimes.com/2017/05/22/us/trucking-jobs.html (accessed 30.07.18).

[19] The Guardian. Women in Logistics: There's More to the Industry Than Just Moving and Lifting, 2013. Retrieved from: https://www.theguardian.com/careers/women-logistics-diverse-workforce-career-opportunities (accessed 14.0618).

[20] Trucking Moves America Forward. About Us, 2018. Retrieved from: http://truckingmovesamerica.com/aboutus/.

[21] Association of American Railroads. Freight Rail Works for America, 2018). Retrieved from: https://www.aar.org/railroad-101/.

[22] The Rutgers Business School. Supply Chain Education Partnership Program, 2018. Retrieved from: http://www.business.rutgers.edu/pre-college/supply-chain-management.

[23] Women in Trucking. About Us, 2018. Retrieved from: https://www.womenintrucking.org/about-us.

[24] US Departments of Education, Health and Human Services, and Labor, 2012. Letter issued.

[25] US Department of Labor. Committee on Supply Chain Competitiveness, 2015.

[26] The North American Marine Environmental Protection Association. Marine Industry Learning Guide: Interactive Lessons for Educators, Seafarers, and the Public, 2018. Retrieved from: https://namepa.net/wp-content/uploads/2018/06/FINAL-marine-industry-guide.pdf.

[27] Port Houston. The Port of Houston Partners in Maritime Education Scholarship, 2018. Retrieved from: http://porthouston.com/maritime-education/.

[28] SREB High Schools that Work. Global Logistics & Supply Chain Management, 2014. Retrieved from: https://www.nj.gov/education/cte/career/Transportation/global.pdf.

[29] Council of Supply Chain Management Professionals. SCPro Certification, 2018. Retrieved from: https://cscmp.org/CSCMP/Certify/SCPro__Certification_Overview.aspx.

[30] Executive Order Establishing the President's National Council for the American Worker, 2018. Retrieved from: https://www.whitehouse.gov/presidential-actions/executive-order-establishing-presidents-national-council-american-worker/ (accessed 29.07.18).

[31] US Department of Labor. The Workforce Solution for Transportation, Logistics & Distribution, 2018. Retrieved from: https://www.dol.gov/apprenticeship/industry/transportation.htm.

[32] TransPORTS. Step-by-Step Guide to Designing and Launching a Successful Apprenticeship Program, 2017. Retrieved from: http://transportsapprenticeship.com/wp-content/uploads/2018/03/TransPORTs-Guide-to-Designing-and-Launching-an-Effective-Apprenticeship-Program.pdf.

[33] UPS. UPS Registered Apprenticeship Program, 2018. Retrieved from: https://military.jobs-ups.com/culture-benefits/article/ra-faq.html.

[34] The Port Authority of NY and NJ. Making Connections: Port Hosts Transportation, Logistics, and Distribution (TLD) Job Expo, 2018. Retrieved from: https://www.portbreakingwaves.com/tldjobexpo/.

[35] Federal Motor Carrier Safety Administration. New USDOT Pilot Program Provides Boost to Military Recruitment, 2018. Retrieved from: https://www.fmcsa.dot.gov/newsroom/new-usdot-pilot-program-provides-boost-military-recruitment (accessed 01.08.18).

[36] US Xpress Inc. US Xpress Announces Industry Leading Team Bonus, 2018. Retrieved from: https://www.usxpress.com/2018/02/14/us-xpress-announces-industry-leading-team-bonus/ (accessed 22.06.18).

[37] Anne Strauss-Wieder, North Jersey Transportation Planning Authority, Presentation on the New Last Mile, 2016 Transportation Research Board Annual Meeting.

[38] Greater Mercer TMA. About Us, 2018. Retrieved from: http://gmtma.org/the-association/.

[39] Greater Mercer TMA. About Us, 2018. Retrieved from: http://gmtma.org/wp-content/uploads/2018/03/z_line_dec_26_2017_web.pdf.

CHAPTER NINE

Does transportation access affect the ability to recruit and retain logistics workers?

Marlon G. Boarnet[1], Genevieve Giuliano[1], Gary Painter[1], Sanggyun Kang[2], Saumya Lathia[3] and Benjamin Toney[3]

[1]Professor, Sol Price School of Public Policy, University of Southern California, Los Angeles, CA, United States
[2]Postdoctoral Researcher, Center for Transportation Equity, Decisions and Dollars, University of Texas, Arlington, TX, United States
[3]Graduate Student, Sol Price School of Public Policy, University of Southern California, Los Angeles, CA, United States

Contents

Empowering the New Mobility Workforce.
DOI: https://doi.org/10.1016/B978-0-12-816088-6.00009-2

Introduction

Workers need to get to their jobs. This truism holds for transportation as well as it holds for any other industry. Yet ironically, for an industry that produces transportation as a good, there has not been much analysis of how transportation workers themselves get to and from their jobs. Many transportation job sites are clustered in locations that may be distant from residential areas. To explore this possible mismatch, we examine the logistics industry in metropolitan Los Angeles as a case study of access to work. The logistics industry in greater Los Angeles employs approximately 290,000 workers [2015 Longitudinal Employer-Household Dynamics Origin-Destination Employment Statistics (2015 LODES)], with average annual salary approximating $40,000 [2016 Integrated Public Use Microdata Series (IPUMS)]. Logistics jobs—trucking, shipping, warehousing—are spatially concentrated. The locations of these logistics jobs have shifted over recent decades as the industry has consolidated into larger distribution centers and expanded into the Inland Empire [1]. As this landscape has evolved, transportation access for logistics jobs poses an important question with implications for regional economic stability, prosperity, and equity.

In this chapter, we examine the spatial access to logistics jobs as a workforce issue in the Los Angeles-Long Beach, CA Combined Statistical Area (Los Angeles CSA). Where are the logistics job concentrations in this area of Southern California? Where do existing workers live? How well do transportation networks—via car and public transit—connect the locations of residences and workplaces for these workers? How do these connections appear for potential workers? For this study, we identified potential workers who are likely to rely on public transit and who also meet demographic characteristics that could help diversify the logistics industry workforce. We examine whether access for these groups is different than for existing industry employees.

Our motivation for this study is the literature on the link between transportation access and employment. For decades, scholars have examined whether and how a person's transportation access to jobs influences their likelihood of being employed. The logistics industry has been working to diversify its workforce, largely through training and targeted recruitment programs. Is transportation access also a barrier? Are logistics jobs in greater Los Angeles accessible from locations with large concentrations of nonwhite populations? And if not, how might policymakers and the logistics industry respond to improve access to worksites? While our focus is logistics, these questions apply throughout the economy. The solutions in the transportation and warehousing industry might prototype approaches that could work in other industries as well.

The remainder of this chapter is organized as follows: Section "Theory and evidence on transportation access to employment" discusses theory and evidence related to transportation access and employment. Section "Data" introduces the data sources we use in our analysis. Section "Logistics Industry in Los Angeles" presents a description of the Southern California logistics industry, and the following section presents results. Section "Conclusion and Interpretation" presents our conclusions and policy implications.

Theory and evidence on transportation access to employment

Spatial mismatch

Half a century ago, John Kain first proposed the spatial mismatch hypothesis. Kain [2] argued that residential segregation in the housing market forced African-Americans to live farther from job centers, and that this "spatial mismatch" might help explain higher unemployment rates for blacks in the United States. He also found evidence in support of his hypothesis, and it was soon applied to other population groups such as Hispanics and Asians, low-income individuals, or women. His general question is as follows: When persons live far from jobs, does that reduce their success in the labor market?

Decades of research have examined this hypothesis (mostly in the United States). Kain's evidence from Chicago and Detroit [2] found that the fraction of black employment decreases with increasing distance of Ghettos from job clusters. Many but not all studies found results along the same lines. A study of 25 Standard Metropolitan Statistical Areas, or SMSA's using 1960 data [3] showed that although black employment rates are positively associated with the fraction of blacks employed in suburbs and with increased job decentralization the effect is swamped by the local unemployment rate. A similar study in Pittsburgh [4] highlighted that black residents were less likely to be employed at more distantly located jobs. Another study in Cleveland, Detroit, and St. Louis [5] showed that a large proportion of poor residents from the city center commute to job clusters in suburbs, and that black residents working in suburbs had on

average a 10% higher hourly wage than those working in the inner city.
Decades later, a study of all SMSAs larger than 250,000 [6] highlighted
that black males in suburbs earn 40% more than those in inner cities.
Another study based in Chicago, Philadelphia, and Los Angeles [7] indicated that average travel time had significant impacts on black employment.

Despite the evidence supporting the "spatial mismatch hypothesis,"
debate emerged immediately. Offner and Saks [8] found that Kain's original results were sensitive to model specification. In some models, the
impact was reversed. Studies like this one in Los Angeles [9] observed that
there were no significant impacts between job access and black or teen
employment. Many reviews of the spatial mismatch hypothesis have noted
the empirical challenges in identifying the causal link between residential
segregation and job market outcomes in the United States [10].

Recently, researchers have argued that spatial mismatch is less important than other types of mismatches. Modal mismatch is defined as access
disadvantage due to lack of car ownership. Skills mismatch may exist due
to lower level of skills and education than required for the local labor
market. Social mismatch can disadvantage those with limited social networks related to obtaining or retaining jobs [11−13].

Modal mismatch

Spatial mismatch fails to address two key concerns that are important for the
logistics industry today. First, in economies that are close to full employment, transport access may not be linked to unemployment, but rather
whether transportation access influences which job a person can find and
keep, and hence the composition of an industry's labor force. For example,
if a certain population has less transport mobility in an economy near full
employment, then that population may be dependent on a much more
localized labor market, leading to placement in less preferred jobs. While we
do not formally test this concept, we provide evidence on transportation
access from residential locations of existing or potential workers to logistics
jobs in the Los Angeles region to get insight into this question.

Second, spatial mismatch focuses mostly on distance from homes to
workplaces. However, travel time to work varies substantially depending
on whether one travels by car or public transit. In 2009 mean travel time
to work for persons commuting by public transportation was 47.8 minutes
compared to a 24.2-minute one-way commute for persons who drove
alone [14]. Therefore, scholars have begun to focus on modal mismatch.
Several studies have demonstrated that in contemporary US cities, poor or
nonwhite populations might live close to jobs, but the travel time penalty

of public transit causes transit-dependent persons to have poor job access even if they live "close" to jobs [15−17]. Blumenberg [18] showed that from near-central neighborhoods in Los Angeles such as Boyle Heights, Pico-Union, and West Adams—all relatively close to downtown—residents could access from 5 to 10 times as many jobs commuting by car than by public transit. Boarnet, Giuliano, Hou, and Shin [19] documented differences that are approximately 30-fold in the number of jobs that residents from the 37 lowest income census tracts in San Diego County can access by car versus by public transit.

As a result of these two effects, urban planners and transportation analysts today focus on the mode of travel to work and the characteristics of the transportation system used. Consistent with the concept of modal mismatch, we examine job access by focusing on commute times from workers' residential locations to logistics jobs concentrations by two travel modes—car and transit. To conduct our analysis, we proceed in three steps—(1) analyzing where logistics jobs are in greater Los Angeles, (2) analyzing where the current and potential future logistics workforce lives, and (3) examining the transport links (by car and by transit) between those concentrations of residences and jobs. This analysis will provide insight into the underlying job accessibility issues that logistics workers face using personal vehicles or public transit. This research could inform development of public policy efforts that have largely been informed by anecdotal evidence.

Data

Our study area is the Los Angeles Combined Statistical Area (CSA)—the second largest in the nation with a population of nearly 19 million in 2018. Our analysis of jobs, workers, potential workers, and access could not be accomplished using a single dataset. Information on industry and jobs is collected by the Bureau of Commerce, and information on population is collected by the US Census. Information on transportation and travel times is typically available from metropolitan planning organizations. Using different data sources results in some inconsistencies. For example, a count of the number of jobs in a metropolitan area will not be the same as a count of the number of workers, because of differences in when and how the data are collected. These differences are small and will not affect our conclusions. The main data sources are described below. We identify the data sources used throughout our analysis.

2015 Longitudinal Employer-Household Dynamics Origin-Destination Employment Statistics

LODES is produced by the US Census Bureau Center for Economic Studies. It is based on Unemployment Insurance records, the Quarterly Census of Employment, and various Office of Personnel Management datasets. LODES gives the most comprehensive and spatially detailed data on employment available from the US government. Annual employment statistics are provided, but the year range differs by state. In California, annual data from 2002 to 2015 are available. The LODES dataset provides employment counts by two-digit NAICS industry sector at the census tract level. It also includes the three-digit subsector statistics for rail and postal service. However, census tract level numbers are suppressed when numbers are small to preserve confidentiality. Census tracts typically range from 1200 to 8000 persons in population, and the borders of census tracts usually follow boundaries of municipalities, counties, and states and/or major barriers such as rivers, major roads, or other delineating features. There are 3925 census tracts in the five-county region. We use the 2015 LODES data to examine the locations of logistics jobs and existing workers.

Integrated Public Use Microdata Series

IPUMS is produced by the US Census and provides person-level data drawn from individual responses to the decennial census up to 2010 and the American Community Survey from 2000.

The trade-off for individual-level data is geographic aggregation; IPUMS data are available at the Public Use Microdata Area (PUMA) level. PUMAs consist of populations of at least 100,000, and they share boundaries with census tracts. We use the 2016 IPUMS data to identify the characteristics of workers and location of potential workers in the logistics sector.

Southern California Association of Governments Travel Model

The third main data source is the Southern California Association of Governments (SCAG) 2016 travel model. The SCAG travel model has information on both the highway and transit networks. The geographic unit is the Traffic Analysis Zone (TAZ). The size of a TAZ is similar to that of a census tract, but the boundaries are set so that highways and arterials are included within the TAZ boundaries. There are 3999 (TAZs) in the study area. When combining the LODES and SCAG data, we convert the census tract data to TAZ data. The SCAG travel model provides zone-to-zone travel times by car or transit by multiple time periods of the day. The research in this study focused on morning peak travel times.

Logistics industry in Los Angeles

The Los Angeles CSA consists of five counties: Los Angeles, Orange, San Bernardino, Riverside, and Ventura. It has 18.46 million population and 7.66 million jobs in 34,000 square miles.[1] The two central counties—Los Angeles and Orange—have the highest average population density in the United States with 2650 people per square mile. Two other counties located to the east—San Bernardino and Riverside, commonly known as the Inland Empire—house intense logistics and freight transportation activity. The Los Angeles CSA is one of the nation's top foreign trade centers. It has rich transportation infrastructure (seaports, airports, rail-to-truck intermodal terminals, and highways), through which 32.4% of all US container trade in terms of TEU was processed in 2015.[2] The region's cargo service airport system is ranked seventh nationwide [20]. Two Class I railroads operate in the region: Union Pacific (UP) and Burlington Northern Santa Fe (BNSF). Fig. 9.1 presents major freight transportation infrastructure.

Definition of the logistics sector

We define the logistics sector as the North American Industrial Classification System (NAICS) two-digit sector 48—49, Transportation and Warehousing.[3] The sector consists of 11 subsectors (Table 9.1). The data source is the 2015 County Business Patterns published by the US Census. It is the only public data source that provides three-digit sector statistics, but it excludes NAICS 482 Rail and NAICS 491 Postal service sectors. There are a total of 276,000 NAICS 48—49 jobs and 12,000 establishments. Four subsectors with the largest number of jobs (484: truck, 488: support activities, 492: couriers and messengers, and 493: warehousing and storage; in italics) comprise 81.7% of the total logistics jobs (226,000) and 86.5% of all logistics establishments (10,456).

---

[1] American Community Survey 2012—16 and LODES 2015.
[2] US Department of Transportation, Maritime Administration, US waterborne foreign container trade by US customs ports in 2015, total trade (imports and exports) in twenty-foot equivalent units (TEUs).
[3] NAICS definition available at: <https://www.census.gov/eos/www/naics/>.

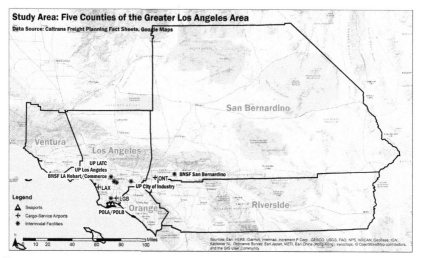

Figure 9.1 Study area and freight transportation infrastructure.

Table 9.1 Number of establishments and employment in the logistics sector in Los Angeles CSA (2015 County Business Patterns).

Sectors	Establishments	Percent	Employment	Percent
481 Air transportation	252	2.1	22,687	8.2
482 Rail transportation	No data	—	No data	—
483 Water transportation	76	0.6	3,575	1.3
484 Truck transportation	*5289*	*43.8*	*59,301*	*21.5*
485 Transit and ground transportation	1117	9.2	21,437	7.8
486 Pipeline transportation	40	0.3	774	0.3
487 Scenic and sightseeing	145	1.2	1,823	0.7
488 Support activities	*3230*	*26.7*	*64,192*	*23.2*
491 Postal service	No data	—	No data	—
492 Couriers	*846*	*7.0*	*41,460*	*15.0*
493 Warehousing and storage	*1091*	*9.0*	*61,136*	*22.1*
48–49 Transportation and Warehousing Sector sum (excluding 482 Rail and 491 Postal service)	12,086		276,385	

We use 2010 IPUMS data to summarize the characteristics of the current logistics industry workforce. As noted in Section "Data," IPUMS is a sample of a larger population, hence the numbers are not equivalent to actual population counts. However, the samples are drawn to be representative of the total population. Table 9.2 give descriptive statistics for

Table 9.2 Characteristics of logistics workers and all workers, 2010 IPUMS data.

Variable		Number of observations	Mean	Std. Dev.	Min.	Max.
Age	Logistics	23,189	43.43	13.22	16	90
	All industries	531,584	42.12338	14.25963	16	94
Income	Logistics	23,189	$40,935.81	$42,449.09	$0.00	$504,000
	All industries	531,584	$44,743.88	$60,973.84	$0.00	$504,000
			Less than high school diploma	*High school diploma*	*Some college*	*Bachelor's degree or above*
Educational Attainment	Logistics		18.45	38.39	40.25	2.91
	All industries		15.79	26.43	46.08	11.69
		White only	*African–American only*	*Hispanic only*	*Asian only*	*Non-Hispanic other*
Race/Ethnicity	Logistics	25.11%	9.47%	50.63%	12.8%	1.99%
	All industries	35.95%	5.16%	41.63%	14.81%	2.43%
					Employed	*Unemployed*
Employment Status	Logistics				93.92%	6.08%
	All industries				91.57%	8.43%
					Male	*Female*
Sex	Logistics	23,189			74.86%	25.14%
	All industries	531,584			53.54%	46.46%

NAICS Industry 48 and 49 data calculated from 2016 Integrated Public Use Microdata Series (IPUMS).

logistics workers and all workers based on the IPUMS sample of 23,189 logistics workers and 531,584 total workers.[4] Logistics workers have about the same age distribution as all workers, but have a substantially lower annual income. Logistics jobs tend to include more workers with high school education or less. African-Americans and Hispanics are overrepresented in logistics compared to all industries. Perhaps the most striking disparity is the dominance of male workers relative to the gender distribution among all workers. Logistics jobs tend to be in traditionally male dominated occupations (e.g., truck driver), or in occupations that require physical strength (e.g., warehouse worker).

Locations of logistics jobs, logistics workers, and the travel time connections between workers and jobs

In this section, we present our analysis of logistics jobs, workers, and commuting patterns. We consider current and potential workers, particularly those who may have limited access to private vehicles and may be more reliant on public transportation.

Spatial distribution of logistics jobs

We begin our analysis with an examination of the distribution of logistics jobs. We use the 2015 LODES data. There are 293,292 logistics jobs and 284,898 logistics resident workers reported in the LODES data for the CSA.[5] The number of jobs and workers do not exactly match—likely due to vacancies or workers who might reside outside of the Los Angeles CSA. Out of the total 3925 census tracts in the Los Angeles CSA, almost two-thirds (2495) have at least one logistics job.

Are the jobs concentrated in certain places, such as around the ports or other major intermodal facilities? We use quintiles to divide the 2495 tracts with logistics jobs into five groups based on job density, measured as the number of jobs per acre. The spatial distribution in density quintiles is shown in Fig. 9.2. There are distinct concentrations around the ports,

---

[4] The IPUMS sample includes unemployed workers. For unemployed individuals, the data refer to their most recent job, if it was within the previous 5 years.

[5] Different data sources yield slightly different counts, hence the difference between the total in Table 9.1 that is based on CBP data, which excludes two subsectors (rail and postal service), and the total based on LODES.

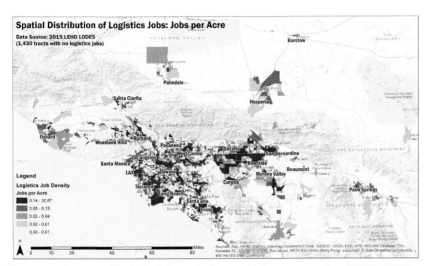

Figure 9.2 Density of logistics jobs, quintiles, and jobs per acre. *From 2015 LODES.*

LAX, in the old industrial core of Los Angeles, along the eastward free-way corridors (Ontario), and in Moreno Valley. There are also secondary clusters around the periphery, including Oxnard, in Ventura County; Santa Clarita and Palmdale, in northern Los Angeles County; Hesperia and Barstow, in San Bernardino County; and Palm Springs.

Given this evidence of clustering, can we identify areas with particu-larly high concentrations of logistics jobs? In order to identify specific job clusters, we identify tracts in the 90th percentile of jobs per acre. We identify 392 tracts, and these tracts account for 85% of all the logistics jobs. If any given tract in this group shares a boundary with another tract in the group, we combine the tracts. We continue to combine tracts until there are no qualified neighbors remaining. We then add up all the jobs in each cluster, and rank order the clusters based on total logistics jobs. This process yields a total of 133 clusters, which account for 85% of all logistics jobs. However, the number of jobs in the clusters varies widely from 51,000 to just a few jobs. Therefore, we set an arbitrary size thresh-old of 3000 jobs to identify those with intense logistics activity. There are 12 clusters that satisfy this size cutoff, and they account for 68% of all the logistics jobs. Fig. 9.3 maps the results, and Table 9.3 describes the 12 clusters and gives the main access factors related to the cluster. The largest cluster is the Inland Empire cluster. It includes Ontario, Riverside, and San Bernardino. The clusters around LAX and around the ports and warehouse districts to the north are basically tied for rank two. Cluster 4

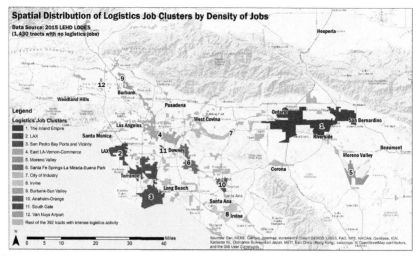

Figure 9.3 Distribution of logistics job clusters by density of jobs. *From 2015 LODES.*

Table 9.3 Logistics job clusters with more than 3000 jobs.

Name	Number of logistics jobs	Factors for clustering
1. The Inland Empire	51,606	Ontario airport, intermodal terminals, highways
2. LAX	38,629	LAX airport
3. San Pedro Bay Ports and Vicinity	38,481	SPB ports
4. East LA-Vernon-Commerce	24,799	Intermodal terminals, highways
5. Moreno Valley	11,322	Highways
6. Santa Fe Springs-La Mirada-Buena Park	9468	Highways
7. City of Industry	7702	Intermodal terminals, highways
8. Irvine	4848	Highways
9. Burbank-Sun Valley	3436	Burbank airport
10. Anaheim-Orange	3167	Highways
11. South Gate	3113	Highways
12. Van Nuys Airport	3076	Van Nuys Airport
Sum of logistics jobs in the clusters	199,647	68.1% of all logistics jobs
Total logistics jobs in Los Angeles CSA	293,292	

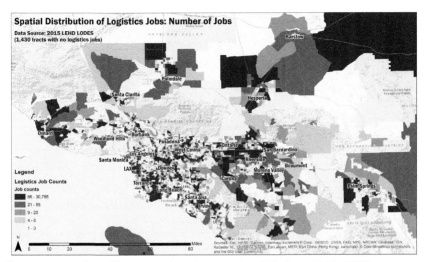

Figure 9.4 Number of logistics jobs in Los Angeles CSA. *From 2015 LODES.*

runs along the I-5 corridor, the old industrial zone of the city, and includes major intermodal facilities. The clusters are consistent with our general knowledge of the region; they are all located in well-known industrial/manufacturing/transportation zones.

We conducted the same exercise using job counts per tract rather than job density. Fig. 9.4 gives a quintile map based on job counts. It can be seen that the spatial pattern is mostly consistent with Fig. 9.2 in dense urban areas, but is substantially different in the outlying areas such as Hesperia, Barstow, Palm Springs, Palmdale, and Santa Clarita. These locations are mostly rural and have very large census tracts. The size of these tracts influences the counts (e.g., relatively small number of jobs spread over a large area). The 292 rural census tracts include approximately 5.0% of all logistics jobs (14,569). Using count data emphasizes large but low density tracts. We also conducted the same exercise of identifying clusters based on count data. The resulting clusters are generally consistent with those based on density (results not shown). We conclude that for jobs, using job density provides a more accurate picture of spatial distribution.

Spatial distribution of logistics workers

It is well known that the spatial distribution of the population is more decentralized than that of jobs. We therefore expect that on average logistics workers will be more spread out than jobs. But precisely how spread out are logistics industry workers? Where do they colocate? We follow

Table 9.4 Spatial distribution of jobs and resident workers.

Measure	Jobs	Workers
All tracts	3925	3925
Average density	0.117	0.237
S.D. of density	0.744	0.226
Min.	0	0
Max.	32.671	1.933
Tracts with at least one job/worker		
Number of tracts	2495	3919
Average density	0.185	0.238
SD of density	0.927	0.226
Min.	0 (not exactly but close to)	0 (not exactly but close to)
Max.	32.671	1.933

the same method as with jobs; the question is whether worker density or worker counts give a better picture of the distribution. In general, density measures are effective when there is a lot of variation in spatial concentration and not effective where there is little variation. With any type of ranking, the density measure will capture more of the distribution in the top ranks when a distribution is concentrated, but little of the distribution when it is less concentrated. The reverse is true for count measures.

We examine the logistics workers by place of residence distribution also using the 2015 LODES data. We generate quintile maps with respect to both density and counts. Table 9.4 gives information on the spatial distributions of jobs and resident workers. It suggests that the resident worker distribution is notably less concentrated.

Fig. 9.5 maps resident workers by density quintiles, and Fig. 9.6 maps them by count quintiles. In Fig. 9.5 worker concentration is highest in the urbanized core of the region. There are other concentrations along the I-5 corridor to the north, the I-10/SR 60 corridors in the Inland Empire, and around Moreno Valley. These latter concentrations are consistent with the job density distribution. Also, as seen in the job density distribution, we observe concentrations in the periphery in Santa Clarita, Palmdale, Hesperia, and Palm Springs.

Fig. 9.6 gives a very different picture. We notice almost the inverse of Fig. 9.5 (note that the two maps are of the same scale). Now the highest counts are in the Inland Empire, followed by the peripheral areas with very large census tracts. The central core has fewer counts, mainly due to the small size of the tracts. Tracts highlighted in the San Fernando Valley in Fig. 9.5 have disappeared. Those tracts were in higher quintiles more

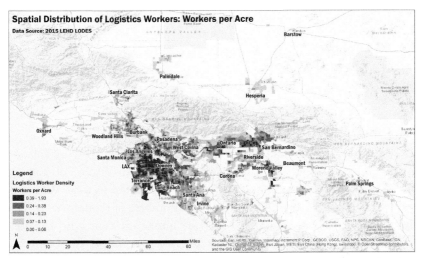

Figure 9.5 Density of resident logistics workers, persons/acre, and quintiles. *From 2015 LODES.*

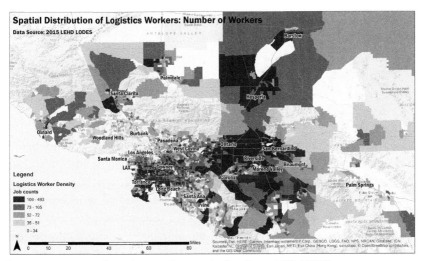

Figure 9.6 Counts of resident workers, quintiles. *From 2015 LODES.*

due to their small acreage than due to having many logistics workers. Both metrics—counts of workers and density of logistics workers—help us understand the spatial pattern of worker residences.

There is some suggestive evidence that resident workers in the peripheral areas may be subject to spatial mismatch if, for example, many of the workers have to travel to more distant job clusters because nearby jobs are scarce. Public transit would clearly not be an option for commutes in these areas.

In contrast to the concentration of jobs, the distribution of workers is far more spread out. The upper 90th percentile of census tracts with respect to density account for just 14% of resident workers. Therefore creating resident worker clusters would not tell us much about the actual distribution of workers.

Commute patterns of existing workers

The third step in our process is to examine the journey to work for current logistics workers. Given the spatial distribution of jobs, do logistics workers incur longer commutes than workers in other sectors? While the LODES data gives us numbers of jobs and numbers of resident workers at the census tract level, it does not provide information on who has what job. Given the limits of the data, we are able to examine the following: the average distance between all logistics jobs and all logistics workers from the LODES data.

Distance between workers and jobs by sector

Functional form:

$$\text{Average distance between two groups} = \frac{\sum_{j=1}^{N} \left[\frac{\sum_{i}^{n}(e_i \times d_{ij})}{E} \right] \times w_j}{W}$$

where e_i, number of jobs in census tract (i); E, sum of e_i; w_j, number of workers in census tract (j); W, sum of w_j; d_{ij}, Euclidean distance to census tract (i) from census tract (j) $(i = 1, 2, \ldots, n; j = 1, 2, \ldots, N)$.

Table 9.5 gives results. We are using all jobs and all workers across a very large region, and therefore the average distance is quite high. Note that this is not a measure of commute distance—workers choose jobs much closer to home than the average distance from all workers to all jobs. The important point of Table 9.5 is that the average distance is about the same for all jobs.

Fig. 9.7 shows the data in a different way. The worker distribution is given by count per tract, and the logistics employment clusters are laid on top. It can be seen that there are large numbers of logistics workers within and around all the employment clusters, but, in addition, there are larger numbers of logistics workers in the outlying areas that are not close to employment clusters.

Table 9.5 Distance between workers and jobs by sector.

From all census tracts (N = 3925)	To all census tracts (N = 3925)	Distance (miles)
All sector workers	All sector jobs	38.89
Logistics workers (NAICS 48−49)	Logistics jobs (NAICS 48−49)	36.31
Manufacturing workers (NAICS 31)	Manufacturing jobs (NAICS 31)	34.69
Retail/wholesale workers (NAICS 42−45)	Retail/wholesale jobs (NAICS 42−45)	37.50

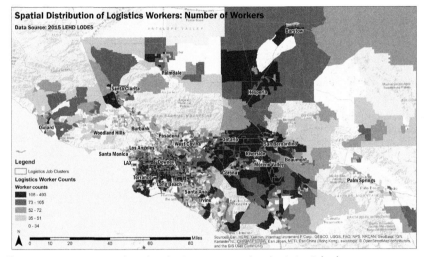

Figure 9.7 Logistics worker distribution compared to logistics job clusters.

Lastly, we further examine the distribution of jobs and workers by comparing the ratio of logistics jobs and logistics workers between census tracts in outlying areas (rural) and those otherwise. We use the 2016 urban area definition published by the US Census. The urban–rural classification is based on the location of the centroid of each tract. Fig. 9.8 shows the distribution of the urban and rural census tracts, and Table 9.6 shows the number of census tracts by urban/rural by county. In Table 9.7 we present mean ratios of logistics jobs per logistics workers by urban/rural by county. In Fig. 9.9 we show the same ratios by census tract. In total, as expected, the ratio is larger for rural tracts than urban. Land-intensive logistics businesses are more likely to be located in nonurban areas. Across counties, the ratio varies. Los Angeles, logistics jobs are more concentrated in urban areas than logistics workers as all major transportation

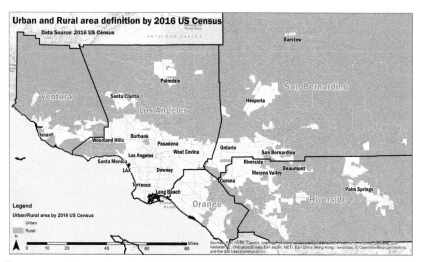

Figure 9.8 Urban and rural areas in the Los Angeles CSA.

Table 9.6 Number of census tracts by county by urban or rural.

County	Urban	Rural
Los Angeles	2260	85
Orange	561	24
Riverside	367	86
San Bernardino	304	65
Ventura	134	39
Total	3626	299

Table 9.7 Mean ratio between logistics jobs per logistics workers by county by urban or rural.

Urban/rural	Urban		Rural	
County	Mean	SD	Mean	SD
Los Angeles	2.24	30.37	0.43	1.72
Orange	0.80	3.29	3.55	14.87
Riverside	0.83	4.06	0.76	2.08
San Bernardino	1.06	5.14	14.51	111.75
Ventura	0.52	1.24	0.50	0.93
Total	1.71	24.10	3.89	52.89

infrastructure—port, airport, and intermodal terminals—is located within the urban area. In Orange and San Bernardino, the ratio is much higher for rural areas. In Riverside and Ventura, the ratio is comparable. This exercise explains that the job—worker ratio differs across location and between urban or rural settings.

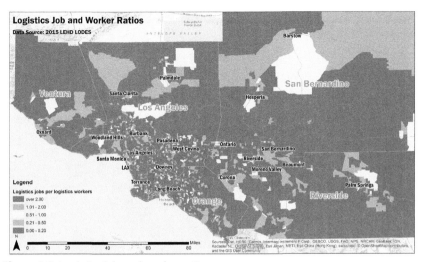

Figure 9.9 Logistics job and worker ratios.

Potential workers

We now turn to the future workforce. The data in Table 9.2 show that the current workforce is representative of the region's population of workers, and in fact overrepresents African-American and Hispanic workers. However, questions about the future workforce remain. Where are the potential workers, and are locations of potential workers well connected to logistics jobs? Are potential workers more reliant on public transport than existing workers?

To classify potential workers that the logistics industry might target, we consulted literature on the recent strategies to bolster the industry's workforce. Strategies often revolved around education, training, and outreach. While many jobs do require certification and postsecondary degrees, the majority of positions require high school diploma as the threshold education level [21–23]. Higher skill, higher wage positions on average tended to represent smaller portions of the workforce, but also had less gender and racial diversity [24]. Ultimately, we identified potential workers as those who meet the minimum requirements for entry (high school diploma) who also occupy groups that are traditionally underrepresented in the broader economy (African-Americans, and Latinos). In addition we consider women, given the large gender gap in this industry.

We choose the high school diploma criterion for two reasons. First, the vast majority of positions projected to grow in the coming years only require a high school diploma [21]. Second, workers with lower educational attainment are more likely to depend on public transportation.

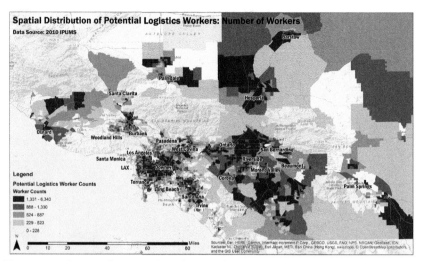

Figure 9.10 Counts of potential resident workers, quintiles. *From 2010 IPUMS.*

In order to identify potential workers as we have defined them, we must identify persons who have a high school diploma as their highest degree, and who are African-American or Hispanic. We also must determine who is available or capable of being employed. We use being in the workforce as the indicator of availability. IPUMS is the only data source that allows us to select persons based on multiple attributes. We therefore use the IPUMS data to calculate the proportions of individuals who meet the education and identity characteristics at the PUMA level and apply those percentages to the corresponding populations for census tracts within a given PUMA. This process generates a total potential workforce of 2,014,316. The number is large, because about 47% of the region's workforce is Hispanic or African-American (Table 9.2). The sample of the potential workforce is 56% male, 89% Hispanic, and 11% African-American. We map the potential worker counts in quintiles in Fig. 9.10. The spatial distribution of existing (Fig. 9.6) and potential workers (Fig. 9.10) is very similar except for a few locations. The concentration of potential workers is less pronounced in Central Los Angeles (areas near the San Pedro Bay ports and intermodal facilities), the Inland Empire, Burbank-Santa Clarita, and Yorba Linda. Worker statistics are different for several large census tracts in Palm Springs.

In addition, we also compare the statistical distribution between existing and potential workers. We employ three methods: Gini coefficient, frequency distribution, and sum of absolute differences. The Gini

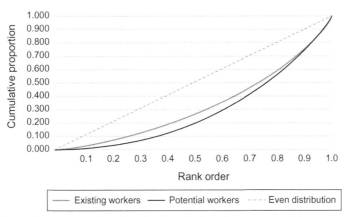

Figure 9.11 Comparison of rank-order distribution (Lorenz curve) between existing and potential workers.

coefficient calculates the extent to which an activity is concentrated in a small area. If an activity is evenly distributed over spatial units, the Gini is 0. If an activity is concentrated in one spatial unit, the Gini is 1. The Gini coefficient can also be visually presented (Fig. 9.11). We show two curves — the cumulative rank-order distribution of existing and potential worker shares from the census tract with the lowest value to that with the most workers. The gray curve represents existing worker distribution, whereas the black curve potential worker distribution. The dotted line represents even distribution. Visually, the Gini is equivalent to the proportion of the crescent area between the even distribution and plotted curves and the area below the even distribution line. Results are given in Table 9.8—potential workers are slightly more concentrated (0.42) than existing workers (0.35), as can be seen in Fig. 9.11.

Second, we plot frequency distribution of the census tracts by number of existing and potential workers (Figs. 9.12 and 9.13). Results are similar to the previous observation. There are more census tracts with a smaller count of potential workers than existing workers. In other words, a larger number of potential workers are concentrated in a smaller number of census tracts, hence more concentration.

Third, we calculate the sum of absolute differences for every paired census tract between existing and potential workers. To account for the big difference in terms of total workers (285 thousand existing workers vs. 2.01 million potential workers), we weight potential workers to the same total as existing workers. The hypothetical maximum difference is 285

Table 9.8 Comparison of the Gini coefficient between existing and potential workers.

	Existing workers	Potential workers
Gini coefficient	348	0.422

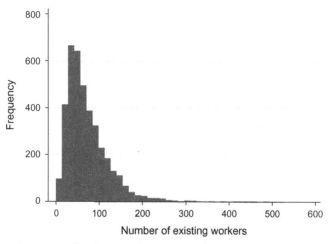

Figure 9.12 Frequency distribution of existing workers by census tract.

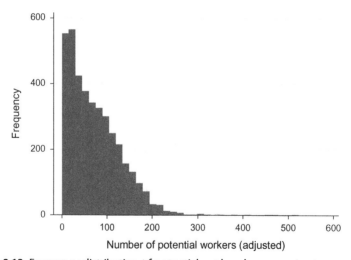

Figure 9.13 Frequency distribution of potential workers by census tract.

Table 9.9 Summary statistics of the absolute difference between existing and adjusted potential workers.

	Sum	Mean	Min.	Max.
Absolute difference	137,653	35.1	0	392.9

thousand, and the minimum difference 0. Results are given in Table 9.9. The mean is 35 workers per census tract. The sum is the total difference between numbers of existing and potential workers across all census tracts. Results of all the three methodologies show similar results: the distributions of existing and potential workers are only moderately different.

Job access analysis

Considering potential workers requires us to consider job access more generally. How accessible are existing jobs to potential workers? What is the difference between access by car and access by public transport? In this section, we develop accessibility measures and apply them to logistics jobs and potential workers.

We define job accessibility as the number of jobs one can reach within a given travel time by a particular mode of transport. We examine two aspects of accessibility: (1) car versus public transit access and (2) job accessibility for existing and potential logistics workers. In order to calculate zone-level travel times, we use the 2016 travel model from the SCAG. As noted in Section "Theory and Evidence on Transportation Access to Employment," the travel model data is based on TAZs, hence our data was converted from census tract to TAZ. There are 3999 (TAZs) in the study area. The SCAG travel model provides zone-to-zone travel times by car or public transit by multiple time periods of the day. We use AM peak travel times. We define job access as the number of jobs that can be reached within 30, 45, and 60 minutes. It is calculated as follows:

$$\text{Job accessibility}_i = \sum_{j=1}^{J} e_j \times t_{ij}$$

where e_j = number of logistics jobs in TAZ (j); t_{ij} is an indicator based on the travel time between TAZ (i) and (j); $t = 1$ if travel time is less than the threshold (30, 45, or 60 minutes), $t = 0$ otherwise.

Car versus transit

We first compare job accessibility by mode. Table 9.10 presents the average number of logistics jobs accessible in 30, 45, and 60 minutes by car and transit. We also present the percentage of all logistics jobs accessible by each mode. The difference between car and transit access is large: within 60 minutes, almost half of all jobs can be reached by car, but just 3% can be reached by transit. As the time constraint is relaxed the number and share of jobs that can be reached increases, but the patterns for car and transit are different. Doubling travel time results in access to 3 times as many jobs by car, but 20 times as many for transit. Almost no jobs are accessible within 30 minutes for transit.

The same data is presented in map form in the following figures. Figs. 9.14, 9.15, and 9.16 show job accessibility by car for 30, 45, and

Table 9.10 Average number and percentage of logistics jobs accessible in 30, 45, and 60 minutes, by car and transit.

Travel time	Average number and percentage of logistics jobs accessible in a given travel time from all TAZs in the Los Angeles CSA (N = 3999), Percentage in parenthesis			
	Car		Transit	
30 min	48,310	(16.5%)	478	(0.2%)
45 min	93,663	(31.9%)	3071	(1.0%)
60 min	141,958	(48.4%)	9765	(3.3%)

Data source: SCAG travel model 2016.

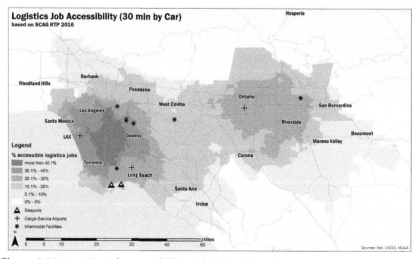

Figure 9.14 Logistics job accessibility within 30 minutes by car.

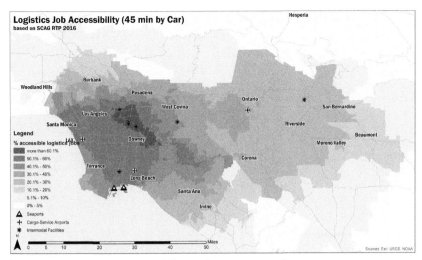

Figure 9.15 Logistics job accessibility within 45 minutes by car.

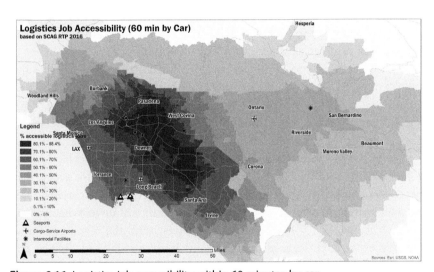

Figure 9.16 Logistics job accessibility within 60 minutes by car.

60 minute travel times, respectively. Fig. 9.14 shows the highest concentration of accessibility in the urbanized core, where job density is high and the road network is dense. There is a second concentration in the Inland Empire. Reducing the time constraint to 45 minutes, Fig. 9.15 shows the highest access along the I-5 corridor, as well as a large high access area that covers all of Los Angeles County south of the foothills and the northern part of Orange County. Fig. 9.16 shows that a

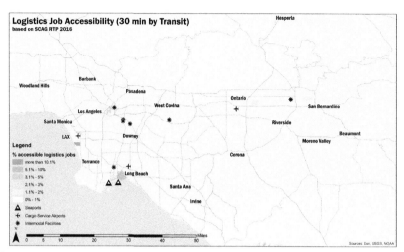

Figure 9.17 Logistics job accessibility within 30 minutes by transit.

60 minute time constraint further expands high access zones to cover a good part of the entire region. Within the 1-hour time limit by car, the most accessible zones have access to 80% of all jobs.

Transit shows a very different pattern. Small areas immediately adjacent to major logistics infrastructure (San Pedro Bay Ports, LAX, and Downtown Los Angeles) have relatively better job accessibility (Fig. 9.17) within the 30-minute time constraint, With the increase in travel time, significant job access improvement is observed in Figs. 9.18 and 9.19, but even with the 60-minute time limit, the most accessible zones have access to just 25% of all jobs. Fig. 9.19 shows that the highest transit access is in the Los Angele core, where extensive transit service and job clusters coincide. However, that level of access pales in comparison to what can be accessed by car. Fig. 9.19 also shows that even with the 60-minute time limit, access to logistics jobs in the Inland Empire is limited, despite the large number of jobs in the area. We conclude that public transit is an inferior mode for access to logistics jobs, particularly to those jobs located outside the core of the region.

Job accessibility comparison between existing and potential logistics worker residence locations

We now compare accessibility between existing and potential workers. We use the same method employed in the previous section, but this time we calculate accessibility from logistics job clusters to existing and potential worker

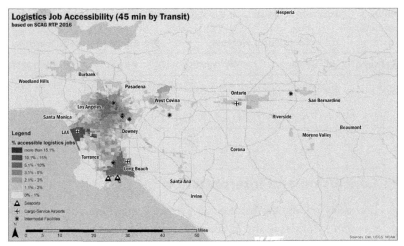

Figure 9.18 Logistics job accessibility within 45 minutes by transit.

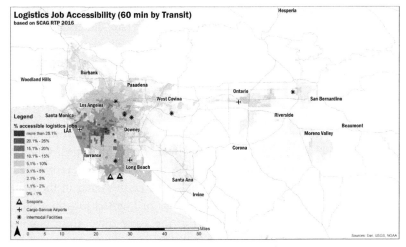

Figure 9.19 Logistics job accessibility within 60 minutes by transit.

residence locations. We use the 12 logistics job clusters identified in Fig. 9.3 as job clusters and calculate number of workers available in 30, 45, and 60 minutes. We also use the adjusted potential worker counts (as noted earlier) to make statistics comparable. Results are in Table 9.11.

Again, the difference between car and transit access is large. Within 60 minutes, 55.9% of all existing workers can be reached by car from logistics job clusters, whereas just 4.6% can be reached by transit. Compared to that, potential worker accessibility is very similar (55.1%) by car and is very slightly greater by transit (5.4%).

Table 9.11 Comparison of existing and potential worker accessibility by mode by travel time.

| | To existing workers | | To adjusted potential workers | |
Travel time	By car	By transit	By car	By transit
30 min	64,099 (22.5%)	558 (0.2%)	63,653 (22.3%)	729 (0.3%)
45 min	113,181 (39.7%)	4061 (1.4%)	111,389 (39.1%)	5074 (1.8%)
60 min	159,178 (55.9%)	13,048 (4.6%)	156,803 (55.1%)	15,357 (5.4%)

Conclusion and interpretation

Our analysis indicates that logistics jobs are more clustered than the locations of existing workers in the industry. As with population and employment distributions more generally, employment is more spatially concentrated than population. Six of the top ten job clusters are located in the southern portion of Los Angeles County, with the remaining four split between the counties of Orange, Riverside, and San Bernardino. Workers are dispersed across the region in small clusters that sometimes overlap with job clusters. In contrast, some small clusters of workers in peripheral areas are far removed from the major centers of employment. Whether or not workers live relatively close to job opportunities, those who must rely on public transit may face accessibility barriers due to sparse or infrequent public transit options.

We used peak morning travel times to measure access from all 3999 TAZs to the 399 TAZs that correspond with top job clusters. Our findings indicate that transportation access is extraordinarily different between car and transit users. By car, averaging across all census tracts in the region, travelers can reach 16.5%, 31.9%, and 48.4% of logistics jobs in a 30, 45, and 60 minute window, respectively. For the same travel time windows, and averaging across all census tracts in the region, transit users can reach 0.2%, 1.0%, and 3.3% of logistics jobs. Areas with strong transit accessibility to logistics jobs are areas where job clusters and worker clusters already overlap. Modal mismatch appears strong for both existing and potential workers, with potential workers able to access 3−4 percentage points fewer jobs by automobile and negligible numbers of jobs by transit. As a result, it appears that transit infrastructure may pose a barrier for individuals seeking logistics jobs that are located far from home or outside of the central core of the region, where transit service is most available. However, we do not find strong evidence that potential workers face distinct transit barriers as compared to the current workforce.

There are a number of policy strategies that can help bridge the spatial gap between workers reliant on transit and jobs in the logistics industry. Workforce housing strategies (e.g., SB 540, 2017) have become more popular as a response to the housing crisis in California. These initiatives can carry the cobenefit of locating workers' residences near job locations. If local planning agencies and developers can work together to build housing for workers located closer to key employment clusters, they can reduce the spatial mismatch. Although workforce housing strategies may help eliminate mismatch, these strategies often face considerable political, economic, and temporal obstacles.

Transit accessibility may help connect potential workers with jobs, but it does not appear to be a likely causal factor in the composition of the logistics industry workforce. When clustered by density or by count, existing and potential workers have very similar ability to reach logistics jobs by a given mode of transportation. Transit may well be a barrier some workers face to entry and retention, which calls for more research at a detailed level to determine the extent of those barriers. Industrial psychologists and human resource specialists could gather data on employee retention in the logistics sector to gain a richer understanding about how long workers stay with a given company and the reasons they choose to stay or resign. Meanwhile, leaders in public transportation can use the findings in this research to explore new options in lower density regions where conventional fixed-route transit is not the answer. In this era of digital connectivity, platform-based carpooling, carsharing, or vanpool models may provide better access to workplaces located on urban fringes for workers who do not have access to personal vehicles. Vanpools could become more flexible with respect to schedule and route. And just as vanpools may find new relevance in the modern digital mobility era so too may carpooling. Considering the popularity of services like Uber and Lyft, it seems more than possible that new digital platform-based carpool software applications could help logistics workers find new ways to get to and from work.

Lastly, it should be noted that our preliminary analysis identifies women as among the most highly underrepresented groups in the industry. In order to both diversify the workforce and identify a large population that can support the industry as large numbers of workers reach retirement age, the industry may want to determine how to include female workers in a systematic way. Whether this is an issue of transportation access, barriers to entry, or barriers to retention, forward-thinking and visionary leadership would recognize the current historic political moment as an opportunity to bring more women into the workforce. The logistics industry can simultaneously choose to affirm the resurgent movement for women's rights, diversify the workforce, and also build resilience and stability as the industry grows in the coming decades.

References

[1] J.D. Lara, Inland Shift: Race, Space, and Capital in Southern California, University of California Press, Oakland, 2018.

[2] J. Kain, Housing segregation, Negro employment, and metropolitan decentralization, Quart. J. Econom. 82 (1968) 175−197.

[3] J. Mooney, Housing segregation, Negro employment, and metropolitan decentralization: an alternative perspective, Quart. J. Econom. 83 (1969) 299−311.

[4] P. Hutchinson, The effects of accessibility and segregation on the employment of the urban poor, in: G. Von Furstenburg, B. Harrison, A. Horowitz (Eds.), Patterns of Racial Discrimination, vol. 1, Lexington Books, Lexington, MA, 1974.

[5] S. Danziger, M. Weinstein, Employment location and wage rates of poverty area residents, J. Urban Econom. 3 (1976) 127−145.

[6] J. Vrooman, S. Greenfield, Are blacks making it in the suburbs? Some new evidence on intrametropolitan spatial segmentation, J. Urban Econom. 7 (1980) 155−167.

[7] K. Ihlanfeldt, D. Sjoquist, Job accessibility and racial differences in youth employment rates, Am. Econom. Rev. 80 (1990) 267−276.

[8] P. Offner, D. Saks, A note on John Kain's Housing segregation, Negro employment, and metropolitan decentralization, Quarter. J. Econom. 85 (1971) 147−160.

[9] J. Leonard, Space, time, and unemployment, Unpublished manuscript, University of California, Berkeley, 1985.

[10] H. Holzer, The spatial mismatch hypothesis: what has the evidence shown? Urban Stud. 28 (1) (1991) 105−122.

[11] Y. Fan, The planners' war against spatial mismatch: lessons learned and way forward, J. Plan. Literat. 27 (2) (2012) 153−169.

[12] S. McLaffery, Spatial mismatch, Int. Encycl. Social Behavior. Sci. 23 (2) (2015) 157−160.

[13] J. Lau, Spatial mismatch and the affordability of public transport for the poor in Singapore's new towns, Cities 28 (2011) 230−237.

[14] B. McKenzie, R. Melani Rapino. Commuting in the United States: 2009, American Community Survey Reports. United States Census Bureau, Washington, DC. <https://www.census.gov/prod/2011pubs/acs-15.pdf>, 2011.

[15] J. Grengs, Job accessibility and the modal mismatch in Detroit, J. Transport. Geogr. 18 (1) (2010) 42−54.

[16] D.B. Hess, Access to employment for adults in poverty in the Buffalo-Niagara region, Urban Stud. 42 (7) (2005) 1177−1200.

[17] M. Kawabata, Job access and employment among low-skilled autoless workers in U. S. metropolitan areas, Environ. Plan. A 35 (9) (2003) 1651−1668.

[18] E. Blumenberg, En-gendering effective planning: spatial mismatch, low-income women, and transportation policy J. Am. Plann. Assoc. 70 (3), 269−281.

[19] M. Boarnet, G. Giuliano, Y. Hou, E.J. Shin, First/last mile transit access as an equity planning issue, Transport. Res. A Policy Pract 2017, 103.

[20] FAA (Federal Aviation Administration), 2017. Passenger Boarding and All-Cargo Data for U.S. Airports. Accessible at. http://www.faa.gov/airports/planning_capacity/passenger_allcargo_stats/passenger/.

[21] C. Cooper, S. Sedgwick, S. Mitra. Goods on the move! Trade and logistics in Southern California. LAEDC, JP Morgan Chase. <https://laedc.org/wp-content/uploads/2017/06/TL_20170515_Final.pdf>, 2017 (accessed 15.03.18).

[22] Goods movement & transportation cluster workforce analysis: labor market and gap analysis. Pacific Gateway Workforce, ICF International. <http://www.pacific-gateway.org/pacific%20gateway%20task2%20report_final.pdf>, 2013 (accessed 24.03.18).

[23] J. Dimon, M. Barnes. New skills at work: strengthening Los Angeles. JP Morgan Chase. <http://www.laocrc.org/media/page/57/JP%20Morgan%20LA%20GapAnalysis.pdf>, 2015 (accessed 24.03.18).

[24] Job needs and priorities report, Phase 2; Southwest Region, Southwest Transportation Workforce Center. <https://www.swtwc.org/wp-content/uploads/2016/06/FHWA_Job-Needs-Phase-2-Report-_Southwest.pdf>, 2016 (accessed 27.03.18).

CHAPTER TEN

Preparing the public transportation workforce for the new mobility world

Xinge Wang
Transportation Learning Center, Silver Spring, MD, United States

Contents

Introduction

In their 2004 book, Levy and Murnane asserted that human drivers could not be easily replaced with machines because "executing a left turn against oncoming traffic involves so many factors that it is hard to imagine discovering the set of rules that can replicate a driver's behavior" [1]. Today, the debate continues to be intense about the speed of business adoption and the exact impact of automation on the global workforce. But driverless vehicles are becoming an inevitable reality, and the development and testing of other automation technologies have been increasingly fast moving, particularly in the last 5 years.

Empowering the New Mobility Workforce.
DOI: https://doi.org/10.1016/B978-0-12-816088-6.00010-9

In September 2016, the U.S. Department of Transportation and the National Highway Traffic Safety Administration (NHTSA) published policy guidelines for autonomous vehicles (AVs), touting its potential to not only improve vehicle safety, but also "transform personal mobility and open doors to people and communities" [2].

Just recently, the Federal Transit Administration (FTA) has announced an ambitious roadmap for Strategic Transit Automation Research (STAR) [3]. Between FY 2018 and 2022, FTA will publish notice of funding opportunities for seven demonstration projects to understand the effectiveness of automated buses, consumer acceptance, and their potential workforce impacts. These projects will investigate topics covering a wide spectrum of automation levels (see Fig. 10.1 for list of SAE-defined automation levels):

- Implementing advanced driver assistance systems (ADAS) in transit buses (SAE Automation) (Levels 1−2);
- Low-speed shuttle buses automation (e.g., circulator services, first/last-mile access to transit networks) (Level 4);
- Automation for maintenance and yard operations such as precision movement for fueling, maintenance, bus wash, automated remote parking and recall (Level 4);
- Automated ADA paratransit (Level 5);
- Automated first/last-mile service (Level 5);
- On-demand shared ride service (Level 5); and
- Automated bus rapid transit (BRT) service (Level 4).

For the public transportation industry, these new technological innovations raise many possibilities and many questions. To what degree will automation replace the need for human drivers and even some

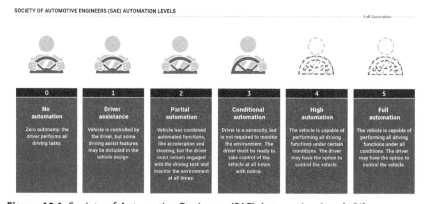

Figure 10.1 Society of Automotive Engineers (SAE) Automation Levels [4].

maintenance workers? Which occupations will be affected the most? What skills will be in demand, and what will become obsolete? What is the social impact for the reshuffling in the labor market, and what can we do to make the transition less disruptive?

The following section aims to synthesize several recent studies and provide additional analysis to quantify what recent technological progress is likely to mean for the future of employment in public transportation. In general, the focus in this section is on the frontline employees, as they represent the majority share of the workforce in public transportation and the potential impact on their employment looms large.

The future of transit operating environment

It is essential to understand the landscape of the future transit operating environment in order to perform a well-grounded analysis of the corresponding workforce trends. Nationally, transit ridership declined 1.3% in 2015 [5] and 2.3% in 2016 [6] according to the American Public Transportation Association (APTA). In 2017, transit ridership fell in 31 of 35 major metropolitan areas in the United States, making 2017 the lowest year of overall transit ridership since 2005 [7]. Bus ridership alone fell 5%. APTA's 2018 report "Understanding Recent Ridership Changes" stated that "The new mobility landscape is bringing new innovations that can have positive impacts on public transit, but elements of this landscape are holding back growth" [8]. In its analysis of factors influencing and causing these ridership declines, TransitCenter cited "[t] he cost of driving, the advent of Transportation Network Companies (TNCs), and other external factors, along with transit fares and service quantity and quality" [9].

At a 2018 summit organized by APTA on the Future of Mobility, many transit leaders defined the priority problem facing transit in the new mobility world as: "How does transit remain relevant in the community?" For other communities where tremendous economic growth is underway, the question becomes: "Can transit grow fast enough to keep up with the expectations and demand for transit?"

Competition from emerging mobility modes

Transit is facing increasing competition from emerging passenger transportation models, most prominently TNCs such as Uber and Lyft. A 2017 report from UC Davis suggested that these ride-hailing services can be complementary to public transportation. However, "the net effect across the entire population is an overall reduction in public transit use and a shift towards lower occupancy vehicles," as they "attract passengers away from public transportation, biking, and walking" [10].

This has manifested in the experience of many cities. For example, the New York Economic Development Corporation (NYCEDC) assessed in its recent report "Transportation Trends" that the recent ridership drop in bus and subway is "fueled in part by apps-based services" [11]. "Uber, Lyft, Via, Juno, and Gett provided roughly 93 million trips in 2016, up from 41 million in 2015," the report observed. Meanwhile, public transit ridership continued to fall. According to the report, "Subway and bus ridership fell by 5.6 percent from March 2017" to March 2018 [11]. Deterioration of the transit system, from years of insufficient funding and backlog of maintenance work, only drives more passengers to app-based services.

Shift of public transportation service delivery

Some transit agencies are venturing into the realm of "microtransit" and exploring options to satisfy the diverse transportation needs and fit into people's lifestyles. For example, the Sacramento Regional Transit District (SacRT) recently received $12 million from the Sacramento Transportation Authority to begin shuttling people between residential and commercial places where transit options are scarce [12] (Fig. 10.2). This option will connect people to the Fulsom business district and the nearby train station, a major transit hub for the rest of the region. Other cities that are moving in this direction of operating flexible route, on-demand microtransit include Washington, Los Angeles, and Detroit [13]. These new services provide residents with better connections to fixed transit, and officials are hoping they will help boost transit ridership.

Agencies are also building partnerships of new mobility models with health care industry and community organizations, assisted by the use of app-based technology. An example is PennDOT's paratransit scheduling and dispatching app FindMyRidePA covering multiple PA counties [14]. FindMyRidePA allows individuals to identify transportation options and book a ride through the FindMyRidePA website. Currently, the transportation services available through FindMyRidePA are limited to local public transportation options but will be expanded overtime to include commercial services (e.g., taxi, train, private bus carriers) and other non-profit transportation services [15].

Figure 10.2 Sacramento Regional Transit (SacRT) SmaRT Ride shuttle. *Reproduced with permission from Business Wire.*

Deployment of new technologies within transit

New and innovative technologies are being tested and implemented in various aspects of transit operations and maintenance. And many can have a potential effect on the workforce.

Autonomous or driverless vehicles, which can be seen as a specific application of artificial intelligence (AI), is the buzzword that is not only seeping into everyday conversations but also playing a potentially larger role in the operations of transit vehicles. Contactless fare systems and transit planning apps that are integrated with TNC interfaces and other transportation modes are used to help riders navigate the system more efficiently. At the same time, public transportation agencies are adopting various new tools for the maintenance of the equipment. Some examples include: the emerging predictive maintenance (as opposed to corrective or preventive maintenance), which uses connected sensors and devices to track the live status of equipment and predict failures in the future; automation and use of robotics in maintenance tasks; use of 3D printing for parts; use of drones for track maintenance; and the federally mandated Positive Train Control (PTC) technology on commuter railroads.

Driverless buses and shuttles

In the United States, automated buses and shuttles are already operating in selected communities [16]. For example, the Regional Transportation Commission of Southern Nevada (RTC) partnered with the French company Navya to provide driverless shuttle service in Las Vegas. However, within hours of hitting the road, a truck collided with the Navya shuttle. Small-scale pilots are also taking place in Minneapolis, Denver, Gainsville, and San Ramon. The technology still need to be fully tested in the larger market and allowed to mature before wider deployment.

Automation in rail transportation

Unlike Europe or Asia, driverless trains or unattended train operation (UTO) are not common in the United States, except for trains connecting airport terminals. However, automation in passenger rail has occurred in several other ways. According to the Federal Railroad Administration, automated systems are currently used for "dispatching, meet and pass trip planning, locomotive fuel trip time optimization, and signaling and train control" [17]. Trains are equipped with sensors and intelligent information systems to provide operating employees in the locomotive cabs with data for real-time situational awareness. PTC is statutorily mandated by Congress for implementation on commuter railroads to prevent train accidents by automatically controlling train speeds and movement if a train operator fails to take appropriate action.

In addition, railroads use automated equipment and track inspections technologies to augment manual inspection methods. The most prominent application is the use of drones or Unmanned Aerial Systems (UAS). In 2017, Denver RTD's rail system started using drones for their State of Good Repair (SGR) reporting [18]. The agency's two FAA-certified pilots who were allowed to fly drones inspected the rail corridors, producing high-definition photography and videos from above. This substituted earlier practice of rail inspectors walking the rails, in a flagged work zone, to check light rail alignment. Other rail agencies have also experimented with drones for other functions. For example, the Santa Clara Valley Transportation Authority (VTA) began employing drones to assist contractors working on the Bay Area Rapid Transit Silicon Valley Berryessa Extension projects [19].

Although challenges such as lagged regulations and legal concerns still exist, automation in rail transportation has picked up such momentum that in March 2018 the Federal Railroad Administration (FRA) issued a Request for Information (RFI) seeking to "understand the current stage and development of automated railroad operations and how the agency can best position itself to support the integration and implementation of new automation technologies to increase the safety, reliability, and the capacity of the nation's railroad system" [17]. This request covers varying levels of automation that already are, or could potentially be, implemented in the railroad industry, including future implementation of fully automated rail operations.

FRA specifically pointed out its interest in comment and data in response to Workforce Viability. The three questions posed by FRA are very relevant to the analysis in this chapter:

1. What is the potential impact of the adoption of these technologies on the existing railroad industry workforce?

2. Would the continued implementation of these technologies, including fully autonomous rail vehicles, create new jobs and/or eliminate the need for existing jobs in the railroad industry?

3. What railroad employee training needs would likely result from the adoption of these technologies? For example, if the technology fails en route, will an onboard employee be trained to take over operation of the vehicle manually or be required to repair the technology en route?

Impact of automation on workforce—data perspective

Current employment and Bureau of Labor Statistics projections

According to the 2017 APTA Fact Book, the public transportation industry had 433,000 total employees in 2015 [20]. The majority of these employees work on the frontline of the public transportation systems, operating and maintaining bus and rail vehicles. We will examine projected employment growth by looking at a few occupations defined under the Standard Occupational Classification (SOC) system that are closely aligned with transit frontline jobs—Bus Drivers, Transit and Intercity (SOC 53—3021) and Bus and Truck Mechanics and Diesel Engine Specialists (SOC 49—3031). According to Bureau of Labor Statistics (BLS), there will be a total of 240,000 job openings for Bus Drivers, Transit and Intercity and 282,000 for Bus and Truck Mechanics and Diesel Engine Specialists between 2016 and 2026 [21]. Their net employment growth rates (9.2% and 9.4%) are both higher than the average of all occupations in the economy (7.4%) [21]. Bus Drivers, Transit, and Intercity also demonstrate a higher occupational separation rate than many other occupations (11.9 vs 10.9 on average), largely due to the high labor force exits, a measure for the projected number of workers leaving an occupation and exiting the labor force entirely (e.g., due to older ages as workers retire) [21]. This comes as no surprise given the demographics of these workers. In 2018, the median age of bus drivers (transit and school combined) was 53.2, significantly higher than all US employed persons at 42.2 [22]. In fact, the public transportation industry is experiencing a silver tsunami overall. In 2018, 41 percent of the workers in the Bus Services and Urban Transit industry are 55 years or older. The 2018 median age of this workforce is 50.8, compared to 44.7 of the transportation and warehousing industry [23].

What are we to make of these projections in the context of the AVs and other automation enabling technologies for transit service provision? First of all, BLS employment projections are based on historical staffing patterns. Secondly, they generally consider changes in normal technological progress, and not on any breakthrough technologies that may be speculative [24]. When we examine the factors that affect occupational utilization in BLS's employment projections, none of the key occupations in public transportation are listed as being affected by technological innovations, or experiencing capital/labor substitutions or demand changes [25]. This may not indicate that researchers never considered the effect of these factors. A more likely scenario is that, after careful evaluation of the circumstances, researchers determined that this effect may not materialize in the current projection cycle (2016−26), as a lot of the new technologies under discussion are only in the early stages of development. That can be an important insight in itself.

BLS's analysis of two occupations related to public transportation provides a preview of how new technology may affect occupational utilization (Table 10.1). In the case of First-Line Supervisors of Transportation and Material-Moving Machine and Vehicle Operators, labor demand decreases as "establishments adopt automated guided vehicles, resulting in fewer machine and vehicle operators, and, in turn, fewer supervisors." It is worth noting that although Bus Drivers are not cited as being affected by automated guided vehicles, Industrial Truck and Tractor Operators are. It is possible that BLS deemed the projected labor demand decrease of the Front-Line Supervisors during the 2016−26 timeframe as stemming primarily from the warehousing and storage industry, rather than public transportation.

Table 10.1 Factors affecting occupational utilization, projected 2016–26 [26].

Occupation title	Occupation code	Industry title	Industry code	Factors affecting occupational utilization
First-Line Supervisors of Transportation and Material-Moving Machine and Vehicle Operators	53–1031	Warehousing and storage	493000	Demand change—share decreases as establishments adopt automated guided vehicles, resulting in fewer machine and vehicle operators, and, in turn, fewer supervisors
Locomotive Firers	53–4012	Rail transportation	482000	Capital/labor substitution—share decreases as the tasks of watching for rights-of-way, train signals, and looking out for obstructions will be automatically handled by Positive Train Control (PTC)

The BLS 10-year projection suggesting fairly large replacement needs for bus drivers is corroborated by current anecdotal evidence from the industry. According to recent reports, there is an industry-wide driver shortage, forcing transit agencies to work overtime to recruit more bus drivers [27]. To give a few examples, "King County Metro in Seattle, Washington, needs about 100 more people to make up their operator gap. Ray Greaves, the New Jersey State ATU chair, believes New Jersey transit needs at least 200 more bus operators across the state" [27]. As of December 2017, Denver RTD was short 127 bus drivers [27]. Other large agencies like L.A. County Metro are also scrambling to fill staffing gaps. This driver shortage has contributed to some agencies straining services. For example, Toledo, Gainesville, and Louisville have all experienced service cuts or delayed arrival times in recent years due to operator vacancies. Expansion of bus services in certain cities is putting pressure on driver recruitment. However, there are a myriad of factors in the industry's struggle to retain its current drivers and attract new ones—aging of the workforce (see BLS driver age data cited earlier), and high turnover due to undesirable working conditions, health and safety concerns, stress dealing with schedules and customers, and wages that have barely kept up with the rate of inflation.

Analyses beyond Bureau of Labor Statistics

The scope and timeframe of BLS data present limitations for a detailed analysis of the long-term impact of technologies on the key frontline jobs in public transportation. Findings from three recent research reports are examined next to gain additional insights on the subject. Many of these analyses emphasize the potential effect of AVs on the employment of drivers. However, they help shed light on other related occupations that can potentially be affected by other types of automation.

Oxford University study

In their 2013 working paper [24], Oxford University researchers Frey and Osborne examined how susceptible jobs are to computerization, including AVs. Their model predicted that computer capital would mainly substitute for low-skill and low-wage jobs in the near future, whereas high-skill and high-wage occupations are the least susceptible to computerization.

The table below displays the authors' rankings of occupations according to their probability of computerization (from least- to most-computerizable) (Table 10.2). We extracted data for a selection of occupations that are closely related to transit and railroading. This data indicates a high probability of computerization for many frontline occupations, from bus and rail operations and maintenance, to track laying and dispatching. Of the 702 occupations listed, most of these frontline occupations fall in the half that are more computerizable. The authors, however, did not provide a projected timeline for the realization of such computerization or the number of jobs likely affected.

Table 10.2 Computerization—occupations related to public transportation [24]. Computerizable

Rank	Probability	SOC code	Occupation
105.	0.029	53−1031	First-line supervisors of transportation and material-moving machine and vehicle operators
184.	0.13	19−3051	Urban and regional planners
256.	0.37	53−7061	Cleaners of vehicles and equipment
322.	0.57	33−3052	Transit and railroad police
328.	0.59	11−3071	Transportation, storage, and distribution managers
338.	0.61	43−4181	Reservation and transportation ticket agents and travel clerks
372.	0.67	53−3021	Bus drivers, transit, and intercity
404.	0.73	49−3031	Bus and truck mechanics and diesel engine specialists
412.	0.75	53−6061	Transportation attendants, except flight attendants
458.	0.83	53−4021	Railroad brake, signal, and switch operators
459.	0.83	53−4031	Railroad conductors and yardmasters
494.	0.86	53−4041	Subway and streetcar operators
521.	0.88	49−3043	Rail car repairers
528.	0.89	47−4061	Rail-track laying and maintenance equipment operators
538.	0.9	53−6051	Transportation inspectors
553.	0.91	53−4013	Rail yard engineers, dinkey operators, and hostlers
554.	0.91	49−2093	Electrical and electronics installers and repairers, transportation equipment
627.	0.96	43−5032	Dispatchers, except police, fire, and ambulance
638.	0.96	53−4011	Locomotive engineers

Department of Commerce study on the workforce impact of autonomous vehicles

The U.S. Department of Commerce 2017 report is the one of the first to quantify the potential impact on labor demand from the introduction of AVs [28]. It identified 15.5 million U.S. workers (2015 employment) in occupations that could be affected (to varying degrees) by the introduction of AVs—about one in nine workers. These occupations were divided into "motor vehicle operators," for which driving vehicles to transport passengers or goods is a primary activity, and "other on-the-job drivers," who use roadway motor vehicles to deliver services or to travel to work sites. The 3.8 million or so motor vehicle operators were predominately male, older, less educated, and compensated less than the typical worker. Motor vehicle operator jobs are most concentrated in the transportation and warehousing sector. Transit and intercity bus drivers take up 4.4% of the share.

An important conclusion by the authors is that motor vehicle operators may have less of a knowledge and skills base that could be transferable to other jobs, such as complex problem-solving, social, content, and systems knowledge (Fig. 10.3). On the other hand, "other-on-the-job drivers" may be more likely to benefit from greater productivity and better working conditions offered by AVs because their knowledge and skills are

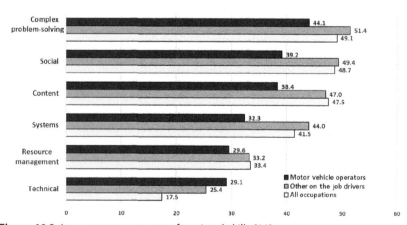

Figure 10.3 Important scores: cross-functional skills [28].
The chart above shows that motor vehicle operators have higher knowledge importance scores for only a couple of categories compared to all occupations, and, except for technical skills, substantially lower cross-functional skill importance scores than all occupations. In contrast, other-on-the-job drivers have higher knowledge and skills importance scores in many categories compared with motor vehicle operators.

more similar to other occupations in the economy and less specialized in transportation knowledge than motor vehicle operators.

Securing America's Future Energy analysis of autonomous vehicles impact on workforce

Commissioned by Securing America's Future Energy (SAFE), a series of recent reports looked at precedents in history for adoption of transformative technologies, their implications about AVs' impact on society and the economy, and the medium- to long-term impact of vehicle automation on the workforce, among other themes [29].

The reports predict that deployment of AVs will result in an estimated $800 billion in economic benefits annually by 2050. The benefits will come from cost savings related to public benefits including congestion mitigation, accident reduction, reduced oil consumption, and consumer benefits from value of time and reduction in cost of taxi service. These estimated benefits, however, do not factor in the potential unintended effect of AVs putting more cars on the road and increasing congestion.

The reports indicate that "the labor market is very good at reabsorbing small numbers of displaced workers—it is when many workers are displaced in a short time that large-scale unemployment emerges as a possibility" [30]. Therefore, the pace of AV adoption and worker displacement is deemed more important than the total number of workers displaced. The commercial sector, including public transportation, is likely to experience more concentrated adoption during a certain period than privately owned vehicles. The authors depict two scenarios to represent two different timelines for AV adoption in trucking, and the ensuing models are applied to a myriad of related occupations, including bus drivers:

- Slow: where trucking takes about 30 years adapting to driver-assisted AV before proceeding to fully AVs that do not need drivers.
- Fast: where trucking AV technologies gain adoption on a more accelerated timeline, possibly as much as a decade in advance of the "slow" scenario.

The authors consulted industry experts and estimated that the share of positions in Bus Driver, Transit and Intercity that will be eliminated is 0.7−0.75 (with actual employment level in 2016 as 1) under the scenarios of slow to fast adoption of AV, respectively. These shares of potential displacement are among the highest of all the related occupations the authors examined. The authors then multiplied these shares by the 2016 employment in this occupation (75,000 according to the American Community

Survey from which the authors extracted data). The potential layoffs associated with slow or fast adoption is 53,000 to 56,000, respectively.

The 75,000-baseline employment represents a somewhat conservative estimate of the number workers in this occupation. The Occupational Employment Statistics (OES) survey from the BLS puts the 2016 employment at 169,680 [31]. Using this as the baseline and following the authors' methodology, we estimate that between 118,776 and 127,260 bus drivers may potentially be displaced due to AV adoption, in the slow (roughly 30 years) and fast (as fast as 20 years) scenarios, respectively.

Job displacement, creation, and skills training

As these selected analyses demonstrate, automation can result in significant benefits in terms of increased productivity, improved safety, and convenience of lives. However, they can also substitute existing work activities we currently carry out [32]. Generally, fewer jobs are needed to make a certain amount of product or services with the adoption of automation [30]. Workers with low skills and low wages tend to be affected more by technological substitution of labor, and the transferability of their existing skills is also more limited. Widespread technological unemployment is cited by John Maynard Keynes as stemming from "our discovery of means of economizing the use of labor outrunning the pace at which we can find new uses for labor" [33].

According to the SAFE reports, though, there is significant time before the impacts of AVs on employment are fully realized, and the overall effect on national employment will be relatively small: "Simulations of the impact of AVs on employment showed a range of impacts that would be felt starting in the early 2030s but would only increase the national unemployment rate by 0.06−0.13 percentage points at peak impact sometime between 2045 and 2050 before a return to full employment" [29].

Undoubtedly, automation, including AVs, will also create new jobs that will, in time, replace jobs that are eliminated. More transportation services will be consumed as personal mobility becomes more affordable and convenient, especially for populations with accessibility needs. In the world of public transportation, cyber security specialists will be in great demand to keep sophisticated automated control systems safe from malicious cyberattacks. And data analysts and scientists will be highly sought after during the transition from corrective, preventive maintenance to predictive maintenance. Other jobs will experience task modifications. For transit mechanics, troubleshooting using a laptop connected to the vehicle and deciphering fault codes has become an essential part of the job, as they continue to acquire new skills associated with the automation or computerization of other tasks. As industry adoption of AVs starts to increase, transit agencies will need qualified individuals capable of managing, monitoring, and maintaining automated buses. Also, customer service may become an expanded role in public transportation, as transit agencies direct their focus on personalized, user-friendly experience and community engagement.

Technological innovations are not new. Literature is abundant with examples of previous disruptive changes and their labor market impacts, such as the industrial revolution in England, autopilot in aviation, and Computer Numerical Control (CNC) in machine tools, to name a few [30,32]. In the early 20th century, the growth of the auto industry eliminated many jobs in the carriage industry and railways, but created ten times more new jobs in automobile manufacturing and trucking [32].

In the end, human labor has only prevailed because of its ability to adopt and acquire new skills through education [30,34]. There is general consensus among researchers that strong workforce development infrastructure needs to be in place to mitigate employment disruption and speed the evolution of worker skill requirements that will contribute to full employment and economic growth [24,30,35]. The economic and societal benefits of AVs are sufficiently large to enable investment of adequate resources in assisting impacted workers [30]. But an intentional effort needs to be made to redirect these resources for this important purpose.

An effective system for worker education requires the investment of both the industry and the government. However, when it comes to investment in workforce training, the U.S. public transportation industry has lagged in general. A Transit Cooperative Research Program quick study report documented the level of investment going into worker training at public transportation agencies [36]. The average across the US transit industry was an equivalent of between 0.66% and 0.88% of payroll. By contrast, the Federal Highway Administration had a target of 3% of payroll for training on its projects. The Paris Metro spent more than 8% of payroll on training.

Labor implications

Public transportation is heavily unionized, with close to 95% of transit operating and maintenance employees belonging to unions [37]. The majority of them today are represented by three major unions:

- The Amalgamated Transit Union (ATU) is the largest labor organization representing transit workers in the United States and Canada, with over 190,000 members in 213 U.S. locales and 39 Canadian locales [38].
- Transport Workers Union of America (TWU) represents nearly 140,000 members across the airline; railroad; transit, universities, utilities, and services; and gaming sectors [39].
- The International Association of Sheet Metal, Air, Rail and Transportation Workers (SMART) was formed by the merger of United Transportation Union (UTU), a broad-based, transportation labor union and the Sheet Metal Workers' International Association [40].

As with any workplace changes that could potentially affect the job security and well-being of their members, labor unions have and will continue to voice concerns with the impending wave of technological changes. According to the Eno Foundation of Transportation, on the considerations to implementing automation technologies, "workforce resistance stands out in particular, as labor unions could mount opposition to agencies procuring automated buses if there are concerns of worker displacement" [3]. For example, in 2005 when New York MTA experimented with running a few late-night trains equipped with Communication-Based Train Control (CBTC) without conductors, TWU Local 100, which represent the majority of the MTA's frontline workers, objected, citing safety reasons and job elimination [41].

Many of these concerns are largely warranted. Driverless trains usually operate in systems that have barriers at the platform edge, like the ones in most airport rail systems. In the United States, none of the metropolitan rail systems have platform edge doors [42] and the track beds are completely open. This lack is exacerbated by some platforms, such as NY MTA, which slope subtly toward the tracks, so that water flows off. This gentle slope is known to cause strollers and wheelchairs to roll off, not to mention the intoxicated or the disoriented [41]. There are also threats of terrorist attacks, which necessitate the presence of transit employees trained in emergency preparedness and response. As many leaders from transit management and labor agree, long and heavy trains that carry lots of passengers are simply not capable of traveling safely through complicated terrains, some of which include street-level crossings, without any crew member on board [41]. Even with sophisticated technologies such as CBTC and PTC, operator intervention may be needed as extensive trials in several cities have shown that these technologies are not fail-proof (for example, stopping the train a few feet from the precise spot).

Similarly, current drawbacks in driverless buses also mean that frontline bus employees are needed in the driver's seat at least for some extended period of time [16]. One FTA official suggested that the potential impact on bus drivers is "pretty unclear as of yet," and that even a self-driving bus may need an operator on board for fare collection, rider safety, and customer service [3]. In the near term, it is almost certain that bus agencies would not choose to send an expensive vehicle on the road with no employee present to deal with incidents and emergencies. Also, passengers may not readily accept the notion of riding in unattended buses with total strangers.

Consider the history of employment on transit vehicles. It used to be that both a conductor and an operator were on all trolleys, streetcars, and buses. The conductor's job involved a lot of tasks, including passenger safety, but from the perspective of the private owners of the vehicle, the conductor's primary function involved collecting fares. The advent of the fare box eliminated that job. If technology moves in the direction of eliminating or at least lessening the role of the operator, reviving the role of the conductor could help ease displacement among drivers while improving passenger safety and service. It should be noted that in the full range of AV bus technology, full implementation of Level 5 autonomy does not seem to be realistic in the short term. With Level 3 or even Level 4 implementation, someone with the skills and ability to drive the vehicle needs to be on board. If that person doesn't need to drive for the majority of the time, the focus of the job can be on serving customers. That really is the primary and most difficult part of an operator's job now. With increased competition from TNCs, customer service can be a critical competitive advantage for public transit agencies. The modern conductor can assist Americans with Disabilities Act passengers more effectively than the driver currently can, and they can help tourists find their way around the transit system and the general area. As with railroad conductors and airline flight attendants, the first job priority needs to be guaranteeing customer safety. As with maintenance occupations, this modern conductor will need significant and ongoing training. A modern, highly skilled conductor can be the public face of the agency.

Even if the industry embraces the transition in operator roles, however, some worry that turning vehicle operators into customer service agents "would turn a trend to reduce the need for labor into a scheme to further de-skill workers, replacing relatively well-trained and paid bus drivers with low-wage customer service or security workers" [16].

For many transportation unions, another key issue is who gets to perform the new jobs or tasks created by automation. For example, railroad unions are concerned about independent contractors who are hired instead of union members to control the drones that inspect tracks for problems, download the reports, and analyze the data for follow-up. One way some unions are trying to get ahead of the wave is to equip their members with the knowledge and skills to prepare for the new technologies, through training programs such as a union or joint apprenticeship.

Ultimately, unions are voicing concerns the represented transit workers are troubled by—that jobs will be replaced by machines sooner or later and that no safety net will be in place to catch those that are negatively affected.

As Armstrong and Sotala stated in "How We're Predicting AI—or Failing to," making predictions about technological progress is notoriously difficult [43]. Projecting its impact on jobs is even more so. It is true that the projections cited here are only based on current simulations and expert estimates and come with a lot of assumptions that may not materialize. For example, the speed of adoption may be slowed by regulation or other factors. However, there is an increasing volume of literature and analysis corroborating the high probability of driver displacement in the next 20−30 years.

If AV alone has the potential of displacing an estimated 53,000 (low end estimate by Groshen et al.) to more than 127,000 (high-end estimate using OES 2016 employment as the baseline) transit and intercity bus drivers in 20−30 years, the total effect of all automation in mobile transit and fixed transit workplaces is likely much larger. For the overall economy, this may represent a relatively small number of workers. But in an industry with a total of 400,000 employees, the impact can reverberate, especially considering the pattern of commercial adoption where entire fleets may be replaced within a short period of time. While the debate is still ongoing as to the exact timeline and quantitative impact, it is important not to lose sight of the big picture trends and stay proactive. It takes years, if not decades, for the paradigm shifts in the industry and government workforce policies to happen, for training investment to reach an adequate level, and for a robust workforce development system to be established for the future of the new mobility workforce.

As Groshen et al. rightly state, "Technology is not deterministic of any particular outcomes, and examples are abundant of how the same technology can be implemented in very different ways with very different consequences, certainly for jobs and skills" [30]. In conversations with transit industry professionals, many remain cautiously optimistic that the benefits of automation can outweigh the costs if it is implemented in a responsible fashion. Stakeholder engagement is key in this equation. Groshen et al. suggest that worker voice is an important factor in job creation and mitigation of income losses:

> *Institutions and regulations that surface workers' voices to facilitate the sharing of productivity gains and preserve the value of employees' human capital may be lacking. When displaced workers have no voice in allocating productivity gains or in reorganizing work, insufficient resources may be directed toward retraining or other assistance they need to smooth their adjustment. Workers can have a voice through unionization, employer practices, and the political system. Without this voice, wages are more likely to remain depressed as the laid-off workers crowd into and compete for the few jobs available for workers like them. In addition, the new jobs created will be less likely to be 'good jobs,' that offer high wages, stability, a chance for advancement, etc. [30].*

While some of the previous major transformations in the United States have occurred without coordinated engagement of stakeholders to mitigate damage to those left behind [30], we have the opportunity to choose the high road of proactive engagement and collaborative problem-solving.

Recommendations

To help assess the impact of new technology on the future of transportation workforce, mitigate the potential effect of worker displacement in large numbers, and prepare for the new skills demands from emerging technologies, the author makes the following recommendations :

1. The industry needs to dramatically increase overall workforce training and training investment particularly as new technologies are introduced. Increasing training overall is an important objective for transit agencies. Better training will ease adaptation of new technologies.

Better training will address skills gaps that get in the way now of meeting demand for vehicles in service. Better and more frequent training, connected to the everyday working life of current employees, also makes possible career ladder and career transition moves. Training that occurs after job displacement has a poor record of helping workers secure comparable employment. By contrast, there is a rich literature documenting success of career ladder and career lattice programs that help people who are employed move into better jobs.

2. Joint labor—management partnerships have successfully addressed issues around the adoption of new technology. Similarly, public transportation agencies and unions can establish these partnerships to provide assistance to displaced workers, retraining, pre-apprenticeship and apprenticeship programs, and other job placement programs.

3. National, regional, and local stakeholders' forums—involving government, employers, labor unions representing affected workers, educational partners, and communities—can be organized by relevant government agencies, industry associations, labor organizations, nonprofits or research organizations for ongoing discussions of upcoming challenges and opportunities, and strategies for mitigating negative effects.

4. There is a strong need for data to drive policy and regulation in federal oversight of any deployment of AV in transit. Collection of data will inform policy makers and the general public about whether those positive outcomes are achieved. Data can also inform government agencies and the general public about scenarios where AV buses can strengthen public transportation systems and scenarios where use of AV buses by private vendors may cannibalize the most desirable and profitable transit routes, thus undermining the ability of current public providers to maintain viable systems. Data also need to be collected through industry organizations, third-party researchers, or government entities, to track the ongoing impact of AV and other automation technologies on the workforce. As suggested by Groshen et al., BLS may collect the needed data through initiatives such as quick-response surveys of employers [30].

5. The industry can develop national training standards, curriculum, and training programs to be used by multiple transit employers and educational partners, with increased focus on the new technologies. Since public transit agencies generally serve single local markets and do not compete with each other, it is possible to leverage resources from

multiple agencies to develop standardized curricula to assist with the smooth implementation of new technologies, and the upskilling for the career transition of the affected transit employees. Standards-based training development effort has been underway for a decade for various frontline operations and maintenance occupations, led by the Transportation Learning Center, in partnership with the APTA, International unions representing transit workers, public transportation agencies, and local unions.

6. Transit agencies should, individually and collectively, explore new roles within the industry that utilize the industry knowledge and talents of the existing workforce to improve rider experience. Agencies should also make efforts to design new jobs created by AVs to take advantage of the transferable skills that people in the disrupted occupations already have. For example, bus drivers who may be displaced can be upskilled to become dispatchers, control center specialists, or maintenance employees. Many of these labor categories are continuing to experience a shortage of qualified personnel.

7. In addition to technical skills training, focus should also be placed on soft skills such as customer service, interpersonal communications, and problem-solving.

Even with the rise of AI, AV, and other fast-paced technology, interactions between human beings cannot be replaced. Through stakeholder engagement and partnerships, data-driven decision making, and strong policies and investment in skills training and transition assistance, the industry has the opportunity to leverage these technological transformations to upskill workers and boost the overall quality and safety of public transportation services.

References

[1] F. Levy, R.J. Murnane, The New Division of Labor: How Computers Are Creating the Next Job Market, Princeton University Press, 2004.
[2] Federal automated vehicles policy: a voluntary approach to accelerating the next revolution in roadway safety, National Highway Traffic Safety Administration, 2016.
[3] G. Rogers, FTA launches 5-year research initiative for transit automation, The Eno Center for Transportation. <https://www.enotrans.org/article/fta-launches-5-year-research-initiative-transit-automation/>, 2017 (accessed 31.07.18).
[4] Automated vehicles for safety, National Highway Traffic Safety Administration. <https://www.nhtsa.gov/technology-innovation/automated-vehicles-safety> (accessed 03.10.18).
[5] Americans took 10.6 billion trips on public transportation in 2015, American Public Transportation Association. <https://www.apta.com/mediacenter/pressreleases/2016/Pages/160331_Ridership.aspx> (accessed 03.1018).

[6] Public transportation ridership report: fourth quarter 2016, American Public Transportation Association. <https://www.apta.com/resources/statistics/Documents/Ridership/2016-q4-ridership-APTA.pdf> (accessed 03.10.18).

[7] Siddiqui F. Falling transit ridership poses an "emergency" for cities, experts fear, Washington Post. <https://www.washingtonpost.com/local/trafficandcommuting/falling-transit-ridership-poses-an-emergency-for-cities-experts-fear/2018/03/20/ffb67c28-2865-11e8-874b-d517e912f125_story.html>, 2018 (accessed 03.08.18).

[8] Understanding recent ridership changes, American Public Transportation Association, 2018.

[9] Lessons on ridership, from the National Literature, TransitCenter. <http://transitcenter.org/2018/01/29/lessons-on-ridership-from-the-national-literature/>, 2018 (accessed 31.07.18).

[10] R.R. Clewlow, New research on how ride-hailing impact travel behavior, Planetizen. <https://www.planetizen.com/features/95227-new-research-how-ride-hailing-impacts-travel-behavior>, 2017 (accessed 03.03.19).

[11] Transportation trends in NYC, NYCEDC's Blog. <https://www.nycedc.com/blog-entry/transportation-trends-nyc>, 2017 (accessed 03.10.18).

[12] SacRT awarded $12 million to expand SmaRT ride service on-demand—Sacramento Regional Transit District. <http://www.sacrt.com/apps/sacrt-awarded-12-million-to-expand-smart-ride-service-on-demand/>, 2018 (accessed 01.08.18).

[13] Lazo L. For public transit agencies losing riders, microtransit might be an answer. Washington Post. <https://www.washingtonpost.com/local/trafficandcommuting/for-public-transit-agencies-loosing-riders-microtransit-might-be-an-answer/2018/02/03/37771f46-0070-11e8-9d31-d72cf78dbeee_story.html>, 2018 (accessed 04.08.18).

[14] Ecolane. Ecolane and PennDOT complete software implementation across Pennsylvania. <https://www.ecolane.com/news/ecolane-and-penndot-complete-software-implementation-across-pennsylvania>, 2018 (accessed 31.07.18).

[15] What is FindMyRidePA. <http://www.findmyridepa.com/#/about> (accessed 03.10.18).

[16] A. Levy, Flagging down driverless buses, The American Prospect. <http://prospect.org/article/flagging-down-driverless-buses>, 2018 (accessed 31.07.18).

[17] FRA RFI: "Automation in the railroad industry"—railway age, Railway Age. <https://www.railwayage.com/regulatory/fra-rfi-automation-railroad-industry/>, 2018 (accessed 31.07.18).

[18] J. Lotus, RTD drones keep light rail moving. Denver, CO, Patch 2018. <https://patch.com/colorado/denver/rtd-drones-keep-light-rail-moving> (accessed 31.07.18).

[19] D. Niepow, Railroaders contemplate drones to secure tracks, cargo. Progressive Railroading. <https://www.progressiverailroading.com/passenger_rail/article/Railroaders-contemplate-drones-to-secure-tracks-cargo--45836>, 2015 (accessed 31.07.18).

[20] M. Hughes-Cromwick, 2017 Public Transportation Fact Book, American Public Transportation Association, 2018.

[21] Employment projections 2016 to 2026. <https://www.bls.gov/emp/> (accessed 03.10.18).

[22] Employed persons by detailed occupation and age 2018. <https://www.bls.gov/cps/cpsaat11b.htm> (accessed 31.07.18).

[23] Employed persons by detailed industry and age 2018. <https://www.bls.gov/cps/cpsaat18b.htm> (accessed 28.02.19).

[24] C.B. Frey, M.A. Osborne, The future of employment: how susceptible are jobs to computerisation? Technol. Forecast. Soc. Change 114 (2017) 254−280.

[25] Employment projections methodology. <https://www.bls.gov/emp/documentation/projections-methods.htm>, 2018 (accessed 31.07.18).

[26] Factors affecting occupational utilization. <https://www.bls.gov/emp/tables/factors-affecting-occupational-utilization.htm>, 2017 (accessed 31.07.18).

[27] L. Bliss, There is a driver shortage. And no wonder. <https://www.citylab.com/transportation/2018/06/why-wont-anyone-drive-the-bus/563555/>, 2018 (accessed 15.10.18).

[28] D.N. Beede, R. Powers, C. Ingram, The employment impact of autonomous vehicles, SSRN Electr. J. (2017).

[29] America's workforce and the self-driving future—realizing productivity gains and spurring economic growth, Securing America's Future Energy (SAFE), 2018.

[30] E.L. Groshen, S. Helper, J.P. MacDuffie, C. Carson, Preparing U.S. workers and employers for an autonomous vehicle future, Securing America's Future Energy, 2018.

[31] National occupational employment and wage estimates. <https://www.bls.gov/oes/2016/may/oes_nat.htm#53-0000>, May 2016 (accessed 31.07.18).

[32] J. Manyika, S. Lund, M. Chui, J. Bughin, J. Woetzel, P. Batra, et al. Jobs Lost, Jobs Gained: What the Future of Work Will Mean for Jobs, Skills, and Wages, McKinsey Global Institute, 2017.

[33] J.M. Keynes, Economic possibilities for our grandchildren (1930), Essays in Persuasion (1931) 358–373.

[34] C. Burke, C. Goldin, L.F. Katz, The race between education and technology, J. Am. Hist. 96 (2009) 246.

[35] D.M. West, The Future of Work: Robots, AI, and Automation, Brookings Institution Press, 2018.

[36] Transit Cooperative Research Program (TCRP) Project J-11 Task 12 Final Report: Survey of Existing Resources, Practices and Metrics of Workforce Development Programs in the U.S. Transit Industry, Transportation Learning Center, 2010.

[37] H.H. Oestreich, G.L. Whaley, Transit Labor Relations Guide, Mineta Transportation Institute, San Jos é State University, San Jose, CA, Norman Y. Mineta International Institute for Surface Transportation Policy Studies, 2001.

[38] Amalgamated Transit Union—Wikipedia. <https://en.wikipedia.org/wiki/Amalgamated_Transit_Union>, n.d. (accessed 31.07.18).

[39] TWU—Transport Workers Union. <https://www.twu.org>, n.d. (accessed 31.07.18).

[40] International Association of Sheet Metal, Air, Rail and Transportation Workers—Wikipedia. <https://en.wikipedia.org/wiki/International_Association_of_Sheet_Metal,_Air,_Rail_and_Transportation_Workers>, n.d. (accessed 31.07.18).

[41] W. Finnegan, Can Andy Byford save the subways? The New Yorker. <https://www.newyorker.com/magazine/2018/07/09/can-andy-byford-save-the-subways>, 2018 (accessed 31.07.18).

[42] Platform screen doors—Wikipedia. <https://en.wikipedia.org/wiki/Platform_screen_doors#cite_note-37>, n.d. (accessed 31.07.18).

[43] S. Armstrong, K. Sotala, How we're predicting AI − or failing to, Beyond Artificial Intelligence (2015) 11–29.

PART III

The Changing Role of Transportation Providers in the Future Transportation Ecosystem

CHAPTER ELEVEN

LA Metro: changing the mobility game—inspiring and training a new workforce, filling leadership voids, and creating farm teams for the future

Phillip A. Washington[1] and Joanne Peterson[2]
[1]Chief Executive Officer, LA Metro
[2]Chief, Human Capital and Development, LA Metro

Contents

Introduction

In the early 1920s the St. Louis Cardinals "were fighting for their life in the National League." They struggled to obtain "players of merit from the minors" and were outbid by teams with more money [1]. The Cardinals had a serious workforce development problem. In response, Branch Rickey developed the farm system and forever changed the way Major League Baseball cultivated new players. In developing the farm team system, Rickey created a "production line of talent" for the Cardinals [2]. When assessing his accomplishment, Rickey told *The Sporting News*, "I do not feel that the farming system we have established is the result of any inventive genius—it is the result of stark necessity. We did it to meet a question of supply and demand of young ballplayers" [1].

Empowering the New Mobility Workforce.
DOI: https://doi.org/10.1016/B978-0-12-816088-6.00011-0
247

So how does Branch Rickey's farm system relate to a chapter on the transportation workforce and transit providers? The answer is simple. At a time when the mobility workforce is graying, and transformational technologies are deploying at breakneck speeds, leaders at transit agencies around the country are trying to figure out how to build the transportation workforce of the future while competing against other industries who are vying to recruit future professionals of merit. This is what keeps us up at night at the Los Angeles County Metropolitan Transportation Authority (LA Metro).

Leaders at LA Metro know the perfect storm looms on the horizon—a silver tsunami—50% of the transportation industry eligible to retire in the next 10 years [3]. Metro will be losing 42% of our workforce to retirement in the next 5 years; 68.5% of our workforce is over 40 years of age [4]. Even more alarming is that 27% of our workforce could walk out the door today due to retirement. All while we are implementing the largest and most ambitious transportation expansion program in the country.

In November 2016 the voters of Los Angeles County overwhelmingly approved Metro's Measure M transportation sales tax ballot measure. The plan will deliver 40 major transit and highway projects over the next 40 years with funding carved out for other elements like expanding bus and rail operations; local transportation projects in all 88 cities and unincorporated areas in LA County; bike and pedestrian connections; programs for seniors, students, and the disabled; and maintaining a state of good repair to keep our system in good working condition. All of these programs are projected to create 778,000 jobs over the next four decades [5]—but who will fill those jobs?

LA County will continue seeing a growth in population, with 2.3 million people expected to move here over the next 40 years [6]. So, we will have the people, but will they be able to be part of our transportation transformation? Furthermore, do the Millennial and Digital Native Generations see themselves joining the new mobility workforce? The answer is no. Most young people are gravitating toward startups, coding, and IT-focused jobs. Our job is to help them understand that joining the new mobility workforce means quite literally rebuilding the way America moves—one algorithm, semiconductor rail line, and cubic foot of cement at a time.

When we consider helping to build the new mobility workforce in the LA region, we have to consider two important factors: the high cost of living and accessibility to healthcare. Many people, of all ages, are moving farther outside the urban core to places where they can afford the rent or buy a home. Meanwhile, healthcare costs are becoming increasingly burdensome to Angelinos already overwhelmed by housing costs that are among the highest in the nation. At LA Metro, we know that offering great healthcare and other benefits for our union and noncontract staff helps retain employees, but we also know that much more must be done for us to develop and retain a sustainable mobility workforce.

In addition to the brass tacks of income and affordability, the LA Metro team believes that people join our ranks to make a difference. At Metro, we have worked hard to create a culture that allows people to do so. The work we are doing will change the landscape of Southern California, especially if we can reduce traffic congestion and improve mobility in our communities. We are excited to take on these new challenges. Our people see themselves in this movement. In fact, LA Metro employees were a key part of the development of Metro's Strategic Plan: Metro Vision 2028 [7]. This Strategic Plan was the result of a comprehensive and engaging 2-year process with Metro's workforce as a key stakeholder every step of the way. This chapter will draw upon a few initiatives that strive to establish Los Angeles as the Transportation Center of Excellence.

The Transportation Center of Excellence

We talk a lot about how we believe that LA County is positioned to be the Transportation Center of Excellence. Not only we are implementing the largest transportation expansion program in America, but Los Angeles World Airports is also in the midst of a redevelopment of Los Angeles International Airport that includes an Automated People Mover connection to our rail system. Our ports—Los Angeles and Long Beach—are expanding, and Elon Musk's SpaceX, which is based in Hawthorne, is taking space travel to new heights. Musk's The Boring Company is leading the way in revolutionizing underground tunneling to enhance mobility options.

At Metro, we have mapped a "five-point plan" that is contributing to making LA County the Transportation Center of Excellence. Our plan builds upon our strategic plan goals:
- *Implement mobility innovation*
     Goal 1: Provide high-quality mobility options that enable people to spend less time traveling.

- *Capture the hearts and minds of the people*
  Goal 2: Deliver outstanding trip experiences for all users of the transportation system.
- *Embrace equity*
  Goal 3: Enhance communities and lives through mobility and access to opportunity.
- *Step into leadership voids*
  Goal 4: Transform Los Angeles County through regional collaboration and national leadership.
- *Build the industry*
  Goal 5: Provide responsive, accountable, and trustworthy governance within the LA Metro organization.

Point one in our five-point plan focuses on *implementing mobility innovation*. We mentioned earlier that Metro's Measure M is the most ambitious and comprehensive voter-approved transportation program in America, with 40 major transit and highway projects in 40 years. Through our "Twenty-Eight by '28" initiative, we are working to get 28 of those projects done in time for the 2028 Olympic and Paralympic Games hosted by the LA region. We are also partnering with the private sector to evaluate new ways of conducting our business. Our Office of Extraordinary Innovation evaluates unsolicited proposals that we receive through our Unsolicited Proposals Policy—some for small projects, some for mega projects.

As a result of some of those proposals, we are pursuing public–private partnerships on some of our major construction projects (Fig. 11.1).

We are also implementing a Microtransit On-Demand Bus Service Pilot Project to improve our customers' experience and help "drive" new customers to connect with our transit system. This is a potentially huge opportunity for LA County that could help solve one of our key transit challenges. Microtransit would perform like an infinite, continuous van-pool service to provide point-to-point service to a fixed-route transit line in a given area. Routes would be dynamically created based on real-time rider demand. Such a service could help us boost ridership via increased trip-taking and the creation of new users. It could help optimize our existing bus system and drive ridership to the rail network. Importantly, Microtransit could help Metro's underserved areas and become a first-and-last mile solution to our expanding transit system.

In April 2018 we contracted with three different companies to plan, design, test, and evaluate Microtransit. We are looking for the best

---

Metro's Project Labor Agreement/Construction Career Policy (PLA/CCP) encourages construction employment and training opportunities on Metro projects to those who reside in economically disadvantaged areas near Metro construction projects. Metro adopted the CCP in conjunction with the Project Labor Agreement (PLA), which applies to certain local (non federally) funded and federally funded construction projects with a construction value greater than $2.5 million.

Metro is the first transit agency in the nation to adopt such a PLA that includes national targeted hiring goals for federally funded projects with Federal Transit Administration. The PLA and CCP were approved by Metro's Board of Directors on January 26, 2012. Both were subsequently renewed on January 26, 2017 and negotiated with the Los Angeles/Orange County Building Construction Trades Council (LAOCBCTC) to help facilitate the timely completion of transit projects in LA County.

Figure 11.1 *Project labor and construction career policy.*

solution that will help determine if this service is feasible. If these companies can demonstrate that it is, we will give them first dibs at negotiating rights to implement and evaluate Microtransit further down the road. Each company will deliver feasibility studies for a range of Microtransit tasks, including transportation planning and analysis, a software/technology solution plan, a performance plan, cost structure, payment and recovery, capital programming, and innovation [8].

We are embracing the ways technological advancements and changes can better our modes of transportation. But in order to ensure proper implementation of these systems, and a skilled workforce that is equipped with the new, necessary competencies, we need to be involved at the beginning and end of workforce development. Strategically, we have pivoted toward engaging and connecting with people through proper training and education, and marketing transit jobs to a new demographic of people.

Point 2 is *capturing the hearts and minds of the people*. Like other transit agencies across North America, Metro has been experiencing a reduction in ridership. As we look at how to reclaim former riders, retain current riders, and recruit new riders, we are reimagining our bus service for the first time in 25 years. Through our NextGen Bus study, we want to reflect the way people now move around LA County. We have learned from our riders that bus traveling takes too long. We need to do a better job getting them where they need to go quickly, reliably, and conveniently.

We are embedding active transportation and first-and-last mile efforts into our plan. Approximately half of all trips people in our region take are 3 miles or less, which is generally a distance that can be biked. Approximately one-quarter of trips are less than 1 mile, which is generally a distance that can be walked. Several times a year, Metro sponsors Open Streets events in our partner cities where streets are closed to cars and open for the public to walk, bike, and skate. These events help remind people that there are other ways to get around than driving and help expose more members of the public to our transit system (Fig. 11.2).

Empowering Veterans
by Phillip A. Washington

As a retired US Army Command Sergeant Major, I know first-hand the challenges that Military Veterans face when trying to transition from serving their country to serving in a new career in mainstream society. Many Veterans feel like they are on an island with no shore in sight. We realize that vets have the transferable skills we need in the transportation industry. Veterans bring strong technical skills combined with discipline and character.

While 4% of the overall population are Veterans, we have been able to make Veterans 7% of our annual hires. This has been accomplished by building partnerships with Veteran Service Organizations, active military bases and community-based service providers. We have dedicated staff members assigned to support Veterans through the hiring process by interpreting their military experience to the transportation industry. In addition, we support our Veteran employees to connect with Veteran candidates through job fairs and outreach activities. We have found that if people can see themselves in our organization, they are more likely to succeed.

Our path for Veterans includes an annual celebration of their service to our country and to our organization. In 2017, over 450 Veteran employees joined the LA Metro team for lunch and recognition of their contributions. The evaluations of this event rate over 97% positive, and this gesture of gratitude goes a long way to honor the Veteran employees at Metro.

Figure 11.2 *The path for veterans.*

Furthermore, we have been converting static signs to digital information displays at our rail stations. We are also installing digital information kiosks at our busiest stations that provide amenities such as free Wi-Fi, charging stations, interactive tablets to search for community information, and the ability to make free phone calls—right from the panels on the kiosks.

The auto industry has done an outstanding job of glamorizing their industry. Beautiful people with flowing hair are depicted experiencing freedom by driving. We need to find a way to make public transportation more appealing to capture the hearts and minds of people. All of this is designed to enhance the customer experience as we continue our commitment to give people back one of life's most precious commodities—the time they waste sitting in traffic.

Point 3 is *embracing equity*. We want to enhance communities and lives through mobility and access to opportunity. In Spring 2018 the Metro Board of Directors approved an Equity Platform—a guide to ensure that we are considering all people as we plan, build, and operate transportation. The Platform is especially targeted at those who have experienced significant and persistent disparity in access to jobs, education, healthcare, and other quality-of-life indicators.

Knowing that transportation is a critical link to bridging disinvested communities and these opportunities, Metro is taking a proactive and committed role to advance equity in how we do business.

There are Four Pillars of the Equity Platform Framework:

1. *Define and measure*: Define what "equity" means for Metro, its partners, and the community it serves; and develop measures to determine how well we are achieving those goals and objectives.

2. *Listen and learn*: Authentically listen to the community; embrace peoples' current and past experiences in which equity has and has not been realized related to Metro and Metro's larger context; and develop actions to address where equitable outcomes are lacking.

3. *Focus and deliver*: Commit to specific Metro activities where equity will be woven up-front and meaningfully.

4. *Train and grow*: Metro leadership commits to training and supporting its staff (and the Board) to deploy "state of the art" research and practices to guide more equitable transportation projects, investments, and services; and be prepared to work and partner with the diverse communities Metro serves.

We have a very active Joint Development Program that fosters the development of transit-oriented communities that help the indigenous people of a neighborhood to thrive and prevent their displacement. Metro's Transit-Oriented Communities policy requires that at least 35% of the housing built by developers on Metro's property is affordable housing. We continue to evaluate how to reduce, reuse, or consolidate parking to better utilize our property to enhance communities.

Point 4 is *stepping into leadership voids* to transform transportation in LA County through regional collaboration and bold leadership. While our mission is better transportation, we are stepping into leadership voids in several areas to influence, impact, and instigate. While we do not control everything, we can influence, impact, and instigate a great number of things, such as affordable housing, reducing homelessness, and all aspects of bettering people's lives (Fig. 11.3).

We can influence others and encourage them to step out front to tackle the many issues that hold communities back; we are here to enable socioeconomic changes through the transit industry. Earlier in this chapter, the issue of soaring housing costs for Angelinos was raised; LA Metro's advocacy for affordable housing is part of a holistic strategy to improve livability for not only our own workforce but also the Los Angeles community as a whole.

The fifth point of our five-point plan is *building the industry* by providing responsive, accountable, and trustworthy governance within the LA Metro organization. This is the basis on which we are building the workforce of the future with a career pathway that provides opportunities for people to move into transportation jobs, and then move up through the ranks.

The transportation industry is facing a major challenge to build a qualified workforce to fill jobs as our industry workers age and retire. These are jobs in construction, special trades, and hard-to-fill positions such as track and signal inspectors, bus mechanics, and engineers. We are actually nearing a crisis where we will not have enough people to keep the industry moving. So, building the workforce of the future is one of our main priorities at LA Metro.

In 2017, Metro began a Women and Girls Governing Council of Metro employees. The council examines Metro policies, programs, and services and works together for effective, innovative, and collaborative change. The council applies a gender lens in three areas: Metro as an employer, Metro as a service provider, and Metro as a catalyst for economic development. The council makes recommendations to the CEO to help impact, advance, and empower women and girls.

The Business Case for the Council:

- 51% (5,134,000) of LA County residents are women and girls and they comprise 13% of the state's population.
- 6% of the 288,590 veterans living in LA County are women.
- Less than 1% of LA County women work in construction.
- LA County has the second highest concentration of women-owned businesses in the nation (437,000).
- LA County women who are under the age of 35 graduate from high school and attain postsecondary degrees at significantly higher rates than both their men peers and women over the age of 35.

    Yet, women and girls suffer from disproportionate disadvantages and burdens due to poverty, violent crime, and workforce parity.

- One of five women in LA County live below the federal poverty level.
- The poverty rate for African American women and Latinas is significantly higher.
- Women make up a third of the county's homeless population.

    Women earn 80 cents to every dollar men make.

Metro has made it a priority to look at our agency through a gender lens as an employer, as a service provider and as a catalyst for economic development.

Metro's Female Workforce:

- 10,830 full-time staff.
- 3169 (29%) of Metro staff are female.
- 2471 (78%) are staff represented by a Labor Union .
- 697 (22%) are staff not represented by a Labor Union.
- 26% of All FTE contract staff are female.
- 47% of All FTE noncontract staff are female.

Figure 11.3 *Stepping into a critical leadership void—forming the Women and Girls Governing Council.*

- 37% of the 129 executive/senior management positions are held by female staff.

Metro has numerous supportive policies and programs with women in mind:

- Equal opportunity employer/Office of civil rights.
- Child care center and mother's rooms at Metro headquarters.
- Women's safety workshop.
- Metro today lunchtime forum.
- Mandatory sexual harassment training for Managers.
- Zero tolerance for sexual harassment at Metro and with contractors.
- Gender pay equity review.
- Veteran/veteran spouses hiring initiative.
- Work-life flexibility policies.
- Peace over violence hotline for customers.
- Homeless task force.
- Transit watch app for customers.
- Human trafficking campaign (nationally recognized).
- Youth on the move (age 18–24 foster youth).

Metro's Female Customers

- 55% of Metro bus riders are female.
- 47% of Metro rail riders are female.
- 34% of Metro bikeshare users are female.
- 50% of Metrolink riders are female (Metrolink is heavily funded by Metro).
- 62% of Access trips are by females.
- 17% of homeless individuals on Metro Rail/Bus are female.

Metro also has women in mind through our opportunities for economic development:

- Project Labor Agreement – single mother category/female utilization.
- Women build Metro Los Angeles.
- WIN-LA.
- SBE/DBE Programs–40% of SBE firms are women owned.

Figure 11.3 *Continued*

The Transportation School

The most significant effort in building the transportation workforce is getting young people to realize they can have a career in transportation. The Transportation School model draws from the same basic logic and inspiration that inspired Branch Rickey's farm team system. Metro initiated a Transportation School concept that we call E3—expose, educate, and employ youth in the transportation industry. The goal is to provide students 12 to 18-years old with STEAM (science, technology, engineering, arts, and math) programs, mentorships, hands-on learning, and other opportunities as an early pathway into the transportation industry (Fig. 11.4).

The centerpiece of the E3 initiative is an actual transportation school. Metro, in partnership with the County of Los Angeles, is developing a transportation academy [9], an educational and vocational program to train high school students to become the next generation of transportation workers.

The pilot program is a boarding school on 4.2 acres of land at Vermont Avenue and Manchester Boulevard in South Los Angeles that was left vacant for more than 25 years after the civil unrest of 1992. Los Angeles County Supervisor and Metro Board Member Mark Ridley-Thomas represents this area and embraced this effort from the onset. He has become the political champion for the project. The supervisor worked with his four colleagues on the Board of Supervisors to purchase the property to transform it into a thriving mixed-use development, with the transportation school as the centerpiece of the project [10]. The entire County Board of Supervisors deserves great credit for committing to this landmark investment.

Metro and LA County are working with the LA County Department of Children and Family Services to target and recruit at-risk youth from underserved communities to attend the school. Fundraising is a big component of the project so that these young people can attend the school free of charge and benefit from a top-notch STEAM curriculum and get the wrap-around services they need to support them in their life needs.

In addition to the transportation academy, Metro also offers a range of supplemental E3 programs that provide middle and high school students across LA County with direct exposure to Metro and real-world experiences through tours, field trips, educational sessions, mentorships, and

This ethos, logos, and pathos inspired our June 2018 transportation school kickoff with the County of Los Angeles to provide educational and vocational training aimed at preparing high school-age youth for entry into the transportation field. The farm team for the future will target disadvantaged and at-risk students who will learn from a curriculum of transferrable industry skills focused on science, technology, engineering, arts, and math.

Figure 11.4 The Transportation School is proposed for a lot at the intersection of Vermont Avenue and Manchester Boulevard in South Los Angeles; the lot has been vacant since 1992. The hope is to get the school open by 2021.

apprenticeships. This is an opportunity to build a qualified workforce for the transportation industry while giving local youth a pathway to quality careers and meaningful lives as we build a community from the ground up (Fig. 11.5).

The Transportation School idea is absolutely bold. We think it is an opportunity to have that singular focus on transportation in preparing the workforce. There are existing schools that do vocational training, but

The Transportation Career Academy Program (TCAP) provides summer internship opportunities to junior and senior high school students who are transit dependent, reside in LA County, live near a Metro Rail station and whose schools are located near Metro's rail expansion efforts. This program offers students an opportunity to learn about careers in transportation and how to apply classroom theories and concepts to "real-world" work situations at one of the nation's largest public transportation agencies. Project details:

- TCAP is a 7-week program.

- Interns work Monday through Friday, 8:30 a.m. to 3:30 p.m.

- Fridays are designated for "in-service training" and Metro tours.

- Pay rates are based on LA minimum wage requirements.

Program Goals:

- Offer high school students an opportunity to explore careers in transportation.

- Connect learning from high school coursework to real-world work experience.

- Provide an on-the-job work experience in a specific career pathway or in a specific technical area.

- Establish a professional mentorship relationship for interns and their mentors.

- Provide an innovative approach to how LA Metro promotes transportation, antigraffiti, and safety education programs.

Eligibility:

- Junior and senior high school students who have met program requirements.

- Must be between the ages of 16 and 18

- Must have a Grade Point Average (GPA) of 2.5 or better.

- Must be a US citizen, permanent resident or be high school students who have legal authorization to work in the United States.

- Must have work permit (if under 18 years of age).

Figure 11.5 *Summer internship for young people.*

they do not have that focus solely on transportation. This method is allowing us to really bring people into the industry early and build commitment early. The whole approach of giving youth the chance to see themselves as a meaningful resource, and realize that we see them as a meaningful resource, is powerful. There is a marriage of people needing purpose and direction and young people needing skills. If they choose to learn about transportation, Metro absolutely believes these young people can be upskilled to become the future of the industry.

Creating a career pathway

The people side of our business is the most important part of everything we do. Our employees are our most important resource. This reality is central to our approach for recruiting employees and retaining them. We have thought a lot about how we open the door for the five generations of people currently in the workforce to do the meaningful work happening at Metro, highlighting the steady benefits of these careers.

We have a very hierarchical structure allowing for transition into management. A lot of younger workers strive for upward mobility without having to spend years in lower level positions taking orders. So, one thing we are trying to do is create a different narrative for the organization and create real career pathways that we can use to show people that you can build a career at Metro (Fig. 11.6).

Young people need to see a bit of themselves in an organization. If candidates do not see someone who they can relate to—whether by race or gender or sexual orientation or something else—then they are not going to choose to join the Metro workforce. We can do a better job of showing that our work has strong living wages, great benefits and security, and makes people comfortable in building their families.

We do need to be more relevant in today's workforce, but we are not going to be Google or have the environment of some of these other tech companies. We are on a path in which we become an organization that is rich in opportunity, inclusive, and welcomes the best talent in the industry. We want to be the farm team for the industry, and one that develops the future talent and all-stars of the transportation industry. In addition, in the past, Metro employees got into a lane and stayed there. If you were

Workforce Initiative Now-Los Angeles (WIN-LA) is Metro's workforce development program established to focus on creating career pathways in the transportation industry. WIN-LA career pathways consist of: construction, operations/maintenance, administration and professional services. WIN-LA focuses on increasing opportunities by inclusion of priority populations from historically underrepresented communities that have met challenges such as emancipated foster youth, homeless, involvement with the criminal justice system, those lacking a GED; and veterans. In the spirit of diversity and inclusion, WIN-LA will also outreach community college students throughout the region with focus on the inclusion of women.

The core objective of WIN-LA is to help people obtain the education and training they need to get a career at Metro and in the transportation industry; which is being achieved through our collaboration with the regional Workforce Development Board consortium including the Los Angeles Regional Community College Consortium, Transportation Workforce Institute and others.

WIN-LA supports Metro's pledge to be a learning organization that attracts, develops, motivates and retains a world-class workforce; and fosters Metro's promise of being a community partner as we build the future of public transportation for LA County.

Figure 11.6 *Workforce Initiative Now-Los Angeles (WIN-LA)*

in Accounting, you did not think about going to Human Resources. That is why we revised all job descriptions while considering what skills are transferrable so that people could change lanes if they want. We believe that creating opportunities for people within the company to make lateral or hierarchical moves will make leadership happen at all levels.

The goal for our comprehensive Career Pathways program is to develop an innovative and progressive learning environment and training model to better prepare tomorrow's transportation leaders to steward our ambitious expansion plans for decades to come. We want to nurture the best management and leadership skills that our industry requires. The program begins with youth and progresses with every new stage of an employee's career. We call it a program that goes "from cradle to grave"—teaching 9th—12th graders about the opportunities in transportation with rungs along the way that lead all the way to the CEO position.

Once people join the Metro team, we make training available to contract and noncontract employees. We have mandatory training that keeps employees informed about ethics, emergency preparedness, sexual harassment prevention, and transit terrorism awareness, among others. Our Metro Employee Development program includes self-paced courses in presupervisory training, certificate programs, and professional skill development. To further develop our management and leadership teams, we have a series of programs such as the Transportation Leadership Academy, a year-long structured program for a group of emerging leaders who want to better understand their personal leadership, workplace, and industry. These and other programs are helping Metro develop and cultivate the most important asset we have: our people (Fig. 11.7).

A major milestone for Metro was settling our labor union contracts as 5-year contracts, which went into effect on July 1, 2017. We never had 5-year contracts before. In essence, we put our money where our mouth

The mission of our Leadership Academy is to build Metro's leaders of the future. This year-long intensive program is open to all levels below the C Suite, which feeds into the culture of inclusion that we are trying to foster. In the past we tended to promote people who were technicians and we have not put enough emphasis on being able to inspire them and teach them what leadership means. We are trying to better assess people's ability to lead. The program emphasizes the difference between management and leadership, and that leadership happens at all levels of our organization. The focus is on intrinsic development by focusing on the employee's use of their influence. Participants are often reminded that management roles can be granted to individuals, but leadership cannot be granted or taken away. The use of feedback, collaborative problem solving, and personal action planning are some of the key learning tools for the program.

The Program is based on the senior leadership team competencies and values. In the Leadership Academy we begin to paint a picture of what leadership looks like in the organization. We not only teach leadership skills, but measure leadership behaviors through our performance evaluations. The demand for this Program is greater than our capacity; however, we are making great progress in building Metro's leaders of the future.

Figure 11.7 *The Leadership Academy.*

Senior Leadership Team Charter

MISSION & OBJECTIVES

The members of the Senior Leadership Team, individually and as a group, support the vision and mission of Metro to lead, direct and manage the agency to provide effective and efficient transportation planning, construction and operations to the region. The team must have a level of alignment on how they work together, and in turn, what behaviors and thinking they should be reinforcing on a daily basis to meet the Senior Leadership Team objective. In fulfilling its role, the Senior Leadership Team will demonstrate the following 10 Leadership Competencies.

LEADERSHIP COMPETENCIES

LEADING CHANGE – ability to bring about strategic change, both within and outside the Agency, to meet Agency goals.

1. **Act as a Champion for Change & Strive for Innovation** – Encourages people to question existing methods, practices, and assumptions; supports people in their efforts to try new things.

2. **Set a Strategic Vision** – Creates and communicates a compelling vision that motivates others; conveys the purpose and importance of the corporate vision and mission; links department, team, and individual initiatives to those of the organization.

RESULTS DRIVEN – ability to meet organizational goals and customer expectations.

3. **Act Decisively** – Makes timely and informed decisions; commits to a clear course of action; comfortable making necessary decisions based on partial information (P=40-70); takes appropriate risks to maintain momentum; decision-making and problem-solving skills are respected and sought after.

4. **Manage Resources** – Manages resources to achieve maximum value with minimum cost. Accurately estimates, invests and monitors resources and budgets to optimize returns and control waste.

LEADING PEOPLE – ability to lead people toward meeting the Agency's vision, mission and goals. Ability to provide an inclusive workplace that fosters the development of others, facilitates cooperation and teamwork and supports constructive resolution of conflicts.

5. **Build Effective Teams** – Blends people into teams when needed; creates strong morale and spirit in his/her team; shares wins and successes; fosters open dialogue; lets people finish and be responsible for their work; defines success in terms of the whole team; creates a feeling of belonging in the team.

6. **Commit to Performance Management as a Daily Practice** – Engages with staff by establishing clear goals; commits to development planning; conducts meaningful performance evaluations; provides coaching and feedback; creates an environment for high-performers to thrive and be energized.

7. **Manage Diversity and Work Well with Diverse Populations** – Works well with people of diverse backgrounds both internal and external to the agency; sees the value of cultural, ethnic, gender, and other differences in people and leverages those differences effectively; considers diversity when hiring; supports equal and fair treatment and opportunity for all.

8. **Inspire and Motivate Others** – Emphasizes the importance of each person's contributions; communicates why the work is important and how it benefits self and others; employs unique motivation strategies to get the best out of each person; empowers direct reports to perform tasks and make decisions; invites input.

LEADING SELF – enhancing personal effectiveness.

9. **Act with Empathy or Compassion** – Demonstrating an active concern for people and their needs by forming close and supportive relationships with others.

10. **Act with Integrity** – Follows through on commitments; lets others know his/her true intentions.

TEAM BEHAVIORS

1. Resolve conflicts with each other before resorting to joint escalation.
2. Include, when at all possible, all relevant team members in meaningful decision making (SITREPS).
3. Visit one-on-one to see how to be of service to each other.

TEAM MEMBERS

We, the undersigned, commit to each other on this day, April 18, 2017, to the leadership competencies and teaming behaviors above:

Phillip A. Washington, CEO

Nalini Ahuja	Debra Avila	Richard Clarke	David Edwards
Chief Financial Officer	Chief, Vendor/Contract Management Officer	Chief, Program Management Officer	Chief, Information Officer
Diana Estrada	James Gallagher	Karen Gorman	Elba Higuereos
Chief Auditor	Chief Operations Officer	Inspector General	Chief Policy Officer
Gregory Kildare	Daniel Levy	Therese McMillan	Joanne Peterson
Chief, Risk, Safety & Asset Management	Chief, Civil Rights Programs Officer	Chief Planning Officer	Chief, Human Capital & Development Officer
Charles Safer	Joshua Schank	Pauletta Tonilas	Alex Wiggins	Stephanie Wiggins
County Counsel	Chief Innovation Officer	Chief Communications Officer	Chief, System Security & Law Enforcement Officer	Deputy Chief Executive Officer

Metro

Figure 11.8 Members of Metro's Senior Leadership Team have committed to building the industry's future leaders.

was and put together very attractive packages. We started working on those contracts almost a year earlier, in August 2016. Our old labor agreements had outdated and archaic language that supports a type of hierarchy and control that was not working. We had a backlog of employee grievances and complaints and put resources into tackling that backlog and we have made a lot of progress.

As part of the contract negotiations, we had workshops that explained industry trends, ridership issues, security concerns, and public–private partnerships to the labor force as an innovative project delivery method. We wanted employees to understand the direction we want to take the agency. We revised the job classification system to keep it relevant and aligned. We now have performance-based compensation. We have made a major shift in moving our workforce into the second and third quartile of their pay range and hanging around the midpoint. We have given our workers a career system and have made them a part of it every step of the way.

We also are encouraging more mentoring. Our senior leadership team spent hours in a retreat crafting our team charter—our values and competencies for how we want to conduct business. We do a periodic check-in to make sure we, as senior leaders, are being the real agents of change: driving change in a meaningful way, being accountable, having integrity, and being a good steward of the public trust. Part of the charter is our commitment to motivate and inspire others—one of the competencies that brings the other competencies along. As we work to ensure that the employees we need to transform transportation in Los Angeles County have the proper training to get the work done, we have built our career pathway to span a wide spectrum of programs to reach various sectors of the community (Fig. 11.8).

Conclusion

The heart of the farm team system is the understanding that people can advance their positions and progress in their skills, given the resources, space, and guidance. LA Metro has taken numerous steps to do just that. In anticipation of a large group leaving the workforce, we understand that it is our responsibility to create economic opportunities for a new generation of Angelenos who will build and maintain Metro's expanding, and technologically advancing, transportation system. These programs are focused on helping our current employees develop further skills while also enabling the socioeconomically disadvantaged.

As we look to the future, our employees and their input will help Metro implement our strategic goals and ensure we are doing all we can to build and operate a transportation system with people at the heart of all we do:

- Building forward-thinking projects;
- Operating faster, safer, and more reliable service that enhances the customer experience;
- Improving quality of life by providing better access to the places our customers want and need to go; and
- Providing careers.

Metro embraces its role in transforming LA County into the transportation center of excellence. We are in the middle of a transportation revolution that will leave an infrastructure inheritance for future generations. We are poised to not only provide high-quality mobility options, but also enhance the communities we serve. Our strategic blueprint for the future recognizes both the concrete improvements needed for the existing Metro system and the innovative workforce, management, and community engagement shifts needed to empower not only the LA Metro workforce but also the communities of Los Angeles. Today and tomorrow, our mission is all about people—the people we move, and the workforce we empower to move those people.

References

[1] A. McCue,, Branch Rickey. Society for American Baseball Research. Available from: <https://sabr.org/bioproj/person/6d0ab8f3>.

[2] K. Kerrane, How Branch Rickey invented modern baseball. Deadspin. Available from: <https://deadspin.com/how-branch-rickey-invented-modern-baseball-1458137692>.

[3] B. Cronin, Attracting, recruiting, and retaining skilled staff for transportation system operations and management. National Cooperative Highway Research Program. Available from: <https://books.google.com/books?isbn = 030923843 >.

[4] METRO for Transit and Motorcoach Business, LA Metro launches workforce development program. Metro Magazine. Available from: <http://www.metro-magazine.com/management-operations/news/724569/la-metro-launches-workforce-development-program >.

[5] Los Angeles County Metropolitan Transportation Authority, Next stop: boomtown. LA Metro. Available from: <https://www.metro.net/projects/main_page/boomtown/ >.

[6] A. Nagourney, The capital of car culture, Los Angeles warms to mass transit. The New York Times. Available from: <https://www.nytimes.com/2016/07/21/us/the-capital-of-car-culture-los-angeles-warms-to-mass-transit.html >.

[7] L.A. Metro's Strategic Plan: Metro Vision 2028 (Goals/initiatives).

Goal 1: Provide high-quality mobility options that enable people to spend less time traveling.

- **Initiative 1.1** To expand the transportation network and increase mobility for all users, Metro will:
  - Target infrastructure and service investments toward those with the greatest mobility needs.
  - Expand the transportation system as responsibly and as quickly as possible.
- **Initiative 1.2** To improve LA County's overall transit network and assets, Metro will:
  - Invest in a world-class bus system that is reliable, convenient and attractive to more users for more trips.
  - Partner with Metrolink, Southern California's commuter rail provider, to increase the capacity of the regional transportation system.
  - Optimize the speed, reliability, and performance of the existing system by revitalizing and upgrading Metro's transit assets.
  - Improve connectivity to provide seamless journeys.
  - Improve safety on the transit system and reduce roadway collisions and injuries.
- **Initiative 1.3** To manage transportation demand in a fair and equitable manner, Metro will:
  - Develop simplified, sustainable, and comprehensive pricing policies to support the provision of equitable, affordable, and high-quality transportation services.
  - Implement the ExpressLanes Tier 1 network within the next 10 years.
  - Test and implement pricing strategies to reduce traffic congestion.
  - Manage congestion and reduce conflicts between the movement of goods and people on streets and highways.
  - Explore opportunities for expanding access to shared, demand-responsive transportation options for everyone.

Goal 2: Deliver outstanding trip experiences for all users of the transportation system.

- **Initiative 2.1** Metro is committed to improving security.
- **Initiative 2.2** Metro is committed to improving legibility, ease of use and trip information on the transit system.
- **Initiative 2.1** Metro will improve customer satisfaction at all customer touch points.
- **Goal 3: Enhance communities and lives through mobility and access to opportunity.**
- **Initiative 3.1** To lift up local communities, Metro will create jobs and career pathways in transportation.
- **Initiative 3.2** Metro will leverage its transit investments to catalyze transit-oriented communities and help stabilize neighborhoods where these investments are made.
- **Initiative 3.3** Metro is committed to genuine public and community engagement to achieve better mobility outcomes for the people of LA County.
- **Initiative 3.4** Metro will play a strong leadership role in efforts to address homelessness in LA County.
- **Goal 4: Transform LA County through regional collaboration and national leadership**
- **Initiative 4.1** Metro will work with partners to build trust and make decisions that support the goals of the Vision 2028 Plan.
- **Initiative 4.2** Metro will help drive mobility agendas, discussions and policies at the state, regional and national levels.

Goal 5: Provide responsive, accountable and trustworthy governance within the LA Metro organization.

- **Initiative 5.1** Metro will leverage funding and staff resources to accelerate the achievement of goals and initiatives prioritized in the Vision 2028 Plan.
- **Initiative 5.2** Metro will exercise good public policy judgment and sound fiscal stewardship.
- **Initiative 5.3** Metro will develop a transparent data management policy that addresses open data, data storage, and data protections.
- **Initiative 5.4** We will apply prudent commercial business practices to create a more effective agency.
- **Initiative 5.5** Metro will expand opportunities for businesses and external organizations to work with us.
- **Initiative 5.6** We will foster and maintain a strong safety culture.
- **Initiative 5.7** Metro will build and nurture a diverse, inspired, and high-performing workforce.

[8] Los Angeles County Metropolitan Transportation Authority. MicroTransit Pilot Project. LA Metro. Available from: <https://www.metro.net/projects/microtransit/>.

[9] Ubaldo, Jose. Metro and L.A. County Partner on Transportation School to Create the Next Generation of Workers. The Source, Available from: <https://thesource.metro.net/2018/06/18/metro-and-l-a-county-partner-on-transportation-school-to-create-the-next-generation-of-workers/>.

[10] Ridley-Thomas, Mark. Laying the Groundwork for Development in Vermont Manchester. County of Los Angeles. Available from: <http://ridley-thomas.lacounty.gov/index.php/laying-the-groundwork-for-development-in-vermont-manchester/>.

CHAPTER TWELVE

Designing our future transportation workforce for supporting seniors and individuals with disabilities

Valerie Lefler[1] and Flora Castillo[2]
[1]Executive Director, Feonix - Mobility Rising
[2]President, Pivot Strategies LLC

Contents

Introduction

In designing a fully inclusive transportation infrastructure, our future workforce must be engaged beyond a planning and engineering educational base. Across the nation, city planning departments and state departments of transportation must include experts in public health, gerontology, and social work to address the vulnerable populations, such as seniors and individuals with disabilities who have remained dramatically underserved over the past 30 years.

Moving forward, engineers and community and regional planners will need to be exposed to and immersed in the realities of supporting transportation ecosystems for our evolving communities—thinking beyond the equation will be required. Immersive experiences such as spending time

Empowering the New Mobility Workforce.
DOI: https://doi.org/10.1016/B978-0-12-816088-6.00012-2

in senior centers, dialysis clinic waiting rooms, and centers for independent living will quickly give a level of education and empathy that cannot
be attained in any classroom. Our future transportation professionals must
learn to be storytellers, community organizers, and proponents of new
partnerships that will require a level of flexibility and trust that has not
been required until today's breakneck pace of innovation in mobility.

Our future workforce and leaders in transportation must lean in and go
beyond the "minimum federal requirements" in serving those who need
help most. In a recent Federal Transit Administration study done on household characteristics, one in five seniors over the age of 65 does not drive,
and, according to American Association of Retired Persons (AARP),
10,000 baby boomers are turning 65 every single day, and this trend is
expected to continue into the 2030s. This means that nearly seven baby
boomers are turning 65 every minute [1]. The demand for alternative transportation options to support the "silver tsunami" that is occurring in
America will have a louder cry and greater social impact than ever before.

Seniors on vacation in Montana overlooking the countryside.

The US Bureau of Transportation Statistics reports that 25.5 million
Americans age 5 and older have self-reported travel-limiting disabilities;
13.4 million are age 18−64, and 11.2 million are age 65 and older [2].
The percentage of people reporting travel-limiting disabilities increases
with age [3]. In thinking about the not-so-distant future, the possibilities
of the autonomous revolution for seniors and individuals with disabilities

have never been brighter, but great care must be taken to design our innovation ecosystems, policies, and regulatory framework to be meaningfully and proactively "accessible."

In regards to seniors and individuals with disabilities in most communities across the United States, the tale will be told of less access to mobility options than ever before, declining quality and frequency as demand increases, and less and less of a voice in the process.

This paradigm must not continue, as the cost of doing nothing is even more unaffordable. Seniors' decision about where to age is not just about preference; it is about cost savings as well. For example, the average month in assisted living is $3,628, which is $43,563 per senior, per year [4]. Multiply that figure by the 10,000 additional baby boomers entering the senior age bracket each day, and the cost balloons to $1,088,400,000 *per month.*

While not everyone age 65 will enter assisted living or require Medicare to cover the cost, even the fraction of that figure that will demonstrates the tidal wave of additional care required and the importance that we address this with more than feigned effort. And even with all that funding invested in additional care, it does not solve the true transportation issue regarding qualify of life. Most assisted living facilities only provide set trips on set days, have limited transportation availability, and rarely provide transportation out of town to specialist medical doctors. Seniors in assisted living facilities also still suffer from isolation, as they are dislocated from their friends and family, and most facilities do not provide on-demand trips such as coffee on Saturday morning with friends or blanket sewing at church Wednesday evening.

"Husband visiting wife in nursing home, drinking coffee together talking about the week ahead."

A US Department of Transportation study titled "Freedom to Travel" demonstrated that 12% of Americans with disabilities reported difficulty getting the transportation they needed, compared to 3% of people without disabilities [5]. The same study found that more than half a million Americans with disabilities could not leave their homes because of inadequate transportation. That is the same as leaving the entire population of Wyoming stranded due to inadequate transportation for those who need additional accommodations.

This is not only an issue of social justice. Consider the impact to our economy. Fig. 12.1 depicts the US DOT FHWA national household survey, reported as part of the 2017 National Household Travel Survey, which shows the increasing percentage of travel-limiting disabilities by age. In 2016 in the United States, an estimated 7.8% of noninstitutionalized persons aged 21—64 years with a disability who were not working were actively looking for work [6]. In other words, 997,800 out of 12,799,900 noninstitutionalized persons aged 21—64 years with a disability who were not working were actively looking for work. Even at the federal mandated minimum wage of $7.25 per hour, that is, $15,046,824,000 lost to the American economy [7]. Not providing equitable and effective transportation for individuals with disabilities is a heavy price to pay—both in dollars and in terms of an individual's identity, social support system, and effective outcomes.

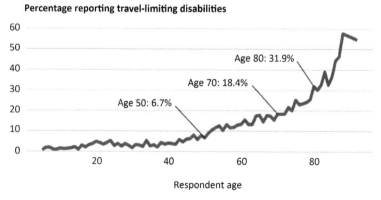

US Department of Transportation, Federal Highway Administration, 2017 National Household Travel Survey.

Figure 12.1 Percentage reporting travel-limiting disabilities.

"Man in Chicago walking home from work using his walking cane."

Integrated and holistic approach

Facilitating a future transportation workforce and planning transportation resources must be more person-centered and based in population health. Not one entity alone has enough funding to address "all" or even "barely minimal" transportation needs to fully serve our vulnerable members of society, so a collaborative effort is required. In addressing not just access to medical care but also jobs, affordable housing, education, and grocery stores, the health of the person must be considered. Considering that, as a nation, missed appointments and the resulting delays in care cost the health system $150 billion each year is mind blowing [8]. The fact that that "cost" is only 20% of what factors into population health improves the business case for person-centered transportation (Fig. 12.2) [9].

As much as stats and dollar signs thrill the hearts and minds of economists and chief financial officers, when it comes to going to the court of

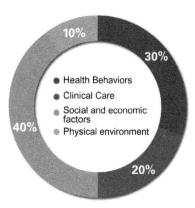

Figure 12.2 Contributing factors of health. *Health Research and Educational Trust, 2017.*

public opinion in approving the funding for bond initiatives, tax increases, and innovative finance models, the stories of those impacted will yield a stronger and more memorable campaign.

Consider the following:

Martha is 89 years old, living in a small town in North Carolina and suffers from severe macular degeneration. She lost her ability to drive 3 years ago when the Department of Motor Vehicles ruled that her vision no longer allowed her to retain her driver's license. Her husband, Alan, age 84, suffers from mild to moderate dementia, but has good vision, and still has a few years left before his license is due for renewal. There is no public transit in their part of the county, and the local town they go to for groceries is about an hour away. In addition, their doctor has a demand-responsive appointment system, but it does not go outside the city limits.

Martha and Alan have lived in their home over 50 years together, and the thought of moving into a nursing home or assisted care is not, financially, an option. Locally, for both of their care, their living costs would skyrocket to over $14,000 a month out of pocket. Their two children live on the west coast with their families and are unable to help financially. Martha doesn't want to call and add more of a burden to her daughter struggling to raise two kids on her own, or her son who just lost his job after a recent factory lay-off.

The nearby assisted living facilities are already at capacity, and if they counted on Medicare to help cover some of these long-term costs, they would have to move almost 70 miles away to find an opening for subsidized care. This option would relocate them far from not only their home, where they are comfortable and familiar, but also all their friends they have ever known, all their doctors, and everyone they care about.

For Martha, the thought of losing her connection with her emotional support system as she watches her brilliant husband fade away is unbearable, so when it is time to get groceries, or go to the doctor, she takes the risk, and gives Alan the keys—and then sits in the passenger seat and prays no one gets hurt.

How do we prepare our future transportation leaders to design solutions and infrastructure that address issues facing the "Martha and Alan's" living in our communities? There are a number of policy, education, public health, and public transit infrastructure failures, and the demand coming has only begun to stress these systems. If Alan runs a red light and injures someone or himself or Martha, who is to blame? How would you solve this issue? In your community, who do you bring to the table to address these issues?

The Community Transportation Association of America (CTAA) recommends an inclusive planning process when designing solutions for vulnerable populations, which engages a diverse taskforce of leaders from across the community as well as everyday members of the impacted communities [10]. These inclusive task forces are an excellent starting point for addressing the issue; however, they must be careful not to get bogged down in each agency's red tape, paperwork, or personal baggage. While those things will be addressed with time, starting these meetings by addressing political controversial topics or complicated issues such as insurance or matching funds is a quick way for the conversation to start to "circle the drain" and lose engagement.

Complementing the CTAA planning process focusing on the "why" is essential. The future transportation workforce must understand and be tied to more than just statistics if they want to see true progress; they need to be able to articulate the "why" and have training on moderating meetings [11].

For example, one of the most pressing needs facing almost every agency is that there is not enough funding to expand transportation. However, alternative paths forward can often lead to innovative solutions.

How does Martha and Alan's situation change with autonomous vehicles? What if Martha could request a ride to the doctor with her voice? What about Alan requesting a ride to see his buddies at the coffee shop on Friday morning? Does there still need to be a person in an autonomous vehicle? How do those logistics work? What happens if Alan requests a ride, then forgets where he is and starts to panic and damage the vehicle? What safety risks emerge in helping Martha on and off the vehicle because she cannot see where she is stepping down onto the street? These are just a few of the factors that must be considered when designing the future mobility ecosystem. All too often "innovation" on the cutting edge is marketed for and created in the vacuum of the start-up community, which is largely young, able-bodied men and women who focus more on cash flow and timelines for investors than on taking the time and resources to address this growing part of the population.

Complex Populations

Individuals of all ages—elderly and nonelderly—with intellectual and developmental disabilities, physical disabilities, behavioral health diagnoses (e.g., dementia), spinal cord or traumatic brain injuries, or disabling chronic conditions require long-term services and supports. Consumers with both chronic physical conditions and a behavioral health condition use significantly more healthcare resources than those with a behavioral health condition alone.

Consider Julia, a 62-year-old White female. She is single and has never been married. She currently lives on the outskirts of Oklahoma City in a rented, single ranch home where she raised her two children who are now deceased. She is receiving care from a network of providers as well as behavioral health and treatment from her community mental health center.

Her current diagnoses include bipolar disorder, general anxiety disorder, posttraumatic stress, diabetes, arthritis, insomnia, and migraines. She receives monthly payments from SSI and is currently working in supportive employment at the local Amazon Fulfillment Center that allow's her to be more involved with her community and keep her active.

She is dependent on others for all her transportation needs and is currently relying on community transportation services offered by her behavioral health provider to go to work and the county's Non-Emergency Medical Transportation (NEMT) services to make it to her medical and behavioral health appointments.

Julia is part of the population known as "super utilizers" that is responsible for the majority of healthcare spending, thanks in large part to high rates of multiple chronic conditions, as noted earlier. Julia is part of the 5% of the US population that account for half (49%) of healthcare spending, with an average expenditure per person per year of $43,212, compared to the 50% of US population that account for only 3% of healthcare spending, with an average expenditure per person per year of $253 [12]. More than 80% of Medicaid super utilizers have a comorbid mental illness and an estimated 44% of super utilizers have a serious mental illness. The medical transportation needs for populations such as individuals with developmental disabilities; serious, persistent mental illnesses; and behavioral health/substance abuse patients often include transportation to treatment related to a variety of medical services as well as nonmedical destinations to support their well-being. These patients with Medicaid coverage generate 40% of the nation's NEMT trips [13].

Insurance providers such as Medicaid Managed Care, Dual Special Needs Plans, and Managed Long-Term Services and Supports are seeking to provide health benefits and programs for these complex populations as State Medicaid Programs are moving populations to address cost pressures on state budgets as well as improve the quality of life and care of their residents who depend on government-funded insurance programs.

In an effort to enhance the care for these complex populations, insurance payers are exploring a variety of integrated care coordination models and are introducing value-based contracting payment models to increase the engagement of these individuals. Healthcare payers and providers are also recognizing that 80% of the factors impacting the care and well-being of individuals are the social determinants of health such as housing, food insecurity, unsafe environments, and lack of education [9]. Our transportation workforce of the future will play a key role and serve as a critical link for healthcare providers and payers in contributing to the population health goals.

A best practice sample is the Johnson County Mental Health Center's wrap-around transportation and peer driver pilot program that identified patients who had the willingness and capacity to provide driving, scheduling, dispatching, and other transportation support services. These "peer drivers and support team members" are patients in recovery who passed both driving and background checks, as county employees do, and are trained in de-escalation/crisis management, first aid, customer service, and call center services. The program's participants reduced ER utilization by 28.7% and inpatient costs by 52.1% [14]. Although a small sample, it does illustrate that peer drivers and wrap-around services reduce costs.

What if professionals within the new mobility workforce were trained to provide feedback loops and peer-support networks to complement person-centered transportation planning for elderly and physically disabled populations? What would that training requirement look like? What if our drivers could serve as mobility managers who are trained in trauma-informed care and can connect seamlessly with the individuals' doctors' intake staff to facilitate a quicker check-in through the individual's electronic medical record? All of these questions suggest a more inclusive and ethical future for the new mobility workforce informed by more holistic approaches to training and education paired with new recruitment strategies to attract qualified healthcare professionals with the competencies required to serve and help these vulnerable populations to thrive and manage their lives.

Embracing Diversity & Community Planning

As our multicultural society continues to grow and continues to age over the years, it is essential that the mobility ecosystem acts as a support system for our aging populations as they seek to thrive and age in place. Demography is indeed our destiny, and the future workforce will be counted upon to serve the diverse needs of our future populations. By 2030, people age 65 and over will make up a full one-fifth of America's population, with a growing percentage of them representing ethnic minorities. The US Census Bureau projects that the number of older adults who are Latino, African-American, and non-Latino White is projected to grow to peak levels in 2036 (54.8 million), reflecting the aging of the baby boomer population [15].

Similarly, the Administration on Aging projects that by 2030, the Latino population aged 65 years and older will increase to 224%, compared to a 65% increase for the non-Latino White population in the same age category [16]. The health and social consequences permeate every aspect of life in this country. The Latino and African-American ages 65 or older populations will grow rapidly through 2060, with Latinos outpacing African-Americans and non-Latino Whites. Data indicate that by 2060, there will be 21.5 million Latinos, 53.6 million non-Latino Whites, and 12 million African-Americans who are age 65 or older.

"Senior woman in New Mexico sitting in her backyard."

Findings from the Centers for Disease Control and Prevention suggest that addressing persistent health disparities based on race and ethnicity must become a national priority and Healthy People 2020 seeks to achieve health equity, eliminate disparities, and improve the health of all groups [17].

The diverse healthcare and mobility needs of our aging and vulnerable populations will necessitate our workforce of the future to be culturally competent and embrace best practices from across sectors to fully and successfully engage and build trust with these multicultural populations. Whether the populations you serve are refugees, Limited English Proficient, or American Asians, we must always begin with a solid understanding of the community and its needs, as well as the local conditions, which allows us to better understand how to provide and design appropriate services for vulnerable communities.

Religion, culture, beliefs, and ethnic customs can influence how patients understand health concepts, take care of themselves, and how they make decisions related to their health. Our future workforce, organizational support systems, and immediate influencers should consider adopting the National Culturally and Linguistically Appropriate Services (CLAS) Standards. CLAS provides organizations with a systems design framework to support the delivery of culturally competent transportation services. The CLAS standards were established by the Office of Minority Health at the US Department of Health and Human Services, in all policies and community design efforts to support and advance health equity, improve quality, and help eliminate healthcare disparities [18].

How might the services' delivery and engagement transform if our future workforce embraces the following 15 CLAS standards?

1. Provide effective, equitable, understandable, and respectful quality care and services that are responsive to diverse cultural health beliefs and practices, preferred languages, health literacy, and other communication needs.

2. Advance and sustain organizational governance and leadership that promotes CLAS and health equity through policy, practices, and allocated resources.

3. Recruit, promote, and support a culturally and linguistically diverse governance, leadership, and workforce that are responsive to the population in the service area.

4. Educate and train governance, leadership, and workforce in culturally and linguistically appropriate policies and practices on an ongoing basis.

5. Offer language assistance to individuals who have limited English proficiency and/or other communication needs, at no cost to them, to facilitate timely access to all healthcare and services.

6. Inform all individuals of the availability of language assistance services clearly and in their preferred language, verbally and in writing.

7. Ensure the competence of individuals providing language assistance, recognizing that the use of untrained individuals and/or minors as interpreters should be avoided.

8. Provide easy-to-understand print and multimedia materials and signage in the languages commonly used by the populations in the service area.

9. Establish culturally and linguistically appropriate goals, policies, and management accountability, and infuse them throughout the organization's planning and operations.

10. Conduct ongoing assessments of the organization's CLAS-related activities and integrate CLAS-related measures into measurement and continuous quality improvement activities.

11. Collect and maintain accurate and reliable demographic data to monitor and evaluate the impact of CLAS on health equity and outcomes and to inform service delivery.

12. Conduct regular assessments of community health assets and needs and use the results to plan and implement services that respond to the cultural and linguistic diversity of populations in the service area.

13. Partner with the community to design, implement, and evaluate policies, practices, and services to ensure cultural and linguistic appropriateness.

14. Create conflict and grievance resolution processes that are culturally and linguistically appropriate to identify, prevent, and resolve conflicts or complaints.

15. Communicate the organization's progress in implementing and sustaining CLAS to all stakeholders, constituents, and the general public.

Community Needs Assessments

Another best practice currently being used to understand the unique needs and pain points of vulnerable communities across the United States are community assessments. Required of hospitals, local and state health departments, federally qualified health centers, community action agencies, and other federal grantees, United Way affiliates, and banks subject to Federal Reserve requirements, these assessments also provide a plethora of insights on the community health priorities, organizational support systems, immediate influencers, and individual's health needs. Requiring our transportation workforce to integrate these insights in their future planning will add to developing person-centered transportation planning.

As human-centered design thinking and inclusive planning approaches take hold, it is crucial to keep front and center the voice of the customer, especially as it relates to how religion, culture, and ethnic customs can influence how aging and vulnerable patients interact with existing support ecosystems and how our future transportation workforce and community designers' practitioners would use these insights to include:

- *Ethnic customs*: Differing roles of women and men in society may determine who makes decisions.
- *Interpersonal customs*: Eye contact or physical touch will be expected in some cultures and inappropriate or offensive in others.

In preparing our future transportation workforce and the community designer practitioners is an emerging evidence-based practice of *Advancing*

Trauma-Informed Care, led by the Center for Health Care Strategies (CHCS) through support from the Robert Wood Johnson Foundation [19].

This is a national initiative aimed at understanding how trauma-informed approaches can be practically implemented across the healthcare sector. This emerging practice should be noted for transportation providers designing and delivering services which may include customers who are homeless, victims of human trafficking and domestic abuse, as well as seniors with special needs.

For example, the San Francisco Department of Public Health is one of six pilot demonstrations committed to improving care for individuals with a history of trauma. The pilot efforts, representing a range of delivery systems and populations, are designed to expand and enhance trauma-informed approaches with a focus on improving patient outcomes, decreasing costs, and increasing staff resiliency.

As transportation and healthcare providers, planners, and influencers, we must dive deep in understanding the specific needs of the diverse populations we are aiming to serve and the unique attributes of a given community and region. As the diversity of the United States continues to grow based on age, race, and ethnic backgrounds, addressing the cultural and linguistic needs of these communities will lead to fully engaging and thriving communities with aging populations that are embracing their differences and achieving well-being in a healthily built environment.

Entrepreneurial safeguards

As hard as it is to find community leaders willing to embrace change and take the time necessary to create effective solutions for seniors and individuals with disabilities, it is even harder to find a venture capitalist willing to risk their "window" of opportunity to race to market for those early adopters with deep pockets. Paratransit transportation for seniors and individuals with a disability has been federally subsidized by the government since the beginning. Creating an innovation that relies on government funding and even more complicated subsidies that could come and go in a single presidential cycle will scare away most venture capital funds.

So how do we create innovation for all when most funding is dedicated to deep pockets looking for a quick win? Even when the government tries to step in and require accessibility modification as part of the innovative ecosystem, they face incredible hurdles and backlash. For example, Uber, Lyft, and Via banded together and filed a petition in New York State Supreme Court in April 2018 asking that the mandate "within 12 months 5% of all trips dispatched by the operators be in wheelchair accessible vehicles" be vacated and annulled [20].

Public—private partnerships

Recent trends show government agencies taking the lead in creating innovation for all, creating a safety net for large and small businesses to apply for funding, and taking the time to craft and implement thoughtful design and solutions. For example, Michigan Department of Transportation dedicated an $8 million fund to spur innovative technologies and solutions helping seniors and individuals with disabilities [21]. They set up a full day of workshops and listening sessions and invited established companies and start-ups to unpack and understand the issues facing Michigan resident seniors and individuals with disabilities. State, county, and municipal transportation leaders in small and large communities also came together to meet with the private sector organizations that were invited to plant the seeds of partnerships to come.

Across the pond, Ireland recently launched a €600 million National Development Plan fund to establish innovation programs focused on disruptive technologies, which aim to create a healthy and vibrant country by 2040 [22]. In addition to creating pots of funding for innovators to apply for, some of the largest government agencies are cutting through the red tape themselves and taking a risk, because the cost of doing nothing far outweighs the cost of trying. For example, in Japan, autonomous buses are being rolled out in Nishikata, a small rice-farming town about 71 miles north of the capital city of Tokyo. The town is inhabited largely by older residents (about a third of its 6300 inhabitants are age 65 or older), and the number of public transportation and taxi options has decreased over the last several years, leaving many of the city's residents high and dry [23].

Another example of government taking the lead is one of the biggest public transit networks in the United States moving forward with an innovation that will allow riders to plan a trip with a car share, bike share, or other mobility providers, all within its own system—a framework known as "Mobility as a Service." LA Metro in Los Angeles is putting the finishing touches on upgrades to its Transit Access Pass—known to riders as simply the TAP card—to allow the agency to build relationships with third-party private mobility providers like Uber, Lyft, Lime, and others [24]. The system will boost equity by allowing unbanked customers to load to their TAPWallet using cash. Those customers are instructed to go to the website, download a bar code, and take that code to the nearest CVS or 7-Eleven store where they can pay the cashier to load their account.

Cross Program Functionality

Benefits	PROGRAM	BIKESHARE	TRANSIT	TOLL LANES	PARKING	EV CAR SHARE
	Membership - Level	Flex Monthly			Monthly	Monthly
	Products	$	Metro 30 Day Foothill Day	$	$	$
	Group Discounts	Senior, Low-Income	Sr65, Disabled, Low-Income, Student K-12	Low-Income, AARP, AAA	AAA	Sr60
	Earn Rewards Redeem	🚲 x 5 = 🚆	🚆 x 50 = 🚌	I-110 x 16 = $5	(P) x 30 = (P)	🚗 x 20 = 🚗
	Badges	(🚲 x 10) + 🚆 + 🚌 = ⭐		⭐ + ⭐ = ⭐		Environmentalist Level 2
	Promo Codes	🎟 = 🚲	PROMO = 🚌	Refer Friends and Family = $10 credit		Use Code XER6553 = 🚗
	Trust Level	Trust Increase Min. Balance	"Super-Pass" loaded to select TAP Card	Trust Increase Min. Balance	Program doesn't use	Trust Increase Min. Balance

What this means for the future transportation workforce is that we will see continued cross-pollination of the private and public sector, with employees crossing from the private sector to the public sector to work on both sides of the innovation. It will also mean additional education for the budding private sector transportation staff to better understand government safeguards for the public and data security, and it will likewise require the respect of the public sector to understand that sharing of data and profit are required to stay in business.

The future of transportation without a framework to equitably and effectively support individuals with disabilities is not going to be easy, but the cost savings gained by supporting seniors aging in place, as well as the economic gains for individuals with disabilities, cannot be ignored. Those communities who put in the effort will see the reward socially and economically.

Side bar: "Fernando's Journey"

Fernando has been fighting since the day he was born. Born premature and weighing only 2 pounds while also suffering from congenital disabilities, he beat the odds by making it to 1-week old. The doctor had already told his mother to go home and take care of his siblings as there was no hope. He continued to defy odds by first walking, then being able to go to school, and is still fighting today.

Today, Fernando is in his 50s and has an undergraduate degree in sociology and a master's degree in counseling; he works for the Coastal Bend Area Agency on Aging and the Center for Independent Living. As he is unable to drive, his mother used to take him the roughly 20-minute drive to work every morning so he could be to work at 8 and then pick him back up at the end of his shift at noon. Due to the nature of his disability, sitting and holding himself upright for several hours is painful. Therefore he worked until noon and then went home to rest.

However, as Fernando's mother began to age, things began to change. One day as they sat in the car after their regular trip to church, his mother looked at him and in a scared voice told him she couldn't see anymore. That was the last day she ever drove, and Fernando now faced even greater mobility challenges. He managed to continue to work, take over all of the housework, and take more and more responsibility in caring for his aging mother. Without his mother driving, he began to take a local bus to work. He soon had to change his schedule, however, to work from 10:30 to 2:30 as that was the only time the bus was able to help him. Then in 2014, on the way home from work, Fernando was in an accident on the bus that transports him. He ended up shattering the knee cap of this left leg, further hindering his ability to walk and move around. When he finally made it back home from the hospital, she met him in the doorway with tears claiming if he had died they both would have, because even with his injury she was still dependent on Fernando to care for her.

Fernando's mother passed away in the summer of 2018. Fernando still takes the same bus to and from his job at the Area Agency on Aging. He pays $40 every week to be ready for the bus whenever it comes, typically around 8:15 or 8:30. He then rides the bus for several hours as he fights to hold himself up over the bumps and hopefully make it to work on time by 10:30. After his shift at 2:30, he waits for the bus to pick him up again whenever it can get to him, often being around 1 hour late but sometimes up to 3. He then again endures a rough ride to make it home late in the afternoon. Due to the pain of sitting so long and remaining upright on the bumps of the bus on rough rural roads, he must then lay down and rest to relieve some of the pain on his back.

As hard as it may seem to believe, everyday there are millions of individuals with disabilities who endure extreme pain and long wait times just to have the *opportunity* to work. Fernando with his disability could stay at home and collect his benefits, but he wants to work, he desires to give back and make a difference, and most importantly enjoy a full life. However, that comes at a high price.

If you were Fernando, would you endure hours of pain each day just to have the opportunity to work? Every Center for Independent Living or Area Agency on Aging Director in America can name men and women facing similar challenges.

Now consider that as tax payers, Fernando's round trip using the rural public transit is costing easily over $100 per day. When Fernando could use Lyft or Uber, the cost would be approximately $60 and provide him door to door service, allow him to work the morning hours he prefers that are easier on his body, and give him the opportunity to meet new people in the community. As we consider the future of mobility, we must consider alternative models, for the sake of not only ROI but also social justice for incredible individuals like Fernando—fighting to retain the basic right to work.

"Fernando in front of his family home in Taft, Texas."

References

[1] AARP Public Policy Institute calculations based on driving status by age and gender using Highway Statistics 2016 (Federal Highway Administration) and 2016 Population Estimates (US Census Bureau).

[2] S. Brumbaugh, Travel Patterns of American Adults With Disabilities, Bureau of Transportation Statistics, 2018.

[3] S.H. Murdock, M.E. Cline, M. Zey, D. Perez, P. Wilner Jeanty, Population Change in the United States: Socioeconomic Challenges and Opportunities in the Twenty-First Century, Springer Science + Business Media, Dordrecht, 2015. Chapter 7.

[4] A. Lisa, The average cost of senior care in every state, MSN. <https://www.msn.com/en-us/money/retirement/the-average-cost-of-senior-care-in-every-state/ss-BBBrCEH>, 2017 (accessed 01.11.18).

[5] US Department of Transportation, Bureau of Transportation Statistics, Freedom to Travel, BTS03-08, US Department of Transportation, Washington, DC, 2003.

[6] Cornell University, Disability statistics: Online resource for U.S. disability statistics. <http://www.disabilitystatistics.org/reports/acs.cfm?statistic = 3>, 2016 (accessed 01.11.18).

[7] Center for Poverty Research, University of California, Davis, What are the annual earnings for a full-time minimum wage worker? Minimum wage basic calculations and its impact on poverty. <https://poverty.ucdavis.edu/faq/what-are-annual-earnings-full-time-minimum-wage-worker> (accessed 01.11.18).

[8] J. Sviokla, B. Schroeder, T. Weakland, How behavioral economics can help cure the health care crisis, Harvard Business Review. <https://hbr.org/2010/03/howbehavioral-economics-can-h>.

[9] Health Research & Educational Trust, Social determinants of health series: transportation and the role of hospitals, Health Research & Educational Trust, Chicago, IL. <www.aha.org/transportation>, 2017 (accessed 01.11.18).

[10] Administration for Community Living, Inclusive planning techniques. <http://web1.ctaa.org/webmodules/webarticles/articlefiles/Inclusive_Techniques_TheArcCT.pdf>, 2016 (accessed 01.11.18).

[11] Start with why. Simon Sinek on leadership & finding your calling. <https://startwithwhy.com/>, 2018 (accessed 01.11.18).

[12] https://leadership.openminds.com/wp-content/uploads/2017/09/082517PreCon.pdf.

[13] https://www.kff.org/medicaid/issue-brief/medicaid-non-emergency-medical-transportation-overview-and-key-issues-in-medicaid-expansion-waivers/.

[14] Johnson County Kansas Commissioners meeting - January 2019 - Presentation by Johnson County Mental Health Center

[15] https://www.census.gov/prod/2010pubs/p25-1138.pdf.

[16] https://www.census.gov/content/dam/Census/library/publications/2018/demo/P25_1144.pdf.

[17] https://www.healthypeople.gov/2020/about/foundation-health-measures/Disparities.

[18] https://www.thinkculturalhealth.hhs.gov/clas/standards.

[19] https://www.chcs.org/project/advancing-trauma-informed-care/.

[20] M. Flamm, Uber, Lyft and Via sue to block wheelchair-accessibility mandate, CrainCommunications, Inc. <https://www.crainsnewyork.com/article/20180413/NEWS/180419917/uber-lyft-and-via-sue-to-block-wheelchair-accessibility-mandate> (accessed 01.11.18).

[21] Michigan Department of Transportation, $8 Million Michigan mobility challenge. <https://www.michigan.gov/mdot/0,4616,7-151-9621_17216_86614---,00.html>, 2018 (accessed 01.11.18).

[22] Government of Ireland, Disruptive technologies innovation fund. <https://www.gov.ie/en/campaigns/disruptive-technologies-innovation-fund/>, 2018 (accessed 01.11.18).
[23] L. Chang, Japan focusing on a curious demographic with driverless cars—senior citizens, Designtechnica Corporation. <https://www.digitaltrends.com/cars/japan-self-driving-bus-elderly/>, 2017 (accessed 01.11.18).
[24] K. Musulin, LA Metro to develop MaaS system for TAP smart card program, Industry Dive. <https://www.smartcitiesdive.com/news/la-metro-to-develop-maas-system-for-tap-smart-card-program/529316/>, 2018 (accessed 01.11.18).

CHAPTER THIRTEEN

Cultivating a rural lens: successful approaches to developing regional transportation corridors through professional capacity building

Susan Gallagher and Stephen Albert

Western Transportation Institute, Montana State University, Bozeman, MT, United States

Contents

Introduction

The nation's transportation network is an integrated system, in which connectivity between various segments is necessary to the safe and efficient passage of people, goods, and services to and through cities, towns, and regions of all sizes. While transportation systems management and operations have traditionally focused on urban corridors or rural "hot spots," policymakers and practitioners are increasingly moving away from this piecemeal approach toward a more systems wide approach. An

Empowering the New Mobility Workforce.
DOI: https://doi.org/10.1016/B978-0-12-816088-6.00013-4

intermediary step in this evolution is the implementation of regional systems that cross multiple jurisdictions to seamlessly link urban and rural areas throughout a larger corridor.

Regionally integrated corridors present both challenges and opportunities. Ensuring equity of access to transportation services both within and between urban population centers and throughout rural landscapes with low population densities is an important benefit. The potential to address pressing national needs related to the safety and efficiency of the transportation network overall for both passenger travel and freight is an equally exciting prospect. Advances in data collection, processing, and communications over the past few decades have opened new opportunities to address roadway safety, efficiency, and connectivity issues through implementation of new technologies and operational management systems. Integration of regional data collection and traveler information systems, emergency response, Intelligent Transportation Systems (ITS), and coordination of multiple transportation service providers can deliver many targeted system improvements. To achieve these ends, however, challenges related to coordination between multiple agencies, jurisdictions, and technology systems, as well as data ownership and use must be addressed.

The California-Oregon border provides an excellent example of how state agencies can drive operational improvements through corridors that cross state boundaries. Interstate 5 climbs steeply through southern Oregon to reach Siskiyou Summit at an elevation of 4310 feet before dropping over the pass and descending into northern California. This portion of interstate along the border includes one of the highest passes and some of the steepest grades in the nation's interstate system [1]. Each state employs different winter maintenance policies and practices, which can result in varied roadway conditions on either side of the border. When extreme weather, wildfire, or other incidents make travel inadvisable, getting road closure information to upstream users in two states as quickly as possible is critical, as few alternate routes are available through the area. Road closures can therefore result in significant traveler delays and costs. In these conditions, how can transportation agencies address the need for better real-time information and streamline communications between different roadway maintenance and operations districts in two states as well as to local and long-distance travelers?

In many regions in the late 1990s, planning and widespread implementation of road weather information systems, roadside cameras, automatic messaging systems, and other ITS technologies were in their early stages. There was a lack of evidence for the effectiveness of ITS systems in rural contexts to justify costs, and agency personnel were largely unfamiliar with the technical requirements for operating and maintaining various emerging ITS technologies. The California and Oregon Departments of Transportation responded by partnering to develop regional ITS strategic planning efforts, rural traffic management centers, and systems architecture, and to identify early deployment projects. As will be discussed, this initial bistate effort has spawned a multistate forum that fosters peer exchange, professional capacity building, technology transfer, and multijurisdictional networking, planning, and project implementation. The evolving focus on addressing training and other challenges faced by staff, particularly in rural districts, is instructive and points to a path forward for transportation managers seeking to improve regional corridor operational efficiencies.

This chapter focuses on the challenges faced by the workforce (e.g., state and local transportation agency staff, systems engineers and technicians, local and regional planners, and service providers) in the successful implementation and maintenance of regional and multistate corridors. Issues related to rural systems integration are emphasized to highlight the unique obstacles faced by professionals at smaller local agencies, which must be effectively addressed to implement large-scale transportation corridors successfully.

The context of rural

Traditional thinking about the rural/urban divide can be likened to a simple map of the United States; on the map, black dots represent urban centers of various population sizes. In this scenario, "rural" is envisioned as all the space between the black dots [2]. The reality is much more nuanced, and neither transportation systems nor system users fit neatly into a single category. Within the illustrative map's geographically expansive "white space" lies 70% of the nation's publicly owned surface roads [3]. Rural transportation system users include those passing through the area, such as freight carriers or tourists, users traveling between population centers or between urban centers and outlying suburban communities (e.g., intercity and commuter travel), as well as rural residents living in small towns and rural areas [2].

The extensive rural road network crosses multiple jurisdictions, including state and county lines, as well as tribal and publicly managed lands. It also crosses over more rugged terrain than found in urban areas and is prone to severe weather events [2]. Exacerbating these institutional and operational issues are the higher speeds, more severe alignment features, and longer incident and emergency response times found in rural areas, where traffic fatalities occur at a higher rate than in urban areas [2]. However, the vast majority of the US population lives in urban areas, and state and federal transportation dollars tend to be allocated primarily toward addressing urban challenges (i.e., the "black dots") [2,4]. More sparsely populated rural areas have a lower tax base and subsequently less funding and personnel resources to devote to new infrastructure, maintenance activities, and transit services [4].

The workforce in rural and urban areas can be likened to schools found in each context. In cities, public schools tend to be large. Teachers at a larger school have more opportunities to specialize in a specific subject or subarea. Large schools can offer more diverse courses and extracurricular activities, and students are able to elect from a variety of specialized interest areas like music, sports, culinary arts, science fiction writing, or manufacturing and trade classes.

In a smaller rural school, teachers and students will likely have fewer and more general resources. Instead of specialization, a teacher may need to be able to teach a wider variety of topics and offer content to a greater range of grade levels. A rural Midwestern teacher who teaches AP physics, chemistry, and welding during the school day, and then drives the school bus after school provides an excellent example. Taking this scenario to its extreme, one can picture the one-room classroom of yesterday, where one teacher provided basic education to students ranging from kindergarten to secondary school and had to cover all general education topics.

In a similar vein, rural transportation agency staffs are less likely to have opportunities to specialize relative to their urban counterparts. Difficulties in attracting and retaining professional staff with specialized skillsets to work in isolated rural areas may restrict staffing decisions; and in any case, local agency professionals tend to play many organizational roles in their day-to-day activities. They therefore require knowledge in multiple subject areas to afford them the ability to cross over between a variety of task areas like planning, operations, maintenance, and management. With fewer personnel, it is likewise difficult for rural agencies to carve out time for specialized training without leaving mission critical activities unstaffed. Staff training opportunities that address skills specific to rural areas—such as animal–vehicle collision mitigation measures or wildlife crossing structures—may likewise be more limited. In less populated areas, staff may also have less exposure to addressing specialized service needs, such as Americans with Disabilities Act (ADA) paratransit eligibility or travel training, or less familiarity with specific technologies. Interviews conducted by the Western Transportation Institute to assess training issues related to providing rural ADA and paratransit services highlighted the importance rural agencies place on information exchange with other peer agencies, to fill in knowledge gaps or brainstorm solutions to common challenges [5]. During an outreach effort conducted by ITS America to assess impediments to deploying connected vehicle technologies in rural areas, one interviewee pointed out that while cities tend to have entire ITS teams, a rural area might be fortunate to have a single person with specialized ITS knowledge [4]. In this environment, rural transportation personnel utilize strategies that rely heavily on peer exchange and professional networking and problem-solving to address workforce issues.

Doing more with less is a common theme for rural agencies. The US National Park System provides a relevant example. Park visitation has been steadily increasing over the years with over 56 million additional visits made to national parks in 2016 as compared to 2008. In comparison, park staffing over the same period remained relatively stagnant. In fact 500 fewer NPS employees were responsible for managing the additional resource and service demands of the huge visitation increases experienced over this 8-year period [6]. Gateway communities rely on the economic activity generated by park visitation, which in 2016 was estimated to generate over $18 billion in communities within 60 miles of a park [7]. In addition to supporting increased visitation, public land managers are also entrusted with the (sometimes competing) responsibility of protecting the habitat, wildlife, and other natural resources within the park that draw visitors to it in the first place (Photo 13.1). Strategies to reduce congestion, improve traveler information, manage parking, and support transit and other modes are critical in attaining the two primary park objectives of stewardship and visitation [2]. However, few parks have specialized transportation staff. Recent public financing trends offer little optimism that land management agencies will be able to increase staffing to meet rising demand or to address a growing complexity of transportation management issues (Photo 13.2).

The situation for state, regional, and local transportation agencies is similar. Progress toward greater environmental sustainability and safety,

Photo 13.1 Animal–vehicle conflicts in Yellowstone National Park.

Photo 13.2 Rural congestion in recreation areas.

improved equity and access to transportation services for all, and accommodation of multimodal users, including nonmotorized, is increasingly expected by the public. Although demand for high-quality transportation services in both rural and urban areas is high, public financing and investment in transportation systems remains flat or is decreasing [4]. In this environment, transportation agencies are under pressure to provide a greater variety of services with fewer personnel and fiscal resources.

Making connections and connectivity across jurisdictions

Potential transportation systems management solutions focus on increasing efficiency through pooled resources, innovation, and coordination. Workforce solutions likewise encompass strategies that leverage technical assistance and training resources among multiple organizations, facilitate coordination of services, and provide opportunities for peer exchange, technology transfer, and professional networking. Perhaps because rural agencies out of necessity have long valued information exchange with their peers in other rural communities, some formalized peer-to-peer relationships have provided a longstanding foundation upon which regional corridor collaborations and projects can build and expand. One such locally initiated effort centered on the unique operational and workforce challenges found along the California/Oregon border. As such, the evolution of the partnership from a few rural districts located in two states into a 4-state regional consortium and 11-state regional traveler information system is instructive.

Growth of a regional coalition

A collaborative effort was initiated in 1998 between the California Department of Transportation (Caltrans), the Oregon Department of Transportation (ODOT), and the Western Transportation Institute (WTI) at Montana State University to facilitate implementation of ITS in the bistate rural area along the California/Oregon border. Known as COATS, the California Oregon Advanced Transportation Systems project supported the deployment and evaluation of rural ITS demonstration projects. As the COATS collaboration progressed, participants recognized a need for a technology transfer mechanism so that technology implementers, practitioners, and researchers could share information about problems encountered as well as insights gained with ITS deployments. To meet that end, members initiated the Western States Rural Transportation Technology Implementers Forum (WSF). The forum is designed to allow implementers of rural transportation technologies an opportunity for frank and open discussion about what works and what does not work in the field, and to delve into a greater level of technical detail than would be possible in a typical conference format.

First offered in 2006 the benefits of peer-to-peer information exchange that the annual forum provided, as well as the opportunities for greater research and technology transfer collaborations between states, were quickly recognized. In 2009 the neighboring states of Nevada and Washington expressed interest in joining the COATS partnership and it evolved into the four-state Western States Rural Transportation Consortium (WSRTC). The consortium "provides a collaborative mechanism to leverage research activities in a coordinated manner to respond to rural transportation issues among western states. The Consortium focuses on technology transfer/education and incubator projects centered on the pillars of technology, operations and safety [8]." Successful incubator projects sponsored by the consortium have the potential to lead to more geographically expansive applications.

The formal institutional structure provided by the COATS project over the past two decades has afforded vital opportunities for project participants to build cumulatively on past research and development results, as well as coordination and collaboration experiences over time. One early COATS project explored the feasibility for a rural Integrated Corridor Management (ICM) system to optimize travel through adjoining Caltrans districts and ODOT regions, located in a mountainous area frequently challenged by weather events that could cause vehicle movement restrictions along some routes. The project concluded that ICM could be applied to rural areas where alternative corridors were present and technologies were in place to collect data on current road conditions [9]. The project identified two key ingredients to make rural ICM systems operable:

- A data sharing mechanism between agencies within the corridor; and
- Multiagency stakeholder buy-in to ensure all applicable data are made available in usable formats and to coordinate agencies' response to events.

A subsequent consortium incubator project that successfully expanded from one rural district to encompass all four consortium states and beyond utilized these important lessons learned. The One-Stop-Shop for Rural Traveler Information (OSS) project progressed using a multiphased approach. In Phase 1, the goal was to provide a proof-of-concept for a traveler information system that aggregated a variety of real-time information into one easy-to-use website. Traveler information can provide an important safety and efficiency tool by allowing travelers to learn about possible delays, inclement weather, or other hazards that could impact their trip and to plan accordingly. The system was designed to address the lack of easily accessible real-time traveler information for rural travelers, which can be scattered across multiple sources [10]. These systems can also be used by roadway operators and maintenance crews to identify and address nonrecurring congestion events, maintenance needs, or other events requiring coordinated response through the corridor. The Phase 1 project was limited to Caltrans District 2 but was designed to be scalable and to provide a platform for a site encompassing a much larger geographic area. Experience gained from the ICM project in engaging stakeholders from various agencies, knowledge of available data sources, and development of data sharing platforms were all valuable in the early OSS development phase. Phase 2 of the project utilized the prototype web application for rural northern California and expanded it to all four consortium states. Further refinements of the system in Phase 3 included adding a mobile interface and further expansion into seven additional western states (Photo 13.3).

OSS received ITS America's Best of ITS Award for *Best New Innovative Practice—Research Design and Innovation* at the 2014 ITS World Congress. The pioneering aspect of the project is that it provided route-oriented, real-time or near real-time traveler information on a single website over a multistate region that crossed multiple jurisdictional boundaries. Underlying this achievement was a longstanding institutional structure to support and facilitate collaborative research, education, and technology transfer efforts related to transportation operations, safety, and technology implementation challenges in rural regions of the west.

Photo 13.3 Passenger consults the One-Stop-Shop traveler information site to obtain information on current road conditions.

Challenges and a roadmap forward

Multistate corridor coalitions provide a foundation for regional coordination and systems integration, creating a patchwork national system of regional corridors [2]. The Rural ICM, One-Stop-Shop traveler information, and related ITS deployment and evaluation projects undertaken under the COATS/Western States Rural Transportation Consortium umbrella highlight the many challenges of establishing multistate corridor coalitions. To successfully accomplish regional integration, coalitions need to obtain multijurisdictional stakeholder buy-in, shared data platforms, and a competent workforce capable of dealing with the many technical, planning, and operations issues that arise. Technical staff must be cognizant of establishing interoperability between systems and ensuring data quality and consistent data formats to facilitate cross-agency data sharing. Roadside infrastructure in rural areas is often difficult to maintain, and rural communications and power issues further complicate operational and technical issues (e.g., lack of backhaul networks to facilitate communication networks, inconsistent cellular coverage, etc.) [4]. Technical and systems engineering staff need to work with planning and operations personnel to find creative ways to address issues with gaps in information on road conditions or other data due to lack of power, communications, or other infrastructure in rural areas.

The evolution of COATS into a regional consortium of western states, which provided an organizational structure for regional communication and collaboration, technology transfer, and leveraged resources for workforce development, provides an excellent example of how state departments of transportation (DOTs) can provide leadership and support to local and regional agencies to facilitate the development of smart, safe, and efficient transportation corridors that cross jurisdictional boundaries. The consortium model highlights a path forward to overcoming many of the challenges found in rural areas. In the absence of Metropolitan Planning Organizations (MPOs) or other oversight organizations to facilitate communication, planning, and development efforts across jurisdictions in rural areas, state DOTs can take the lead in supporting regional collaborative efforts as demonstrated by Caltrans and ODOT. Even small-scale projects can set the groundwork for wider-scale implementation by creating a foundation and mechanisms for engagement and communication with a variety of regional stakeholders. Productive relationships established in demonstration projects can help overcome some of the communication and coordination challenges inherent in multijurisdictional corridors and facilitate collaborative strategic planning processes.

While much attention is paid to the technical and institutional issues inherent in regional corridor systems integration, less focus has been placed on the workforce issues. The WSRTC established education and technology transfer as core organizational purposes. The Forum provides a regular opportunity for regional DOT and other agency staff to network and discuss implementation issues at a highly technical level. These opportunities for peer information exchange are especially critical in rural areas where fewer resources and specialized staff are available. Common technical challenges identified in the process have sparked support for professional capacity building projects to tackle high-priority issues that existing agency staff do not currently have the technical background to address. For example, Caltrans worked with the Western Transportation Institute to develop curricula for topics on rural ITS communications systems, to include: plant wireless technologies and Radio Frequency (RF) system basics, IP fundamentals, plant wired communications and optical fiber, and Telco wireless. These were areas deemed of high importance to ITS communications engineers where few training resources existed and where rapid technology changes necessitate continuous updating. The WSRTC's emphasis on integrating workforce development needs into project discussions and research is especially important as technological advancements accelerate. As complexity and variety of available transportation technologies grows, it will become increasingly difficult for engineers, technicians, and other agency staff to stay current on the latest technology. Unless addressed, this can lead to reductions in system functionality and operational efficiencies.

Lessons learned from western states that are of value to transportation leaders pursuing corridor management projects throughout rural America include the following.

Integrate research into technology deployments
Collaboration with universities can assist agencies to integrate research and evaluation into local and regional deployment efforts. This integration is vital as ITS, CV or other technology deployments, and systems integration projects will be a tough sell to resource-strapped agencies, elected officials, and the public in the absence of proof-of-concept work and documented benefits [4]. During periods of public financing contractions,

information gathered over time on system benefits may make the difference in justifying further investments. An additional benefit of university/agency collaborations is the transportation project experience they provide to undergraduate and graduate students. Such experiences can be instrumental in demonstrating to students the transportation applications of disciplines across the academy (e.g., electrical engineering, systems engineering, computer science, planning, as well as civil engineering). They also provide a pipeline of talented new entrants to fill difficult-to-recruit transportation technology occupations with knowledge of the latest technologies as applied to transportation safety and operational issues.

Provide regular formal or informal forums for cross-agency information exchange and technology transfer

Establishing regular opportunities and mechanisms for multijurisdictional agencies to meet and discuss common challenges can lead to new project collaborations. Such opportunities should be supported and champions identified from each locality who possess the capability of transforming ideas into on-the-ground implementation projects. Agency staff typically do not have the time and resources to devote to coordination. Having an organizational framework and an outside coordinator to oversee the logistics of meetings and follow-up tasks will help staff to view forums as opportunities rather than one more duty on an overburdened docket. Universities and other external collaborators can provide this important function.

Design new projects to be scalable

The value to starting small and testing a proof-of-concept should not be overlooked. However, even small-scale projects should begin with a larger end in mind. That means involving as many stakeholders as possible in the planning and development process early on to avoid problems in the implementation or expansion phases. Fostering strong institutional commitment and organizational structures from the outset allows small proof-of-concept projects to successfully scale up.

Shift from project-to-project funding to long-term commitments to support regional efforts

Public funding cycles tend to promote short-term 1 to 2-year individual projects. Setting organizational priorities that support long-term regional efforts will allow related research and education initiatives to ripen and build off each other and will provide the time necessary for collaborations to take hold and bear fruit. Multiphase projects produce higher returns on investment when lessons learned and platforms developed from previous phases can evolve and be integrated into new project aspects or expansion efforts.

Integrate education, technology transfer, and professional capacity building efforts into all regional coalition efforts

An absence of specially trained technicians or systems engineering staff, difficulties in keeping personnel abreast of rapidly changing technologies, high turnover, and recruitment challenges are common themes for urban and rural transportation agencies alike. Without a competent and skilled workforce, successful advancements in transportation system safety and operational efficiencies cannot be achieved. Despite the risk that agencies will be unable to meet mission critical mandates, workforce development is often treated as a side issue, relegated to human resource and training departments. As technology innovations multiply, transportation leaders need to move workforce development front and center and make it a key component of all regional efforts. Mechanisms for peer-to-peer networking, information exchange, and technology transfer should be embedded into all project tasks. To make regional systems feasible, coalitions should look to identify common professional capacity building needs and to leverage support for the development of needed training resources as new technologies emerge or new skills are identified.

New technologies—same issues

As an increasing number of revolutionary transportation technologies begin market penetration, many smaller rural agencies have adopted a "wait and see" approach toward these advancements. Potential benefits relevant to rural areas are expected from technologies like connected and autonomous vehicles in terms of driver safety, freight efficiency, and improvements in real-time traveler information, incident management, and emergency response. However, new technologies are not a panacea and bring familiar challenges. For vehicle-to-infrastructure (V2I) deployments, the same issues with power and communication gaps in rural areas must be addressed; and while Dedicated Short Range Communications (DSRC) are currently the most reliable for safety applications in rural areas, DSRC can also present greater expense as well as new deployment and operations challenges [4]. Uncertainty about competing technologies, such as vehicle-to-vehicle communication systems (V2V) and autonomous vehicles, also mutes enthusiasm for significant investment in deployments of unproven systems by cash-strapped rural agencies [4]. Federal and state leadership can help overcome these barriers by investing in small proof-of-concept rural projects. The Wyoming Department of Transportation's connected vehicle pilot project on I-80 provides a relevant example. Funded by the US Department of Transportation, the pilot is deploying and testing a variety of CV communication systems to improve safety and efficiency along the I-80 corridor, which experiences significant freight traffic and extreme weather events. Lessons learned through the pilot development and implementation process will be of interest to other agencies wishing to assess what potential safety and operational benefits connected vehicle technologies offer in rural corridors.

Challenges faced by state agencies with initial rural ITS deployments mirror those observed during connected vehicle and other emerging transportation system technology implementations. To address the urban/rural gap, agencies will need to devote resources to better quantify the benefits and costs of rural technology deployments and maintenance. The greatest return on investment to initial proof-of-concept projects will be gained by following the same guidelines as outlined earlier—integrating research (e.g., system reliability testing, assessment of operational, safety, and other system benefits), scalability, professional capacity building, and peer-to-peer networking and technology transfer mechanisms—into all aspects of pilot deployment projects. This process will help to establish the multijurisdictional institutional structures and coordination mechanisms necessary to support further developments. Establishing proof of concepts, quantifying benefits, and identifying local champions will additionally assist rural areas to build on initial results and to make smart, targeted investments with the limited resources available. The establishment of formal structures for long-term collaboration and coordination between multiple agencies, jurisdictions, and stakeholders, as well as mechanisms for peer-driven professional capacity building and networking creates the institutional foundations necessary for incremental regional corridor safety and operational improvements, regardless of the latest technology at hand.

Smart cities to smart corridors: regional planning writ large

Expanded capabilities for information collection and dissemination on the transportation network's level of service in real time present significant benefits for urban and rural areas. As such, the Federal Highway Administration observes opportunities to employ and leverage the same institutional, operational, and technical integration strategies for both Integrated Corridor Management and Smart Cities applications [11]. Establishing shared goals is critical to instituting synergies, and common objectives for both corridors and smart cities often extend beyond city limits to address challenges associated with broader trends related to regional demographics, economics, and associated travel patterns. To address the wider array of regional interests, an expansion of stakeholder participation in the process is necessary to include organizations that extend beyond traditional transportation-focused agencies, encompassing health and human services, sustainability, public safety, economic vitality, and quality of life concerns [11]. Despite the inherent coordination challenges such an approach presents, when done well, the result is a more holistic, systems wide, cross-disciplinary, and participatory approach to transportation planning and decision-making, which can help mitigate equity and access issues that plague many urban and rural areas (Fig. 13.1).

One of the issues many rural agencies face is the lack of an organizational entity to ensure the incorporation of local input into statewide transportation plans. While MPOs have long contributed Long Range Transportation Plans (LRTPs) and Transportation Improvement Programs (TIPs) to state agencies, lack of representation from smaller urban and rural communities as part of the statewide planning process can result in less attention being paid to rural transportation needs. Recognizing this challenge, federal transportation legislation (MAP-21) asserts that state DOTs shall cooperate with affected local officials in nonmetropolitan areas when carrying out planning in rural areas, and further pronounces that a state "may establish and designate regional transportation planning organizations to enhance the planning, coordination, and implementation of statewide strategic long-range transportation plans and transportation improvement programs, with an emphasis on addressing the needs of nonmetropolitan areas of the State [12]."

Figure 13.1 Participatory approach to transportation planning: expanding stakeholder input into decision-making processes.

DOT leadership in states without Regional Transportation Planning Organizations (RTPOs) may want to explore whether planning processes currently in place effectively capture multijurisdictional input from non-metropolitan areas of the state. RTPOs can provide: a forum for public participation in the planning process for rural residents, a structure for two-way communication between regions and state DOTs, increased equity in transportation project funding between urban and rural regions, and better integration of rural needs into state transportation plans [13]. RTPOs often combine multiple planning operations within a single agency, which helps bring into the transportation decision-making process a wider array of overlapping focus areas, such as economic development, human services, housing, and land use, ultimately leading to improved transportation planning outcomes to the benefit of the public. In addition, RTPOs must participate in national, multistate, and state-level policy and planning processes, and therefore provide an excellent institutional framework for fostering collaboration with neighboring RTPOs and MPOs and for implementing multijurisdictional regional transportation project planning.

However, creation of an RTPO is not enough without developing the transportation expertise of the organization's diverse members. As such, RTPOs can additionally provide a conduit for peer mentorship and transportation professional capacity building. Ohio provides an excellent case study. Prior to 2013, regional transportation planning was conducted by 17 MPOs, representing 30 out of the 88 counties in the state. To obtain better geographical coverage and to better incorporate participation of nonmetropolitan stakeholders in statewide transportation planning, the Ohio Department of Transportation (ODOT) first turned to the state's five Rural Planning Organizations (RPOs) for assistance [14]. The Ohio RPOs had a long history of conducting a variety of planning functions for their local communities, including economic development, housing, and land use planning. However, ODOT found that these organizations had no transportation planning experience. To develop this expertise, the agency initiated a 2-year pilot program to develop the transportation capabilities of the RPOs so that they could effectively function as RTPOs. A key component of the pilot was a process that teamed RPOs with MPO mentors to help build RPOs' regional transportation planning capacity and to coach them through the process of developing multimodal Long-Range Transportation Plans. By the end of the pilot program, all five RPOs produced LRTPs and were subsequently formally designated by the governor as RTPOs. As a result of this initiative, Ohio added five designated RTPOs, covering an additional 34 counties, and has new pilots underway (Figs. 13.2 and 13.3).

RTPO expansion ensures that more nonmetropolitan areas across the state are involved in a variety of transportation planning components, including corridor studies, safety planning, transit and coordinated human services transportation plans, and freight planning. This valuable benefit could not be realized without the time and effort dedicated to capacity building and mentorship of RPOs, to ensure that transportation planning products delivered by these entities are comparable in content and quality to those produced by MPOs.

Innovations to foster regional equity

Whether focusing on planning efforts, technology deployments, or systems operations, the creation of effective regional transportation networks capable of seamlessly connecting urban and rural spaces is a complex process. Connectivity in terms of on-the-ground mobility is increasingly

Ohio MPOs and Large Cities

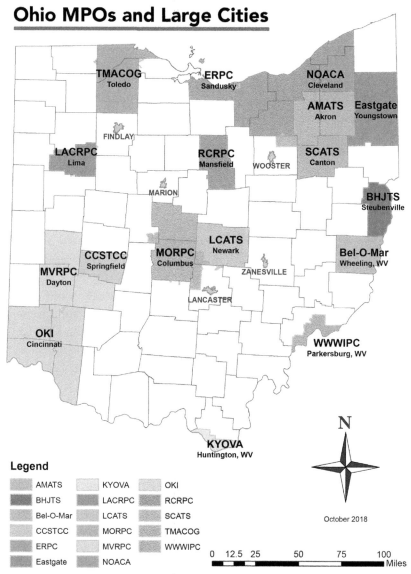

Figure 13.2 Transportation planning organization geographic coverage in Ohio. Original coverage by 17 MPOs.

equated with cellular, internet, and other computer and communication systems connectivity. This is especially true in the observed shift, particularly in urban centers, to a mobility-on-demand model facilitated by the widespread market penetration of smart phones and cellular connectivity.

Ohio MPOs and RTPOs

Figure 13.3 Transportation planning organization geographic coverage in Ohio. Additional coverage gained by creation of five RTPOs through pilot program as of March 2018.

Private companies and service providers are more heavily involved in this emerging mobility market. However, in smaller rural communities, private sector investments can be less profitable and therefore slower to penetrate. Lower investment in assets like broadband or other communications infrastructure in smaller urban and rural areas can cascade into further inequalities when new systems like V2I are implemented that rely on having a communications infrastructure already in place. In response, some smaller communities are taking matters into their own hands, for example, by funding public broadband networks [15]. Other public entities have pursued partnership opportunities with private companies to improve equitable access.

State DOTs can play an important role in improving rural broadband access. According to the US Department of Transportation, per-mile broadband deployment costs in rural areas can be 40 times more expensive than for urban communities, primarily due to excavation costs. To address this issue and the resulting inequalities in broadband access between rural and urban populations in the state, the Utah Department of Transportation (UDOT) instituted "Dig Once" measures to lower fiber optic installation costs for private telecommunications companies, thereby expanding broadband coverage in rural areas. The policy formalizes a process for private—public partnerships in which private companies gain access to public rights-of-way, while also ensuring that broadband installation occurs during road construction projects [16]. By fostering collaborations with private companies to extend broadband connectivity statewide, UDOT has been able to install new ITS devices in remote locations with high-speed data links to its Advanced Transportation Management System, improving statewide systems management. In the process, rural residents have gained quality of life benefits in terms of improved access to 911 emergency services as well as reliable high-speed communications for economic development and other community purposes [17].

Transcending academic siloes to create next generation transportation professionals

The increasing importance of computer and communications connectivity and data management in transportation systems and applications, and the greater involvement of private sector entities as service providers, technology implementers, and data collectors and brokers add complexity to the transportation workforce picture. So too does the need for better assessing the interaction between the transportation system and a variety of other community assets, such as open space, public health, affordability, economic development, and livability. In the emerging transportation environment, new paradigms are evolving that many current professionals feel ill-equipped to deal with. For multistate, regional systems, organizations are applying different business models to move management and fiscal responsibilities away from a single DOT. In the process, different approaches to project oversight, contractual relationships, profit generation, and intellectual property are being explored. The role of state DOTs is also changing from providers of infrastructure to providers of mobility, whereby agencies must work with a wider group of industry and local stakeholders to assist localities in reaching their mobility goals [18]. These shifting priorities and practices will necessitate new competencies not traditionally associated with the transportation workforce.

When organizations face major changes in the environments in which they operate, they must transform the way they conduct business, and sometimes their core missions, to maintain their relevance and effectiveness [19]. An organization's ability to change and reinvent itself to address changing dynamics is critical to its success; and in today's rapidly transforming transportation environment, more organizations will be forced to optimize limited resources and to play more entrepreneurial roles than they have traditionally played [20]. Transportation agency leaders should seek innovative adaptations to traditional workforce development approaches to meet the changing environment and to better encompass the increasingly multidisciplinary demands being made on organizations to manage complex data and relationships. In addition to integrating professional capacity building as a core element of all aspects of the organization's activities, transportation leaders will need to address future organizational competency needs and capacity building through collaborations with education providers.

Agency partnerships with education institutions are not new. Traditionally, agencies have provided internship or co-op opportunities to postsecondary students, participated on departmental advisory boards or in career fairs, or provided guest speakers. These activities help expose students to transportation career options and to professional development opportunities. Research partnerships with undergraduate and graduate student involvement represent another successful mechanism for developing students' transportation problem-solving skills and expertise in a specific topic. However, most of these activities have primarily targeted civil engineering or other disciplines conventionally associated with transportation. Just as transportation planning and project implementation have benefited from the participation of a wider array of stakeholders, approaches to transportation workforce development also need to change to encompass a greater variety of academic disciplines and skillsets.

Public agencies can play a greater role in shaping the next generation of transportation professionals by becoming change agents. One approach to addressing the cross-disciplinary expertise gap in transportation decision-making is by involving students from multiple disciplines in transportation project-based learning opportunities through capstone, design, service learning or other project-based or experiential learning courses. In the process, agencies gain access to student capacity, creativity, and multidisciplinary expertise; at the same time, students learn to apply their disciplinary expertise to solving real-world transportation issues. This approach can help cultivate a more cross-disciplinary future transportation workforce capable of addressing the growing complexity of transportation systems and operations. Beyond workforce development, it also exposes young community members to the role transportation plays in various facets of their lives, which can lead to better public understanding and participation in the decision-making process (Fig. 13.4).

The University of Oregon successfully implemented this approach with city governments. In 2009, it launched its Sustainable City Year Program, which integrated sustainability-focused city projects into project-based learning course components across a variety of academic

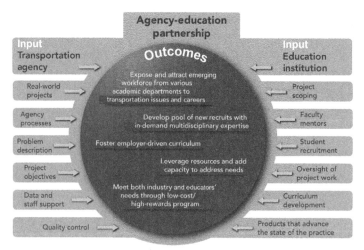

Figure 13.4 Collaborative project partnerships between transportation agencies and educational institutions add problem-solving capacity while training the next generation workforce.

departments. In its pilot year, the program involved students in 19 courses across 8 academic disciplines in community-engaged project work with a single city government partner [21]. The program has since been replicated and similar programs, utilizing the same basic framework, have been implemented at universities across the country. Although most programs continue to focus primarily on city government partnerships and urban issues, some programs have begun to initiate partnerships with smaller communities.

Implementing sustained engagement of this kind between universities and rural communities will take substantial time, effort, and support, given the considerable personnel and funding resource constraints small agencies face. State transportation agencies can provide leadership by proactively supporting new collaboration opportunities between education institutions and local agencies. Such partnerships can be instrumental in building a pipeline of multidisciplinary talent with heightened awareness and understanding of rural issues as well as project-based expertise in addressing them. In addition to impacting the next generation workforce, agency partners benefit from these partnerships in the near-term, by gaining access to multidisciplinary expertise and the ability to apply student capacity and creativity to address rural transportation issues.

Conclusion

As state transportation organizations strive to develop smart, safe, and efficient transportation corridors that connect regions made up of both higher and lower population densities, agency leadership will need to understand the unique challenges rural personnel face in terms of funding and human resource constraints. Similar to rural schools, staff in small urban and rural areas often must undertake a variety of roles and responsibilities within their agencies, and there are less resources available to hire technology or other niche area specialists or to obtain specialized training. Against the backdrop of these workforce constraints are the difficult safety and operational challenges found in rural regions: higher fatality rates, power and communication infrastructure gaps, terrain and weather, higher maintenance and per passenger public transit costs, high seasonal demand and congestion in recreation areas, fewer available alternate routes, among others. Institutional barriers present additional challenges to regional corridor integration. As roadways cross multiple jurisdictional boundaries, data platforms and data collection systems may not be able to communicate seamlessly with one another. Establishing good communication among the various community stakeholders can be equally difficult.

However, necessity can be a generator of innovation. While demand on the transportation network is increasing in many areas, as is demand for a greater variety of mobility services, funding and staffing for public agencies are not. Faced with personnel and resource constraints, rural agencies have long relied on opportunities for peer networking and information exchange to fill knowledge gaps or discuss solutions to common issues. These formal and informal professional networks can provide a foundation for both workforce development and for the development of regional coalitions and corridor systems integration.

As wildfires spread through Northern California in the summers of 2017 and 2018, at times leading to closures of Interstate 5, State Route 299, and even the Caltrans District 2 regional office in Redding, the One-Stop-Shop traveler information system proved an invaluable resource. Providing easy access to multiple layers of information along the route, to include road closures, CMS messages, California Highway Patrol incidents, fire detections, CCTV images, and weather, the system was used by the traveling public to access real-time updates as well as by transportation agency staff to better manage response. A dispatcher from the Caltrans Transportation Management Center noted, "In recent lightning induced fires in Northern California, [OSS] was instrumental in gauging where the fires could be headed based on wind speed... This allowed our center to be better prepared for all the many 'what if' situations we were faced with [22]." The OSS system is one of many positive outcomes resulting from long-term commitment and investment in regional planning efforts, technology deployments, and professional capacity building.

State DOT leadership can play an important role in fostering regional peer-to-peer relationships for the dual purpose of workforce development and regional corridor development. The Western States Rural Transportation Consortium demonstrates how state DOT support for demonstration ITS projects in a bistate region led to a larger multistate coalition of technology implementers. This coalition has provided a forum for addressing technology deployment, workforce, and multijurisdictional coordination challenges; in so doing, it laid the groundwork for an 11-state regional traveler information system. Ohio DOT's innovative pilot program fostered collaboration and mentorship relationships between MPOs and RPOs, thereby expanding rural stakeholder input into regional transportation planning processes. Utah DOT's support for public/private partnerships with telecommunications companies has helped address the inequities in broadband access between rural and urban communities, strengthening the reach of the state's transportation management system in the process. Leadership in developing the next generation workforce—as demonstrated by University of Oregon's partnerships with local agencies—can yield both immediate and long-term benefits, by providing agencies access to the skillsets needed to accomplish changing organizational roles.

As shown through these case studies, placing professional capacity building as a core organizational purpose at the center of all transportation planning and implementation projects leads to additional benefits. By ensuring that mechanisms for technology transfer, peer exchange, and professional networking are embedded into project tasks, agencies can provide a framework for cross-jurisdictional communication and coordination upon which regional collaborations can build and expand. Development of regional professional networks can provide the institutional structures necessary to improve regional transportation networks as well as provide a pathway for building the new professional capacities and competencies increasingly called for in a dynamically changing transportation environment.

References

[1] G. Kramer, The Interstate Highway System in Oregon: a historic overview. Report prepared for the Oregon Department of Transportation. <https://www.oregon.gov/ODOT/GeoEnvironmental/Docs_CulturalResource/Oregon_Interstate_Highway_Overview_2004.pdf>, 2004 (accessed October 2018).
[2] S. Albert, ITS e-Primer: Module 10: Rural and Regional ITS Applications. United States Department of Transportation. Intelligent Transportation Systems Joint Programs Office. <https://www.pcb.its.dot.gov/eprimer/module10.aspx> (accessed May 2018).
[3] U.S. Department of Transportation Federal Highway Administration. Highway Statistics 2016. <https://www.fhwa.dot.gov/policyinformation/statistics/2016/> (accessed May 2018).
[4] Intelligent Transportation Society of America, Rural connected vehicle gap analysis: factors impeding deployment and recommendations for moving forward., FHWA-JPO-18-612, August 25, 2017.
[5] S. Gallagher, I. Karapetyants, N. Villwock-Witte, Comparative approaches to fostering an accessible transportation environment in the United States and Russia, in: 2018 Transportation Research Board Annual Meeting, Washington, DC, 2018.
[6] U.S. Office of Personnel Management, National Park Services Salaries of 2017. <https://www.federalpay.org/employees/national-park-service> (accessed May 2018).

[7] C. Cullinane Thomas, L. Koontz, 2016 National Park Visitor Spending Effects. Economic Contributions to Local Communities, States, and the Nation. Natural Resource Report NPS/NRSS/EQD/NRR—2017/1421, April 2017.

[8] Western States Rural Transportation Consortium, WSRTC factsheet, <http://www.westernstates.org/Documents/WSRTC_Factsheet-web.pdf> (accessed May 2018).

[9] Western States Rural Transportation Consortium, Integrated Corridor Management, <http://www.westernstates.org/Projects/ICM/Default.html> (accessed May 2018).

[10] D. Veneziano, D. Galarus, D. Richter, K. Bateman, S. Wang, Rural Traveler Information Phase 1: rural traveler information needs assessment and pilot study. Final Report. California Department of Transportation, Division of Research and Innovation, 2010.

[11] U.S. Department of Transportation Federal Highway Administration, Integrated Corridor Management and the Smart Cities Revolution: leveraging synergies. FHWA-HOP-16-075 (October 2016) <https://ops.fhwa.dot.gov/publications/fhwahop16075/index.htm#toc> (accessed May 2018).

[12] Moving Ahead for Progress in the 21st Century Act (MAP-21). Public Law 112-141. Subtitle B, Section 1202(m). July 6, 2012. <https://www.gpo.gov/fdsys/pkg/PLAW-112publ141/pdf/PLAW-112publ141.pdf> (accessed July 2018).

[13] U.S. Department of Transportation. What is a Regional Transportation Planning Organization? RTPO 101 Fact Sheet Series. <https://www.planning.dot.gov/documents/RTPO_factsheet_master.pdf> (accessed June 2018).

[14] National Center for Rural Road Safety (Producer), Creating a Rural Transportation Planning Organization (RTPO) [Webinar]. <https://ruralsafetycenter.org/resources/list/creating-a-rural-transportation-planning-organization-rtpo/>, 2018 (accessed July 2018).

[15] A. Marshall, The broadband boost small-town America needs, in: Governing the States and Localities, April 2018. <www.governing.com/columns/eco-engines/gov-rural-broadband-publicly-owned-internet.html> (accessed July 2018).

[16] A. Coleman, Dig once: using public rights-of-way to bridge the digital divide, in: The Current State, E-newsletter of the Council of State Governments, July/August 2017. <www.csg.org/pubs/capitolideas/enews/cs41_1.aspx> (accessed July 2018).

[17] Z. Whitney, UDOT honored with America's Transportation Award, in: UDOT Transportation Blog, June 13, 2018. <https://blog.udot.utah.gov/category/awards/> (accessed July 2018).

[18] CAVita, LLC, National Cooperative Highway Research Program CEO Leadership Forum 2017. White Paper on Connected and Automated Technologies and Transportation Infrastructure Readiness, Prepared for NCHRP 20-24(111), September 15, 2017. <http://apps.trb.org/cmsfeed/TRBNetProjectDisplay.asp?ProjectID = 4223> (accessed July 2018).

[19] KFH Group, Embracing Change in a Changing World: Case Studies Applying New Paradigms for Rural and Small Urban Transit Service Delivery, vol. 99, Transportation Research Board, 2004.

[20] K.I. Hosen,Innovative Rural Transit Services, vol. 94, Transportation Research Board, 2011.

[21] University of Oregon, Sustainable City Year Program website. <https://sci.uoregon.edu/homepage> (accessed July 2018).

[22] Western States Rural Transportation Consortium, Impacts of the one-stop-shop. <http://www.westernstates.org/Impact/OSS/Default.html> (accessed October 2018).

PART IV

Creating Transportation Innovation Networks for the New Mobility Workforce

Inspiring the next generation mobility workforce through innovative industry—academia partnerships

Stephanie Ivey
Associate Dean for Research, Herff College of Engineering, University of Memphis, TN, United States

Contents

Introduction

My commitment to fostering interest in STEM fields comes from two major inspirations: my parents and my first teaching experience. My father, himself very logical and open-minded, recognized my love of math, science, and solving mysteries, and helped me articulate these inclinations into a life path. My passionate and strong-willed mom instilled in me the love of teaching, a calling I discovered for myself during my first job out of school.

Empowering the New Mobility Workforce.
DOI: https://doi.org/10.1016/B978-0-12-816088-6.00015-8
317

After earning a bachelor's and master's in Civil Engineering from the University of Memphis, I accepted a position teaching math and science at Immaculate Conception, an all-girls high school that was lacking a calculus, physics, chemistry, and geometry teacher. I realized that by developing STEM curriculum for those young women, I was extending the same purpose-driven guidance and opportunities that my parents provided for me. This experience was transformational. While intending for the job at Immaculate Conception to be a short-term deviation in the life of my career, I realized how deeply the profession resonated with me and decided to pursue academia.

I went on to complete a PhD in engineering, secure tenure at the University of Memphis, and take on various leadership roles in research and education. Throughout all of it, my priorities have remained engaged scholarship and positive community impact, particularly in terms of inspiring the next generation to enter into the vibrant, dynamic fields within STEM. As I work to help others find and explore their passions, I thank my parents and the students at Immaculate Conception for being the reasons I was able to find a meaningful path myself.

The evolving mobility workforce

The next generation mobility workforce will undoubtedly face challenges that currently cannot be conceived as the transportation industry moves toward an entirely new landscape of autonomous and connected vehicles, smart infrastructure, big data, artificial intelligence, IoT, emerging modes, and ever-evolving technologies that change the way we do work. With these changes come shifts (often dramatic) in required skills and abilities for existing occupations and new jobs with work functions and requirements that did not previously exist. Science, technology, engineering, and math (STEM) competencies will be required for all workers in this new era, whether in STEM fields or not. Effective communication, teamwork, and leadership skills become "core" rather than "soft" skillsets. Next generation workers will need to continuously adapt and learn new skills in order to effectively integrate transformative technologies. And, workers must understand and assess impacts of technologies on people and issues regarding data—including privacy, security, and ethics. They must make decisions regarding the best way forward for their company or organization to meet the demands of the communities they serve.

These changes create exciting opportunities for the new mobility workforce, but also require new approaches to how we attract, educate, and retain workers. Siloed educational practices and traditional models of formal education are not flexible or rapidly adaptable to the current pace of progress. And, as the need for more interdisciplinary education and cross-cutting skills increases, institutions from K-12 to postsecondary will need to transform the way education takes place in order to appropriately prepare students for the future workforce. Most importantly, effective strategies for transportation workforce development must be coherent and collaborative—the right agencies, people, modes, and industries must all be at the table to ensure varied and wide-ranging perspectives are included and comprehensive solutions across the workforce continuum (K-12 to career) are developed. Thus it is imperative that we deploy innovative approaches to attracting and inspiring new workers and industry−academia partnerships are at the core of transformative workforce development approaches (Box 14.1).

Box 14.1 National Network for the Transportation Workforce: creating strategic partnerships (author: Dr. Martin Lipinski, Professor Emeritus, Herff College of Engineering, University of Memphis)

The National Network for the Transportation Workforce (NNTW), sponsored by the Federal Highway Administration, is dedicated to advancing a national transportation workforce agenda. Five regional transportation workforce centers make up the NNTW, with each dedicated to a broad transportation workforce mission as well as expertise in certain disciplines unique to each center. As part of the NNTW agenda, more than 100 strategic partnerships were developed over the past 4 years that engage public and private sector industry representatives, K-12, and institutions of higher education (technical colleges, community colleges, universities) and community organizations in innovative approaches to addressing critical and emergent workforce challenges. One example is the National Transportation Career Pathways Initiative that is a collaborative effort across regional centers (described in detail in Chapter 17: Creating communities of practice for the new mobility workforce: lessons from the National Transportation Career Pathway Initiative). This initiative is engaging industry and academic stakeholders in five core areas of the transportation industry: engineering, environment, operations, planning, and safety. These groups of experts are focusing on identifying priority occupations for the future, determining critical knowledge, skills, and abilities necessary for success, and developing career pathways and implementation plans to create experiential learning opportunities for postsecondary students that will inspire them to consider transportation professions.

The mobility workforce crisis

The US transportation industry has a disproportionally aged workforce, with more than 50% of state transportation agency workers at retirement age, and the rest of the industry following closely behind [1,2]. This is in stark contrast to the US workforce as a whole, also feeling the brunt of the aging baby boomer population, where employees over age 55 will comprise 25% of the total workforce by 2026 [3]. This potential for industry exits on a massive scale coupled with competition from other workforce sectors for talent and a limited pipeline of interested workers creates significant challenges for the industry [4–7]. And, these issues are only expected to increase in the future. Demand for STEM professionals from all industry sectors is on the rise. Job growth is forecasted to be greater than average (average annual growth rate projected at 0.7%) [3] for all STEM occupations relevant to the transportation workforce, as well as other occupations that are shared across modes as shown in Table 14.1 [8]. The result is increasing competition for qualified workers.

Table 14.1 Growth projections for transportation occupations, 2026 (Bureau of Labor Statistics, 2018).

SOC code	Occupation title	Current # employees, 2016	Projected # employees, 2026	Percent change
53–6041	Traffic technicians	6600	7200	9.10
17–2071	Electrical engineers	188,300	204,500	9.00
17–2051	Civil engineers	303,500	335,700	10.60
49–3031	Bus and truck mechanics and diesel engine specialists	278,800	305,300	9.50
15–2031	Operations research analysts	114,000	145,300	27.40
17–2112	Industrial engineers	257,900	283,000	9.70
53–3021	Bus drivers, transit, and intercity	179,300	195,100	8.80
15–1111	Computer and information research scientists	27,900	33,200	19.20
15–2041	Statisticians	37,200	49,600	33.40
11–3021	Computer and information systems managers	367,600	411,400	11.90
15–1122	Information security analyst	100,000	128,500	28.40
11–9161	Emergency management directors	10,100	10,900	7.70
11–1021	General and operations managers	2,263,100	2,469,000	9.10
19–3051	Urban and regional planner	36,000	40,600	12.80
47–2111	Electricians	666,900	727,000	9.00

As new technologies continue to emerge, required knowledge, skills, and abilities for industry competence become a moving target, and workers must constantly adapt [9–13]. For example, diesel technicians had primarily skilled labor roles until technology advances in heavy vehicles changed the job requirements. Diesel workers now must possess STEM competencies, as much of the work they do requires understanding computers and diagnostic software and electronics technology.

Another example is found in the public sector with state Departments of Transportation (DOT) in the Transportation Systems Management and Operations (TSMO) workforce. This specialization did not exist prior to the rise of Transportation Management Centers (TMCs). TMCs integrate a variety of technologies to collect and assess highway traffic data in real time to improve roadway operations through mitigating congestion and enhancing safety. Civil engineers have historically comprised the majority of technical staff for state DOTs. Civil engineers in TSMO roles must possess competencies well outside the range of traditional civil engineering education, to include advanced data analytics, modeling and optimization, electrical and electronics technology, and other technology-oriented skills. This rapid rise of technological innovation means 21st century skills, and in particular STEM competencies are crucial. However, finding qualified workers, particularly in the numbers needed, is a major challenge [7,14,15].

Diversity is another issue that the transportation industry has struggled with for years. Progress and representation varies by mode and occupation, particularly with regard to gender. While women account for 50% of the population and 46% of the total workforce in the United States, they make up only 4%–25% of the workforce in specific transportation occupations [16]. African Americans (13% of US population) account for 12%–20%, and Hispanic workers (19% of US population) make up 9%–19% of these same occupations [16,17]. Women are underrepresented at all levels broadly in STEM and specifically in transportation—and the numbers get worse the higher up the career ladder you look [18,19]. This is important because a diverse workforce is a critical component to supplying not only the needed workers but also the variety of perspectives and skillsets required for successfully solving the mobility challenges of the future. Thus efforts to recruit and retain a skilled workforce must target points all along the career pipeline, from K–12 to postemployment, and must consider diversity at the forefront rather than as an afterthought (Box 14.2).

Box 14.2 APEC women in transportation (WiT) data framework

The Asia-Pacific Economic Cooperation forum's WiT initiative is an exemplar for building robust partnerships to advance women's representation at all levels in the transportation industry around the globe. Two key resources have recently been released—the APEC WiT Data Framework and Best Practices Report (2015) and the APEC WiT Best Practices Compendium Update (2017). In the Data Framework, the stage is set for identifying actions, indicators, and data sources needed to move the needle with regard to women in transportation in five primary areas or "pillars":

- Education;
- Entry into the Sector;
- Retention;
- Leadership; and
- Access and Use.

The framework is unique in that it considers not only pinch points in the talent pipeline but also the question of whether women have equal access and safety in using public transportation systems. This is the only comprehensive data framework developed specifically for women in transportation, and it includes a global perspective given the APEC member countries. The framework was developed through extensive research and numerous stakeholder forums in APEC economies. The best practices compendium catalogs existing programs for all pillars that show evidence of positive impact. The overarching goal of the initiative is to make significant and lasting impact through a data-driven approach to advancing women in transportation.

Compendium cover

With these issues in mind, it is necessary to consider the following key questions in considering new ways to inspire the next generation mobility workforce:

- When (and how) do we engage students to showcase transportation career paths?
- What messages are important for inspiring future mobility professionals?
- What must we do differently to attract diversity to the industry?
- What role do industry—academia partnerships play?
- How do we develop productive and sustainable partnerships?

Attracting the next generation

In thinking about how to attract the new mobility workforce, there are several important factors to consider—factors that can both accelerate and inhibit workforce entry. Employers still struggle to attract and retain workers in an industry that has been largely invisible, modally disconnected, and fraught with misperceptions. Even industry professionals themselves often fail to recognize connections between public and private practice, translation of skillsets and experience across realms (such as traffic, transit, and freight), and opportunities to retain workers in the industry at large. Moreover, a large number of professionals describe their career path as "stumbling" into a transportation career rather than consciously choosing it from the outset [20]. Thus awareness and messaging are crucial components of an effective strategy for attracting the next generation of mobility workers.

When (and how) do we engage students to showcase transportation career paths?

Increasing awareness of mobility occupations requires early intervention. Studies show that students as young as preschool begin forming perceptions of career identity and cement these ideas as early as age 12 [21]. Even more concerning, gender stereotypes are prevalent in elementary school and remain in place as children grow older [21]. Thus it is important to intervene very early in the education-workforce continuum so that students are aware of options available to them and see opportunities in the new mobility workforce as accessible to all.

Equally as important as making students aware of opportunities in transportation is raising awareness with parents. Numerous studies show that parents are one of the most important (if not the most important) factor influencing students' choices of career pathway [22–24]. If students do not perceive that their parents are supportive of a particular career decision, they often change course toward a more apparently acceptable trajectory [25]. Awareness efforts must target a range of stakeholders, from students to parents to teachers and guidance counselors, for real impact to be made (Box 14.3).

Box 14.3 The American Society of Civil Engineers (ASCE) : Dream Big (author: Patrice Thomas, STEM Director, InventHer)

ASCE leadership began "dreaming big" several years ago in thinking about how to attract more students to STEM. And so, the leading civil engineering professional organization began the journey to create a feature film that would showcase the world of engineering and inspire the next generation. Dream Big: Engineering Our World, the result from ASCE's partnership with MacGillivray Freeman Films and the Bechtel Corporation, is a film dedicated to changing the conversation about engineering. "The project is so big, it is more than a movie—it's part of a movement aimed at bringing engineering into the forefront of our culture. Dream Big is the first giant-screen film to answer the call of the STEM (Science, Technology, Engineering, Math) initiative, which aims to inspire kids of diverse backgrounds to become the innovators who will improve the lives of people across our entire planet as we head into the 21st Century and beyond" (ASCE, Bechtel, and MacGillivray Freeman Fillms, 2016). The Dream Big Project:

- Provides continuing educational, museum, and community involvement opportunities in STEM.
- Informs the public about the importance of engineering by showcasing what engineering really means, providing high-interest and inspiring looks into engineering careers through personal stories, and creating a new perception of engineering careers.
- Addresses the demand for K-12 engineering curriculum aligned with the Next Generation Science Standards (NGSS) through an Educator Guide and website with video and other resources.

The Dream Big Educator Guide is a companion resource to the film. It includes multidisciplinary activities for students in grades K-12 and has been written to meet NGSS, as well as common state science objectives. Each lesson presents students with an engineering challenge inspired by the work of

(Continued)

Box 14.3 The American Society of Civil Engineers (ASCE) : Dream Big (author: Patrice Thomas, STEM Director, InventHer) (Continued)

real engineers and can be used to help introduce the engineering mindset to the classroom. To maximize impact, ASCE encourages its members to "adopt" local schools through local chapters to bring the theater experience to as many students as possible. In addition, through funding from the United Engineering Fund, ASCE is working toward its goal of providing a copy of the film and educational materials free of charge to all public schools in the United States. The initiative, which launched in February 2018 during National Engineers Week, encourages ASCE members to sponsor the $5 shipping cost to send the materials to schools.

This truly innovative and groundbreaking effort highlights the impact that can be made through partnerships at massive scale. Everything about "Dream Big" is extraordinary—the giant IMAX screens through which it is presented in 3D, the high-quality educational toolkit, and the access provided to public schools. Through the vision of one professional organization and its primary partners, the power and reach of its membership, and the creativity, imagination, and support of countless others, students (and parents, teachers, and the general public) across the United States now have a completely new image in their minds of engineering and are inspired to "Dream Big."

Students in the 2018 Girls Experiencing Engineering program at the University of Memphis attend a viewing of ASCE's Dream Big.

For awareness strategies to be effective, repeat and varied exposures are necessary [23]. This means students must learn about mobility careers at multiple points along their educational journey, in both formal and informal settings, and through varied approaches such as through connections to academic content, experiential learning, media, success stories of near-peers, mentoring, and role models [23,26,27]. With limited time to integrate additional content into already packed K-12 and postsecondary curriculum, we must look for opportunities to better align existing curriculum with industry practice along the pipeline. This includes reconsidering how we approach formal education (typically slow to react to change) to ensure students exit educational institutions career ready. A new approach is required to integrate industry input into formal education through expanded experiential learning and continuous evaluation of necessary competencies [13,23,28,29]. We must also address the fact that in industry, unlike education where curriculum and programs of study remain largely entrenched in silos, disciplinary lines are no longer so distinct [13]. In fact, employers are moving toward recruiting candidates based on skills, rather than on particular degrees [30].

It may be that the traditional boundaries of disciplinary focus—reflected in the undergraduate "major" and the graduate area of concentration—are becoming increasingly blurred, resulting in a need for greater emphasis on interdisciplinary and transdisciplinary approaches to classroom instruction and labs.

Developing a National STEM Workforce Strategy,
National Academies Press (2016)

Students begin seriously considering career options and selecting coursework to prepare them for the future in secondary schools. However, students typically get limited exposure to the range of transportation career choices in these settings. For example, in high schools in the United States, transportation-related curriculum is found across a spectrum of Career and Technical Education (CTE) pathways including transportation, STEM, and construction. The career cluster obviously associated with transportation is titled "Transportation, Distribution, and Logistics," and integrates a spectrum of pathway opportunities including operations, maintenance, planning, infrastructure management, logistics, safety, environmental management, and sales [31]. The comprehensive framework also points to connections to jobs in the public and private sector and across modes. The problem arises, however, when these pathways are implemented at the local level. School districts rarely have the resources to provide students with the full scope of pathway selections and tend to focus on a very narrow range of opportunities, such as auto repair or warehouse operations. This does little to broaden students' understanding of careers in transportation, and certainly does not address the changing landscape of the industry and the future of mobility. And, because construction and most STEM pathways to mobility jobs are located in other career clusters, these connections are not obvious to students or teachers (Box 14.4).

Box 14.4 Spotlight on K-12 academies of innovation (Author: Dr. Martin Lipinski, Professor Emeritus, Herff College of Engineering, University of Memphis)

The Port of Long Beach Academy of Global Logistics (AGL) at Cabrillo High School

Cabrillo High School is home to a unique program designed to make students aware of logistics careers and to prepare them to pursue these career pathways upon high school graduation. In partnership with the Port of Long Beach, California State University Long Beach, Long Beach Unified School District, and numerous other partners, the program was launched to prepare the next generation of workers for supply chain and logistics careers, given the massive number of jobs and tremendous impact of this sector on the local economy. The 4-year program is designed to provide rigorous academic content and innovative career readiness programming to empower students to pursue global trade and logistics professions through certifications, 2-year, or 4-year degrees with academic partners after graduation. First-year students are engaged in an introduction to the industry, including the basics of supply chain and security considerations. In the sophomore year, students are exposed to more in-depth and multimodal experiential learning as they begin developing career portfolios. The junior year includes networking opportunities at trade/professional association meetings, leadership development, and resume and interview preparation. By the time students reach their senior year, they are ready for a multitude of networking events with industry professionals and they are prepared, completed portfolio in hand, to pursue the next step toward their career goals.

Transportation-STEM Academy at East High

The Transportation-STEM (T-STEM) Academy at East High is part of Shelby County Schools located in Memphis, TN. T-STEM opened its doors to its first class of freshmen in 2017. The program was conceived and developed in a truly collaborative fashion with an advisory committee of over 30 industry, postsecondary, and community partners who serve on planning and

(Continued)

Box 14.4 Spotlight on K-12 academies of innovation (Author: Dr. Martin Lipinski, Professor Emeritus, Herff College of Engineering, University of Memphis) (Continued)

development teams for T-STEM curriculum, extracurricular engagement, and communication and recruiting strategies. All students in 9th grade must take an engineering course (using Project Lead the Way curriculum). Beginning in the sophomore year, students choose from a focus in engineering, aviation, logistics, or diesel mechanics (new for fall 2018). The diesel program launched as the first implementation of Cummins' Technology Education for Communities (TEC) program in North America. Cummins provided leadership of an intensive working group of local companies and postsecondary institutions to develop a state-of-the-art diesel technology lab, curriculum aligned with postsecondary partners and employer needs, and instructor training. All T-STEM programs of study offer dual enrollment/dual credit options with postsecondary partners and/or industry certifications upon graduation. Students are exposed to a variety of unique experiences including a monthly CEO series speaker session, T-STEM Ambassadors from the University of Memphis (undergraduate STEM majors) who support project-based learning and STEM challenge competition preparation, an annual conference with industry professionals, numerous career preparation events with industry partners, and a summer Transportation Academy at the University of Memphis.

One very specific example of the process of providing awareness is illustrated by looking at the civil engineering pathway to mobility jobs. While this is the most traditional pathway to transportation engineering careers, in most civil engineering programs there is only one required transportation course at the undergraduate level, and this comes typically at the junior year [32]. This means students have limited exposure to the breadth of transportation engineering options (as the required course typically focuses on basics of design, operations, and planning for highway systems), and they receive this exposure at a time in their educational path when many students have already selected a specialization preference within the discipline [32].

These difficulties in providing connections to mobility careers in formal educational settings mean experiential learning and informal experiences outside of the classroom take on greater importance. Transportation-themed competitions and challenges, internships and apprenticeships, and after-school clubs and summer career exploration programs must become commonplace in high school and postsecondary experiences [15,33,34]. The role of professional societies and large public and private sector organizations is critical in raising awareness of specific mobility occupations, as they are tremendous resources for targeted awareness campaigns, volunteers for both informal and formal education programs, development of transportation-related curriculum and creating and hosting competitions or challenge experiences. And, collaboration across the workforce pipeline is key for success in awareness campaigns. All stakeholders, including K-12 and higher education, community and professional organizations, and public and private sector employers must be engaged to move the needle (Box 14.5).

Box 14.5 Spotlight on K-12 transportation curriculum (Author: Patrice Thomas, STEM Director, InventHer)
NanoSonic STEM lessons

NanoSonic and Leidos, Inc., in partnership with STEM teachers in Giles County, VA, have developed a suite of middle and high school STEM lesson plans (focused on transportation). The lessons were developed through funding from the U.S. Department of Transportation via a "Small Business Innovative Research" (SBIR) program, and are available for free on NanoSonic's website (http://www.nanosonic.com/education/). The hands-on activities allow students to develop deeper learning of STEM content and concepts through real-world examples set in an advanced transportation system context. The lesson plans engage students in everything from robotics to mathematics to electronics and coding and build interest through connections to exciting advances in the industry such as connected and automated vehicles and Intelligent Transportation Systems.

Comprehensive lesson plans are specifically tailored for both middle and high school audiences, and include 10 modules:
- Module 1: Crash Prevention_Lesson 1: Physics and Reaction Time
- Module 1: Crash Prevention_Lesson 2: Stopping Distance and Crash Avoidance
- Module 1: Crash Prevention_Lesson 3: Road Weather Information Systems
- Module 1: Crash Prevention_Lesson 4: Traffic Congestion
- Module 2: Connected Vehicles
- Module 3: School Zone Safety Audit
- Module 4: Traffic Signal Design
- Module 5: Sustainable and Intelligent Transportation
- Module 6: Congestion Pricing
- Module 7: Road Trip Board Game
- Module 8: RADAR and LIDAR Systems in Intelligent Transportation Systems
- Module 9: Dynamic Message Signs
- Module 10: Intelligent Transportation Systems - Smart Work Zones.

(Continued)

Box 14.5 Spotlight on K-12 transportation curriculum (Author: Patrice Thomas, STEM Director, InventHer) (Continued)

This partnership led by NanoSonic has also resulted in the development of a transportation-themed board game, *Road Trip*. Designed to increase middle and high school students' knowledge of advanced technologies and their impact on transportation engineering and safety, the game inspires students as they take a trip toward the future of transportation. These distinctive resources empower teachers to integrate transportation-themed STEM content in an academically rigorous but highly engaging format and encourage students to learn advanced content through a fun and active setting.

Transportation careers: a resource for teachers

Transportation Careers: A Resource for Teachers was developed with funding from the US Department of Transportation and the US Department of Education working in partnership with Advance CTE. Developed by teachers for teachers, all lesson plans also include input from industry partners. This free resource (http://www.transportationcareers.org) of over 500 lessons features problem-based learning in Transportation, Distribution, and Logistics (TDL). Targeting middle and high school audiences, the units introduce students to careers in TDL and the knowledge and skills required for success. The tailored lessons are designed to address the TDL cluster standards and appropriate academic standards for the seven TDL pathways available through CTE programs:

- Transportation Operations Pathway
- Logistics Planning and Management Services Pathway
- Warehousing and Distribution Center
- Facility and Mobile Equipment Maintenance
- Transportation Systems/Infrastructure Planning, Management and Regulation Pathway
- Health, Safety and Environmental Management Pathway
- Sales and Service Pathway.

The resources enhance curriculum CTE teachers deliver through relevant real-world applications. In addition, the site features a 180-hour course designed specifically to US Department of Education standards entitled, *An Introduction to Transportation Careers*. This course is part of the CTE TDL pathway curriculum, and is created for 9th and 10th grade students. The course is designed in a modular fashion so that individual schools can adapt it to the specific needs of their program and students. The site also provides background on the TDL industry, links to additional resources for teachers, and support for problem-based learning. This thorough resource makes the transportation industry visible and accessible to students by enhancing content and facilitating delivery of TDL curriculum for teachers.

What messages are important for inspiring future mobility professionals?

While raising awareness of mobility careers is important, the messages that are being delivered about the industry are critical. And, addressing misperceptions is just as big an issue as getting the messages across in the first place. A comprehensive strategy for creating a campaign to attract the new mobility workforce requires first identifying the misperceptions that are commonplace, and then thinking carefully about the messages that need to be conveyed.

In thinking about the struggles in attracting new workers to transportation, Eric Plosky of the US Department of Transportation Volpe Center reflected, "Every kid thinks transportation is cool. My question is when did people 'fall out of' transportation?" [35]. This statement underscores the issue of rampant perceptions of transportation roles as being low skill, "tough" jobs, having no connections to STEM, and being generally undesirable [20,26,36]. Connections between transportation roles and societal impact are also poorly understood. As discussed previously, because K-12 and higher education programs typically have narrow and siloed offerings for transportation programs of study, students tend to have an incomplete perspective of what a transportation career may encompass. In addition, care must be taken in all outreach and recruitment materials to be sure images or content do not inadvertently reinforce stereotypes, particularly when trying to reach underrepresented populations [26].

Kids all seem to be 'into' transportation — they love cars and trucks and buses and trains and boats and planes. But, for some reason, as they grow up, they seem to 'fall out' of transportation. Well, I never did! So, when people ask me, 'How did you get into transportation?' I ask, 'How did you get out of transportation?!'

Eric Plosky (2018)

These perceptions, of course, could not be further from reality. Transportation is inherently an inter- and transdisciplinary field. STEM occupations (at all levels) dominate the industry [37]. And, while there are many roles that do not require a 4-year or advanced degrees, a large number of these are high-skill (requiring specialized certifications) and high-wage opportunities [2,37]. Median wages in 2016 for high growth transportation occupations are shown in Table 14.2, along with educational requirements. It is important to note for comparison purposes that the median annual wage for all occupations in the US economy was $37,920 [8].

Understanding how a career can lead to making a difference in our communities is a primary motivator for our next generation workforce, and is

Table 14.2 Median salaries for high growth transportation occupations, 2016 (Bureau of Labor Statistics, 2018).

SOC code	Occupation title	Typical entry	Median hourly	Median annual
		Level of education	Wage, 2017	Wage, 2017
53−6041	Traffic technicians	High school diploma/ specialized certifications	$21.96	$45,670
17−2071	Electrical engineers	Bachelor's degree	$45.70	$95,060
17−2051	Civil engineers	Bachelor's degree	$40.75	$84,770
49−3031	Bus and truck mechanics and diesel engine specialists	High school diploma/ specialized certifications	$22.29	$46,360
15−2031	Operations research analysts	Bachelor's degree	$39.13	$81,390
17−2112	Industrial engineers	Bachelor's degree	$41.29	$85,880
53−3021	Bus drivers, transit, and intercity	High school diploma/ specialized certifications	$19.61	$40,780
15−1111	Computer and information research scientists	Master's degree	$55.06	$114,520
15−2041	Statisticians	Master's degree	$40.41	$84,060
11−3021	Computer and information systems managers	Bachelor's degree	$66.93	$139,220
15−1122	Information security analyst	Bachelor's degree	$45.92	$95,510
11−9161	Emergency management directors	Bachelor's degree	$33.89	$72,760
11−1021	General and operations Managers	Bachelor's degree	$48.27	$100,410
19−3051	Urban and regional planner	Master's degree	$34.37	$71,490
47−2111	Electricians	High school diploma/ specialized certifications	$26.01	$54,110

even more influential for women and persons of color [38]. The next generation also expects clarity around how their roles (even at entry level) contribute to the organizations' goals and the path forward for advancement [39]. Mobility professionals have a tremendous impact in society through focus on the safety of our transportation systems, community planning and design, supply chain and logistics resulting in rapid delivery of goods, managing and operating public transportation, and designing next generation technologies to improve transportation system experiences and create new modes. These are the stories we need to share with the next generation workforce and those that influence them so that mobility careers become careers of choice.

The incredibly diverse nature of the transportation industry provides opportunities for people with varied interests, talents, and academic preparation—but, this message needs to reach the pipeline of future workers. And, the exciting technological advancements that are occurring in the industry are changing the landscape of transportation—children being born today may never drive a car [40]. This is an incredible time in history to be engaged in transportation. Transportation is dynamic, challenging, and at the leading edge of technology and innovation. In order to change the conversation around transportation (or mobility) careers, we must effectively communicate the following ideas to our next generation:

- There is a diversity of opportunity in this rapidly evolving industry—students can find their "fit" in transportation no matter what their interests.
- Multiple pathways to GOOD jobs are available through transportation, from technical certifications to 4-year degrees and beyond.
- Transportation professionals make a difference, impacting lives of people in their communities and around the world on a daily basis.
- The industry is at the cusp of transformational shifts—the next generation workforce will be on the front lines innovating, designing, and deploying advanced technologies that will fundamentally change the way our society views mobility (Box 14.6).

What must we do differently to attract diversity to the industry?

Attracting diversity is crucial in addressing the talent crisis. Organizations must look to expand the pool of potential workers through specialized initiatives to increase the diversity of all types including gender, ethnic/cultural, generational, and veterans. The best approaches for attracting diversity may vary based on the group in question. For example, for women, primary strategies may include interventions at earlier ages, programs designed specifically for girls that showcase female role models, or other outreach activities intended to debunk negative stereotypes that limit women's interest in transportation roles. For veterans, difficulties often arise in the transition process as they are unsure how their military experience translates to civilian occupations, so strategies to provide more seamless transition are needed.

Veterans are a particularly strong candidate pool, as nearly 60% of military jobs are in high growth occupations for the transportation industry, meaning that many of the skillsets and competencies veterans have developed through military service are directly transferrable to civilian transportation roles [41]. Numerous programs have been developed to help with military transition to the civilian transportation workforce. One specific example is the Military Crosswalk Search tool developed and

Box 14.6 SETWC Transportation Spotlights

Transportation Spotlights are an initiative of the Southeast Transportation Workforce Center to showcase professionals from a variety of transportation occupations. The Spotlights are intended to demonstrate diversity—in career path, gender, ethnicity, level of experience—such that students understand that the transportation industry provides an opportunity for people from every background and area of interest to make an impact in our society. Spotlights are shared via social media weekly on "Transportation Tuesday."

CATALINA ECHEVERRI

COMPANY:
Gannett Fleming

TITLE:
Project Manager

TRAINING ORGANIZATION OR COLLEGE/UNIVERSITY:
University of South Florida

CERTIFICATION/DEGREE:
Bachelor in Industrial Engineering, Master in Civil Engineering (Transportation)

memphis.edu/setwc

Q: How did you select your certification program or college major?
A: I decided to study Industrial Engineering because of the degree concentration in engineering management. I became interested in transportation projects during my years in the undergraduate research program. The Center for Urban Transportation Research (CUTR) is located in the USF Tampa campus and they had many interesting projects where industrial engineers were involved. I became interested in traffic and intelligent transportations systems (ITS) projects. Therefore, I decided to do a master's degree in transportation, while being a graduate research assistant at CUTR with the ITS group.

Q: What was the biggest influence in your selection of career pathway?
A: The biggest influence was CUTR. This program helped me understand how all engineering majors play a role in the future of transportation.

Q: What attracted you to the transportation industry?
A: I've always been fascinated with interchanges and how incredible the highway system is.

Q: What is your favorite aspect of your job?
A: I like that we can make a difference on everyone's daily lives and our own. Traffic operations is an exciting field to be in right now with all the upcoming connected and automated vehicles technologies and smart cities. I enjoy participating in the discussions of how technology can change the world that we live in now.

Q: How do you/your company make a positive impact on society/our community?
A: We are encouraged by the company to give back and part of that is through charities. Some of the regional offices organize volunteer days. We always try to get involved with the local community donating not only money but also our time.

Q: What's the most interesting thing you have been able to do in your professional career?
A: I would say working in the design of a tunnel management system in the Middle East. There are only two (2) tunnels in Florida so we don't really have an opportunity to constantly get involved in this type of work. Also, I was working with mechanical, electrical, and communication's engineers. We all contributed in one way or another to this project.

Q: What makes you get up each morning excited about your profession?
A: It feels good to contribute to quality of people's lives. Traffic is something that we experience every day and we are constantly looking for ways improve the transportation system.

Q: If you could go back to high school and select any elective course to take that would have better prepared you for college, what would it be?
A: I would recommend design and programming courses. Engineers have only one required course of each and those skills are always helpful after graduation.

Q: What advice would you share with students or anyone considering your profession?
A: Take as many science classes as possible. Most of the engineering majors have a hard time and sometimes drop out the first two years of math, physics, and chemistry. After the basic classes are done, you can concentrate on the engineering track chosen.

This material is based upon work supported by the Federal Highway Administration under Agreement No. DTFH6414H00005 & DTFH6116H00030. Any opinions, findings, and conclusions or recommendations expressed in this publication are those of the Author(s) and do not necessarily reflect the view of the Federal Highway Administration.

 U.S. Department of Transportation
Federal Highway Administration

 THE UNIVERSITY OF **MEMPHIS.** | Southeast Transportation Workforce Center

Transportation Spotlight of transportation professional Catalina Echeverri hosted by the US Department of Labor on O*Net OnLine [42]. This tool allows users to select their military branch and input their current Military Occupational Classification and the search will return a listing of relevant civilian occupations with detailed information such as job titles, work tasks and knowledge, skills, abilities, education and credentialing requirements, and wage detail. Links are also available to help veterans find training programs if additional education is required. Tennessee's Highways for Heroes program provides a commercial driver's license (CDL) skills test waiver for veterans with military driving experience [43]. Veterans must still take the knowledge component of the test. The effort is designed to make the transition easier for veterans to obtain CDLs. Another example from the private sector is that of Schneider, where nearly 30% of the company's employees have military experience. Schneider's military program offers veterans credit for military service years toward pay, an apprenticeship program in partnership with the Department of Veterans Affairs providing up-skilling opportunities, flexible and predictable work schedules, and a range of other benefits [44]. And, the USDOT recently announced plans to launch a pilot program to allow veterans ages 18−20 with the military equivalent of a CDL to operate commercial vehicles in the civilian workforce. Driving records will be monitored throughout the pilot period, which may last up to 3 years. If successful, this change may make a significant impact on the tremendous driver shortage in the United States [45].

In the case of women, early and frequent intervention is needed to attract them to transportation. Women tend to be more other-oriented rather than self-oriented, and want to know how their work will make a difference [18]. Girls may still face gender stereotyping that limits their awareness of experiential learning and outreach programs as they may not be made aware of opportunities that teachers and parents may consider more oriented to boys [46]. This is one reason that programs specifically designed for girls can be very impactful [26]. The University of Memphis designed and developed the Girls Experiencing Engineering (GEE) program in 2004 to encourage more young women to consider STEM careers. GEE is designed to attract young women to STEM fields by increasing their awareness of career opportunities, addressing misperceptions and stereotypes, and providing hands-on learning experiences that build confidence and offer leadership opportunities. Annual workshops for parents and teachers are also part of the comprehensive program model. Through longitudinal evaluation, it is apparent that the model is working. From 2004 to 2017, the GEE program engaged 1574 middle and high school girls (including 1016 unique participants as nearly 1/3 are repeat attendees), nearly 750 teachers, and over 300 peer mentors. Importantly, approximately 88% of these young women represent ethnicities (African American and Hispanic students) traditionally underrepresented in STEM fields. Program evaluation indicates that 98% of tracked high school graduates (506 girls) are now attending college and 35% are in STEM majors [47]. And, of the high school girls selected to serve as peer mentors, 76% are now in engineering majors, 88% are in a STEM major, and 100% are in college. These statistics are particularly impressive given the fact that there is no academic performance or preparation requirements required for acceptance to the program, and a significant number of GEE graduates are first-generation college students (Box 14.7).

Box 14.7 Spotlight on impact through informal education
Girls Experiencing Engineering: opening doors and minds to STEM professions

Girls Experiencing Engineering (GEE) attracts young women to science, technology, engineering, and math (STEM) fields by increasing their awareness of career opportunities, addressing misperceptions and stereotypes, and providing hands-on learning experiences that build confidence and offer leadership opportunities. GEE was first offered in 2004 as a 1-week summer program for middle school girls. Today, GEE has grown to include multiple weeks each summer of general engineering, discipline specific (transportation), and leadership programming for middle and high school girls. GEE is hosted by the University of Memphis Herff College of Engineering and has been funded since inception by the Women's Foundation for a Greater Memphis and a variety of corporate partners, including CN. Insight Into Diversity Magazine recognized the GEE program as one of 2018's top Inspiring Programs In STEM.

Beyond simply a summer outreach program, a variety of support is offered to encourage these young women to pursue STEM majors, and to remain in them once in college. GEE staff hosts academic year events, including after-school STEM clubs and fall and spring socials. All events reinforce requirements for academic preparation and provide support for STEM skill development (and particularly for math). GEE participants are also strongly encouraged to attend multiple GEE summer sessions, to remain connected to program staff, and to apply to serve as peer mentors for younger students.

Young women that choose to attend the University of Memphis receive priority consideration for STEM Ambassador jobs with the Herff College of Engineering's STEM Ambassador program. This program employs undergraduate STEM majors to work in K-12 settings as math or science tutors, STEM club leaders, STEM competition coaches, and other STEM educational

(Continued)

Box 14.7 Spotlight on impact through informal education (Continued)

activities. Engaging GEE graduates as STEM Ambassadors develops a sense of community and provides a network of support through faculty, staff, and peers, as well as builds confidence and commitment to STEM majors by employment that reinforces STEM learning. These young women are also tapped to serve as GEE mentors each summer during their college career.

And, the model is working. Former participant Patrice Thomas is one such success story. Patrice began the GEE program as a high school student. She had low expectations for the experience, having been signed up by her mother without her knowledge. However, something about the program sparked her interest, and she returned each summer until graduating high school as both a participant and mentor to students in the middle school sessions. She then chose to major in civil engineering at the University of Memphis, and became the lead GEE mentor throughout her undergraduate career. She is now a transportation professional, and has experience with several organizations, both public and private sector. Even more impressive, she returns each year to share her story with the GEE participants and cofounded an annual conference to increase Memphis area high school girls' awareness of STEM careers. When asked to reflect on her experience, Patrice stated, "Prior to attending GEE I had no idea what engineering was. I met so many influential women who were making an impact and changing the world around them. I have always had the heart to help others, so that inspired me so much! My involvement in the camp left me feeling as if I could do and be anything I put my mind to. I'm so grateful that I was exposed to the various possibilities that a career in engineering entailed; otherwise, I do not think I would have chosen a career in Transportation Engineering."

Patrice Thomas (center) mentors Amanda and Kristen Haltom in the GEE program. Amanda and Kristen are now both engineering professionals.

(Continued)

Box 14.7 Spotlight on impact through informal education (Continued)

Women In trucking: advancing women in the industry—starting with girl scouts! (Author: Patrice Thomas, STEM Director, InventHer)

The Women In Trucking (WIT) Association has been a leader in advancing women in the trucking industry since its inception. From elevating the status of driving occupations for women, keeping tabs on industry progress toward diversity at all levels, and to increasing awareness of the range of possibilities that provide tremendous career opportunities for women, WIT is at the forefront. The innovation and large-scale impact of their efforts are exemplified through their partnership with Girl Scouts of America to encourage more women to look at careers in transportation and supply chain. This partnership has created an opportunity for young girls across America and Canada to earn a Transportation Patch. The purpose of the Transportation Patch is to expose young girls to these careers through hands-on learning activities that explore multimodal content—from trucks, to boats and airplanes and pipelines. An estimated 800 young girls have now earned the Women In Trucking Transportation Patch. Girl Scout troops can request to earn the patch directly, but WIT members (and drivers) also reach out to local troops to make them aware of the patch and sponsor events that allow girls to earn the patch.

To earn a patch, the girls learn about all modes of transportation, but more importantly, they learn from a range of professionals—from female engineers who design trucking systems to the female drivers who operate them—about the impact of trucking and the variety of roles in the industry. WIT developed the curriculum and the patch alongside the Greater Chicago/Northern Indiana Girl Scout regional office. A supplemental activity guide to provide girls with a real-world understanding of supply chain is under development. The guide depicts the importance of the supply chain path of Girl Scout cookies from the field to the final mile, placing supply chain firmly within a context that all Girls Scouts understand.

WIT Girl Scout Patch

Another program targeting young women is the USDOT's Women and Girls in Transportation Initiative (WITI). This program provides a spectrum of support to increase women's participation in the transportation industry through providing paid internship experiences with industry partners, educating WITI interns on the variety of opportunities available in the industry (particularly through STEM), and providing resources to female-owned small businesses to overcome barriers to economic competitiveness in the transportation industry [48].

WTS also provides an outstanding example of supporting women across the pipeline. This professional organization, whose mission is to advance women in transportation, offers a program for high school students (Transportation You), supports collegiate student chapters, and serves as a leading professional organization for women in the industry who are in STEM occupations [49]. WTS partnered with the USDOT to create Transportation You, and through this program provides a mentoring for young women through local WTS chapters, a website and blog targeting girls age 13–18, and an annual DC Youth Summit [50]. The DC Youth Summit features a 5-day experience for 20–30 girls from around the country each year. Youth travel with their WTS mentors to DC, and participate in an intensive event that includes a multitude of industry tours, female guest speakers, and culminates with a STEM Challenge project.

Beyond increasing awareness and support and sending the right messages during K-12 and college years, it is important to convey the business case for diversity so that organizations coalesce around the true benefits of diversity and inclusion rather than simply working to "check a box." A 2018 report released by McKinsey and Company documented continued evidence that companies with greater numbers of women in leadership roles significantly outperform those with less female representation [51]. They also showed a significant correlation between increased profitability and companies with greater ethnic/cultural diversity in leadership. Specific to the transportation industry, the 2017 APEC Women in Transportation Data Framework Report highlighted the numerous evidence-based benefits of a more balanced representation of women in the workforce, including increased organizational productivity and performance, greater innovation, improved consideration of safety issues, and improved competitiveness [19]. Both studies also point to increased diversity as a prime strategy to attract more (and diverse) workers.

Diversity and inclusion is still a work in progress in the transportation industry. It is clear, however, that it is imperative for the industry to excel. The following recommendations are vital to moving the needle related to diversity in the new mobility workforce:

- Targeted initiatives with tailored messages are important for reaching varied segments of the population.
- Awareness campaigns must start early and be repeated often-repeat exposure is an essential aspect for motivating students to pursue a particular career path.
- We must remove barriers to entry into transportation careers. These vary but include eradicating stereotypes, clarifying occupational roles, and smoothing transitions from military to civilian careers.
- Expanding mentoring programs, development of role models via media, guest speakers, and other sources, and engaging target populations in challenge projects or other experiential learning can help potential workers envision themselves as transportation professionals.
- For real change to occur, organizations must embrace the true value of diversity, and approach diversity recruitment through this lens.

Industry–academia partnerships in workforce development

Industry–academia partnerships are essential for inspiring the new mobility workforce. Industry must take an active role in developing K-16 curriculum, developing outreach programming, creating awareness campaigns, and designing other initiatives to increase participation in the mobility workforce of the future [15,26]. Only through a collaborative approach can true innovation occur. This is because while academia has expertise in pedagogy, engaging students, and delivering content, industry holds the key to ensuring what is taught is state of the art and practice, experiential learning is tied to real-world applications, and role models in aspirational careers engage with prospective workers. And, as technologies continue to rapidly transform the workplace and thus workforce needs, this approach is even more critical. Both communities must be at the table for the best approaches to building a robust mobility workforce to emerge.

What role do industry—academia partnerships play?

Direct interaction with industry professionals is one of the most effective ways to change perceptions of technical career paths [24]. While guest speakers can debunk stereotypes and inspire future workers, it is even more impactful when students have an opportunity to participate in experiential learning-through field visits, industry-designed challenge projects, internships, and apprenticeships, and develop more meaningful interactions with these professionals [15,34,52]. This can be even more important for underrepresented students, as experiential learning allows them to explore content and context and to begin to envision themselves in a related role [15,30] (Box 14.8).

Box 14.8 National Operations Center of Excellence (NOCoE): leading the way in TSMO workforce partnerships

Created to address specific workforce challenges in the TSMO realm, the NOCoE was established through a partnership between the American Association of State Highway and Transportation Officials, the Institute of Transportation Engineers, and the Intelligent Transportation Society of America and support from the Federal Highway Administration. Led by Patrick Son, the center's mission is to, "...address the need for a more centralized and comprehensive set of resources to serve the TSM&O community." NOCoE provides support and facilitation for technical forums and peer exchanges targeted toward partnering state DOTs. NOCoE also develops and maintains a comprehensive clearinghouse (www.transportationops.org) of state of practice research, technical reports, case studies, and news relevant to TSMO.

In 2016, NOCoE commissioned a series of white papers on the emergence of the TSMO specialty and state of the workforce and convened a national stakeholder group to identify top workforce challenges and priorities for action plans. In response to findings from these efforts, NOCoE launched two programs targeting college students to raise awareness and interest in TSMO. The first is an e-Portfolio competition for students to showcase their TSMO-related research. The inaugural event was held in the fall of 2018, with winners receiving trips to the annual Transportation Research Board conference and extended networking opportunities with NOCoE staff. The Transportation Technology Tournament was developed in partnership with the USDOT ITS Joint Program Office PCB. The competition pairs interdisciplinary teams of students with state DOTs to solve real-world challenges relevant to ITS and TSMO. The program included training webinars, multiple progress check-ins, and a preliminary round of presentations to determine finalists. The finalists competed live at the 2018 ITE Annual Meeting in Minneapolis, MN in August 2018.

How do we develop productive and sustainable partnerships?

There is clear support for a collaborative approach to transportation workforce development, and particularly for the criticality of industry—academia partnerships [1,53,54]. However, for partnerships to be effective, they must be carefully created. It is important to have a formalized structure for partnerships and to ensure each partnering organization has not only a voice but also a stake in the planned outcomes [30,34]. Approaching partnership development in this way can ensure successful talent pipeline programs are created. One example is that of the West TN STEM Hub (Hub), one of six STEM centers comprising the Tennessee STEM Innovation Network. The Hub was established in 2012 through state funding. The Hub's initiatives, impact, and funding have grown each year, even after the initial grant funding ended [55]. This sustainability is due in large part to the fact that a steering committee, comprised of a large number of industry and academic representatives, was organized from the Hub's inception. This group was actively engaged in creating a strategic plan, planning and developing the Hub's primary initiatives, and crafting a plan for sustainability from the moment the Hub was conceived. The Hub's leadership carefully facilitated all partner engagement, and made sure that each meeting resulted in a set of action items, and that "quick wins" were achieved so that partners viewed the time invested as valuable. This resulted in a clear business case for the Hub's initiatives and led to investment from numerous public and private sector partners of both time and financial support [34].

Several guides for creating successful partnerships for workforce development have been put forth over the last several years. The Business-Higher Education Forum (BHEF) released a report in 2013 championing the value of and need for industry—academia partnerships across the board, but particularly for STEM, to address local and regional workforce challenges [28]. The report outlines a framework for developing successful partnerships that address key workforce issues. The steps in the process include research into high-demand sectors to identify the most significant workforce gaps for a region, narrowing the focus of interventions to these specific industry segments to achieve economic impact, determining the range of professionals that could fill the gaps, and developing interventions targeting these specific needs. BHEF also highlights the importance of having the leadership of partnering organizations meaningfully engaged so that there is top-down buy-in, creating a joint vision, framing the involvement of industry in terms of philanthropy to create a sustainable model, and ensuring a corporate volunteer is part of the partnership [28]. BHEF concludes the approach results in, "...learning incubators designed to resolve America's toughest workforce issues in today's high-demand fields" [28].

A more detailed framework was developed by MHI and Smart Workforce Strategies based upon case studies in the supply chain industry [56]. The framework includes 13 questions organized into 4 primary categories: problem need/definition, developing partnerships, producing results, and leveraging results. DeLong points out that educational institutions and employers often have agendas and goals that are not in sync, and thus it is very important to develop clarity around organizational objectives. He also highlights the fact that it takes time to develop meaningful relationships and productive partnerships [56]. The report further highlights the need to engage leadership from partnering organizations, to start with a pilot-scale approach, consider from the outset how sustainability (from a funding perspective) can be achieved, and to continuously evaluate partnership progress and address obstacles or challenges as they are encountered [56].

There are many examples that these approaches work. A similar framework to those proposed by BHEF and DeLong was used for the NNTW's development of regional Job Needs and Priorities reports and subsequently Phase II reports that included gap analyses and action plans [37,57−61]. The result of this process is multiple active action plans in each of the five regions where business and academia are working together to address local workforce concerns. These initiatives target a variety of points along the pipeline, from K-12 to higher education to career retraining and reentry. For example, SETWC facilitates active partnerships focused on priority occupations in the greater Memphis area. These collaborations have resulted in a new Transportation-STEM high school within Shelby County Schools, an annual transportation career fair for regional postsecondary students, and development of a pilot program framework designed to help impoverished women access support leading to employment in high-demand transportation jobs [20].

Thus productive partnerships that lead to impactful workforce development share at the core:

- research to identify regional needs and target occupations,
- a well-thought out statement of value highlighting the business case for intervention,

- a conscious effort to attract the right partners to the table, including organizational leadership,
- clear articulation of the problem to be addressed and goal(s) to be achieved,
- clear definition of expectations from all partners—everyone must have "skin in the game,"
- well-planned meetings so that specific tasks are accomplished each time partners get together, and opportunities for "quick wins" are leveraged,
- a plan for sustainability from the outset, and
- a long-term vision and metrics for evaluating progress—all partners must be on the same page and know how to gauge impact of the initiative.

Conclusion

The evolving transportation industry requires a robust and highly prepared workforce to address the challenges of the future. As the industry changes, so must our approach to attracting the new workforce. Successful approaches to inspiring the next generation must change the conversation about what it means to be a transportation or mobility professional by:

- showcasing transportation as an exciting, challenging, and high-tech industry that impacts people's daily lives and communities,
- highlighting the diversity of career opportunities in the industry,
- carefully crafting messages to appeal to a diversity of audiences,
- providing varied opportunities for exposure and impact—messages must be repeatedly reinforced and students must have the opportunity to deepen career exploration,
- engaging not only students but also their influencers (parents, teachers, guidance counselor, community organization leaders), and
- leveraging networks of professionals to share success stories and "put a face" on the industry.

At the crux of these efforts, strong industry—academia partnerships are essential for creating impactful and sustainable initiatives. Collective impact is the key to catalyzing workforce transformation. All partners must have a voice, a united vision, and a shared commitment to move the needle for the new mobility workforce.

Acknowledgments

This material is based on work supported by the Federal Highway Administration under Agreement No. DTFH6114H00025 & DTFH6116H00030. Any opinions, findings, and conclusions or recommendations expressed in this publication are those of the author(s) and do not necessarily reflect the view of the Federal Highway Administration.

References

[1] B. Cronin, L. Anderson, B. Heinen, C.B. Cronin, D. Fien-Helfman, M. Venner, Strategies to Attract and Retain a Capable Transportation Workforce, Transportation Research Board, Washington, DC, 2011. National Cooperative Highway Research Program.

[2] Strengthening Skills Training and Career Pathways Across the Transportation Industry. US Department of Education, Department of Transportation, Department of Labor, Washington, DC, 2015.

[3] Bureau of Labor Statistics, Employment Projections, 2016-2026, US Department of Labor, Washington, DC, 2017.

[4] R. Noonan, STEM Jobs: 2017 Update, U.S. Department of Commerece, Office of the Chief Economist, Washington, DC, 2017.

[5] MHI, Material Handling & Logistics U.S. Roadmap 2.0, MHI, Charlotte, NC, 2017.

[6] S. Lockwood, G. Euler, Transportation System Management & Operations (TSM&O) Workforce Development White Paper 1: Background and State of Play, NOCoE, Washington, DC, 2016.

[7] T. Adams, J. Collura, National Transportation Workforce Summit Summary of Results, April 26, 2012. Retrieved October 15, 2015, from Council of University Transportation Centers <http://www.mycutc.com/wp-content/uploads/2014/09/NTWS_Summary-of-Results.pdf>.

[8] Bureau of Labor Statistics, Occupational Outlook Handbook, April 13, 2018. Retrieved June 30, 2018, from Bureau of Labor Statistics <https://www.bls.gov/ooh/>.

[9] Mckinsey Global Institute, Jobs Lost, Jobs Gained: Workforce Transitions in a Time of Automation, McKinsey & Company, 2017.

[10] USDOT Federal Highway Administration, Impacts of Technology Advancements on Transportation Management Center Operations, USDOT, Washington, DC, 2013.

[11] Materials Handling Institute. Materials Handling and Logistics US Roadmap 2.0. MHI, 2017.

[12] Intelligent Transportation Systems Joint Program Office, ITS Research Fact Sheets, n.d. Retrieved 02 17, 2017, from USDOT OST-R <https://www.its.dot.gov/communications/its_factsheets.htm>.

[13] National Academies of Science, Engineering and Medicine, Information Technology and the U.S. Workforce Where Are We and Where Do We Go from Here? National Academies Press, Washington, DC, 2017.

[14] E.S. White, A.F. Shakibnia, State of STEM: Defining the Landscape to Determine High-Impact Pathways for the Future Workforce., STEM connector, Washington, DC, 2018.

[15] J. Alper, Developing a National STEM Workforce Strategy: A Workshop Summary., National Academies Press, Washington, DC, 2016.

[16] Bureau of Labor Statistics, Labor Force Statistics from the Current Population Survey, June 22, 2018. Retrieved June 30, 2018, from Bureau of Labor Statistics <https://www.bls.gov/cps/demographics.htm#women>.

[17] United States Census Bureau, Quick Facts, July 2017. Retrieved June 30, 2018, from United States Census Bureau <https://www.census.gov/quickfacts/fact/table/US/PST045217>.

[18] E. Cruz, The gap between women and men in STEM. LinkedIn Talent Trends.

[19] Nathan Associates, Inc., APEC Women in Transportation Data Framework and Best Practice Report. APEC, 2015.

[20] Southeast Transportation Workforce Center, Job Needs and Priorities Report, 2016. Retrieved June 30, 2018, from Southeast Transportation Workforce Center <http://www.memphis.edu/setwc/job_needs_and_priorities_report/index.php>.

[21] N. Chambers, E. Kashefpakdel, J. Rehill, C. Percy, Drawing the Future: Exploring the Career Aspirations of Primary and Secondary School Children from Around the World, Education and Employers, 2018.

[22] L.B. Otto, Youth perspectives on parental career influence, J. Career Dev. 27 (2) (2000) 111−118.

[23] W.S. Rullo, Impacting career choice, in: G. Eliason, J. Patrick, J. Samide, T. Eliason (Eds.), Career Counseling Across the Lifespan: Community, School, Higher Education, and Beyond, Information Age Publishing, Inc, Charlotte, NC, 2014, pp. 415−446.

[24] S. Ivey, M. Golias, P. Palazolo, K. Ford, V. Wise, P. Thomas, Transportation engineering careers: strategies for attracting students to transportation professions, Transpor. Res. Record: J. Transport. Res. Board 2414 (2014) 45−51.

[25] R.C. Chope, Influence of the family in career decision making: identity development, career path, and life planning, Career Plan. Adult Dev. J. 17 (2001) 54−64.

[26] Nathan Associates, Inc. APEC Women in Transportation (WiT) Data Framework and Best Practices Initiative: Update of the WiT, APEC, 2017.

[27] S. Ivey, M. Golias, P. Palazolo, S. Edwards, P. Thomas, Attracting students to transportation engineering: gender differences and implications of student perceptions of transportation careers, Transport. Res. Record: J. Transport. Res. Board 2320 (2012) 90−96.

[28] Business-Higher Education Forum, The National Higher Education and Workforce Initiative: Forging Strategic Partnerships for Undergraduate Innovation and Workforce Development, Business-Higher Education Forum, Washington, DC, 2013.

[29] A. Cota, A. Dua, M. Laboisseiere, J. Lin, Rethinking 101: a New Agenda for Universities and Higher Education System Leaders? McKinsey & Company, 2012.

[30] Committee on Improving Higher Education's Responsiveness to STEM Workforce Needs, Promising Practices for Strengthening the Regional STEM Workforce Development Ecosystem, National Academies of Sciences, Engineering, and Medicine, Washington, DC, 2016.

[31] C.T.E. Advance, Transportation, Distribution, and logistics, 2018. Retrieved June 30, 2018, from Advance CTE <https://careertech.org/transportation>.

[32] R. Turochy, J. Fricker, H. Hawkins, D. Hurwitz, S. Ivey, M. Knodler, et al., Assessment of introductory transportation engineering course and general transportation engineering curriculum. Transportation Research Record, 2014.

[33] Southeast Transportation Workforce Center, Transportation, Distribution, and Logistics: Apprenticeship Acceleration in West TN, Tennessee Department of Economic and Community Development, Nashville, 2018.

[34] S. Ivey, A. Hall, L. Allen, P. Bridson, West TN STEM hub: cradle to career collaborations for STEM, Crit. Convers.: J. Tennessee Board Regents 1 (2) (2015) 215−233.

[35] E. Plosky, Workshop 873: Addressing the impact of disruptive/transformative technologies on the transportation workforce, in: 97th Annual Meeting of the Transportation Research Board (N. N. Workforce, Compiler), Transportation Research Board, Washington, DC, 2018.

[36] PwC Global, Transportation and Logistics 2030: Winning the Talent Race. PwC Global, 2015.

[37] National Network for the Transportation Workforce, US Transportation Job Needs and Priorities Report, Phase 1: National Overview, Report Prepared for Federal Highway Administration, Washington, DC, 2015.

[38] C. Corbett, C. Hill, Solving the Equation: The Variables for Women's Success in Mathematics and Computing, AAUW, Washington, DC, 2015.

[39] J. Kuhl, J. Zephirin, S. Hewlett, Misunderstood Millenial Talent: The Other Ninety-One Percent., Center for Talent Innovation, Los Angeles, 2016.

[40] J. Schroer, The future of transportation, in: 4th Annual Choosing Transportation Summit, 2018.

[41] Bureau of Labor Statistics, Occupational outlook handbook: military careers (2017). Retrieved June 30, 2018, from Bureau of Labor Statistics <https://www.bls.gov/ooh/military/military-careers.htm#tab-2>.

[42] US Department of Labor, Military Crosswalk Search, (2018). Retrieved June 30, 2018, from O*Net Online <https://onetonline.org/crosswalk/MOC/>.

[43] Tennessee Department of Safety and Homeland Security, Highways for heroes, (2018). Retrieved June 30, 2018, from Tennessee Department of Safety and Homeland Security <https://www.tn.gov/safety/driver-services/h4h.html>.

[44] Schneider. Military, Retrieved June 30, 2018, from Schneider Jobs, (2018) <https://schneiderjobs.com/company-drivers/military>.

[45] E. Miller, DOT to launch pilot program for former military veteran drivers ages 18−20, (2018).Retrieved 07 07, 2018, from Transport Topics <http://www.ttnews.com/articles/dot-launch-pilot-program-former-military-veteran-drivers-ages-18-20>.

[46] J. Gaines, Women in male-dominated careers, Cornell HR Review, 2017.

[47] University of Memphis Herff College of Engineering, Program impact (2017). Retrieved June 30, 2018, from Girls Experiencing Engineering <http://www.memphis.edu/gee/announcements/index.php>.

[48] US Department of Transportation, USDOT's Women & Girls in Transportation Initiative (WITI) (2018). Retrieved June 30, 2018, from Transportation.gov <https://www.transportation.gov/osdbu/women-and-girls>.

[49] WTS International, Homepage (2018). Retrieved June 30, 2018, from WTS <https://www.wtsinternational.org>.

[50] WTS International and WTS Foundation, Transportation you (2018). Retrieved June 30, 2018, from Transportation You <http://www.transportationyou.org>.

[51] V. Hunt, S. Prince, S. Dixon-Fyle, Y. Lareina, Delivering Through Diversity, McKinsey & Company, 2018.

[52] A. Bunshaft, P. Cornwell, S. Heimlich, B. Albrecht, Career focused experiential learning, STEM Connector, Advancing a Jobs-Driven Economy, Morgan James Publishing, New York, 2015, pp. 166−181.

[53] C. Martin, Connecting the employment dots, Public Roads 79 (3) (2015) 22−25.

[54] S. Lockwood, G. Euler, Transportation System Management & Operations (TSM&O) Workforce Development White Paper No 3: Recruitment, Retention and Career Development, NOCoE, Washington, DC, 2016.

[55] T.N. West, STEM Hub., About us (2017). Retrieved June 2018, from West TN STEM Hub - Annual Impact Statement <http://westtnstem.org/about-us>.

[56] D. DeLong, The Myths & Realities of Successful Workforce Solutions: Lessons From Supply Chain's Leading Edge, MHI and Smart Workforce Strategies, Charlotte, NC, 2017.

[57] Midwest Transportation Workforce Center, Job needs and priorities report (2016). Retrieved 06 2018, from Midwest Transportation Workforce Center <http://mtwc.org/resources/job-needs-and-priorities-report-phase-i/>.

[58] Northeast Transportation Workforce Center, FHWA job needs and priorities report (2016). Retrieved June 30, 2018, from Northeast Transportation Workforce Center <http://netwc.net/fhwa-job-needs-and-priorities-report/>.

[59] Southeast Transportation Workforce Center, Job needs and priorities report (2016). Retrieved June 30, 2018, from Southeast Transportation Workforce Center: <http://www.memphis.edu/setwc/job_needs_and_priorities_report/index.php>.

[60] West Region Transportation Workforce Center, Labor market analysis report (2016). Retrieved June 2018, from West Region Transportation Workforce Center <http://wrtwc.org/resources/labor-market-analysis-report/>.

[61] Southwest Transportation Workforce Center, Labor market analysis (2016). Retrieved June 2018, from Southwest Transportation Workforce Center <https://www.swtwc.org/labor-market-analysis/>.

CHAPTER FIFTEEN

Building an innovation network for the transit workforce

David M. Stumpo
Executive Director SCRTTC

What is the Southern California Regional Transit Training Consortium (SCRTTC) and why was it needed?

Contents

Introduction

In 2002 the public transportation industry faced numerous workforce issues due to the rise of innovative advances in technology and equipment. During this time I retired to Point Roberts, Washington, after completing work for a public transit agency in Vancouver, British Columbia, when the late Jim Ditch, who served as the Executive Director of Maintenance and Facilities for Long Beach Transit for 19 years, dropped by my residence on the way to an Alaskan cruise. Jim raised several concerns regarding the limitations of the Southern California transportation industry to address an aging workforce, a lack of

Empowering the New Mobility Workforce.
DOI: https://doi.org/10.1016/B978-0-12-816088-6.00016-X

training materials, and a lack of agreed upon work standards for the maintenance of those transit systems. Jim and I shared decades of work in the transportation industry and together we thought of the initial idea that would grow to become the Southern California Regional Transit Training Consortium (SCRTTC).

With the help of Rich Wong, Manager of Maintenance for the Orange County Transit Authority (OCTA), and Alan Fox, Lawyer and Vice-Chair of the Long Beach Planning Commission, the SCRTTC was legally established as a nonprofit organization. Alan Fox was recruited early on to ensure that the organization was properly formed, in meeting the State and Federal requirements as a nonprofit 501c(3) organization, and to have the required legal sign off to qualify for Federal grants. The strategic intent of the SCRTTC was to develop a new "learning model" to address this human capital challenge through a systematic, regional approach to develop curricula, to eliminate training duplication, and to reduce costs for designing and producing training materials. Establishing a consortium through the utilization of the various colleges and universities to support the development of these new innovative approaches toward training and development would introduce transportation as a career pathway for new entrants, increase productivity of current employees, and improve the quality of work for the transit agencies involved.

Early on we established our goals in a clear charter and business plan. It is critical to approach the launch of any new organization with a business plan so that it can move forward with direction and strategies to accomplish initial goals. Our intent was to logically think through the process in writing and try to foresee any obvious missteps on paper. The process gave us direction and helped us map out our strategies to achieve the initial goals set. I cannot emphasize the importance of drafting a business plan; it helped us move beyond abstract goals to a tangible game plan for implementation that included a timeline for the consortium to accomplish the start-up phase. Here is the earliest version of our business plan [1]:

Purpose and Mission (2004)

The purpose of the consortium was to provide a resource network comprised of public and private organizations focused on the development of the regional transit industry's workforce, and to assure the workforce is knowledgeable of ITS standards, practices, and procedures.

Goals and Objectives

- *Develop industry-driven, competency-based curriculum that meets present and future needs;*
- *Develop partnerships with transit systems, colleges, and educational institutions;*
- *Develop partnerships with private industry and public agencies;*
- *Provide immediate use of the SCRTTC network and shared information;*
- *Provide a reliable source of technical and regulatory information;*
- *Optimize training resources;*
- *Develop State-of-the-art training facilities and mobile training labs;*
- *Provide distance learning and Internet-based learning systems;*
- *Establish industry-wide recognition and develop business relationships that lead to mutual support and assistance;*
- *Develop Mentor/Internship programs that enhance promotional opportunities;*
- *Replicate the SCRTTC model nationally;*
- *Promote* and market transit industry—related careers and education to the general public.

We saw the need to begin implementing a streamlined training program as soon as possible. In Southern California, transit agencies are made up of smaller systems and municipal systems. Smaller systems, at the time, did not have the capacity to train as needed—many were trained by peers on the job due to a lack of dedicated trainers. Larger agencies, like LA Metro, Long Beach Transit, and Orange County Transit, had the training rooms but would often conduct classes with only two or three attendees, while also supplementing their internal training with subcontracting with outside trainers. It became clear to us that the resources and needs of both the smaller and larger agencies could be much more efficient. So we approached the region's transit agencies with the consortium idea, which allowed us to move forward with standardized training and efficient use of resources for everyone in the region. The SCRTTC consortium model introduced a broad range of innovations and efficiencies including:

- establishing standards for training;
- providing a level of efficiency so that funding was spent on doing more training in the region;
- reducing the duplication of training already delivered; and
- finally, everyone was being trained the same way with the same content.

In short the SCRTTC consortium model brought a level of professional training from college instructors to teach the transit courseware.

The overriding philosophy of the consortium was to provide an education and training process that would enhance the skills of transit employees and the ability for transit agencies to provide more efficient, effective, and safer public transit services using "state of the art" technologies and systems. The consortium design philosophy heavily emphasized the *civic partnership* between regional transit agencies, interested educational institutions, federal and state governments, private industry stakeholders, and the represented employees of the affiliated labor unions within transit agencies. There was a mixed reaction to the consortium model from all stakeholders but, once our intent was made clear and implementation was a success, positive news about the consortium spread quickly.

The first product of the SCRTTC was the Digital Volt Ohm Meter class, which was clearly needed around the region based on discussions with various transit agencies. We thought that the consortium model could be best demonstrated through the delivery of this class. In a matter of months with the assistance of the late Long Beach City College instructor Cal Macy, the SCRTTC had a DVOM course ready for delivery. Our first class sold out with 20 students and instantly the consortium model was understood.

It was easy to get the transit agencies on board initially, but other stakeholders expressed their hesitancy and concerns. Colleges and universities did not want to sign up for an organization that would not move forward. Transit agencies were worried that existing training positions would be eliminated and people would lose their jobs. Yet once they realized the power of collaboration toward a common cause, they saw the potential for what the consortium was trying to achieve. Once the consortium was up and running we garnered positive press attention in industry magazines like Passenger Transport, Metro and BusRide, and transit agencies in Northern California, Oregon, Colorado, and New York were all interested in the idea of a consortium.

How did the organization come together?

Jim, Alan, Rich, and I brought together an ad hoc group with personnel from both Long Beach Transit and the Orange County Transit Authority (OCTA). The intent was to bring together subject matter experts who were familiar with the new technologies being implemented in public transit and identify the need to provide an up-to-date training program that could be offered in a cost-effective manner. This would enable the transit agencies to reduce duplication and operate more cost effectively. In addition, many colleges wanted to be at the table to discuss the implementation and the colleges are Long Beach City College, Cerritos College, Goldenwest Collect, Santa Monica College, Citrus College, Cypress College, LA Trade-Tech College, Rio Hondo College, College of the Desert, and San Bernardino Valley College were among the first of many that participated.

A preliminary study of available training programs was discussed. In the opinion of the ad hoc group, each of the existing programs had its advantages and disadvantages. It was concluded by the group that existing programs were not structured to provide the training required and not cost effective in either time or money. The alternative training programs were reviewed in Fig. 15.1.

With this analysis completed, and opinions rendered, the ad hoc group decided to formalize its structure for the purposes of identifying the type of training program that would be required to meet the needs of the transit properties in the Southern California area.

After we more formally decided upon our intent and purpose as an organization, we needed *to establish SCRTTC as a credible consortium.* In 2004 the formal bylaws of the organization were developed, the name search completed, and the website registered. The organization was approved under the IRS regulations as a 501(c) 3 "nonprofit" and subjected to the California Nonprofit Corporation laws and regulations. The ad hoc group initially formalized its structure by *organizing into three committees, Organization, Planning and Legislative.* The committees were designed to study the feasibility of the consortium structure to ensure that the needs of all members were met. Initial membership was composed of

Method/ Criteria	Educational content	Delivery process	Domain knowledge	Cost effective
Federal and Association Programs[1]	Good—limited integration of content	Decentralized	Excellent	Travel and out of office time excessive
University programs	Good	Classroom oriented	Limited	Requires travel to college facilities; can be done on site
Vendor training	Limited to specific product or system sold	On site—good	Limited to specific product or system sold	Usually limited in time and scope not an integrated program
Consortium	Will be specific to consortium and will be a fully integrated program	Training will be regional and centralized for agencies involved	Excellent and will be specific to technologies and systems being implemented at the agencies involved	Shared cost for consortium members will reduce cost to each agency involved.

Figure 15.1 Alternative training programs.

public transportation agencies, colleges, universities, associations, labor unions, and private industry partnerships. The purpose, mission, and short-term goals were to be identified and agreed upon by all consortium stakeholders.

How did we get the organization off the ground?

As a nonprofit organization, we pursued government funding opportunities. In June 2004 the Federal Highway Administration (FHWA), through the Intelligent Transportation Systems of America's (ITSA) Joint Program Office (JPO), Larry Schulman and Mike Kushner, awarded a training study contract to the consortium. The purpose of this contract was to continue a study and perform a detailed "Needs Assessment and Skill Gap Analysis" to identify training needs of public transit agency employees in the Southern California area and provide professional capacity building for the region with the mindset to replicate their program nationally. At the time, Nina Babiarz from the College of the Desert performed the very first assessment for the SCRTTC. The results of the "Needs Assessment and Skill Gap Analysis" were invaluable for transit agencies. For example, a need for digital volt ohm meter class was identified, and this training was available and provided almost immediately. Additionally, this endeavor helped to further enhance the choices, options, replication, and availability of the transit training throughout the Southern California region.

The results also provided further input to identify and prioritize the course development and training delivery requirements for the transit agencies. Input came from college and transit members, who helped to cement and promote this new learning model of the consortium. Additionally, the studies have driven how the methodology of instructor-led classes would be conducted, what the length of each course needed to be, and how the courses would circulate around the region to reduce travel time of those attending. Finally the studies determined that all course registrations needed to be developed from a central online portal— hence the development of our Website (www.scrttc.com).

We also discovered some inefficiencies that needed to be addressed. During the inventory of training topics, which was conducted independently with the transit agencies and community college members, we discovered that the current transit training courses available and being conducted by the member entities still needed refinement by the transit agencies. For example, brakes courses had pictures of trucks, not buses. While the fundamental operation is similar the courseware needed to be updated to specific transit applications. And finally, through conducting the updated transit inventory and needs assessment, the consortium had taken steps to anticipate new training gaps and put into play a course of action that addressed them.

Initially the planning committee handled the development of the membership procedure and how fees for membership would be structured through a tiered system based on fleet size. Educational institutions would be a flat fee. These initial fees were used for start-up efforts, which further formalized the organization. The planning group was also tasked with developing the course catalog outline, the standard operating procedure for courseware development and the certification process for instructors to teach consortium courses. Moreover this committee was responsible for the inventory of courses, annual needs assessments, and required course updates.

How has funding support been over the years?

The consortium start-up funding was provided by membership fees based on a model of fleet size. Moreover follow-on funding was provided by the US DOT Joint Program Office and was part of the US DOT Professional Capacity Building Program. This funding was followed with the allocation of Federal Transit Administration (FTA) Program Workforce Development Funds. The detail of the FTA program funding for $1.2 million over 4 years from FY2007 to FY2010 was the initial program funding and ended September 30, 2010. In addition, given the program success after 4 years, FTA provided supplemental funding in the amount of $450,000 that allowed us to continue the learning model development for an addition year ending December 31, 2011.

With the allocation of FTA Funds, leverage was provided to propose and secure additional Workforce Development Funds from Industry Driven Regional Collaborative (IDRC) grants from the member colleges, and the State of California. The state Workforce Development Funds were usually related to green technology programs, and/or clean air programs, or employment and retention, by which represent new technologies requiring retraining of the transit maintenance workforce. The acquisition of state funds provided a training capacity beyond the original planned objectives. Federal and State Workforce Development Funds and

grants represent the largest source of funds that support ongoing operations of the consortium. These funds were used primarily to develop
needed courseware and to pay for in-class training, which includes
instructor salaries, course materials, online registration, administration, and
outreach.

Membership fees from the transit members represent the third largest
funding source for the SCRTTC. Membership fees are based on the size
of the transit property, and are similar to the fee schedule used by the
American Public Transportation Association (APTA). We chose to model
our membership fee structure after APTA because it is a well-recognized
and respected association in the industry. Most transit agencies belong to
APTA and are very familiar with their model. By using a similar
approach, registrants and agencies were signing up for an accessible and
fair fee structure that is based upon fleet size and revenue miles operated.
More importantly the familiarity of APTA made it easier to sell our consortium membership. Membership fees are adjusted on an annual basis.
Other funds for the SCRTTC training program are obtained from private
industry partnerships and a small educational fund called the Jim Ditch
Golf Classic formed in 2009, after the passing of Jim Ditch. Each year,
scholarships are given to students who meet a certain criteria and have a
transportation emphasis with their studies. Jim's idea for scholarships was
to promote transit as a career. He further stated, "Let's give the students
money to buy tools. Tools last a lifetime and it enables them the opportunity to work in public transit."

In addition to these hard cash sources a tremendous amount of in-
kind support has been obtained from all of the SCRTTC members. This
in-kind support continues to be crucial to the ongoing operations. The
list below summarizes each funding source and its relative share of
SCRTTC's total budget:

- Federal, State, and Local Funding—40%
- Membership fees—25%
- Grants—15%
- Private industry partnerships—10%
- Jim Ditch Fund and Scholarships—5%
- In-Kind—5%

With the assistance of transit and college consortium members' government affairs personnel, we decided to attend the legislative conference
in Washington DC in the spring of 2005. We approached the local con-
gressional staff with talking points about the consortium, which led to

Senator Barbara Boxer sponsoring an earmark awarded to the consortium from the Federal Transit Administration (FTA). The federal earmark was for $1.4 million over 4 years from FY2007 to FY2010 with the initial program funding ending September 30, 2010. With the aftermath of Hurricane Katrina in 2005, the earmark was reduced to $1.2 million. Given the program successes after 4 years, FTA provided supplemental funding in the amount of $450,000 to continue the development for an addition year ending December 31, 2011. Federal funding allowed the consortium to fully develop the new learning model and provide specific program approaches to enable the use of the developed materials for future replication across the nation. Moreover, the federal support led the board to eliminate annual membership fees previously collected, which was a crucial error during our start-up stage.

As we progressed in our earlier start-up years and became more experienced in developing and delivering training, we realized our message of providing "free" training was not responsible or appropriate. The perception of "free" or "no charge" meant that what the consortium was offering was not valuable. More specifically, it led to registrants not showing up for scheduled training and taking seats that could have otherwise been filled. To rectify this issue we explicitly stated the costs of attending each course provided with the registration. We further showed that the fee was paid through a grant or college partnerships. We then announced that once a transit agency registered for a course—they had to cancel or substitute within 48 hours otherwise they would be charged the course fee. These actions almost immediately solved the no show issue.

As the consortium board had to scale back to a sustaining mode and were determining the fees schedule for the fiscal year, they decided that the membership fees should always be collected regardless of active grants. Applications for grant deadlines were too far out to be useful in the short run and it took away from the value of the consortium's product offered to attendees and agencies. In many cases, grant awards required an organization to have funds in place in order to be reimbursed.

Along with FTA funding we received college industry-driven regional collaborative funds and in-kind services from members and we anticipated that similar funding could also be sought after. Continued support of the transit property members, the community colleges, private industry partners, and the various state and federal workforce development programs were necessary to maintain the viability of the consortium and to continue the successes that have been achieved to that point.

The administration committee was designed to oversee the bylaws, standard operating procedure cataloging and legal affairs. Once base documents were created, activities for this group were limited on an as needed basis until later when a restructure of the committees was done in 2012.

The business and affairs of the consortium were intended to be managed by or under the direction of the Board of Directors and officers of the organization elected by the members. The Board voted to delegate day-to-day responsibilities of management of the activities of the consortium to a management company. All the policies, standard operating procedures, activities, and affairs of the consortium were to be exercised under the ultimate direction of the Board of Directors. The initial Board of Directors consisted of 10 members including 5 transit members, and 5 college members.

In late 2009 and early 2010 the SCRTTC board formally considered the merits of increasing the number and diversity of its membership to better represent the full scope of the consortium's civic partnerships. The early success of the FTA Earmark demonstrated that the learning model had merit and the board's executive committee took steps to expand the number of board members, increasing the general membership and looking for new funding opportunities.

Our chair at the time, Mr. Jesus Guerra, Director, Transportation Workforce Institute from Los Angeles Trade-Tech College, suggested that many of the local representatives may have some awareness of potential funding sources for education and training. He urged that the college and transit agency members flex their organizational muscles in ways that others do not or cannot and help to aggressively pursue additional funding opportunities on behalf of the consortium [2].

The question was, "How do we emphasize the consortium learning model to gain better access to elected officials and other representatives?" The answer was to expand the message through our membership and leadership. With that in mind, we started to brainstorm which specific areas where we needed more 'organizational horsepower.' We wanted to identify underutilized areas like private industry, but also be inclusive of colleges and transit agencies in areas that we did not serve like central and northern California [3].

In August 2011 the board increased to 15 members, including the addition of Pamela Boswell, Vice President-Workforce Development & Educational Services for the American Public Transportation Association

(APTA), which was a national organization. Later, Mr. Joseph Niegoski, Senior Director—Educational Services, joined to replace Ms. Boswell.

The following year at the annual board workshop held in the spring each year, we created a board responsibility and commitment form that outlined fiduciary responsibilities, general expectations, and commitment to attend meetings. Additionally, we developed a board member orientation program so that new board members were taught about the history and structure of the organization.

By 2013 we had increased the board to 21 members as it still stands today. We included private industry partners, labor union representation, universities, and northern California transit and college members. It was very important for the board at this stage in its life cycle to introduce senior and executive level personnel to the board. The main reason was because of their knowledge, experience, and decision-making abilities. For example, our chair Dr. Thomas O'Brien, California State University at Long Beach and the Executive Director at the College of Continuing and Professional Education Center for International Trade and Transportation METRANS Transportation Center. Board member Ms. Marion Jane Colston, Sr. Director, Strategic & Organizational Planning at LA Metro, has been intimately involved in career pathways, workforce development, and many other applicable areas of expertise. Past Chair Ms. Jannet Malig, State Sector Navigator for Advanced Transportation & Logistics, Cerritos College, provides direction for curriculum development in emerging occupations; expanding industry certificate programs, and determining short- and long-term industry training needs.

President and CEO of Long Beach Transit Mr. Kenneth McDonald, provides a long history of public transit experience, strategic planning, and workforce development to the table, as does Ed King, Transit Director for the Santa Monica Big Blue Bus. Mr. Jess Guerra, Director, Transportation Workforce Institute, and Chair of the Advanced Transportation and Manufacturing, Los Angeles Trade Technical College. In addition, vice-chair Ms. Donna DeMartino, President/CEO of San Joaquin Regional Transit District, who provides a long list of experience from education and transportation background. Finally, our industry partnerships with Complete Coach Works, Immersed Technologies, Clean Energy, Proterra, and BYD creates synergy. These attributes enhance the direction and future of the consortium and opens doors into the unknown areas for funding sources, impact, and workforce development opportunities.

How has SCRTTC evolved from its initial inception?

In 2012 the consortium annual workshop resulted in doing a SWOT analysis which is an exercise to determine strengths, weaknesses, opportunities, and threats [4]. We started using the Kirkpatrick Model when we built SCRTTC's first strategic plan. This model is probably the best known model for analyzing and evaluating the results of training and educational programs. It takes into account any style of training, both informal and formal, to determine aptitude based on four levels of criteria [4]. Following this exercise we initiated a 5-year strategic planning process that was conducted over several months. While I will speak about this further in the chapter, the main result included a change to the mission of the consortium, which is now, "advance the skills of our transit workforce...preparing for the future."

Today the structure of the consortium consists of the Board of Directors and six working committees approved by the board members. The Board Chairperson serves a 2-year term, and Board Chairmanship will be rotated between a transit member and a college member. The board is designed to represent both transit and education with participants signing an annual commitment and responsibility statement that reflects their common understanding. Board members are also actively involved in committees and working groups, allowing for collaborative activity. Communications at quarterly and annual meetings ensures that the consortium moves forward with shared objectives and manageable goals. In essence the consortium is mostly a volunteer organization hence the requirement for steering and working committees.

The executive committee is designed to be a steering committee. The executive committee make-up includes the board chair, vice-chair, immediate past chair, and all the committee chairs plus the executive director. The primary responsibilities are to solve policy conflicts, conflicts of interest, strategic oversight, procurement, and contractual issues, that reinforces the direction of the board and maintains the common agenda. The working committees were structured to assist the consortium membership specifically to seek funding opportunities through the Government Relations Committee, build and maintain the organizations budget and financial needs through the Finance and Budget Committee, develop the training standards through the Education Services Committee, maintain the ongoing administrative duties normally associated with running any organization through the Administration Committee and providing annual scholarships to college students who seek transit as a career through the Scholarship Committee. Other working committees and subcommittees may be formed at the discretion of the Board. For example, an Electric and Hybrid Bus subcommittee was formed under the Educational Services Committee to handle the recent development of the burgeoning need for Electric and Hybrid Bus training. The working committees also handle specific tasks assigned by the Board in their respective areas, with mission statements of each committee identified to synergize with the intent of the organization. Committee chairs are appointed by the board chair and come from the membership population.

The staff positions of the consortium are contracted through a management company. The basic structure includes an executive director who oversees all operations and a training director responsible for day-to-day operations and coordination of all the training programs. In addition, subcontracts with administration assistance, webmaster, and a program coordinator who assists in outreach and strategic intent issues. The organizational objectives include more emphasis on technical and leadership training, technical standards development, assessments, skill gap analysis, and ITS practices. In addition, the need for more succession planning from technician to supervisor and leadership management courses remain key concerns for the transit agencies and goals of the consortium.

The executive director is responsible for day-to-day oversight, strategic issues, and directs the efforts of the training director, the planning coordinator, and the working committees and all contracts. The executive director responsibilities are contracted to a professional management firm (presently the APTREX Institute) because of their vast experience of transit training programs and professional certification for the transit workforce.

The training director, Ms. Nina Babiarz who was an original founding member of the SCRTTC from the College of the Desert and joined APTREX in 2007, is responsible for all day-to-day operations, planning, organizing, registrations, and facilitating all transit training classes and course development. This effort includes coordination with the community colleges that provide the in-class training and instruction. The Training Director also leads the effort to conduct the needs assessment and skill gap analysis periodically in order to identify new and emerging courseware development and delivery needs, prioritize courseware topics for development and establish a training calendar of course delivery for the consortium program plan.

The planning coordinator is responsible for liaison with the Federal Transit Administration, the American Public Transit Association (APTA), and other related transit associations. This responsibility also includes other associated outreach and strategic efforts. The consortium functions and operates under a set of bylaws reviewed and approved by the Board of Directors. A copy of the bylaws is available on the consortium Website.

Board meetings are held on a quarterly basis and conducted in the second month of the quarter in the months of February, May, August, and November. Board members either attend in person by teleconference or videoconference. An annual meeting of all members and affiliated members is held in May/June with the agenda to elect board members as a result of the administration committee. Finally an annual board workshop is held prior to the annual meeting in May or June to develop and recommend approval of annual work plans, budgets, goals, objectives, and strategic plans.

How has the curriculum developed?

The courseware developed by the consortium is built around specific training tracks developed from the "Needs Assessment and Skill Gap Analysis Study" conducted during the initial organization of the consortium and updated periodically [5]. The training tracks were designed to meet the needs of a transit technician, and to move the technician through a programmed course of prerequisites and of skills development with progressively advanced training to meet the goal of increasing the skill set of the technician.

All consortium courses follow a formal courseware development process, industry numbering system and approval, including validation. The validation process includes a beta offering of each course, which incorporates input from the transit rank and file, and transit system/college subject matter experts before the offering becomes a final product for train-the-trainer delivery. Additionally, the subject matter experts, one from a college and one from a transit, are required to sign off on the validation signature page then followed by signatures by the Training Director and Executive Director.

Once fully validated, a train-the-trainer delivery of the completed course is offered. This enables an increase in the pool of certified instructors expanding the training capacity to deliver to the transit systems throughout the regional zones of the consortium. All courses delivered are built with ASE (Automotive Society of Excellence) conformance in mind and are suitable for technicians who seek an ASE certification. A complete catalog of the courses and their relationship to the training tracks is referenced in Fig. 15.2 and can be found on the Website.

All courses are delivered at member community college locations or transit agency facilities. This provides excellent regional accessibility to put courses on in various areas minimizing time and travel expense. Classroom materials include course text materials and worksheets, system simulations and electronic boards, and various test benches that replicate in-vehicle operating systems. Many of the simulated systems and test benches have been provided by participating industry partners, and they have added a richness and practical functionality to the delivery of course instruction.

Today the consortium benefits the transit industry and educational institutions by the development of a bottom-up industry—driven competency-based curriculum and training program that meets present and future needs in California and for the transit industry. This collaboration continues to expand and brings together 52 member transit agencies and community colleges to be the mechanism for prioritization, coordination, courseware development, and delivery of training for the technical

Training tracks

Track A — Basic	Courses: Basic skills, introductions, foundational, measurement, devices
Track B — General	Courses: Engines, transmission, electrical, brakes, doors, body
Track C — Advanced	Courses: Diagnostics, heating ventilation air conditioning, electronics
Track D — Specific Advanced	Courses: Cummins, ZF, hybrid bus, battery electric bus, hydrogen, LNG, CNG, advanced diagnostics, ITS applications, advanced electronics, distance education series

Figure 15.2 Training tracks.

and supervisory workforce within the transportation industry. Over the last 14 years the SCRTTC has delivered 77,612 hours of training and has trained over 5463 transit employees. Now that the development of the policies and standard operating procedures are in place for this new learning model, leveraging this resource for national replication will serve the needs and benefits for other public agencies and educational partners.

What lessons did we learn?

In 2012 the Board of Directors determined that the consortium was experiencing growing pains and had somewhat needed guidance on its strategic direction. In addition, with expansion creeping without a clear vision or in-depth discussion, it was time the board made sense of the direction and whether expansion was applicable. With a strong Southern California presence, membership began to creep outside the region into Central California and Colorado. An additional push was coming from Northern California agencies to also become part of the consortium.

Funding was inconsistent and lacked a long-term plan, which gave the consortium a sense of living paycheck to paycheck. Training course offerings were dictated by funding sources available versus funding acquisition being the need that drove the agency. The consortium thought it had moved out of the "start-up" era in its organizational life cycle and moved into the "adolescence" phase. The groundwork needed was to build a strategic plan that advanced it into the "mature" phase and beyond. However, that was not the case.

According to Judith Simon's "The 5 Stages of A Non-Profit's Life," every nonprofit organization evolves and matures according to phases in a life cycle [6]. Depending on where an organization is in the life cycle, strategies must be employed to ensure it matures and progresses along each phase in a deliberate and methodical way. Nonprofit life cycle transitions occur in seven key categories: Programs and Services, Management, Staffing, Governance Board, Administrative Systems/Operations, Finance, Marketing, and Community Awareness. The Board members rated each category according to where it was in the life cycle. Overall the Board determined that the consortium vacillated between the start-up, adolescent, and mature phases.

In Fig. 15.3 the Board assessed each category below with the highest number of votes shown in each area. While administration reached the

Life cycle transitions	Grass roots-invention	Start-up-incubation	Adolescent-growing	Mature-sustainability	Stagnant and renewal	Decline and shut down
Programs and services			7	3		
Management		2	7	2		
Staffing		4	5			
Governance board		2	2	3	3	
Administrative systems/operations				8	1	
Finances		6	2		2	
Marketing/ community awareness			2	4	4	

Figure 15.3 Nonprofit life cycle chart.

mature stage, other key operations were still in the adolescent stage with some still in the start-up stage.

The consortium realized at that point in its organizational life cycle that the requirement was to reflect, analyze, and decide on the best strategies moving forward. In order to build on the consortium's success and ensure long-term viability, it was important to start developing measurable objectives that got to the quality and effectiveness of the training offerings and ensured that there was a long-term strategic shift organizationally. The consortium centered on a 5-Year Strategic Business Plan focusing on seven key strategic goals found in Fig. 15.4 [5].

Where do we go from here?

I believe that SCRTTC has fulfilled its goal of implementing a transit training learning model to enhance the skills and abilities of transit

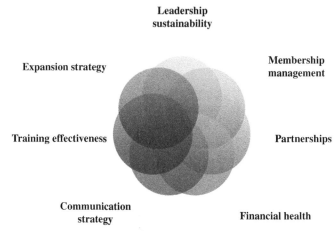

Figure 15.4 Strategic goals 2013–18.

employees and to provide area transit agencies with more efficient and effective training. Collectively, SCRTTC members serve over 750 million boarding passengers on more than 6000 transit vehicles traveling 200 million vehicle service miles. The industry-driven and competency-based curriculum and training meets both present and future needs for transit maintenance and supervisory staff, while also providing consistency in work methods and standards. Our results over this 14-year period speaks for itself.

- 57 transit agencies, educational institutions, private industry partners as members
- 77,612 + hours of training delivered
- 5463 + students trained
- Expansion to Central and Northern California
- Distance-based education course offerings
- Award for Innovation in Transit Training by the National Transit Institute
- Award for Excellent in Transit Training by the California Transit Association.

Because the consortium was born on the need for a coordinated workforce development strategy, the new mission became the foundation: to advance the skills of our transit workforce and prepare for the future. The learning model emphasizes consistency and established baseline standards of training for technicians who now require new technological skills to inspect, maintain, and repair vehicles using alternative fuels, hybrids, or all battery-electric.

With industry and academic partners the consortium has developed more than 33 courses over its life cycle, each rooted in a process that involves transit sector subject matter experts identifying highly specialized technical training required by our transit agencies. Courses are delivered by consortium certified instructors to incumbent workers and students at transit agency locations. Students learn through interactive coursework and laboratory exercises, testing their knowledge and skills on commercial bus system components including electrical, brakes, heating and air conditioning, and engines. The course roster also includes Occupational Health and Safety Administration (OHSA) safety principles, project management and leadership training. The consortium also issues certificates of successful completion to all students who complete the coursework.

In summary, building a similar model must take the key elements of a competency-based training model into consideration. Some of those key elements include industry-supported curriculum, internship/mentorship programs, and pathways to employment. Additionally, the nuts and bolts of any organizational training program must be built on a foundation that includes needs assessment and skills gap analysis, industry-validated courseware, certified instructors, and certification.

For those who are considering using SCRTTC's model, here are a few key takeaways:

- Strengthen the pool of certified instructors;
- Set membership fees and stick with it;
- Do not offer "free" courses;
- Build a comprehensive strategic plan earlier in the process;
- Hire consortium staff to reduce the volunteer work that is relied on to meet goals and objectives;
- Hire a lobbyist or government affairs person who is present in federal government; and
- Establish the use of Kirkpatrick Model sooner to assess results of training and modeling programs (see supra note 4).

If Jim and I met in my living room today to create an organization like SCRTTC, I would not deviate much from what we have already done, except to move away from a mass majority of volunteers to hired positions. The consortium is a practical solution to a need in the industry—with clear objectives, strategic civic partnerships, and a sturdy organizational structure, we continue to succeed by serving members of the transit workforce.

References

[1] D.M. Stumpo, "SCRTTC Business Plan," ninth ed., Aptrex Institute, Point Roberts, February 8, 2005, pp. 3—7, 10—22.

[2] SCRTTC. Secretary Report, Organization and New Business, Board Annual Meeting, 2010, February 17.

[3] SCRTTC. Secretary Report, Organization and New Business, Board Annual Meeting, 2010, May 19.

[4] T. Fisher, "SCRTTC SWOT Analysis Report," first ed., Insight Strategies, Long Beach, November 14, 2012, pp. 3—10, 36.

[5] T. Fisher, "2013—2018 SCRTTC Strategic Business Plan Report," first ed., Long Beach: Insight Strategies, June 14, 2013, pp. 3—4, 9—10.

[6] J.S. Simon, *The 5 Life Stages of Nonprofits*, second ed., Speakman Consulting, 1997, 2002.

CHAPTER SIXTEEN

Creating communities of practice for the new mobility workforce: lessons from the National Transportation Career Pathway Initiative

Thomas O'Brien[1] and Scott Jakovich[2]

[1]Center for International Trade and Transportation, California State University, Long Beach, CA, United States
[2]Southwest Transportation Workforce Center, California State University, Long Beach, CA, United States

Contents

My pathways to both transportation and education were circuitous and accidental. Having a strong undergraduate foundation in languages and policy was fulfilling personally but apparently not immediately of interest to employers. As a result, and upon graduation, I found myself in front of a classroom in Morocco, serving as an English teacher in the Peace Corps. Peace Corps training is highly regarded and very effective, and learning how to teach also taught me how to learn. After completing my service, I returned to the U.S. to a graduate program in urban planning. I had new perspective on the classroom experience and was better able to understand what constituted success for both the instructor and me, the student.

An unexpected assignment as a graduate research assistant introduced me to the world of freight transportation which, in turn, led me back to the classroom as an instructor, this time working with Masters-level students as well as adult

Empowering the New Mobility Workforce.
DOI: https://doi.org/10.1016/B978-0-12-816088-6.00017-1

learners pursuing professional certifications. Many of my students have taken their own circuitous and accidental paths, including the young Moroccan who overcame great odds to become a Washington-based translator and interpreter for world leaders. Others manage the transport networks of global shipping lines, ensure the smooth flow of goods through North America's largest trade gateway or help develop policy for the state's transportation system.

The most successful students do not always demonstrate clarity of purpose from the start. They struggle, as I did, to envision a future beyond the classroom. But they do tend to demonstrate a curiosity about learning, a willingness to look beyond grades toward the value of the educational process, and an openness toward change.

The struggle for the educator is finding the balance between encouraging that creativity and self-reflection, and providing the support that allows a student to not get bogged down in indecision. Indecision is a common outcome for today's students who face a rapidly changing job market, a revolution in both the nature of work and how we learn, and an unlimited number of information resources that do not always prove helpful in charting a course forward. Educational institutions have had to adjust accordingly. We are no longer effective if we are only teaching to or from the text. We have to teach students how to discern good information from bad, how to navigate a world of mediated communication, and how to prepare to be flexible in a world where the job you were hired for disappears with the advent of a new technology. We have to teach students to innovate in a world of innovation.

The desire to innovate is a survival instinct. The people and firms that not only understand the marketplace for new technologies and new ideas but can also drive it — and are willing to risk failure along the way — are the ones that ultimately succeed. And they are also the ones who recognize the need to make self-assessment an integral part of their core philosophy. The world of supply chain management calls it "kaizen," or continuous improvement. It means looking at the structure of a success or failure regularly and recognizing the value of empowering everyone in the firm or on the team, at whatever level, to identify risks and "stop the assembly line" when warranted. [1]

Sometimes the innovation comes in the form of an organizational change, sometimes in the form of a process improvement. Increasingly it comes in the form of a technology that may support both. The world of transportation is confronted with the need to innovate on a regular basis: to reduce accidents, improve turn times for truck drivers, increase transit ridership, and make infrastructure smarter (assuming it's already smart) by developing data-driven systems that provide real time feedback to planners from users of the system and from the system itself.

The education sector is not exempt from the need to innovate, and new learning tools, approaches, methods of delivery, and student assessment have all undergone significant changes in recent years because of new ways of thinking and the application of new technologies. The ability of educational institutions to respond to these pressure points is somewhat constrained however. The educational mission is not — and shouldn't be — driven by the same market forces that drive business, but the academy does our students no favors if we are not developing our own key performance indicators (KPIs, to borrow another term from supply chain management) that match learning objectives with outcomes in the classroom and in the real world.

It is not uncommon for educational programs across the entire educational continuum to rely upon advisory boards to direct the development of new courses and degree programs. Community colleges have historically had a much more direct link with industry because of their workforce development mission. However, the ability of schools to succeed in a world where not only the nature of education — but the very nature of work itself — are constantly changing, depends upon a new approach to engagement within and across education, industry, and government and the community in which they all operate. It is not a need I could have articulated back when I first set foot in the classroom in Morocco. Today, it is essential.

This chapter explores the development of a community of practice (CoP) approach to workforce development. While communities of practice have their foundation in work-based learning — in the apprenticeship concept in fact [2] — and have been applied within education, the new mobility workforce will need a broader application of the community practice model that extends beyond often siloed government, education, or industry networks to a crosscutting system that involves all three. After investigating the origins of CoPs, we consider the potential structure and range of partnerships that constitute a community of practice. We then present the findings from a transportation planning career pathway demonstration that had as one of its goals establishing the foundations of a cross-functional CoP. We conclude with some comments on the challenges of sustaining the model.

Thomas O'Brien.

Taxonomy of a pathway partnership: defining a CoP and the partnership continuum

Communities of Practice involve a "group of people who share a concern or passion for something they do and learn how to do it better as they interact regularly" [3]. They foster innovation by bringing together people with the same interest (domain) and a common set of resources and tools available for problem solving (practice) in a forum in which social capital can be developed and knowledge shared (community) [3]. The concept suggests a shared culture of learning and a common set of practices that the community has normalized in the development of social capital. The approach has been applied in a number of settings in both the public and the private sector and, since the term was coined in the early 1990s and now in the wake of the Internet revolution, applies to virtual communities as well [4].

Central to the concept of a community of practice (CoP) is active participation on the part of individuals for their own growth as well as for the growth of the community. The process of developing a shared purpose via shared common knowledge is one way in which CoPs have found their way into organizational development [4]. The notion of active, regular, and meaningful participation is also central to communities of practice. CoP theory recognizes that the development of the community involves significant negotiation, realignment of purpose, and brokering, particularly as individual or group practices can often be "imported" into a new CoP in what is referred to as a "boundary encounter" [4]. As a result the community requires people who are not only adept within the domain, but at translating between various members of the community and with new members as they learn to negotiate community standards for knowledge management.

Communities of practice are messy, particularly if they exist in a dynamic and rapidly changing work environment. They involve some people who identify themselves as leaders and others whose participation is more irregular based upon areas of interest. There are others who may exist at the edges of different CoPs and those who serve as the aforementioned translators [5].

Where CoPs differ from organizational management or business theory is in the emphasis on knowledge accumulation and management rather than cost. And while the CoP clearly involves "transactions" between members, the approach is much less transactional or project-focused than it is constantly evolving to reflect community priorities [6]. Because it lacks a top-down structure and sometimes even resists a well-defined organizational chart, it only exists if the community sees value in continuing the exercise of knowledge transfer.

Despite the CoP's focus on community, the willingness of the participant to first join and then to remain active depends in part on a little motivated self-interest. CoPs work best when they find ways to harness the interests of community members with varying knowledge bases, skill sets, level of interest and, frankly, time to commit to development of the community. As a result, the ability to form partnerships both internal and external to the CoP plays a critical role in its success.

Because a CoP is somewhat more organic than a highly structured organization with clearly defined chains of command and lines of reporting and accountability, the CoP can take advantage of a wider (and more flexible) array of agreements to provide guidance on standards of community behavior for the group as a whole and between individual members [7].

The community's principle goal of knowledge sharing can be accomplished in a number of ways, ranging from the simple exchange of ideas via networking to a formal agreement to partner in a way that aligns goals and shares resources. In between are increasingly more structured approaches to working together that move from cooperation on sometimes disparate goals, to coordination on shared goals and then collaboration on a common goal, while maintaining a level of independence with regard to decision-making. The CoP allows for them all and even all at the same time.

In a workforce-focused CoP education is central to the mission but it is merely a means to an end. The partners who constitute the community members are those who inform the development of the educational content as well as deliver it, but they also include those who ensure job readiness and those who study and assess market forces and employment trends. Simply put, the community validates the educational mission by ensuring that program participants and graduates are workplace ready. The Workplace Development CoP (Table 16.1) draws upon the skills of partners at all levels of the education continuum, from government and industry to workforce development specialists and workforce development agencies. There is also a role to be played by community leaders who shape perceptions of valued work and education within a community. In some communities they might be political leaders and elected officials; in others, it might be faith-based organizations. With multiple perspectives come opportunities to experiment with new approaches to workforce development.

Table 16.1 Characteristics of a workforce development community of practice (CoP).

WORKFORCE COMMUNITY OF PRACTICE GOALS	CRITICAL COMMUNITY MEMBERS/PARTNERS
Identify skills gaps and develop competency models.	
Create communication channels across education, industry and government (build multi-stakeholder ecosystem).	
Integrated planning, execution, and monitoring (quality assurance).	Employer base
Continuity of workforce supply.	Labor groups
Workforce readiness.	Research community (labor market analysis)
Establish opportunities to adapt to new technologies in learning and working.	Education community (K-12, Community College, University)
Create an infrastructure for student support (mentoring, financial counseling, career guidance).	Workforce development agencies Faith-based groups
Plan for and manage disruption to workforce.	Private foundations
Facilitate movement in and out of career pathways.	School boards and Departments of Education
Create opportunities for work-based learning.	Social service providers
Develop sustained funding for training, reskilling and program development.	Technology service providers
Build capacity of training network (emphasis on Train-the-Trainer).	
Contextualize problem solving.	

While establishing measurements of success is crucial to the purpose of a CoP, inherent in the concept is the notion of trial and error. In the educational sector, where the end game of a degree or certification is standard, trial and error is usually counterproductive and if nothing else, costly in terms of time and money. In a CoP, however, the freedom to experiment outside of the norms of traditional processes is not only permissible, it is desirable. It is the opportunity to develop workforce training programs on a small-scale basis, using a cooperative model that engages a cross-section of partners using innovative financing, with a focus on assessment that ultimately benefits the more traditional programs in the end. Demonstrations of feasibility of a particular concept, or small-scale rollouts of a program on a pilot basis, permit necessary readjustments in strategy before significant investments are made. In this way the CoP encourages learning from failure. At a minimum the experience reveals challenges that may not have been foreseen. It is not uncommon for a demonstration to reveal key institutional hurdles (bureaucratic processes, legal roadblocks) that have nothing directly to do with the program or technology being tested.

It is also possible, however, that the demonstration will succeed. In demonstrating the feasibility of an approach, even at a small scale, the participants can claim victory. This serves multiple purposes, not the least of which is generating interest among other participants who can contribute resources to a broader implementation effort.

Demonstrating workforce success through community of practices

In April of 2012 the Council of University Transportation Centers (CUTC), in cooperation with the US Department of Transportation, brought together a diverse range of stakeholders to develop a cohesive strategic framework for addressing the challenges that face the current and future workforce responsible for the design, operation, and maintenance of the nation's transportation infrastructure. One outcome of this convening was to identify four areas of concern: an upcoming wave of generational retirement, poor career awareness within the K-12 system, increased skills gaps due to the adoption of new technologies, and a growing demand on the expectations of transportation agencies. Collectively, these factors—retirement, recruitment, training, and retention—would loom over the future effectiveness of a workforce that was anticipated to grow dramatically in response to a national need for transportation infrastructure improvements.

> "DOT invests in the future of transportation through its University Transportation Centers (UTC) program, which awards and administers grants to consortia of colleges and universities across the United States" [9]

To the Federal Highway Administration (FHWA), it became clear that a greater investment was needed to "*provide national leadership, coordination, and assistance that support initiatives to develop and expand the nation's transportation workforce* [8]." Part of this investment included establishing a national collaborative of regional centers that could provide a strategic and efficient approach to workforce development across the country. Formally established in 2014 this collaborative launched as the National Network for the Transportation Workforce (NNTW); a university-based research powerhouse comprised of five well-regarded UTC's. Then as it does now, the NNTW operates as an FHWA extension into the industries, agencies, and workforce that represent the nation's highway transportation infrastructure. Each of the NNTW's five regional centers, collectively representing the 49 contiguous states, supplies the people, planning, resources, and coordination necessary to address workforce development priorities unique to their respective demographics (Fig. 16.1). A critical factor to the success of this mission lies within partnerships: the NNTW actively seeks industry engagement at all levels of center activity, in both steering and advisory capacities, to drive the development of tangible workplace solutions that will increase the effectiveness of the transportation workforce.

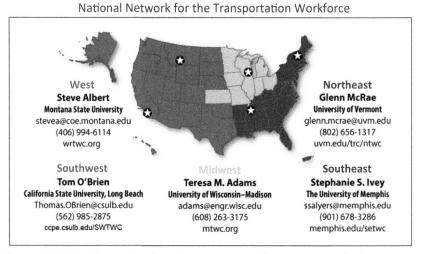

Figure 16.1 The five regional transportation workforce centers of the National Network for the Transportation Workforce (NNTW) [10].

Since its formation the NNTW has worked to expand FHWA's connections into and understanding of the highway transportation workforce, by providing rigorous regional labor market analysis, establishing workforce development action plans, and developing meaningful and sustainable partnerships within the transportation industry. In 2016 the NNTW published its "Job Needs and Priorities Report," a study that revealed the workforce challenges and opportunities reflecting the unique social, economic, political, and demographic characteristics of the five regions.

By June of 2017 FHWA had also devised a plan to deepen its understanding of the highway transportation workforce; to identify which jobs would be most critical over the next 15 years and how the impact of transformative technologies—like Intelligent Transportation Systems and shared mobility—may be reshaping the requirements for those jobs. The plan was to fund a 2-year investigation into five key transportation disciplines; engineering, planning, operations, safety, and the environment. The goal was to identify a set of current and emerging jobs that were critical to the continued advancement of each of those disciplines, then craft new educational pathways that would be effective at preparing workers to qualify for and excel at those job opportunities. Ultimately, these "career pathways" would then be seeded into the nation's postsecondary education space, so that over time, a new class of worker would start to emerge in numbers sufficient to satisfy the expected demand of this future workforce. FHWA understood that "*a highly skilled workforce is necessary to address the ever-changing US transportation [system], including the evolving areas of automation, information technology, vehicle-to-vehicle and vehicle-to-roadway technologies, intelligent traffic management systems, environmental stewardship, land use, livable communities, rural access, and facility and system design* [11]."

Strategically, this initiative also aligned well with the US DOT's 2017 Performance Plan, which advocated for economic competitiveness through the creation of a dynamic workforce. The idea was to build workforce CoPs that would identify and advance career and technical education (CTE) pathways that supported transportation jobs, addressed STEM (science, technology, engineering, and mathematics) education, and promoted transportation-related academics for K–12 students. These CoPs would include stakeholders from partnering Federal agencies, public and private employers, educational institutions, and workforce and labor organizations; stakeholders who could convene without the burden of formal management to formulate new ideas, share in experiential knowledge, and create strategies and solutions critical to their common success. With the formation of informal CoPs becoming more commonplace, both DOT and FHWA foresaw the value in building-out these networks of partner practitioners, who would ultimately confer, advise, and advocate around all things transportation.

For FHWA's pathway initiative to be successful, it would require the work of a national

> "This Federal Highway initiative creates sustainable partnerships between industry and education to prepare students for critical transportation career pathways."
>
> *NTCPI Mission Statement.*

collaborative capable of establishing regional CoPs, each focused on identifying the workforce needs and workplace challenges for one transportation discipline; a collaborative both versed in the methodologies of
workforce research AND capable of crafting new pathway strategies that
would attract and prepare students for this underrepresented job sector.

With the NNTW now firmly established as an FHWA partner in the
development of strategic and efficient workforce solutions, its five regional
centers seemed ideally suited to take on this responsibility. In October of
2017 the NNTW was awarded the "National Transportation Career
Pathways Initiative," or NTCPI. It was agreed that each NNTW center
would focus on one discipline (Fig. 16.2), and the Southwest center,
founded on the campus of Long Beach State University, would act as the
initiative's programmatic lead. This structure, it was thought, would allow
the regional centers to pursue their individual lines of research, while still
keeping them collaboratively working in sync toward the common goals
of the initiative.

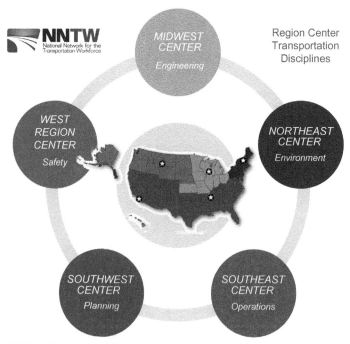

Figure 16.2 For the National Transportation Career Pathways Initiative, each NNTW
regional center focused their research on a specific transportation workforce
"discipline" [10].

Each center quickly took on the responsibility of identifying critical occupations and related competencies for each discipline. This research involved a cross-analysis of historical labor market data versus real-time employment demand, the latter characterized by web-based job listings mined by Burning Glass software. In the Southwest this analysis was further validated using job postings from regional transportation planning organizations and a survey of transportation planners, circulated on behalf of the initiative by the American Planning Association Transportation Division and the California Department of Transportation.

These preliminary lists of occupations and competencies were then reviewed and retooled by "Discipline Working Groups"; small CoPs formed in each region to represent the public, private, and academic interests of their respective transportation discipline. In the Southwest the final list (Fig. 16.3) included some very traditional jobs (Planner, Analyst) as well as some that combined occupations with much needed competencies or skill sets (Modeling, Forecasting, GIS Analysis).

Critical Planning Occupations in Highway Transportation

SOC code	Occupation	Survey results	Current # employees, 2016	Projected # employees, 2026	Percent change	2016 Median annual wage
n/a	Transportation planner	87.1%	n/a	n/a	n/a	n/a
19-3051	Urban and regional planner	81.5%	36,000	40,600	12.8%	$70,020
n/a	Land use planner	74.2%	n/a	n/a	n/a	n/a
n/a	Environmental planner	65.3%	n/a	n/a	n/a	n/a
17-1021	Cartographers and photogrammetrists	32.5%	12,600	15,000	19.4%	$62,750
n/a	GIS analyst/technician	n/a	n/a	n/a	n/a	n/a
17-3031	Surveying and mapping technician	42.2%	60,200	66,600	10.6%	$42,450

Figure 16.3 The Southwest center identified seven occupations that play a significant role in the long-term success of the nation's transportation planning workforce [10].

This overlap between occupation and competency was also revealed in the position descriptions for the job postings reviewed as part of the initial data analysis. In addition to having technical transportation planning or modeling skills, planning agencies and the private sector are seeking candidates who are also capable of critical thinking, problem solving, public outreach to diverse audiences, teamwork, report writing, preparing and delivering presentations, project management, and geospatial analysis. This highlighted a key takeaway from the NTCPI research: identify workforce demand and workforce readiness in terms of high-demand skills and skills gaps rather than traditional job titles. Or put more simply, follow the competencies, not the occupation.

Together with its Discipline Working Group, the Southwest center sought to validate this new characterization of a competency-driven workforce by designing a demonstration pilot that would integrate occupational and technical competencies into classroom curriculum. The goal of the pilot would be straightforward: enrich the student learning experience while also broadening awareness and interest in transportation career opportunities.

The National Transportation Career Pathways Initiative demonstration

An essential feature of NTCPI was the pathway demonstration: a discrete, focused implementation meant to test-out the various strategies of a center's disciplinary career pathway. The evaluation of this demonstration would inform and advise the design of a pathway's full-fledged implementation plan; a plan that lays out the steps required to deploy that pathway within the structure of postsecondary education.

To demonstrate the strategies of its Planning career path design, the Southwest, in partnership with the Los Angeles Trade Technical College (LATTC), formally launched "ARC 341" on February 24, 2018; a pilot class in metropolitan GIS planning systems with a transportation focus. The decision to focus on GIS was driven by the center's earlier research analyzing the occupations and competencies of the Planning discipline, which revealed geospatial analysis to be critical to the job function of a transportation planner as well as an independent job category in its own right for many planning agencies. GIS also proved useful as a "bridge" competency for students, particularly those in high school or community college who were interested in transportation-related issues, but who did not have access to a formal program of study in transportation or urban planning. As a result the Southwest's demonstration sought to test the feasibility of a career pathway in a transportation planning area of specialization—GIS—built through an accumulation of competencies. The hope was that these competencies could translate easily into a traditional undergraduate program in planning. To ensure this, ARC 341 was offered as a for-credit course at LATTC, but it also qualified for transfer credit recognized by both the University of California and California State University systems, including Long Beach State. To further test the career pathway model (Fig. 16.4) and to assess our effectiveness at using the course to raise awareness of transportation planning as a career choice, the demonstration included 10 students participating under their high school's STEM academy

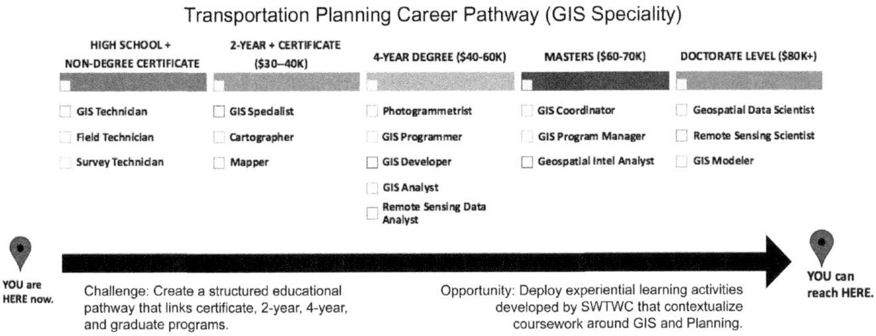

Transportation Planning Career Pathway (GIS Speciality)

HIGH SCHOOL + NON-DEGREE CERTIFICATE	2-YEAR + CERTIFICATE ($30–40K)	4-YEAR DEGREE ($40-60K)	MASTERS ($60-70K)	DOCTORATE LEVEL ($80K+)
GIS Technician	GIS Spedalist	Photogrammetrist	GIS Coordinator	Geospatial Data Scientist
Field Technician	Cartographer	GIS Programmer	GIS Program Manager	Remote Sensing Scientist
Survey Technician	Mapper	GIS Developer	Geospatial Intel Analyst	GIS Modeler
		GIS Analyst		
		Remote Sensing Data Analyst		

YOU are HERE now.

Challenge: Create a structured educational pathway that links certificate, 2-year, 4-year, and graduate programs.

Opportunity: Deploy experiential learning activities developed by SWTWC that contextualize coursework around GIS and Planning.

YOU can reach HERE.

Figure 16.4 The Southwest's demonstration sought to test the feasibility of a career pathway in a transportation planning area of specialization—GIS—built through an accumulation of competencies [10].

dual enrollment program. This meant that students who took part in this one class would obtain high school credit, community college credit and potentially university credit all at the same time.

During this 12-week course, students were introduced to the fundamentals of GIS technology and its application to urban and regional planning, while also receiving an overview of the various modes of transportation—and mobility challenges—found in a metropolitan area like Los Angeles. Throughout the duration of the course, students also received regular exposure to the career opportunities attainable within the transportation planning sector from a variety of professionals who used GIS tools and technologies in different occupations.

One pathway strategy tested by this pilot was the offering of instruction around a flexible schedule that allows for greater access for student learners. Classroom instruction for ARC 341 was scheduled on Saturdays to accommodate the L.A. region's diverse and underrepresented student populations, including the full-time high school students who participated as part of the dual enrollment program. This latter objective—reaching out to underserved students—provided LATTC administrators with an opportunity to fully sponsor the class with funding granted under the California Strong Workforce program, an initiative that seeks to develop workforce opportunities that can lift low-wage workers into living wage jobs. The Strong Workforce program is one of many critical statewide initiatives administered by the California Community College Chancellors Office, whose mission of "Doing What Matters for Jobs and the Economy" responds to the call of our nation, state, and regions to close the skills gap [12].

A second pathway strategy tested was "contextualization," or the delivery of instructional material within the context of the Transportation Planning workplace. One approach to this contextualization was provided by the guest lectures of planning industry professionals, who shared with students their occupational experiences and lessons learned as they themselves "climbed" the planning career ladder. Another approach came in the form of project-based learning activities, where students were challenged to solve transportation/mobility-related problems using tools and solutions found in a typical planning workplace. This included the use of GIS story maps to describe locational and asset-based scenarios and data collection software to capture map-based transportation assets into a GIS database by way of student smartphones (Fig. 16.5).

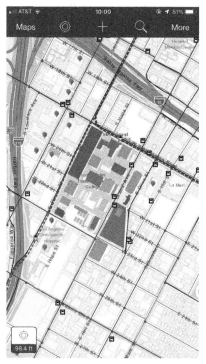

Figure 16.5 For its ARC 341 pilot, the Southwest developed a smartphone-based data collection app to identify and tag transportation assets in the field.

A third strategy tested by this demonstration was experiential learning, or "learning by doing." This was achieved through the use of out-of-class activities including a Data Collection Exercise, where students explored their campus to identify and tag transportation data points. By downloading an Esri ArcGIS Collector application onto their smartphones, students were able to catalog spatially accurate transportation data points onto actual maps of their immediate area using GIS technology. Operating in teams the students set out along the campus perimeter to identify possible freight, transit, and vehicular mobility conflicts that would normally be addressed by an urban/regional or transportation planner. As both an out-of-class activity and a work-based learning experience, this exercise positively engaged students around the application of GIS within a real-world planning scenario, set against the familiar backdrop of an everyday campus setting where a new awareness exposed previously unseen details (Fig. 16.6).

Figure 16.6 GIS students identify campus mobility conflicts using their smartphones, as part of an ARC 341 data collection exercise.

The data collection exercise is further evidence of the CoP approach. The app itself was developed by Long Beach State University GIS graduate students, who also guided the ARC 341 students through this activity. These two student groups were then connected by videoconference during the course of the demo, which served two purposes. First, it allowed the graduate students to do a presentation for the intro-level students on the kinds of skills, including coding, that are developed throughout the course of a GIS-based career. More important, and perhaps more powerful, it allowed the students in the LA Trade Tech class to visualize themselves sitting in a university classroom as a student about to embark on a potentially rewarding career.

The ARC 341 pilot concluded with students showcasing their new skills in story map development, GIS data collection, ArcMap desktop software, transportation planning issues, team collaboration, and narrative reporting, all as part of a group project presentation. Standing before a room of their classmates, the Southwest implementation team, and FHWA leadership, each student team presented a mobility challenge faced during their commute from home to campus, including an analysis of alternative routes using regional traffic maps. Though this class was strictly introductory in nature, professional attendees were impressed by each team's grasp of route planning concepts and use of GIS tools to describe and solve mobility challenges. Students who completed the course with appropriate academic standing were awarded completion certificates as part of a closing graduation ceremony (Figs. 16.7 and 16.8).

Figure 16.7 Students who successfully completed the ARC 341 pilot earned a "Completion Certificate," both on paper and electronically, to help them promote academic achievement to prospective employers.

Figure 16.8 Students of ARC 341 are joined by the Southwest implementation team and guest of honor Virgina Tsu of Federal Highway Administration (FHWA) for a class graduation photo.

Digital certificates were also provided for students to post to their E-portfolios.

The pilot was subsequently added to the official LATTC list of course offerings, and also made available to middle school students engaged in another pilot being offered through the college.

Sustaining the community of practice

The purpose of the National Transportation Career Pathway Initiative was to demonstrate the viability of a career pathway in transportation that focused on postsecondary institutions. The CoP approach (Table 16.2) provided a guidepost in identifying partners and establishing priorities for the effort. The ARC 341 class, while isolated in time and focusing on one on-ramp to the pathway, also met the objectives of a demonstration: to identify potential institutional issues (like those surrounding articulation agreements between institutions of higher learning) and other roadblocks moving forward. Through its successes, which included demonstrating the appropriateness of the material for high school level students and having the course added to the LATTC list of regular course offerings, the class was able to develop its own bandwagon of support from the education sector, industry and government. This support will be critical in moving the transportation planning career pathway from concept to implementation.

Table 16.2 The success of the ARC 341 pilot demonstrates the value of the workforce development community of practice (CoP) approach, which provided a guidepost in identifying partners and establishing priorities for this effort.

WORKFORCE COMMUNITY OF PRACTICE GOALS	ARC 341 APPLICATIONS
Identify skills gaps and develop competency models.	Course development informed by research surrounding critical occupations and competencies.
Create communication channels across education, industry and government (build multi-stakeholder ecosystem).	Discipline Working Group guided selection of critical occupations/competencies and focus of demonstration class.
Integrated planning, execution, and monitoring (quality assurance).	Course development involved coordinated curriculum design, planning, and assessment by Long Beach State, LATTC, and industry expert instructor drawn from ranks of public sector. FHWA provided guidance as grant funding agency.
Continuity of workforce supply.	Incorporating dual-enrolled HS students addressed the need to raise awareness of transportation as a career pathway, furthering efforts to ensure continuity of workforce supply.
Workforce readiness.	Incorporated discrete skills development into curriculum that can be immediately applied in the classroom or the workplace.
Establish opportunities to adapt to new technologies in learning and working.	Incorporated use of a smartphone app in data collection. App development was the responsibility of Masters-level students in GIS, which was itself an example of skills development.
Create an infrastructure for student support (mentoring, financial counseling, career guidance).	The class used the support infrastructure already developed by LATTC supplemented by Long Beach State resources.
Plan for and manage disruption to workforce.	Class content is based on new applications of technology to allow students to develop valuable skills needed by both public and private sector. "Staying ahead of the curve"
Facilitate movement in and out of career pathways.	The demonstration tests the validity of a GIS pathway to a transportation planning career. Skills developed in class can be used in multiple industry sectors (multiple on/off-ramps).
Create opportunities for work-based learning.	The demonstration did not include a work-based learning component, but future implementation of broader career pathway outlined in FHWA grant includes matching students with internship and apprenticeship opportunities.
Develop sustained funding for training, reskilling and program development.	The demonstration design took advantage of available state resources. Students taking course in the future will have access to a combination of resources including financial aid and scholarships to cover the cost of tuition. Additional grant funding will also be applied to program expansion.
Build capacity of training network (emphasis on Train-the-Trainer).	The demonstration links to another grant program to develop a GIS Train-the-Trainer module, building capacity for GIS instruction in underserved communities. Esri has committed support in the form of software licenses.
Contextualize problem solving.	The demonstration uses contextualized learning as the basis for all exercises and class presentations. Career pathways are also incorporated into curriculum design so that students can connect skills development with educational channels, work-based learning opportunities, and earnings potential.

The collaborative model and the financial sustainability model are two positive outcomes of NTCPI that will allow the next phase of the career pathway to move forward, and serves as a useful or at least illustrative model for similar demonstrations in other places. The fact that the course has already been repeated should give community members hope that there is "life beyond the demo."

Two other lessons are worth taking forward, however, and these are relevant for both the demonstration and the broader CoP. The first is the power of storytelling. The tools that the students used in ARC 341—GIS story maps—will be critical in the jobs of the future. Technology, while useful, will often need to be mediated or explained in a way that is relevant to a community that is not familiar with its inner workings. Therefore as a competency, technology-driven storytelling is one that these students will have in their toolkit, regardless of which career pathway(s) they choose. But beyond that, the story of a high school student on a career pathway, giving up a Saturday to take a class for credit, motivated by the desire to learn or to stay one step ahead of fellow students or simply to reduce the cost of future college credits (or some combination of the three) is a story that resonates. It resonates with program designers, instructors, and grant administrators. In a world driven by images, it creates a narrative in both pictures and words that validates the CoP and helps sustain it. The story has meaning to an educator, a parent, or a student facing similar challenges and opportunities.

The second lesson is about the ability of a university to take part in a CoP. Educational institutions are not always the leaders of innovation. The ivory tower is called that for a reason, and there is often good reason why a college or university seeks first and foremost to protect its turf, its standards, and its reputation. But increasingly, what will matter to the students we serve is our ability to be nimble with and for them; to use our research skills to predict the labor market, to deliver some (not all) content in a more menu-driven way that allows students to design their own program, and to create an educational experience that moves seamlessly from the classroom to the boardroom to the laboratory, sometimes via VR goggles or AI.

Furthermore the university will need to come to terms with the fact that our partners include community colleges and trade schools, high schools, and industry-driven training programs. Our students are looking for seamless transitions from one to the other. For them, our attractiveness is enhanced by the paths we forge across and between institutions. We need to see the benefits ourselves.

Once upon a time the university was the end of the pathway. The degree and the school determined your future. Now, we are a stop along the way, one that could even by bypassed. We bring tremendous value to the educational experience, but we need to understand how we fit into the broader plans of our students. As members of a CoP, we give ourselves the best opportunity to get the answer right.

References

[1] G. Greeff, R. Ghoshal, *Practical E-Manufacturing and Supply Chain Management*, Elsevier Science, Burlington, 2004.

[2] E. Wenger-Trayner, B. Wenger-Trayner. Communities of practice a brief introduction. Wenger-Trayner, <http://wenger-trayner.com/introduction-to-communities-of-practice/> 2015 (accessed 31.10.18).

[3] J. Lave, E. Wenger, *Situated Learning: Legitimate Peripheral Participation*, Cambridge University Press, Cambridge, UK, 1991.

[4] E. Wenger, *Communities of practice: learning, Meaning, and Identity*, Cambridge University Press, Cambridge, UK, 1998.

[5] Scaled Agile, Inc. Communities of Practice. <https://www.scaledagileframework.com/communities-of-practice/> 2018 (accessed 31.10.18).

[6] S. Trautman, M. McKee. *The Power of Knowledge Transfer: Preserving Your Secret Sauce While Mitigating Talent Management Risks*. Career Partners International, 2014.

[7] Southwest Transportation Workforce Center, Featured Partnerships, U.S. Department of Transportation Federal Highway Administration, 2016.

[8] FHWA Center for Transportation Workforce Development. <https://www.fhwa.dot.gov/innovativeprograms/centers/workforce_dev/>, 2018 (accessed 7.11.18).

[9] U.S. Department of Transportation, University Transportation Centers. <https://www.transportation.gov/utc>, 2018 (accessed 7.11.18).

[10] National Network for the Transportation Workforce. <http://nntw.org>, 2018 (accessed 31.10.18).

[11] FHWA Cooperative Agreement DTFH6116H000030, Project Background, 2016.

[12] Doing What Matters for Jobs and the Economy. <http://doingwhatmatters.cccco.edu>, 2018 (accessed 31.10.18).

Conclusion

Tyler D. Reeb, Ph.D.
Editor

Recruiting the distinguished roster of subject matter experts featured in this book has given me a richer understanding of the value of teamwork and communities of practice.[1] Looked at through an ethical lens, the mobility of people and goods is an equality issue, and communities of practice should be viewed as "Special Ops" teams assembled to address critical socioeconomic challenges.

Leaders in industry, government, and education who form communities of practice share common values. They seek to create leadership architecture to empower multijurisdictional and transdisciplinary teams to address technological, educational, financial, and policy challenges affecting the new mobility workforce. They build bridges to knowledge empowerment and related career pathways for emerging and incumbent professionals. And they understand the importance of implementing a more comprehensive standard for mobility resilience that draws from expertise in healthcare, safety, information technology, and strategic communications to ensure the integrity of the systems that move people and goods through communities, across borders, and around the globe.

Upholding such values is integral to the vitality of communities throughout the United States and abroad. In this way, critical mobility issues are higher calling issues. People who care about those important socioeconomic mobility issues can find common cause across political, business, education, and social spheres to affect positive change. If formed strategically and inclusively, communities of practice can work together to address situations where the mobility systems that move people and goods are failing. Such failures include situations where:

- Elderly and physically disabled people are unable to access healthcare and basic amenities to survive.
- Tribal community members need to hitchhike on a daily basis to commute to the closest school or college.

[1] For more on communities of practice, read Chapter 16.

- Passenger freight conflicts in rural, suburban, and urban environments are increasing pedestrian death and injury rates.
- Motivated and qualified workers are unable to access meaningful employment due to a lack of available public- and private-sector mass transit options.
- Global and domestic supply chains are vulnerable to terrorist and criminal activity.
- Owners of personal vehicles with smart technologies have their personal and financial information stolen by hackers.
- The systems that move people and goods are emitting toxic emissions due to a failure to implement available clean technologies.

The solutions to these and many other challenges rest on the shoulders of the professionals who will design, develop, operate, and maintain the mobility systems of the future. Said another way, we cannot predict every future mobility workforce challenge, but we can empower the professionals who will address those near- and long-term challenges. Such empowerment will require the coordinated efforts of leaders spanning industry, government, education, and international borders.

Workforce development leaders domestically and internationally face common challenges. Baby Boomer generation retirements, competition from other industries, and difficulty in recruiting women and minorities, as well as transformational technologies, are driving the need for new skills from incumbent workers and an increased demand for qualified pipelines of talent. Fortunately, global leaders in industry, government, and education are making it a priority to invest in the abilities of future mobility professionals to successfully deliver and manage efficient, safe, and effective mobility systems. Toward that end, the Council of Supply Chain Management Professionals (CSCMP) has launched a series of targeted initiatives to promote career development and educational opportunities to recruit women and minorities into logistics and supply chain management professions.[2] The American Society of Civil Engineers (ASCE) partnered with industry leaders to produce the IMAX film "Dream Big: Engineering Our World" to inspire young women and men in K-12 to

---

[2] Read Chapter 8, Ensuring a competitive and adaptive supply chain workforce, to learn more about the Council of Supply Chain Management Professionals and a recent U.S. Department of Commerce Supply Chain Competitiveness Taskforce that brought together leaders in industry and government to address economic, workforce, and diversity issues facing logistics professionals.

pursue engineering occupations to quite literally rebuild their world.[3] Equally inspiring, public- and private-sector leaders at California ports are working together to implement new automation and zero-emission infrastructure in terminals along the West Coast.[4]

In the 21st century, network technology has facilitated the creation of billion-dollar corporations, reshaped the economic landscape, and determined the success and failure of political campaigns. This network awareness underscores what the collection of thought leaders in this text instantiate.

This book is a network of communities of practice writ large.

The architects and champions of the new mobility workforce featured in this text understand the importance of developing innovation networks that connect communities of practice around the nation and the globe to share resources, best practices, and expertise. This open-source approach makes it possible for global leaders in workforce development to move beyond political and financial barriers that have traditionally hindered knowledge transfer to share innovative research, curriculum, business models, and policy innovations.

In the years ahead, this global network of communities of practice dedicated to empowering the new mobility workforce will continue to grow. Industry and educational partners will forge new bonds with international organizations like the Volvo Research and Educational Foundations, the Institute for Transportation and Development, and other leaders who are advancing research addressing sustainable mobility initiatives in advanced and developing locations around the world. The network of communities of practice will continue to grow and include new experts qualified to address emerging skills gaps created by emerging transformational technologies and trends. One such trend is preparing the mobility workforce to protect the systems that move people and goods against criminal and terrorist acts.

Shortly before the completion of this text, Clifford R. Bragdon, author of *Transportation Security*, told this author that by 2024 the United States will face a serious deficit of more than 200,000 mobility

---

[3] Chapter 14 addresses the "Dream Big" film within the larger context of inspiring and recruiting young women and men into mobility professions.

[4] For more on new technologies at ports and within intermodal supply chains, read Chapter 4, What are the best strategies to prepare the supply chain workforce for the technologies that will transform the port and intermodal workforces of the future?: Strategies to Prepare Future Port and Intermodal Workers for Transformational Technologies.

professionals skilled in homeland security and emergency preparedness competencies. If those jobs remain unfilled, the US mobility of people, goods, and information—the lifeblood of the economy—will be seriously impacted, impairing economic growth and fostering the onset of gridlock. To address future mobility systems challenges, Bragdon calls for a more comprehensive notion of resilience—one that integrates safety, security, health, financial integrity, and sustainability as a protector of the built environment. He also calls for a redefinition of urban master planning and homeland security standards to include aerial, surface, and subsurface attributes of our biosphere, as well as the integration of all five human senses, not just vision. He extends notions of resilience into the financial realm, asserting that emerging blockchain technologies will play a central role in the development of new accounting systems that will logarithmically replace current financial technologies that are more vulnerable to criminal and terrorist acts. The future mobility-based workforce, Bragdon contends, should ensure "accountability" coupling "resilient financial institutions with resilient cities." He predicts that a resilient blockchain currency will emerge as the catalyst to support the future built environment [3].

Designing, developing, operating, and maintaining mobility systems that ensure unprecedented new standards for safety, security, health, sustainability, and financial integrity will require a workforce that is as bold and dynamic as the undertaking itself. To ensure that the children riding tricycles today are ready for this new world of mobility will require similarly bold innovations in education and training.[5] This approach will require striking the appropriate balance between competency-driven curriculum and the development of essential communication, critical thinking, and leadership skills. It is not enough to equip emerging and incumbent professionals with technical skills, new mobility professionals will also need the emotional intelligence and professional poise to adapt to the fastest rates of technological change in human history.[6]

Technology and social problems are solved when informed teams identify common calls to action and then step into "leadership voids" and implement solutions. The contributors featured in this text are members

---

[5] Chapter 5, Anticipating and responding to changes in the mobility sector, discusses new industry-facing and competency-driven approaches that community college leaders can implement at their campuses to help workers address skills gaps created by transformational technologies.

[6] Chapter 1, Historical perspectives on managing automation and other disruptions in transportation, offers a historical perspective on technological disruption.

of communities of practice that are responding to critical leadership voids associated with mobility systems. To address leadership voids:

- LA Metro is developing a new Los Angeles-based Transpiration School "to provide students 12-to-18-years-old with STEAM (science, technology, engineering, arts, and math) programs, mentorships, hands-on learning, and other opportunities as an early pathway into the transportation industry.[7]

- The Southern California Regional Transit Training Consortium (SCRTTC)[8] was formed to build a new "learning model" to address human capital challenges through a systematic regional approach to developing curricula, eliminate training duplication and to reduce costs for designing and developing training materials. This award-winning approach can and should be replicated around the country.

- Mobility professionals are working with experts in public health, gerontology, and social work to address the mobility needs of vulnerable populations, such as seniors and individuals with disabilities, who have remained dramatically underserved over the past 30 years.[9]

- Tribal leaders are embracing inherent tribal sovereignty[10] to adopt the policies and inter-governmental agreements necessary to fully participate in the new mobility era. Such approaches seek to empower tribal governments so that they stand on equal footing with their federal and state peers in addressing infrastructure management challenges.

- And, leaders in smart city governance[11] are working with leaders in government and industry to address mismatches between public- and private-sector approaches to mobility to better serve the user base in urban environments.

Across the nation and around the world, people rely on mobility systems to commute from home to work, to school, and to access goods that

---

[7] LA Metro, featured in Chapter 11, LA Metro: changing the mobility game—inspiring and training a new workforce, filling leadership voids, and creating farm teams for the future, uses the term "stepping into leadership voids" to address community issues that impede equal access to social and physical mobility.

[8] The Southern California Regional Transit Training Consortium (SCRTTC) model is presented in Chapter 15.

[9] See Chapter 12, Designing our future transportation workforce for supporting seniors and individuals with disabilities, for more insights on developing mobility systems to serve elderly and disabled populations.

[10] For more on empowering tribal governments, read Chapter 7, Strategies for empowered mobility in Indian country.

[11] For more on innovations in smart cities governance, read Chapter 3, Mobility management for smart cities professionals.

ensure their health and wellness. That notion makes clear the essential role that mobility systems play in supporting human livelihood. That notion further drives home the point that mobility researchers must use data as never before to solve problems while simultaneously looking beyond the numbers to understand the human conditions behind those figures.[12] Addressing the expanding range of fields associated with modern mobility will require experts in planning, policy, organizational psychology, and geospatial information systems[13] to better understand the needs of the new mobility workforce and the populations they serve.

More than the roads, rails, semiconductors, microsensors, blockchains, and any other technology, values above all else will determine the integrity of the systems that will move people and goods in the decades ahead. Values like teamwork, customer service, socioeconomic equality, and environmental stewardship will guide the professionals who will design, develop, operate, and maintain the mobility systems of the future. It is incumbent upon leaders in education, industry, and government to embrace those same values to empower the new mobility workforce.

Reference

[1] Clifford R. Bragdon, author of *Transportation Security*, via email correspondence, November 15, 2018.

---

[12] Chapters 6, 9, and 10 present data-driven methods to study challenges facing the new mobility workforce.
[13] Chapter 2, The great transformation: the future of the data-driven transportation workforce, addresses ways the geospatial information systems can empower leaders to make more informed, data-driven decisions about transportation and infrastructure planning and asset management.

Index

Note: Page numbers followed by "*f*," "*t*," and "*b*" refer to figures, tables, and boxes, respectively.